D0075984

# Warbirds

# Warbirds

*An Illustrated Guide
to U.S. Military Aircraft,
1915–2000*

**JOHN C. FREDRIKSEN**

ABC-CLIO

Santa Barbara, California
Denver, Colorado
Oxford, England

**Library of Congress Cataloging-in-Publication Data**
Fredriksen, John C.
    Warbirds : an illustrated guide to U.S. military aircraft, 1915–2000 / John C. Fredriksen.
        p.   cm.
    ISBN 1-57607-131-6 (alk. paper)
    1. Airplanes, Military—United States.   2. Aircraft industry—United States.   I. Title.
UG1240.F74   1999
623.7'46'0973—dc21                                                                99-16624
                                                                                        CIP

05   04   03   02   01   00   99      10  9  8  7  6  5  4  3  2  1

ABC-CLIO, Inc.
130 Cremona Drive, P.O. Box 1911
Santa Barbara, California 93116-1911

This book is printed on acid-free paper ∞.
Manufactured in the United States of America.

# CONTENTS

# LIST OF AIRCRAFT

# PREFACE

Since their invention in 1903, airplanes have captured the world's imagination. Not surprisingly, aviation literature continues to be one of the most popular facets of the history genre. Year after year, multitudes of picture books, directories, and histories, especially about military aircraft, become available for the enlightenment and entertainment of interested readers, both professional and layperson alike. In fact, the sheer volume of aviation literature available sometimes represents a problem for parties intent on testing the waters of this topic. This is an especially daunting proposition for students possessing little skill in conducting historical research: *Where, exactly, does one begin?* Curiously, despite the well-developed body of information available, aviation reference books have been less numerous, and less successful, in bringing information quickly and easily to the attention of casual users. Most such titles are, in fact, written by specialists with specialists in mind, or at least for readers steeped in the nuances of aviation technology and history. Nor is their coverage of military aircraft uniform in nature. Reference books abound on American aircraft of World War II and jet aircraft of contemporary times, but few, if any, address aeronautical developments of World War I and the so-called Golden Era of 1919–1939. For students and laypersons interested in pursuing the facts and feats associated with these earlier periods, this gap is a genuine detriment to effective research.

The book you hold attempts to rectify this long-standing omission in aviation reference books. It has been specifically designed to address student inquiries about specific airplane types while simultaneously possessing sufficient depth and breadth for advanced researchers. It is a comprehensive compilation of all the major U.S. warplanes, including a good number of lesser-known types. These include not only machines specifically designed for military use but also numerous civilian craft that were either adopted or pressed into service during wartime. And in light of the traditional fixation with aircraft from World War II and the jet age, special consideration has been paid to machines that fought or flew throughout World War I and the Golden Era. Present throughout these pages are *all* the fighters, bombers, trainers, patrol craft, transports, and helicopters that have figured so prominently in war and peace since 1917. Compiling this book proved a tall

order, however, so to keep its length manageable, my selection criteria were somewhat restrictive by necessity. I therefore chose only aircraft that were manufactured and actually deployed by military or naval units. Experimental prototypes—regardless of their celebrity or infamy—have been deliberately omitted. I believe my extensive coverage of airplanes used by the military more than compensates for their deletion.

To facilitate reader access, I chose the relatively simple scheme of arranging the book alphabetically by manufacturer, then alphabetically by name or designation. Each entry consists of a photograph and a succinct account of the craft in question. In it I provide technical specifications such as performance, power plant, armament, and service dates; the narrative contextualizes the craft in terms of development, deployment, and ultimate disposal. Special attention is also paid to any record-breaking or otherwise outstanding service it may have performed. Everything has been rendered in simple, nontechnical prose for ease of understanding. My goal throughout is to be exacting in scope without being burdensome in detail.

To facilitate additional inquiry, two detailed bibliographies are provided in the rear matter of this book. This feature was added to counter a personal pique of mine with many so-called reference books available on military aircraft. On more than one occasion, I became intrigued by entries discovered in the works of such aeronautical mavens as William Green, Bill Gunston, and Kenneth Munson, only to find that no further references have been provided. Such material can, naturally, be uncovered, but only after expending much time and effort. Therefore, I can state unequivocally that this is the first warplane directory with bibliographic listings that are both recent and extensive. The first bibliography ("Further Reading") painstakingly lists printed materials available on an airplane-by-airplane basis. Wherever possible, literature on the parent manufacturer is also provided for great historical perspective. This bibliography has been carefully crafted from *WorldCat* and other online sources to ensure that each book and magazine title is readily available through interlibrary loan. Furthermore, magazine articles, if not borrowed outright, can be copied from many aviation museum libraries for a small charge or ordered directly from the publisher. The second bibliography

("General Bibliography") was culled from a vast amount of titles available. These materials represent some of the most recent and best titles on aviation literature anywhere. As previously noted, their availability was confirmed by *WorldCat*, and all should be easily obtained through loan or purchase.

I next sought to enhance the book's utility through the addition of several appendixes. For the benefit of readers who are unfamiliar with the history or application of military aircraft, I provide two detailed lists. Appendix 1 ("Aircraft by Mission") identifies aircraft by the functions they performed. Wherever an aircraft was employed in more than one mission, it is listed in each category accordingly. Appendix 2 ("Chronological Listing of Aircraft by Historical Period") is a strict chronology that lists aircraft by era. Finally, I conclude the book with a list of the biggest and most well-stocked aviation museums across the United States and Canada, where many of the warplanes listed herein can be viewed (see Appendix 3, "Museums"). Other potentially useful sources, such as photographs and magazines, round out what I hope is a comprehensive, one-stop aviation research guide (see Appendix 4, "Aircraft Journals and Magazines").

I would like to acknowledge and thank Ray Wagner of the San Diego Aerospace Museum, Ken Snyder of the Naval Aviation Museum Library, David B. Hofeling of the U.S. Naval Institute, and Nilda Pergola-Jensen of the Defense Visual Information Center for their cheerful assistance in locating photographs. Special gratitude is also accorded Bill Hooper of the New England Air Museum Library for his help in dredging up the innumerable books and magazine articles reproduced in the bibliography. My editor, Alicia S. Merritt, also merits kudos for exemplary patience and understanding throughout this latest contribution to the aviation largesse. I could neither have commenced nor concluded this work without them.

# INTRODUCTION

Like any other form of technology, aircraft possess a history and evolution unique to their form. But what aeronautical maven could have predicted that the frail contraptions of Wilbur and Orville Wright would develop into the mighty war machines of the mid-20th century and beyond? The battlefield ascendancy of aircraft, achieved in only a scant four decades, has been phenomenal and made control of the air an essential component of military strategy and tactics. In truth, the rise of military aircraft is a story of imagination, daring, and triumph seldom equaled in the history of technology. This is especially true regarding American contributions to the field. Therefore, to better acquaint laypersons with the chronological nuances of this development, I wish to provide a brief overview and highlight significant machines that made a difference.

Not surprisingly, the United States played a large role in abetting and facilitating the rise of aerial weapons, but this was achieved after an embarrassingly slow start. The U.S. Army acquired its first aircraft in 1908, based on the original Wright pushers, but official bureaucracy stifled the growth of military aviation up through the advent of World War I. European aircraft at that time were only slightly more advanced and initially employed for reconnaissance purposes. However, war provides great catalyst for change, and new aircraft—stronger, faster, and better-armed—emerged to demonstrate the utility of flying machines as fighters and bombers. The American aviation industry, unfortunately, had fallen so far behind foreign contemporaries that none of its products was deemed capable of wartime service. Consequently, the hundreds of American pilots who flew combat missions in Europe did so in fighters and bombers of either French or British manufacture. However, once committed to the war effort in 1917 and properly financed, the natural talents and innovation of American designers began exerting themselves. One American machine, the Curtiss JN-4 *Jenny*, was mass-produced and dominated aerial instruction throughout the war years and beyond. Another capable design, the Vought VE-7, was subsequently modified as a fighter during the immediate postwar era and proved itself equal to the best of European pursuits. Furthermore, Curtiss also developed several large and capable flying boats that were demonstrably the best in the world and widely employed by the U.S. Navy and Royal Navy. So, despite a tardy debut into the field of military aviation, America demonstrated potential for designing and fielding world-class aircraft of its own.

Unfortunately, the 1920s proved quiescent in terms of funding and development. Despite ten years' passage, American military aircraft showed little improvement, performance-wise, over their World War I predecessors. What changed dramatically was the tactical approach to aircraft as combat weapons. Aerial exponents such as General William "Billy" Mitchell proved that even lumbering crates such as the Martin MB-3 had the potential for sinking even the most modern battleships—and did so with dramatic results. Other machines, like the Fokker T-2 and the Naval Aircraft Factory PN-9, demonstrated the adaptability of aviation for long-range flying, which in turn had potential for both military and civilian applications. Naval aviation also took a dramatic turn with the introduction of the aircraft carrier and the rise of airplanes specifically designed for that service. These included the earliest dive-bombers and torpedo planes, which wielded tremendous implications for the projection of naval airpower in years to come.

The world began moving inexorably toward renewed conflict in the 1930s, and American aviation introduced many technical innovations that revolutionized aerial warfare. Foremost among these was the all-metal monoplane bomber, the Martin B-10 being the first example. Thereafter, retractable landing gear, enclosed cockpits, and controlled-pitch propellers became standard features worldwide. An epic cross-country flight by these craft under Colonel Henry H. Arnold in 1934 amply demonstrated the feasibility for long-range strategic bombing. This capability was confirmed in 1936 with the advent of an even more important aircraft, Boeing's four-engine B-17, appropriately nicknamed the *Flying Fortress*. Fighter development also closely paralleled that of the bombers, with the Seversky P-35 of 1935 becoming the first all-metal monoplane interceptor with retractable landing gear. However, once again, the pace of developments in Europe and Japan overtook American efforts, and by the outbreak of war in 1939 the modest U.S. aerial armada again verged on obsolescence.

It was not until World War II that the United States finally established its dominant role in military aviation. Not only were thousands of warplanes designed and manufactured; they included the most modern and effective of that conflict. More than any other machine, the splendid North American P-51 *Mustang* was the weapon that cleared the skies over Western Europe and made possible the strategic bombing of Germany by fleets of Boeing B-17s and Consolidated B-24 *Liberators*. In the Pacific, fighters like Grumman's F6F *Hellcat* and Vought's F4U *Corsair* bested the famous *Zero* fighter while an even more impressive bomber, the Boeing B-29 *Superfortress*, brought Japanese industry to its knees. Ending the war at Hiroshima and Nagasaki, the B-29 also ushered in the era of atomic warfare, a crucial chapter in the history of mankind. Nor were the more mundane but equally essential fields of military airlift—cargo hauling—neglected. The venerable Douglas C-47 *Skytrain* was the mainstay of Allied logistics but proved so adaptable that it fought in every conflict up through Vietnam. It was soon joined by redoubtable C-54s, C-119s, and a host of other transports that made large-scale global transportation possible. World War II also witnessed the introduction of two entirely new forms of aerial technology. The Sikorsky R-4 was the world's first vertical-lift platform committed to combat operations and demonstrated the viability of helicopters for rescuing lives. Moreover, the Lockheed F-80 *Shooting Star*, though not the first jet-propelled plane to see combat, was a splendid fighter in its own right—and a harbinger of things to come.

However, it was during the Cold War that aircraft, armed with nuclear weapons, moved to the very forefront of strategic military planning. Boeing dominated the field early on with its futuristic B-47 *Stratojet* and continued that dominance with the famous B-52 *Stratofortress*, which today is nearing a half-century of service. The advent of swept-wing technology also ushered in the age of transonic flight and occasioned the first jet-to-jet combat in Korea. There, the superb North American F-86 *Sabre* established air superiority over the equally impressive MiG-15 and the Republic F-84 *Thunderjet* proved an equally effective ground-support weapon. Soon thereafter, the North American F-100 *Super Sabre* became the first fighter capable of sustained supersonic flight. Military airlift concurrently became enhanced by introduction of the Lockheed C-130 *Hercules*, a four-engine giant still plying the air routes today. More significantly, the urgency for accurate military reconnaissance resulted in the development of Lockheed's U-2, the first of the technologically advanced spy planes.

The trend toward greater sophistication and lethality—and expense—was established by the time of the Vietnam War. McDonnell-Douglas F-4 *Phantoms* and Republic F-105 *Thunderchiefs* bombed enemy targets with greater speed and accuracy than ever previously achieved. Meanwhile, the deadliness of the missile-dominated air environment required reconnaissance planes that flew higher, faster, and farther and culminated in Lockheed's super-secret SR-71 *Blackbird*, the first aircraft to operate at three times the speed of sound. Electronic warfare also had become a standard fixture of the modern battlefield, which in turn generated development of specialized aircraft like the General Dynamics EF-111 *Raven* and the Grumman EA-6 *Prowler*. Military airlift has also reached truly strategic proportions with the advent of Lockheed's gigantic C-5 transport, a machine so large that it was appropriately named the *Galaxy*. In the realm of vertical flight, helicopters evolved from passive transports into full-fledged weapons in their own right. Today, the Bell AH-1 *Cobra* and Hughes AH-64 *Apache* bristle with armaments and can fly at night and in any weather. As highly automated, integrated weapon systems of the modern battlefield, they are the scourge of enemy tanks—and a far cry from the original machines of 50 years ago.

Aircraft produced during the last two decades of the 20th century have advanced the trend toward increasing sophistication and capability. The totally computerized McDonnell-Douglas C-17 *Globemaster III* is the first military transport able to carry almost every piece of the U.S. Army arsenal to anywhere on the globe. Furthermore, the advent of fly-by-wire technology has allowed even greater union between man and machine, with commensurate improvements in performance and deadliness. The Grumman F-14 *Tomcat*, the General Dynamics F-16 *Fighting Falcon*, and the McDonnell-Douglas F-15 *Eagle* certainly represent the highest expression of conventional technology as it relates to fighter aviation. However, current developments also incorporate such futuristic concepts as stealth, or invisibility to radar. The Lockheed F-117 *Nighthawk* and Northrop's B-2 *Spirit* are currently the only aircraft in the world with such amazing capability and symbolize the state of military aircraft since World War II: high-performing, high-tech—and hugely expensive. In fact, the frontline aircraft of the 21st century, which combines all these characteristics, is already flying. Lockheed's F-22 *Lightning II* has yet to be deployed operationally, but it unquestionably represents the ultimate warplane designed during this century. In the 97 years since the Wright brothers lifted off at Kitty Hawk, North Carolina, in 1903, military aircraft have evolved from technological novelties to military necessities with astounding speed. No one can predict the future course of such technology, the trends it will follow, and the new vistas it will establish. But if the past is any indication, the future of aviation is a brilliant one, indeed. The sky, literally, is no longer the limit.

# Warbirds

# Aeromarine 39B

**Type:** Trainer

**Dimensions:** wingspan, 47 feet; length, 26 feet, 3 inches; height, 12 feet, 8 inches
**Weights:** empty, 1,939 pounds; gross, 2,505 pounds
**Power plant:** 1 × 100–horsepower Curtiss OXX-6 liquid-cooled engine
**Performance:** maximum speed, 73 miles per hour; ceiling, 5,000 feet; maximum range, 273 miles
**Armament:** none
**Service dates:** 1917–1923

The Aeromarine was a useful early trainer that made history by becoming the first aircraft to attempt a carrier landing.

By 1916 the United States had commenced gradually rearming in anticipation of joining World War I. On October 12 of that year the Army Signal Corps contracted with the Aeromarine Plane and Motor Corporation of Keyport, New Jersey, to construct six trainers, known as M-1s. These were modest-sized, standard biplanes powered by the troublesome Hall Scott A-7a engine. Preliminary tests showed that the M-1 was unstable in anything but level flight, and most spent the war years packed in their crates. However, the Navy expressed interest in the plane and a willingness to spend time and money to refine it. Accordingly, the fuselage was modified for conversion to either land or seaplane use by adding landing struts or water pontoons as needed. The upper wing bay was also lengthened by four feet, which greatly increased overall stability. The Navy was so pleased by the docile flying quali-

ties of the new design that in October 1917 it ordered 200 machines. The first 50 were known as Model 39A, powered by the Hall-Scott engine. An additional 150, designated Model 39B, were refitted with a more reliable Curtiss OXX engine. This was the largest aircraft order placed by the Navy to that date.

Throughout World War I the Aeromarine 39 successfully trained scores of naval aviators. When the war ended only 104 machines had been delivered, and most were declared surplus. However, a handful of Model 39Bs were retained on account of their excellent slow-speed characteristics, which made them prime candidates for landing onboard a new type of ship, the aircraft carrier. On October 26, 1922, Lieutenant Commander Godfrey Chevalier successfully brought his Model 39B down on the deck of the converted collier USS *Langley*—the first carrier landing. By year's end this revolutionary procedure had become routine, and in 1923 the last of the trusted Aeromarines was retired from service.

**Type:** Liaison

**Dimensions:** wingspan, 35 feet; length, 21 feet, 6 inches; height, 7 feet
**Weights:** empty, 890 pounds; gross, 1,450 pounds
**Power plant:** 1 × 90–horsepower Continental O-205 air-cooled engine
**Performance:** maximum speed, 110 miles per hour; ceiling, 14,500 feet; maximum range, 350 miles
**Armament:** none
**Service dates:** 1947–1956

The L-16 *Defender* was one of the last of the Army *Grasshoppers*. Although light and agile, it proved unable to withstand the rigors of field use and served mostly with the National Guard.

Immediately after World War II, Aeronca resumed construction of its light civilian aircraft. A popular model was the Model 7BC *Champion* sport plane, which roughly duplicated the flying characteristics of Aeronca's successful wartime L-3 *Grasshoppers*. The *Champion* possessed a high strut-braced wing, a cabin fuselage, and tandem seating for a pilot and an observer. Powered by an 85-horsepower engine, the new craft was delightfully acrobatic and destined for commercial success.

In 1947 the Army began looking for an updated liaison craft to equip the National Guard. Given the Army's past experience with Aeronca's designs, it did not hesitate to purchase 509 *Champions* under the designation L-16A. Shortly afterward they also acquired 100 Model 7ECs as L-16Bs, which differed from the earlier version in having a 90-horsepower motor and a small dorsal spine to enhance directional stability.

As a liaison craft, the L-16 was expected to perform a variety of duties, including artillery spotting, observation, medical evacuation, and wire laying. They were also relatively cheap and expendable and, as National Guard aircraft, never intended for frontline service. However, in the panic surrounding the outbreak of the Korean War in 1950, and the shortage of Army aircraft encountered at the time, many L-16As were deployed overseas and thrown into the breach. The handful of L-16Bs, meanwhile, remained at home to serve as light trainers. Unlike other liaison aircraft, they proved less sturdy and dependable than expected and were gradually withdrawn as better fixed-wing airplanes became available. Eventually, all L-16s returned to the United States for reassignment to the Civil Air Patrol, where they lingered until 1956.

# Aeronca O-57/L-3 *Grasshopper*

**Type:** Liaison

**Dimensions:** wingspan, 35 feet; length, 21 feet; height, 7 feet, 8 inches
**Weights:** empty, 835 pounds; gross, 1,300 pounds
**Power plant:** 1 × 65–horsepower Continental O-170 air-cooled engine
**Performance:** maximum speed, 87 miles per hour; ceiling, 7,750 feet; maximum range, 200 miles
**Armament:** none
**Service dates:** 1941–1945

The L-3 was one of the three leading *Grasshoppers*, or light liaison aircraft, employed by the U.S. Army throughout World War II.

The U.S. Army had neglected the concept of light/liaison aircraft until the advent of war in Europe forced a reevaluation. In 1941 it tested and accepted delivery of four O-57s from the Aeronca Aircraft Corporation of Middleton, Ohio. These were militarized versions of Aeronca's popular Model 65 high-wing cabin monoplane. The craft was constructed of a steel tubing fuselage that was fabric covered; it seated two pilots in tandem. The Aeronca also employed dual controls, one for each operator. Like their civilian counterparts, the Aeroncas were light, easy to fly and maintain, and could be operated from relatively unprepared airstrips. In 1942 the category "Observation" was dropped in favor of "Liaison," so the Aeroncas were redesignated L-3 *Grasshoppers.*

Like its Interstate, Piper, Stinson, and Taylorcraft counterparts, the L-3 saw service in World War II and in a variety of functions. A jack-of-all-trades, it was employed in artillery spotting, transport, and courier functions to good effect. Production ended in 1944, by which time 1,487 L-3s had been delivered to Army units across the world. Like the other aircraft in this class, the L-3 gained an uncanny reputation for being able to land and take off from just about anywhere.

An interesting derivation of the L-3 was the three-seat TG-5 training glider. This craft retained the wings and aft fuselage of the standard L-3 but had the engine replaced by an extended canopy, and all three operators had their own sets of flying controls. A total of 250 TG-5s was delivered to Army training units by 1942, and the Navy acquired three examples for evaluation.

**Type:** Transport; Trainer

**Dimensions:** wingspan, 47 feet, 8 inches; length, 34 feet, 2 inches; height, 9 feet, 8 inches
**Weights:** empty, 6,175 pounds; gross, 8,727 pounds
**Power plant:** 2 × 450–horsepower Pratt & Whitney R-984 radial engines
**Performance:** maximum speed, 215 miles per hour; ceiling, 25,000 feet; maximum range, 900 miles
**Armament:** none
**Service dates:** 1940–1964

The *Expeditor* was one of the first mass-produced light cargo aircraft in history. It was widely employed during World War II, and many examples are still flying today.

The Beech D-18 first flew in January 1937 as a twin-engine, twin-rudder light cargo aircraft, of which 8,000 would ultimately be produced. It came to the Army's attention in 1940 with an initial purchase of 11 aircraft and received the designation C-45. Following America's entry into World War II, a total of 1,137 *Expeditors* was acquired in various models. Furthermore, an additional 1,500 JRBs were employed by the U.S. Navy. The type was also exported in quantity to the Royal Air Force and Royal Canadian Air Force.

A significant version of the C-45 was the AT-7 *Navigator*, the first Army aircraft designed as a navigation trainer. This craft featured chart tables and instruments for up to three students and was equipped with a revolving astrodome located behind the cockpit. The Navy version was christened the SNB; a total of 1,141 was purchased.

An equally important version was the AT-11 *Kansan*, designed for bombing and gunnery training. It was fitted with an angular glass nose, a Norden bombsight, and functioning bomb-bay doors. A total of 1,582 was acquired; an estimated 90 percent of the 45,000 American bombardiers in World War II trained in the *Kansan*.

The final derivation was the F-2, a specialized photographic reconnaissance aircraft. The first models were fitted with two overlapping cameras in the cabin and possessed an oxygen system for work at high altitude. Latter models had four cameras. A total of 59 models was built.

After the war the C-45 transport version remained in service with the U.S. Air Force and U.S. Navy until 1963. Privately owned D-18s remain a common sight at airports around the country.

**Type:** Trainer

**Dimensions:** wingspan, 44 feet; length, 34 feet, 4 inches; height, 10 feet, 4 inches
**Weights:** empty, 4,757 pounds; gross, 6,465 pounds
**Power plant:** 2 × 295–horsepower Lycoming R-680-9 radial engines
**Performance:** maximum speed, 200 miles per hour; ceiling, 19,700 feet; maximum range, 770 miles
**Armament:** none
**Service dates:** 1941–1945

The *Wichita* was an advanced, multiengine training aircraft. It was the first Beech aircraft constructed entirely of wood and was the first all-wood aircraft accepted by the Army as a training aircraft.

In 1940 the Army Air Corps approached the Beech Aircraft Company to design and build an advanced, twin-engine trainer constructed from non-strategic materials. This specification was made in anticipation of severe metal shortages if war should arrive. Beech responded with the Model 25, which incorporated many design features of existing Beech twin-engine craft but in fact was an entirely new design. True to Army specifications, it was built entirely of plywood, save for aluminum used in the motor cowlings and the cockpit enclosure. Even the fuel tank was made from wood, although it was lined with neoprene rubber to prevent leaks. The aircraft possessed superior performance when test-flown in 1941 and passed into Army service as the AT-10. It was subsequently christened the *Wichita* after the hometown of the main Beech plant.

During World War II, the *Wichita* proved to be one of the most important training aircraft in the American inventory. Nearly half of the Army Air Force pilots who were rated in multiengine aircraft received their qualifications in AT-10s. Between 1941 and 1943 the Beech factory in Kansas assembled 1,771 AT-10s; the Globe Company of Dallas, Texas, contributed another 600.

After the war numerous AT-10s ended up on the civilian market, but their wooden structure posed long-term preservation problems, and the craft rapidly passed from the scene. However, in 1945 Beech engineers fitted an AT-10 with a V-tail configuration. As anticipated, this arrangement weighed much less than a conventional tail structure, with appreciably less aerodynamic drag. The V-tail subsequently became a standard feature on Beech's famous *Bonanza* aircraft of the 1950s.

**Type:** Trainer

**Dimensions:** wingspan, 32 feet, 10 inches; length, 25 feet, 10 inches; height, 9 feet, 7 inches
**Weights:** empty, 2,055 pounds; gross, 2,900 pounds
**Power plant:** 1 × 225–horsepower Continental O-470 air-cooled engine
**Performance:** maximum speed, 189 miles per hour; ceiling, 20,000 feet; maximum range, 975 miles
**Armament:** none
**Service dates:** 1953–

The *Mentor* was the first postwar military training aircraft. Strong, easy to maintain, and fully aerobatic, it is still in service after 45 years.

By 1950 the Air Force decided it needed a new trainer to replace its aging North American T-6 *Texans*. The craft evaluated was the Beech Model 45, a privately funded project that was an outgrowth of the famous V-tail *Bonanza* of 1948. After three years of deliberation, the Air Force finally accepted delivery of 450 new trainers, designated the T-34A *Mentor*. It was a conventional low-wing monoplane with student and instructor seated in tandem under a large canopy. Because of its training duties, it was specially stressed to withstand the rigors of repeated dives, loops, and stalls. In service the T-34 proved itself to be an excellent aircraft, and in 1954 the Navy purchased the first of 423 T-34Bs. Since that date nearly every Navy, Marine Corps, and Coast Guard pilot has received his first flight in the pleasant-handling *Mentor*. Countless Air Force pilots also utilized it before graduating to the more powerful North American T-28 *Trojan* and the jet-powered Cessna T-37.

In 1973 the Navy sought to upgrade the *Mentor* in an attempt to extend its service life on a cost-effective basis. To accomplish this it fitted a standard T-34B with a 715-horsepower Pratt & Whitney PT-6A turbine engine, and the aircraft scored dramatic improvements in overall performance. Maximum speed increased from 189 to 257 miles per hour, with no degradation in terms of maneuverability. The Navy purchased 334 of these new craft under the designation T-34C, and they are still in use today. In terms of engine response and instrumentation, it closely approximates the small jet aircraft that students will graduate to. Several Latin American air forces also purchased T-34Cs and armed them as light attack aircraft.

## ⭐ Bell AH-1 *Cobra*

**Type:** Helicopter Gunship

**Dimensions:** rotor span, 44 feet; length, 44 feet, 7 inches; height, 13 feet, 6 inches
**Weights:** empty, 6,598 pounds; gross, 10,000 pounds
**Power plant:** 1 × 1,800–horsepower Lycoming T53 turboshaft engine
**Performance:** maximum speed, 141 miles per hour; ceiling, 12,200 feet; maximum range, 315 miles
**Armament:** 1 × 20mm Gatling gun; 8 × TOW antitank missiles
**Service dates:** 1967–

Fast and lethal, the *Cobra* was the world's first helicopter gunship. It served with distinction in Vietnam and has figured prominently in several other American conflicts.

As early as 1962 a report issued by the Army's Tactical Requirements Mobility Board predicted that helicopter gunships would constitute essential parts of the evolving airmobile warfare concept. This point was emphasized during the Vietnam War, when unescorted helicopter transports began taking losses to ground fire. By 1965 the worsening situation prompted the Army to announce competition for an Advanced Aerial Fire Support System (AAFSS), and five companies responded. The winner was Bell, which proposed a radically new type of helicopter based on its proven UH-1 *Huey*. The new craft was sleek, possessing a low profile and thin fuselage. Its crew consisted of a pilot and gunner seated under a long plastic canopy for good visi-

bility. Furthermore, the ship was equipped with a chin turret, and its two stubby wings also doubled as weapons pylons. Test trials were so impressive that in 1966 the new machine went into production and service as the AH-1 *Cobra*. The age of the helicopter gunship had dawned.

The AH-1 was deployed in Vietnam in 1967 and proved to be an effective escort and ground-support weapon. As its name implied, it struck quickly, usually with deadly results. In 1972 *Cobras* equipped with antitank missiles wreaked havoc upon North Vietnamese tank columns and were instrumental in defeating the communist Easter Offensive. They enjoyed similar results during the 1991 Gulf War. Subsequent models have added better armor, stronger engines, and a vast array of ultramodern weaponry to an already effective weapon platform. More than 1,500 AH-1s have been built and deployed by the United States, Japan, South Korea, Pakistan, and Israel.

**Type:** Helicopter Gunship

---

**Dimensions:** rotor span, 48 feet; length, 48 feet, 2 inches; height, 13 feet, 8 inches
**Weights:** empty, 10,200 pounds; gross, 14,750 pounds
**Power plant:** 2 × 1,600–horsepower General Electric T700 turboshaft engines
**Performance:** maximum speed, 218 miles per hour; ceiling, 17,500 feet; maximum range, 395 miles
**Armament:** 1 × 20mm cannon; 4 × 2.75–in. rocket pods or 8 × TOW antitank missiles or 2 ×
 *Sidewinder* air-to-air missiles
**Service dates:** 1969–

The *SeaCobra* is a more powerful version of its Army counterpart. Heavily armed and armored, it provides close air support for amphibious landings and ground operations.

As the Vietnam War unfolded during the mid-1960s, the Marine Corps watched the Army's success with AH-1 gunships, and in 1968 the Marines developed a version of their own. By 1969 a total of 160 AH-1J *SeaCobras* had been ordered; the *Sea-Cobra* differed from the Army version in having two engines to drive the same rotor shaft. This feature was considered essential for Marine operations, which were frequently conducted over water, and an extra-large engine meant a larger margin of safety. Throughout the war, *SeaCobras* fought well as ground support aircraft and clearly demonstrated their versatility. During this period, the Shah of Iran also purchased 202 AH-1Js, which had been configured to fire tube-launched optically tracked wire-guided (TOW) antitank missiles.

After Vietnam, the Marine Corps acquired additional *Cobras* and refined the power plant and armament. In 1975 the AH-1T was developed, featuring a larger airframe for more fuel, a lengthened tail boom, and improved rotor designs. The Marine Corps purchased 57 of these machines, which were also fitted as TOW platforms and became unofficially known as *KingCobras*. However, the ultimate version evolved in 1983, when a standard AH-1T was fitted with more powerful engines and a vast array of sophisticated electronics. Designated the AH-1W *SuperCobra*, this helicopter is equipped with a three-barreled 20mm cannon and can carry TOW, *Hellfire*, or 5-inch missiles for ground attack and *Sidewinder* air-to-air missiles for aerial defense. Furthermore, it possesses nocturnal fighting ability through sophisticated night-vision imaging technology. The Marines have since ordered 154 *SuperCobras;* they served well in Grenada and the 1991 Gulf War. Constant upgrades will keep them flying for years to come.

**Type:** Reconnaissance; Rescue Helicopter

**Dimensions:** rotor span, 37 feet, 2 inches; length, 32 feet, 7 inches; height, 9 feet, 6 inches
**Weights:** empty, 1,936 pounds; gross, 2,850 pounds
**Power plant:** 1 × 260–horsepower Lycoming TVO-435 air-cooled engine
**Performance:** maximum speed, 105 miles per hour; ceiling, 18,000 feet; maximum range, 324 miles
**Armament:** none
**Service dates:** 1946–1973

The ubiquitous *Sioux* rolled out of factories worldwide for nearly 20 years. As the first mass-produced military helicopter in history, it served the Army, Navy, and Marine Corps in a variety of functions.

Larry Bell flew his first helicopter in 1943, and in 1946 the Bell 47 became the first such machine to receive commercial certification. It was a simple, two-seated affair with an enclosed canopy and a unique rotor design consisting of a broad, two-bladed propeller, below which sat two counterweights acting as gyroscopic stabilizers. The Bell 47 became the world's first commercially produced helicopter, and the Army evaluated several examples in 1946. That same year it entered military service, first as the YR-13, then as the H-13 *Sioux*. The Navy acquired several machines, designated as HTLs. These first models featured fully enclosed cabins, but in 1948 the famous Bell 47D emerged, introducing the distinct goldfish-bowl canopy for improved vision.

An open-lattice tail boom with an antitorque rotor on the right side also became standard features. The Army immediately acquired 65 more H-13Bs and another 13 H-13Cs and rigged them as flying ambulances. The Navy also purchased 82 additional HTL-2s, half of which went to the Marine Corps.

The Korean War marked the first time that helicopters were introduced into the battlefield equation. From the onset, H-13s were called upon to perform reconnaissance, liaison, scouting, wire laying, and medical evacuation. The simple yet rugged *Sioux* fulfilled all of these tasks, and during the postwar years military orders continued to be placed with Bell. Moreover, the machine was licensed to be built in England, Japan, and Italy; when production finally halted in 1973, more than 6,000 had been built and deployed worldwide. That year the American H-13 was phased out by more advanced, turbine-powered designs, but several hundred commercial models remain in use around the world.

# ✪ Bell HSL-1

**Type:** Antisubmarine Helicopter

**Dimensions:** rotor span, 51 feet, 6 inches; length, 39 feet, 9 inches; height, 14 feet, 6 inches
**Weights:** empty, 12,540 pounds; gross, 26,500 pounds
**Power plant:** 1 × 1,900–horsepower Pratt & Whitney R-2800 Double Wasp radial engine
**Performance:** maximum speed, 135 miles per hour; ceiling, 15,500 feet; maximum range, 350 miles
**Armament:** 2 × Mk-43 homing torpedoes or 1 × Mk-24 mine
**Service dates:** 1954–1960

The ungainly HSL-1 was the largest helicopter of its day and the first expressly designed for antisubmarine warfare (ASW). Though unsuccessful in that role, it laid the groundwork for better designs and more efficient technology.

In 1950 Bell won a Navy competition to build the world's first antisubmarine warfare helicopter. It did so by designing its only twin-rotor machine, a field previously monopolized by Piasecki. Bell also hoped that a sizable quantity would be purchased by the Royal Navy. The XHSL-1 underwent prolonged development and was plagued by technological problems, which were finally solved in 1953 when the prototype was successfully tested. Despite its large appearance, the HSL-1 was powered by a single engine fitted with two drive shafts. Because the HSL-1 was an ASW craft, the Navy intended to employ it in hunter/killer teams whereby the "hunter," equipped with two sonar operators, would locate an enemy submarine, whereas the "killer,"

flown by only two crew members, attacked with homing torpedoes. In 1954 an initial order for 96 HSL-1s was placed by the Navy, with an additional 18 for the Fleet Air Arm. However, the British eventually lost interest and canceled, and American orders were scaled back to only 50 machines.

During its service this large helicopter flew well yet proved unwieldy and unsuited for effective ASW warfare. Its sheer bulk and hand-folded rotor blades made for awkward handling atop carrier decks, and tremendous engine and rotor noise prevented sonar operators from accurately establishing contacts. The HSL-1 was soon withdrawn from active duty and replaced by the smaller, more manageable Sikorsky SH-34. However, some of the remaining machines were tested extensively as airborne minesweepers and operated with considerable success. A squadron of HSL-1s remained stationed near the Panama Canal until being disbanded in mid-1960.

# Bell OH-58 *Kiowa*/H-57 *Jet Ranger*

**Type:** Reconnaissance; Training Helicopter

**Dimensions:** rotor span, 35 feet; length, 42 feet, 2 inches; height, 12 feet, 9 inches
**Weight:** empty, 2,825 pounds; gross, 4,500 pounds
**Power plant:** 1 × 750–horsepower Allison T703 turboshaft engine
**Performance:** maximum speed, 149 miles per hour; ceiling, 17,200 feet; maximum range, 345 miles
**Armament:** up to 2 × 7.62mm machine guns or 6 × *Hellfire* antitank missiles
**Service dates:** 1969–

The *Kiowa* is based upon a very successful civilian design. It served well in Vietnam, continues to operate as an armed scout, and also functions as a Navy trainer.

In 1963 the Army announced a competition for a light observation helicopter (LOH); the Hughes OH-6 *Cayuse* won out the following year. However, the rather ugly Bell entry, the Model 206, was completely overhauled and given a streamlined fuselage, and in 1968 it entered the commercial field as the beautiful *Jet Ranger*. It was instantly successful, and more than 5,000 were sold worldwide. That same year the Army took a second look and decided it needed a fast machine with greater range and payload than the OH-6. Consequently, an order went out for 2,200 *Jet Rangers*, which in 1969 entered service as the OH-58 *Kiowa*. In Vietnam *Kiowas* served as scout ships and frequently worked as spotters for the Bell AH-1 *Cobra* gunships. After the war the

Army continued refining the basic *Kiowa* design, with the latest being the OH-58D. This is a heavily armed craft and sports a four-bladed rotor rather than the two-bladed rotor used on earlier models. Furthermore, a distinct, mast-mounted infrared laser sight endows the helicopter with night-fighting capability. It is also equipped with laser-guided *Hellfire* antitank missiles and has unofficially been dubbed the *Kiowa Warrior*.

In 1968 the Navy also expressed interest in the *Jet Ranger*, purchasing 40 to serve as the TH-57. This was the first turbine-powered helicopter trainer in the world and differed from civilian versions by having tandem controls, naval avionics, and a longer boom and skids. TH-57s are used to impart the rudiments of vertical flight, basic instrument techniques, and night flying to fledgling helicopter pilots. Both versions—the *Kiowa* and the *Jet Ranger*—will be operational well into the 21st century.

**Type:** Fighter

**Dimensions:** wingspan, 34 feet; length, 30 feet, 2 inches; height, 12 feet, 5 inches
**Weights:** empty, 5,462 pounds; gross, 7,651 pounds
**Power plant:** 1 × 1,200–horsepower Allison V-1710 liquid-cooled engine
**Performance:** maximum speed, 382 miles per hour; ceiling, 35,000 feet; maximum range, 650 miles
**Armament:** 1 × 37mm cannon; 2 × .50–caliber nose guns; 4 × .30–caliber wing guns
**Service dates:** 1939–1944

Bell's P-39 was in many ways a radical design. It was the first Army Air Corps fighter with tricycle landing gear, it was the first airplane mounting an engine behind the pilot, and it was the first fighter designed around a 37mm cannon.

The P-39 was designed and flown in 1939 and incorporated many unique innovations. It was impressively sleek, relatively easy to handle, and carried the heaviest armament of any fighter flown to that date. The prototype, equipped with a turbosupercharger for high altitude, performed well, and the Army placed an order for several hundred in 1940. However, for unexplained reasons the supercharger was removed on production models, which restricted the P-39 to mid- and low-altitude missions.

At the time of the Japanese attack on Pearl Harbor in December 1941, the P-39 was among the most numerous aircraft in the American inventory. It was first committed to combat in April 1942 during the defense of Port Moresby, New Guinea, where, lacking altitude and being less nimble than Japanese adversaries, *Airacobra* took heavy losses in air-to-air combat. However, its performance as a ground-attack craft was impressive, combining as it did a relatively fast low-altitude speed with hard-hitting armament.

In Europe, the P-39's career was equally mixed. The Royal Air Force rejected the design after a few combat sorties, but the American aircraft performed well as a ground-attack craft in the North African and Italian campaigns. There it enjoyed one of the lowest loss ratios of any machine deployed in this fashion until being phased out for more advanced designs in 1944. Curiously, the *Airacobra* found its true niche as a tank-buster on the Eastern Front, where Soviet pilots appreciated its heavy cannon, high speed, and robust design. Of the 9,560 aircraft produced, approximately half went to the Red Air Force.

# ★ Bell P-59 *Airacomet*

**Type:** Fighter

**Dimensions:** wingspan, 45 feet, 6 inches; length, 38 feet, 2 inches; height, 12 feet, 4 inches
**Weights:** empty, 7,320 pounds; gross, 12,562 pounds
**Power plant:** 1 × 1,250–pound thrust General Electric I-A turbojet engine
**Performance:** maximum speed, 413 miles per hour; ceiling, 45,756 feet; maximum range, 525 miles
**Armament:** 1 × 37mm cannon; 4 × .50–caliber machine guns
**Service dates:** 1944–1945

The *Airacomet* was the Army Air Force's first jet aircraft and the only such aircraft acquired during World War II. It was unsuited for combat but laid the foundation for later high-performance aircraft.

In 1939 the Germans scored a technological breakthrough with the first jet-powered aircraft. Two years later the British, under Dr. Frank Whittle, managed the same achievement, and General Hap Arnold began pushing for an American jet program. In September 1941 the British allowed the United States to manufacture the Whittle turbojet engine, and it fell upon the Bell Aircraft Corporation to produce an airframe to go with it. Development moved swiftly, and within a year, on October 1, 1942, the XP-59A first flew. This was a twin-engine, straight-wing design with fully retractable tricycle landing gear. The engines were mounted on either side of the underbelly to keep the fuselage as clean as possible. The testing program also proceeded smoothly, and although the XP-59 flew safely and handled well, its top speed of only 400 miles per hour offered few advantages over piston-powered aircraft already in service. It was also judged unsatisfactory as a gunnery platform.

Despite the *Airacomet*'s shortcomings, the Army Air Force was eager to gain operational experience with jet aircraft, so 13 YP-59As were constructed, followed by an additional 50 production models. They were initially deployed with the 412th Fighter Group in 1945 and extensively flown. At length, it was decided to outfit the *Airacomets* for engine research and as drone aircraft directors. Two units were handed to the Navy for evaluation, and another was exchanged for a British Gloster *Meteor* jet fighter. By the fall of 1945 the P-59's brief service career was eclipsed by Lockheed's P-80 *Shooting Star*. Undistinguished as a fighter, the *Airacomet* nonetheless provided the Air Force with valuable experience and technical information.

**Type:** Fighter

**Dimensions:** wingspan, 38 feet, 4 inches; length, 32 feet, 8 inches; height, 12 feet, 7 inches
**Weights:** empty, 6,375 pounds; gross, 10,500 pounds
**Power plant:** 1 × 1,325–horsepower Allison V-1710 liquid-cooled engine
**Performance:** maximum speed, 410 miles per hour; ceiling, 43,000 feet; maximum range, 450 miles
**Armament:** 1 × 37mm cannon; 4 × .50–caliber machine guns; 1,500 pounds of bombs
**Service dates:** 1944–1946

The *Kingcobra* was one of few American fighters to be developed after U.S. entry into World War II. Although produced in large numbers, it never flew with the Army Air Force and was widely exported abroad.

Deficiencies with the P-39 *Airacobra* prompted the Bell Aircraft Corporation to consider a totally revamped airplane based on the original design. Although outwardly similar to the P-39, the P-63, christened the *Kingcobra*, was an entirely new aircraft featuring low-drag laminar wings, a redesigned tail, and a supercharged engine. In the spring of 1943 two prototypes crashed, but a third prototype prompted the Army to place a production order that autumn. Like its predecessor, the P-63 was only marginally effective as an interceptor, but it excelled in a ground-attack role. It was fast at low altitudes, was heavily armed, and could absorb a great amount of damage.

By 1944 the Army decided not to employ the P-63 and cleared it for export abroad. Of 3,303 *Kingcobras* produced, no less than 2,456 served with the Soviet Union's Red Air Force as a tank-buster. An additional 300 were supplied to the French Armée de l'Air for service in Indochina (Vietnam) after the war. Thus, the P-63 was the only mass-produced American fighter that saw no combat with U.S. forces.

An unusual variant of the *Kingcobra* deployed in the United States was the RP-63, the so-called Pinball Target. This plane was stripped of armament and most other equipment and heavily reinforced with a duraluminum alloy skin and a bulletproof windshield. Painted bright orange, it would buzz training aircraft during gunnery practice and be deliberately shot at with live ammunition. When struck by easily fragmented (frangible) bullets, bright red lights on the fuselage and wings blinked on and off, indicating hits. Production of RP-63s totaled 332; they were retired immediately after the war.

# ☆ Bell UH-1 *Iroquois*

**Type:** Transport; Helicopter Gunship

**Dimensions:** rotor span, 48 feet; length, 41 feet, 10 inches; height, 13 feet, 5 inches
**Weights:** empty, 5,550 pounds; gross, 9,500 pounds
**Power plant:** 1 × 1,400–horsepower Lycoming T-53 turboshaft engine
**Performance:** maximum speed, 127 miles per hour; ceiling, 12,700 feet; maximum range, 777 miles
**Armament:** up to 4 × 7.62mm machine guns or 2 × 40mm grenade launchers; 6 × TOW antitank missiles
**Service dates:** 1959–

The *Huey*, a legendary workhorse of the Vietnam War, has been produced in greater numbers than any aircraft since World War II. It is still operated by 55 air forces around the world.

In 1955 the Army put forth specifications for a new medical evacuation helicopter. The following year, Bell responded with the XH-40, a sleek, single-rotor craft with a wide cabin to accommodate medical stretchers lengthwise. As a military troop carrier, up to six fully loaded soldiers could also be transported. The Army authorized three prototypes, which flew successfully in 1956, and a decision was made to procure them in quantity. The first machines arrived in 1959 as the HU-1 *Iroquois*, but based upon their initials this machine acquired the time-honored nickname "Huey." In 1962 it was redesignated the UH-1, but the nickname stuck fast.

UH-1s were among the first modern helicopters to serve in the Vietnam War, and they became a common sight in the skies over that war-torn country. In 1962 the Army armed several with machine guns and rocket pods for flak suppression, giving rise to version UH-1C. During airmobile operations, these gunships swooped in low while more vulnerable troopships remained aloft until the landing zone was declared safe. Afterward, medical *Hueys* evacuated the casualties. The various UH-1s rendered distinguished service during the world's first helicopter war, although gunship versions were later supplanted by the faster AH-1 *Cobras*.

Vietnam demonstrated the strength and versatility of the basic UH-1 design, and the machines were consequently manufactured under license in Japan and Italy. To date, more than 10,000 have been built and deployed by 65 countries around the world. By the year 2000 most American UH-1s will have been replaced by the more advanced UH-60 *Black Hawks*.

## ⭐ Bell V-22 *Osprey*

**Type:** Transport

---

**Dimensions:** rotor span, 38 feet; length, 56 feet, 10 inches; height, 17 feet, 4 inches
**Weights:** empty, 31,772 pounds; gross; 55,000 pounds
**Power plant:** 2 × 6,150–horsepower Allison T-406 turboprop engines
**Performance:** maximum speed, 315 miles per hour; ceiling, 30,000 feet; maximum range, 2,417 miles
**Armament:** 2 × .50–caliber machine guns
**Service dates:** 1998–

---

The *Osprey* is the world's first tilt-rotor warplane. It features the versatility of a helicopter and the speed of a conventional aircraft.

Military planners have long recognized that helicopters, with their relatively slow forward speed and high operating costs, are unsuited for certain types of combat missions. Bell began addressing the problem as early as 1958, when it fielded the XV-3, a twin-engine tilt-rotor prototype. This combined the vertical takeoff and landing characteristics of a helicopter with the flying abilities of an airplane.

Since that time, advances in technology have allowed great strides in performance and survivability under combat conditions. Successive designs enhanced the practical application of tilt-rotor technology, and in 1983 the Pentagon awarded Bell a contract to construct and test two prototypes of its new V-22. The *Osprey* is a medium-sized aircraft with a capacity to carry 24 fully armed troops anywhere in the world. It is constructed almost completely of high-strength, lightweight composites of graphite and epoxy. Amazingly, metal accounts for only 1,000 pounds of the aircraft's basic structure. Its most dramatic feature is the long, swept-forward wing, whose wingtip engine pods can tilt up or down 90 degrees. This enables the V-22 to operate like a helicopter, that is, without the use of runways, yet fly rapidly to its destination. Furthermore, it is completely automated and employs advanced fly-by-wire computers, which render this complex and sophisticated aircraft easy to fly and control in all flight modes.

Bell successfully tested five prototypes commencing in 1987 while politicians dithered over whether to construct the radical craft or not. In 1997 the U.S. Congress finally authorized procurement of 552 *Ospreys* for the Marine Corps as troop-carrying assault ships. Deliveries began in 1998, and within a few years the V-22 will completely replace the slower, more vulnerable CH-46 *Sea Knight* and CH-53 *Sea Stallion* helicopters.

**Type:** Reconnaissance

**Dimensions:** wingspan, 33 feet, 8 inches; length, 25 feet, 8 inches; height, 10 feet, 10 inches
**Weights:** empty, 3,104 pounds; gross, 3,629 pounds
**Power plant:** 1 × 400–horsepower Pratt & Whitney R-985 Wasp Junior radial engine
**Performance:** maximum speed, 149 miles per hour; ceiling, 15,600 feet; maximum range, 643 miles
**Armament:** 2 × .30–caliber machine guns
**Service dates:** 1933–1940

This was a relatively obscure aircraft from a company known for its design failures. Nonetheless, the OJ-2 proved itself a dependable, useful machine with a long service life.

In 1930 the Navy began looking to replace its Vought O2U *Corsairs* with a more modern observation craft. Like its predecessors, the new machine would have interchangeable wheels and floats and be able to operate at sea from capital ships. At length two contestants, the Keystone XOK-1 and the Berliner-Joyce XOJ-2, emerged, and both were returned to their respective companies for modifications. When the improved XOJ-2 flew it was 100 pounds lighter and almost 30 miles per hour faster, and it was declared the winner. It was a standard biplane of wood and metal construction, fabric covering, and two open cockpits. The wings were staggered and equipped with a high-lift device called a "Zap-flap." This device operated as wing flaps on

takeoff and independently as ailerons in flight, but it was deleted from production models. The new aircraft joined the fleet in 1933 as the OJ-2; 39 were eventually constructed. Considering that Berliner-Joyce had a track record of poorly received prototypes for the military, its success was exceptional.

The OJ-2s were operated exclusively by the scouting squadrons VS-5B and VS-6B for several years. It was standard Navy practice to assign a section of two aircraft to a battleship or cruiser to function as the eyes of the fleet. By 1936 the OJ-2 was gradually replaced by the Curtiss SOC *Seagull*, mainly because the new craft employed folding wings, whereas the Berliner-Joyce did not. The OJ-2s were then shunted over into the Naval Reserves, where they remained several years before being retired in 1941. For the time it operated, the OJ-2 was one of the best observation aircraft of its class.

# Berliner-Joyce P-16/PB-1

**Type:** Fighter

---

**Dimensions:** wingspan, 34 feet; length, 28 feet, 2 inches; height, 9 feet
**Weights:** empty, 2,803 pounds; gross, 3,996 pounds
**Power plant:** 1 × 600–horsepower Curtiss Conqueror V-1570 liquid-cooled engine
**Performance:** maximum speed, 175 miles per hour; ceiling, 21,600 feet; maximum range, 650 miles
**Armament:** 3 × .30–caliber machine guns; 244 pounds of bombs
**Service dates:** 1932–1934

The P-16 was something of a flying anachronism, being the last biplane fighter accepted into Army service. Underpowered and difficult to land, it had a brief and undistinguished service record.

The Berliner-Joyce Aircraft Corporation had been founded in Dundalk, Maryland, in 1929, on the cusp of the Great Depression. Although Berliner-Joyce intended to design civilian and sport aircraft, the ensuing financial distress forced it to compete for military contracts. In 1929 the Army announced competition for a two-seat fighter craft, something it had not attempted since 1923. Ironically, the Berliner-Joyce design managed to beat out competing entries from such well-established firms as Boeing and Curtiss. The ensuing TP-1 prototype was unveiled in the fall of 1929 as a standard biplane, although the upper wing was faired into the fuselage, giving it a distinct gull-wing appearance. The upper wing was also longer than the lower one and placed ahead in a positive stagger. Both fuselage and wings were constructed of metal tubing and fabric covering, and pilot and gunner were seated in tandem. The TP-1 was equipped with a supercharged engine that made for adequate performance, so in 1931 the craft entered the Army Air Corps as the P-16. Soon after it was redesignated the PB-1 for "Pursuit, Biplane."

The new aircraft was assigned to the 94th Pursuit Squadron for service trials. Unfortunately, the 25 preproduction PB-1s acquired by the Army had their superchargers deleted and were fitted with three-bladed propellers. This resulted in greater range but inferior performance at high altitude. Also, tests revealed the aircraft possessed poor forward vision, and its center of gravity was too far forward. This gave it an unsavory tendency to ground loop (tip over) while landing. After only a few months of service, the PB-1 was retired in 1934. Thereafter, the Army Air Corps paid greater attention to more modern, monoplane designs.

# ⭐ Boeing B-17 *Flying Fortress*

**Type:** Heavy Bomber

**Dimensions:** wingspan, 103 feet, 9 nine inches; length, 74 feet, 4 inches; height, 19 feet, 1 inch
**Weights:** empty, 36,135 pounds; gross, 65,500 pounds
**Power plant:** 4 × Wright Cyclone R-1820 supercharged radial engines
**Performance:** maximum speed, 287 miles per hour; ceiling, 35,600 feet; maximum range, 3,400 miles
**Armament:** 13 × .50–caliber machine guns; 4,000 pounds of bombs
**Service dates:** 1937–1945

The B-17 was the world's first modern heavy bomber and a potent symbol of American airpower. It was easy to fly, incredibly rugged, and became the grande dame of the Army Air Force.

Boeing designed the prototype Model 299 as a replacement for the aging Keystone bombers in 1934. It flew the following year as a sleek, four-motor craft with impressive range and speed for its day. The Army Air Corps acquired its first B-17s in 1937, but by the advent of World War II only 30 had been procured. Several of these early Model Cs were loaned to the British, who found them lightly armed and unsuited for high-altitude bombing. Boeing responded by developing the B-17E in 1941; this aircraft possessed a completely enlarged and redesigned tail mounting two .50-caliber machine guns for defense. It also had a unique ventral ball turret to protect its undersides and self-sealing fuel tanks.

The B-17s were present at Pearl Harbor and saw active service in the Philippines and New Guinea. However, as time passed they formed the backbone of the American strategic bombing effort over Germany. From bases in England, armadas of B-17s, in tandem with Consolidated B-24s, hit factories, rail facilities, and petroleum plants with devastating accuracy. However, the unescorted bombers paid dearly, and nearly one-third of the 12,726 B-17s constructed were lost over Europe to flak and enemy aircraft. The toll would have been much higher, save for the B-17's ability to absorb incredible amounts of punishment and stay aloft. It was not uncommon for a *Flying Fortress* to limp back to base with large sections of its wing and fuselage shot off. The final Model G featured a powered chin turret to discourage the lethal, head-on attacks practiced by the German Luftwaffe. By 1945 the B-17 dropped more than 640,000 tons of bombs over Europe, nearly a third again as the more numerous B-24.

**Type:** Heavy Bomber

**Dimensions:** wingspan, 141 feet, 3 inches; length, 99 feet; height, 29 feet, 7 inches
**Weights:** empty, 74,500 pounds; gross, 135,000 pounds
**Power plant:** 4 × 2,200–horsepower Wright Cyclone R-3350 turbocharged radial engines
**Performance:** maximum speed, 358 miles per hour; ceiling, 31,850 feet; maximum range, 3,250 miles
**Armament:** 12 × .50–caliber machine guns; 20,000 pounds of bombs
**Service dates:** 1944–1954

The B-29 was the most technically advanced bomber of World War II and the only aircraft to drop atomic weapons in anger. Even with conventional weapons, the giant *Superfortress* represented a quantum jump in bombing capabilities.

As early as 1938 the Army Air Corps began searching to replace its B-17 *Flying Fortresses* with a more formidable craft. Boeing responded with its Model 345, which represented a radical departure from conventional bomber designs. It incorporated such advanced technology as a pressurized fuselage to protect the crew from high altitudes, a fully automatically powered gun-turret system, and two superchargers on each of the four engines. The prototype flew first in September 1942, but nearly two years were required to make the giant craft operational. Because of the aircraft's enormous range, it was decided to deploy it exclusively in the Pacific, where vast distances often separated bases and targets.

The first B-29 raids were staged in August 1944 from primitive fields in China, and results from the high-altitude bombing were mixed. It fell upon General Curtis E. LeMay to completely alter American bombing strategy. Instead of precision daylight bombing, he stripped his B-29s of armament to save weight, sent them in at low altitudes during the night, and effectively burned out several Japanese cities. In August 1945 the B-29s *Enola Gay* and *Bock's Car* dropped atomic weapons on Hiroshima and Nagasaki, which effectively ended the war. Total production of the B-29 ceased at that point, having reached 3,000 units.

The B-29 remained in the postwar inventory, and many were converted into tanker KB-29s. The bomber was also active during the Korean War and dropped 167,000 tons of explosives on communist targets, although many were lost to the modern MiG-15 jet fighters. This concluded the B-29's front-line service, and it was soon phased out entirely in favor of the faster B-50.

# ⭐ Boeing B-47 *Stratojet*

**Type:** Medium Bomber

**Dimensions:** wingspan, 166 feet; length, 107 feet, 1 inch; height, 27 feet, 11 inches
**Weights:** empty, 78,200 pounds; gross, 220,000 pounds
**Power plant:** 6 × 5,970–pound thrust General Electric J-47 turbojet engines
**Performance:** maximum speed, 606 miles per hour; ceiling; 38,000 feet; maximum range, 3,600 miles
**Armament:** 2 × .50–caliber machine guns; up to 20,000 pounds of conventional or nuclear bombs
**Service dates:** 1951–1966

Sleek and futuristic, the *Stratojet* was one of the most important military aircraft ever conceived. It revolutionized jet bomber design and served as the mainstay of the Strategic Air Command throughout the 1950s.

The advent of German jet fighters in 1944 prompted the Army Air Force to explore the possibility of jet bombers to counter them. The following year, Boeing put forth its famous Model 350, which incorporated the latest German swept-wing technology to reduce drag and increase range and speed.

The prototype XB-47 first flew in December 1947 and was unlike any aircraft ever built to that date. It was the first swept-wing bomber in production; it possessed ultrathin laminar wings for low drag; and it was powered by six podded jet engines. It was also the first aircraft to have tandem bicycle landing gear. Because it depended on speed for defense, guns were dispensed with save for two .50-caliber "stingers" in the tail. Furthermore, it was highly automated, reducing the crew to only pilot, copilot, and navigator/bombardier. The XB-47 proved somewhat underpowered, but it exhibited excellent characteristics and was ordered into production. Numerous technological problems had to be overcome, so the first B-47s were not deployed with Air Force bomber units until 1951.

The *Stratojet* represented a quantum jump in bombing capacities, and with inflight refueling it could hit distant targets quickly and high altitude. Being faster than many jet fighters of the day, it was literally invulnerable to interception for many years. More than 2,000 were constructed, of which 1,600 were bombers; 600 served as reconnaissance or electronic surveillance aircraft. Throughout the dangerous Cold War years of the 1950s it served capably as the backbone of American nuclear deterrence and helped keep the peace. The last B-47s were phased out of service in 1966 and replaced by the equally celebrated B-52s.

**Type:** Heavy Bomber; Reconnaissance

---

**Dimensions:** wingspan, 141 feet, 3 inches; length, 100 feet; height, 34 feet, 7 inches
**Weights:** empty, 81,000 pounds; gross, 173,000 pounds
**Power plant:** 4 × 3,500–horsepower Pratt & Whitney R-4360 Wasp Major radial engines
**Performance:** maximum speed, 400 miles per hour; ceiling, 38,000 feet; maximum range, 4,900 miles
**Armament:** 13 × .50–caliber machine guns; up to 20,000 pounds of conventional or nuclear bombs
**Service dates:** 1947–1964

---

The B-50 was the Strategic Air Command's first frontline aircraft and the Air Force's last propeller-driven bomber. Though a vast improvement over the earlier B-29, it was outclassed by jet aircraft, and several were shot down.

Toward the end of World War II, Boeing fitted a standard B-29 bomber with entirely new engines, a taller tail, and numerous other refinements. Initially called the B-29D, it passed into service as the B-50 *Superfortress* in 1947 and became the first frontline bomber for the newly created Strategic Air Command. Its principal mission was to drop atomic and conventional weapons, presumably on targets within the distant Soviet Union. However, with the invention of aerial refueling, range was no longer a problem. In February 1949 a B-50 named "Lucky Lady" flew nonstop around the world, covering 23,452 miles in only 94 hours. The fact it had been refueled four times in midair underscored that the age of the intercontinental bomber had dawned.

For all its good properties, the propeller-driven B-50 was outclassed by jet fighters and vulnerable to interception. This reality became painfully apparent when several reconnaissance RB-50s were shot down during the Korean War and during peripheral flights around the Soviet Union. As the B-50s were slowly phased out of frontline service by faster Boeing B-47 *Stratojets*, 126 of them were converted to KB-50 aerial tankers with the Tactical Air Command. As the jet fighters gradually grew too fast for aerial refueling at low speeds, several KB-50s were fitted with jet engine pods so that they could keep pace. The B-50 was finally dropped from the SAC inventory in 1958, although a final version, the WB-50 weather reconnaissance craft, lingered in Air Force service as late as 1964. A total of 371 had been constructed.

# Boeing B-52 *Stratofortress*

**Type:** Strategic Bomber

**Dimensions:** wingspan, 185 feet; length, 157 feet, 7 inches; height, 40 feet, 8 inches
**Weights:** empty, 195,000 pounds; gross, 488,000 pounds
**Power plant:** 8 × 17,000–pound thrust Pratt & Whitney TF33 turbofan engines
**Performance:** maximum speed, 595 miles per hour; ceiling, 55,000 feet; maximum range, 8,800 miles
**Armament:** 1 × 20mm Gatling gun; 40,000 pounds of bombs, nuclear weapons, or missiles
**Service dates:** 1955–

The venerable *Stratofortress* is entering its 45th year of distinguished service with the U.S. Air Force. Continual weapons and electronic upgrades will keep it flying well into the 21st century.

Conceived in 1944 as a follow-on to the B-47 *Stratojet*, the XB-52 underwent continual redesign for a decade and first flew in 1954. Like its smaller brother, it featured a high-mounted swept wing, with eight podded engines, and bicycle landing gear. However, it was a full 30 percent larger, with greater fuel and payload capacities. Using inflight refueling, a B-52 could rain nuclear destruction on any target in the world in a matter of hours. This point was underscored in 1957, when three B-52s flew nonstop from Okinawa to Madrid, Spain, in only 45 hours. The latest version, the B-52H, which was deployed in 1961, differed in several respects from previous models. Its eight turbofan jets increased its range by nearly a third, and the fuselage was stressed for op-

erations as a low-altitude penetration bomber. Additionally, all B-52s could be rigged for maritime reconnaissance, ship interdiction, and aerial mining.

Despite Cold War tensions, the B-52 was never called upon to use nuclear weapons in anger. Instead, it fought over Vietnam and later Iraq as gigantic bombing platforms, dropping millions of tons of conventional weapons from ten miles up. During Operation Linebacker in 1972, around-the-clock B-52 raids against Hanoi forced the communists to accept peace negotiations. During the January 1991 war with Iraq, a B-52H flew the world's longest bombing mission by flying nonstop from Louisiana to Baghdad, releasing several cruise missiles, and returning unscathed. Nearly 100 of these craft are still in service today and will remain so for the next 40 years, making it the first warplane with a service life of nearly a century! One of the greatest aircraft of all time.

# ✪ Boeing C

**Type:** Trainer

---

**Dimensions:** wingspan, 43 feet, 10 inches; length, 27 feet; height, 12 feet, 7 inches
**Weights:** empty, 1,898 pounds; gross, 2,395 pounds
**Power plant:** 1 × 100–horsepower Hall-Scott liquid-cooled engine
**Performance:** maximum speed, 72 miles per hour; ceiling, 6,500 feet; maximum range, 200 miles
**Armament:** none
**Service dates:** 1918

---

The Model C was Boeing's first mass-produced airplane and its first military design. Although not entirely successful, it established Boeing as a manufacturer of warplanes.

In 1917 the young Boeing company of Seattle, Washington, submitted a modified version of its C-4 commercial airplane to the Navy as a possible float trainer. This craft was only William Boeing's second design and very similar to its civilian counterpart. It was of all-wood construction and sported two large floats and an all-moving tailplane. The Model C also featured extremely staggered wings with increased dihedral to promote better stability. A controversial aspect was its lack of a conventional horizontal stabilizer, but Boeing maintained that the design was so stable that one was not required. Tests were favorable, so in 1918 the Navy contracted for 50 machines. This act established Boeing as a respectable manufacturer of aircraft.

The Model C was easy to fly and an excellent trainer, but the type was not widely employed. The reason was the Hall-Scott engine, which performed poorly and was unreliable. Consequently, the bulk of Model Cs delivered remained in packing crates for the duration of World War I. In view of this difficulty, the Navy ordered a single example of the C-1F, which was fitted with a reliable Curtiss OXX engine and a single float, but no additional orders were forthcoming. After the war, the entire inventory of Model Cs was declared surplus and put up for sale. In civilian hands, Model Cs were usually refitted with Curtiss OX-5s or Wright-Hispano engines to improve performance. On March 3, 1919, a Model C made history by initiating the first airmail delivery between Seattle and Victoria, British Columbia, Canada. The type soon passed into oblivion, but as late as 1931 two Model Cs were given German markings and deliberately crashed in the famous film *Dawn Patrol*.

# ⭐ Boeing E-3 *Sentry*

**Type:** Airborne Early Warning

---

**Dimensions:** wingspan, 145 feet, 9 inches; length, 152 feet, 11 inches; height, 41 feet, 4 inches
**Weights:** empty, 162,000 pounds; gross, 325,000 pounds
**Power plant:** 4 × 21,000–pound thrust Pratt & Whitney TF33 turbofan engines
**Performance:** maximum speed, 530 miles per hour; ceiling, 40,000 feet; maximum range, 1,151 miles
**Armament:** none
**Service dates:** 1977–

The *Sentry* is the world's most advanced airborne warning and control system (AWACS) aircraft. It is essential to command-and-control functions in modern warfare.

The Air Force pioneered the concept of airborne early warning aircraft with their deployment of the EC-121 *Warning Star* during the 1950s. The placement of a radar platform high over a battlefield gave potentially decisive advantages in lead time and countermeasures. During the following decades computers made great strides in terms of data collection and processing, which in turn enabled radars to look directly down onto the ground to detect rapidly moving objects such as planes and missiles. During the early 1970s it was decided to mount these new computer/radar arrays in a relatively modern airframe. The resulting craft, the E-3 *Sentry*, first flew in 1977, and a total of 34 has been delivered to the U.S. Air Force. The *Sentry* consists of a modified Boeing 707/320 aircraft outfitted with a dazzling array of computing and radar detection systems. Its most conspicuous feature is a 30-foot rotating radar dish, located toward the top rear of the fuselage. This large unit turns at six revolutions per minute while operating and has a detection range of 200 miles. Equipped with computers that can sort out 1.25 million bits of information per second, the E-3 can distinguish military hardware from ground clutter, compute its trajectory, and vector in fighter interceptions.

The E-3 was one of the first American aircraft to arrive in Saudi Arabia following the August 1990 Iraqi invasion of Kuwait and flew around-the-clock surveillance missions up through the successful conclusion of Operation Desert Storm. From their lofty perches, the E-3s helped assist more than 120,000 Allied bombing sorties and vectored in 38 of 40 aerial interceptions. They literally ran the air war over Iraq. Since then, *Sentry* aircraft constantly patrol America's borders searching for aircraft and ships engaged in drug smuggling.

**Type:** Airborne Command Post

**Dimensions:** wingspan, 195 feet, 8 inches; length, 231 feet, 4 inches; height, 63 feet, 5 inches
**Weights:** empty, 460,000 pounds; gross, 800,000 pounds
**Power plant:** 4 × 52,500–pound thrust General Electric F-103 turbofan engines
**Performance:** maximum speed, 602 miles per hour; ceiling, 45,000 feet; maximum range, 7,100 miles
**Armament:** none
**Service dates:** 1974–

In the event of nuclear war, the E-4B will help coordinate America's strategic retaliatory response. It is one of the most complex and automated flying headquarters ever devised.

During the early 1970s the Air Force began looking for a bigger aircraft to replace its aging fleet of EC-135 airborne command posts. At that time Boeing had unveiled its giant Model 747 passenger jet, which boasted five times the endurance and internal volume of earlier transports. In 1973 the Air Force acquired two 747s as part of its Advanced Airborne National Command Post (AABNCP) program, and the following year they went into service as E-4As. Two more were purchased for a total of four. The giant craft were outfitted with a complex array of computers and communications equipment, although not much evolved beyond those employed by the EC-135. Nonetheless, the E-4As acted as giant mobile military headquarters, virtually immune from attack once airborne. Their duty was to coordinate

national defense efforts during time of war, especially if stationary command posts had been eliminated by surprise attack.

As impressive as the E-4A was, its equipment was rapidly overtaken by the latest strides in computer and processing technology. Therefore, in 1979 the Air Force fielded the first of two E-4Bs. They were outwardly identical to the earlier models save for a prominent dorsal blister just aft of the main cabin. Its battle staff consists of 30 members backed by an operating crew of 119. The E-4B has been extensively shielded against the effects of thermonuclear radiation in the event of a near-miss, and it trails a low-frequency antenna of wire stretching five miles. Outfitted with the very latest top-secret technology, the E-4B can launch American ICBM missiles against an enemy and even redirect targeting during flight. These capable craft are also among the most expensive ever flown, costing $258 million apiece.

**Type:** Fighter

**Dimensions:** wingspan, 30 feet, 1 inch; length, 22 feet, 11 inches; height, 9 feet, 2 inches
**Weights:** empty, 1,989 pounds; gross, 2,805 pounds
**Power plant:** 1 × 425–horsepower Pratt & Whitney R-1340 radial engine
**Performance:** maximum speed, 158 miles per hour; ceiling, 21,500 feet; maximum range, 317 miles
**Armament:** 2 × .30–caliber machine guns; 5 × 25–pound bombs
**Service dates:** 1928–1932

The F2B was one of the first radial-engine fighters adopted by the Navy. Although never produced in large numbers, it equipped the country's first precision aerobatic team.

The growing perfection of radial-engine technology offered distinct advantages over more intricate liquid-cooled engines in terms of reliability and combat survival. In 1926 Boeing designed its first expressly carrier-based fighter to be powered by the new Pratt & Whitney R-1340. Model 69 flew later that fall and received the Navy prototype designation XF2B-1. It was a standard biplane design based on the earlier PW-8/FB series of fighters, but it featured several refinements. Like its forebears, the new craft was constructed with fabric-covered steel tubing and unequal-span wooden-frame wings. The difference in span between upper and lower wings, however, was much less pronounced. The prototype was also fitted with a large streamlined propeller spinner and a small unbalanced rudder. It proved itself to be relatively fast, strongly built, and highly maneuverable; in 1927 the Navy ordered 32 machines as F2B-1s. They differed from the prototype in that the spinner was removed and a larger, balanced rudder was installed.

In 1928 the F2B was delivered to Fighting Squadron VF-1B and Bombing Squadron VB-2B onboard the carrier USS *Saratoga*. When no more of these machines were acquired, Boeing exported two examples overseas to Brazil and Japan. When they failed to produce orders, production was switched over to the newer F3B. However, the F2B made aviation history by equipping the Navy's first precision aerobatic team, *The Three Seahawks*. The team toured the country at various national air races and air shows and thrilled thousands with seemingly death-defying acts. A *Seahawks* specialty was to rope their three F2Bs together, then take off, maneuver, and land in unison. By 1934 all remaining F2Bs had been retired from frontline service.

**Type:** Fighter

---

**Dimensions:** wingspan, 33 feet; length, 24 feet, 10 inches; height, 9 feet, 2 inches
**Weights:** empty, 2,179 pounds; gross, 2,946 pounds
**Power plant:** 1 × 425–horsepower Pratt & Whitney R-1340 radial engine
**Performance:** maximum speed, 156 miles per hour; ceiling, 22,500 feet; maximum range, 340 miles
**Armament:** 2 × .30–caliber machine guns; 125 pounds of bombs
**Service dates:** 1928–1932

The F3B introduced forward sweep of upper-wing surfaces to fighters. After several years of frontline service, many F3Bs became the chosen aircraft of high-ranking naval personnel.

Given its success with the F2B, in 1927 Boeing set out to design a multipurpose fighter that could operate off either land or water. Their Model 74 was similar to the F2B but could be fitted with a single float and wingtip pontoons as well as regular landing gear. However, the Navy decided the performance gained was minimal, and it returned the prototype to Boeing with suggested modifications. Because the rise of aircraft carriers made the practice of floatplane fighters obsolete, the concept was dropped entirely. The new Model 77, a totally redesigned aircraft, emerged shortly thereafter. The most drastic change was to the upper wing, which was now swept back for improved performance at high altitudes. The lower wing was kept straight and

mounted farther back. The nose was also lengthened, and the new craft sported all-metal tail surfaces, the first in a Boeing design. The Model 77 possessed impressive performance for its day, so in 1928 the Navy ordered 73 examples that entered the service as the F3B.

F3Bs were employed by VF-2B aboard the carrier USS *Saratoga*, alongside VF-3B and VF-1B on the USS *Lexington*. In service the fast, robust fighter proved popular with pilots and doubled as a capable fighter-bomber. Subsequent modifications included introduction of a streamlined cowling to improve airflow over the engine. The F3B served in frontline capacities until 1932, when it was gradually replaced by faster Grumman designs. However, the F3B remained the choice of ranking naval aviators, and many of them were employed as personal aircraft. They were frequently distinguished by the addition of rakish, nonregulation wheel spats (coverings).

# Boeing F4B/P-12

**Type:** Fighter

**Dimensions:** wingspan, 30 feet; length, 20 feet; height, 9 feet, 3 inches
**Weights:** empty, 2,100 pounds; gross, 2,750 pounds
**Power plant:** 1 × 500–horsepower Pratt & Whitney SR-1340 radial engine
**Performance:** maximum speed, 189 miles per hour; ceiling, 27,000 feet; maximum range, 520 miles
**Armament:** 2 × .30–caliber machine guns; 232 pounds of bombs
**Service dates:** 1929–1937

The popular F4B/P-12 was the most famous Boeing biplane fighter during the interwar period. It was also built in greater numbers than any American warplane prior to World War II.

By 1928 Boeing had accumulated enough aerodynamic expertise to improve upon its F2B/F3B and PW-9 fighters. As a private venture, Boeing designed and constructed Models 83 and 89, which closely resembled each other. These were standard biplanes save for a top wing that was longer than the bottom wing and mounted ahead in a positive stagger. Being smaller and lighter than previous designs, these models' performance was exceptionally better, and in 1929 the Navy accepted 27 aircraft as the F4B-1. During the next six years Boeing continually refined the F4B with an improved tail, a streamlined cowling, and an all-metal fuselage. The last version, the F4B-4, also featured a large hump behind the canopy where a life raft could be stowed away. All told, the Navy acquired 170 F4Bs, which were slowly replaced by the faster Grumman biplanes during the late 1930s. However, some were still flying as radio-controlled drones in 1940.

In 1928 the Army also evaluated the Model 89, and the following year it adopted this model as the P-12. The only difference from the Navy version was the lack of an arrester hook. Over the years the P-12 was continually improved, with better tail surfaces, a metal fuselage, and an engine cowling. The final version, the P-12E, featured a 600-horsepower engine and better performance. This fighter was well liked by pilots on account of its speed and maneuverability, and it was possibly the best aircraft of its class at the time. Unlike the Navy, however, the Army rapidly phased out its P-12s after 1934 because even they could not catch Martin's revolutionary B-10 monoplane bomber. A total of 366 machines had been delivered to the Army, for a grand total of 562 aircraft to both services.

**Type:** Fighter

**Dimensions:** wingspan, 32 feet; length, 23 feet, 5 inches; height, 8 feet, 8 inches
**Weights:** empty, 2,328 pounds; gross, 3,170 pounds
**Power plant:** 1 × 435–horsepower Curtiss D-12 water-cooled engine
**Performance:** maximum speed, 158 miles per hour; ceiling, 21,000 feet; maximum range, 390 miles
**Armament:** 2 × .30–caliber machine guns
**Service dates:** 1924–1928

The PW-9 was the first fighter design from Boeing and the last to bear the Army designation "Pursuit, Water-cooled." With minor modifications, it was subsequently adopted by the Navy for carrier use.

Experience in building the Thomas Morse MB-3 fighter convinced Boeing it could construct fighters with performance equal to the very latest European designs. In fact, it turned to a proven German design from World War I, the Fokker D-7, as an inspiration. Like the Fokker, the new Model 15 was slab-sided and constructed out of welded steel tubing and wooden fabric-covered wings. However, Boeing was first to pioneer electric arc welding on the fuselage, which resulted in stronger construction. The new craft had an upper wing that was longer than the lower one and set with a slight forward stagger. In 1923 the Army Air Corps decided to evaluate the prototype as the XPW-9, and the following year it ordered 12 machines. The PW-9 was no world-beater, but it was dependable and handled well in the air. Subsequent modifications resulted in the PW-9D, which sported a redesigned radiator scoop, larger tail surfaces, and wheel brakes. PW-9s remained in frontline service until 1928, by which time 114 had been built.

In 1925 the Navy also evaluated the PW-9 as a possible fighter and that year ordered 10 examples as the FB-1. These were virtually identical to the Army version and, because they were intended for land use only, lacked arrester gear. The Navy continued refining the design, however, and the next production version, designated the FB-5, was fully capable of carrier operations. They also differed from earlier craft by having a more powerful Packard engine, redesigned landing gear, and greater positive stagger on the upper wing. These remained in service until 1930, being replaced by Boeing's F2B/F3B series. Thereafter, the Navy discontinued liquid-cooled engines in favor of radial ones.

# ✪ Boeing KC-97 *Stratotanker*

**Type:** Tanker; Transport

---

**Dimensions:** wingspan, 141 feet, 3 inches; length, 177 feet, 5 inches; height, 38 feet, 3 inches
**Weights:** empty, 85,000 pounds; gross, 175,000 pounds
**Power plant:** 4 × 3,500–horsepower Pratt & Whitney R-4360 Wasp Major radial engines
**Performance:** maximum speed, 370 miles per hour; ceiling, 30,000 feet; maximum range, 4,300 miles
**Armament:** none
**Service dates:** 1949–1977

The *Stratofreighter* was the first Air Force plane designed for aerial refueling and the last propeller-driven warplane constructed by Boeing.

During World War II the Army Air Force desired a large and ultramodern transport developed from the Boeing B-29 bomber, itself then under development. The result was the XC-97, which employed a unique double-hull fuselage while retaining the same wings and tail unit as a B-29. In January 1945 the prototype flew from Seattle to Washington, D.C., in only six hours while carrying ten tons of cargo. The craft was then put into production as the C-97 *Stratofreighter*, which could carry either 53,000 pounds of payload or 134 fully equipped troops. It was heavily engaged during the Korean War as a cargo ship and a flying ambulance. A total of 76 was built.

By the early 1950s the Strategic Air Command (SAC) needed an aerial tanker to extend the range of its RB-45C *Tornados* and B-47 *Stratojets*. Boeing took a basic C-97 and outfitted it with a flying boom near the bottom rear of the aircraft, which could be lowered and attached to waiting aircraft. After successful testing, this variant went into production as the KC-97, of which 812 were constructed. It could carry and transfer 15,000 gallons of fuel to SAC bombers, thereby extending their reach around the globe. In 1957 KC-97s emphasized this fact by refueling three B-52s on a record-breaking circumnavigation of the world. Toward the end of their service career, numerous KC-97s were outfitted with two J-47 jet engines so that the aging tankers could keep pace with the faster jets they serviced. After 1957 the *Stratotanker* was slowly phased out of frontline service by the more modern KC-135. However, it flew with Air Force Reserve and National Guard squadrons in various capacities until 1977.

# ⭐ Boeing KC-135 *Stratotanker*

**Type:** Tanker

**Dimensions:** wingspan, 130 feet, 10 inches; length, 136 feet, 3 inches; height, 41 feet, 8 inches
**Weights:** empty, 106,500 pounds; gross, 277,000 pounds
**Power plant:** 4 × 22,000–pound thrust CFM International F108-CF100 turbofan engines
**Performance:** maximum speed, 585 miles per hour; ceiling; 36,000 feet; maximum range, 1,150 miles
**Armament:** none
**Service dates:** 1957–

The *Stratotanker* was the first jet aircraft specifically designed for aerial refueling. It also spawned a bewildering assortment of variants, many of which will be operating into the next century.

The art of aerial refueling evolved around the time of the Korean War in 1950, when propeller-driven KC-97s began servicing the relatively slow jets of that era. By mid-decade, however, the newer, faster jets could not slow down sufficiently without risk of stalling. The Air Force clearly needed a faster craft that could keep pace with its latest fighters and bombers. Boeing at that time was developing its Model 707, destined as the first American jetliner, and in 1955 Boeing proposed converting it into a jet-powered tanker. The prototype first flew in 1956, and the following year the Air Force accepted the first of 732 airplanes, designated KC-135 *Stratotankers*.

Though a large aircraft, the KC-135 proved easy to fly and could carry 31,000 gallons of fuel for refueling purposes. This was transferred by means of a winged, 47-foot-long boom that was lowered from the rear end of the plane and fastened to the nozzles of waiting jets. Provisions were also made to carry 80 fully armed troops, although this number could be doubled with some internal arrangements. Deployment of the KC-135 meant that the Strategic Air Command could refuel, and fly, its bombers and reconnaissance craft to any point in the world and back. It could also service a variety of Navy, Marine Corps, and NATO aircraft.

The C-135 family of jets proved itself to be extremely versatile, and numerous EC-135 and RC-135 variants were subsequently developed for electronic surveillance and photographic purposes. Command post, cargo, weather reconnaissance, and staff transport versions have also been fielded. With numerous engine and electronic upgrades, the KC-135 family will continue flying for several decades.

# ⭐ Boeing NB

**Type:** Trainer

---

**Dimensions:** wingspan, 36 feet, 10 inches; length, 28 feet, 9 inches; height, 11 feet, 7 inches
**Weights:** empty, 2,136 pounds; gross, 2,837 pounds
**Power plant:** 1 × 200–horsepower Lawrence J-1 radial engine
**Performance:** maximum speed, 100 miles per hour; ceiling, 10,200 feet; maximum range, 300 miles
**Armament:** 1 × .30–caliber machine gun
**Service dates:** 1924–1929

---

The NB was one of the Navy's first post–World War I trainers. Simple to maintain and easy to fly, it was too safe for instruction purposes because of an inability to spin.

With the success of its PW-9 fighter, Boeing sought to broaden its horizons by producing training planes for the Navy. In 1924 that service began looking for a new craft to replace the aging Curtiss JN-4 *Jenny* and contracted with Boeing to build its Model 21. This was a standard biplane powered by an uncovered radial engine. The crew of two sat in tandem open cockpits and landed on a split-axle undercarriage. Furthermore, according to Navy specifications, the new plane could also be readily converted into a seaplane by the addition of a central float and two wing pontoons. The NB was unusual in one other respect: To improve maintenance, the top and bottom wing panels, along with the left and right ailerons and elevators, were completely interchangeable. In flight the aircraft possessed pleasing characteristics with one important exception. The NB was so intrinsically stable that it could not be made to spin, one of the hazards of violent maneuvering. Consequently, a lengthened fuselage and other changes were introduced to make it spin-prone. However, the aircraft now was incapable of coming out of a spin and had to be flown with some caution.

In 1924 the Navy made an initial acquisition of 41 NB-1s, which were latter refitted with a 200-horsepower Wright J-5 radial engine. A second production batch of 30 was made with 180-horsepower Wright-Hispano E-4 liquid-cooled engines and received the designation NB-2. Both versions were utilized for pilot and aerial gunnery training at Pensacola Naval Air Station, Florida. Several others were modified as crop sprayers and flown by U.S. Marines in Puerto Rico. The NB served dutifully and was finally replaced by the Consolidated NY series in 1929.

**Type:** Fighter

**Dimensions:** wingspan, 27 feet, 11 inches; length, 23 feet, 9 inches; height, 10 feet
**Weights:** empty, 2,200 pounds; gross, 3,075 pounds
**Power plant:** 1 × 600–horsepower Pratt & Whitney Wasp SR-1340 radial engine
**Performance:** maximum speed, 235 miles per hour; ceiling, 28,000 feet; maximum range, 635 miles
**Armament:** 1 × .30–caliber machine gun; 1 × .50–caliber machine gun; 200 pounds of bombs
**Service dates:** 1934–1939

The racy little *Peashooter* was the first all-metal monoplane fighter produced in America. To please the conservatively minded military, it was also the last fighter equipped with an open cockpit and fixed landing gear.

Boeing's earlier success with the *Monomail* transport and XB-9 bomber prompted it to apply the same monoplane technology to fighter craft. Boeing did so sparingly, in order not to produce something too radical for the conservative Army. In 1932 Boeing decided to work in close cooperation with the military to develop the Model 248, a historic aircraft. This diminutive fighter was the first all-metal low-wing monoplane fighter accepted by the Army Air Corps. It was highly streamlined and possessed a sleek, stressed skin exterior. However, it also incorporated such biplane-era features as an open cockpit, fixed landing gear, and extensive wire bracing. After much testing, the Army was pleased with the performance and signed a contract for 113 aircraft. In 1934 they entered into service as the P-26A, but pilots, suspicious of the new craft, commonly referred to it as the "Peashooter."

The P-26A was pleasant to fly and was the first Army fighter to exceed 225 miles per hour in level flight. However, it was considered a "hot" aircraft because its landing speed, 75 miles per hour, was considered excessive. The Army thereafter purchased an additional P-26Bs, which were equipped with landing flaps to slow it down. The P-26 quickly became the Air Corps's frontline fighter and was widely deployed at home, in Hawaii, and in the Panama Canal Zone. By 1937, however, they were slowly phased out by more modern Seversky P-35 and Curtiss P-36 fighters, which featured enclosed canopies and retractable landing gear. Several P-26s were operated by the Philippine Air Force during the early days of World War II, claiming several Japanese aircraft.

# Boeing-Vertol CH-46 *Sea Knight*

**Type:** Transport Helicopter

**Dimensions:** rotor span, 51 feet; length, 84 feet, 4 inches; height, 16 feet, 8 inches
**Weights:** empty, 15,537 pounds; gross, 17,396 pounds
**Power plant:** 2 × 1,870–horsepower General Electric T58 turboshaft engines
**Performance:** maximum speed, 154 miles per hour; ceiling, 14,000 feet; maximum range, 365 miles
**Armament:** 2 × .50–caliber machine guns
**Service dates:** 1964–

The *Sea Knight* was the military's first twin-turbine helicopter. It is still used exclusively by the Navy and Marine Corps for supply and assault missions.

In 1956 Piasecki began work on a twin-turbine helicopter for both civilian and military applications. It emerged with a large, boxlike body whose rear fuselage slanted upwards into a powered cargo door. The two motors were placed on either side of the large tail section and drove two three-bladed propellers in contrarotating fashion. Their placement there kept the cargo area unobstructed. Furthermore, the hull was watertight, permitting operations directly on and off water. In 1958 the work was continued by a successor company, Boeing-Vertol, which initially offered the new Model 107 to the Army. It declined in favor of the forthcoming CH-47 *Chinook*, but the Marine Corps tested it as possible assault craft. A large quantity was ordered in 1964, and the craft entered the service as the CH-46 *Sea Knight*. Eventually, 624 machines were acquired.

The CH-46 can carry and unload 25 fully armed troops or more than 10,000 pounds of equipment. Though nominally unarmed, two .50-caliber machine guns can be mounted for flak suppression. The Navy also employs the UH-46 version, which is utilized for vertical onboard delivery (VOD) purposes. VOD entails the transport of mail, supplies, personnel, or any other commodities deemed useful for individual ship operations.

The *Sea Knight* was actively involved in the Vietnam War and also saw action during the 1983 invasion of Grenada. During the 1991 Gulf War, CH-46s flew 1,601 sorties in Operation Desert Storm, principally from the amphibious assault ship USS *Guam*. With constant engine and avionics upgrades, this versatile helicopter will be flying well into the 21st century. Many are also operated by Saudi Arabia, Sweden, Canada, and Japan.

**Type:** Transport Helicopter

**Dimensions:** wingspan, 60 feet; length, 51 feet; height, 18 feet, 8 inches
**Weights:** empty, 22,452 pounds; gross, 50,000 pounds
**Power plant:** 2 × 3,750–horsepower Avco Lycoming T55 turboshaft engines
**Performance:** maximum speed, 183 miles per hour; ceiling, 8,500 feet; maximum range, 1,279 miles
**Armament:** none
**Service dates:** 1962–

Although more than three decades old, the *Chinook* remains the principal medium-lift helicopter for the Western world. In Vietnam it was responsible for recovering hundreds of downed aircraft and helicopters.

Piasecki began development of a very large helicopter in 1956; its successor company, Boeing-Vertol, completed the work four years later. The Model 114 was a large, twin-rotor craft seating three crew members in a forward cabin. The hull was completely sealed for emergency landings in water, and twin engines were mounted on either side of the rear pylon. This arrangement kept the capacious cargo hull free from obstruction. The new craft could easily lift 44 fully armed troops, 24 stretchers, or 10,000 pounds of cargo into action. Up to 30,000 pounds of externally slung cargo could also be hauled for short distances. Like the earlier CH-46 *Sea Knight*, Model 114 also possessed an upswept rear section that terminated in a cargo ramp door for ease of loading. When the Army decided that the

*Sea Knight* was too small for its purposes, the new machine was evaluated in its place. By 1962 the Army decided to acquire it as its standard cargo helicopter, and the machine entered into production as the CH-47 *Chinook*. More than 1,000 have been built and deployed worldwide.

The CH-47 made its combat debut in Vietnam, where its great strength and lifting ability were markedly demonstrated. It is estimated that *Chinooks* salvaged more than 11,000 downed aircraft and helicopters worth $3 billion. In an unusual experiment, four examples were converted into heavily armed ACH-47 gunships, but the faster Bell AH-1 *Cobra* was deemed far superior. Since then the newest model developed, the CH-47D, has more than twice the lifting power of the original *Chinook*. Another version, the MH-47E, is especially designed for special operations forces deep behind enemy lines. This versatile helicopter is currently operated by 13 nations around the world, including Great Britain and Canada.

**Type:** Fighter

**Dimensions:** wingspan, 35 feet; length, 26 feet, 4 inches; height, 12 feet, 1 inch
**Weights:** empty, 4,630 pounds; gross, 7,055 pounds
**Power plant:** 1 × 1,100–horsepower Wright Cyclone R-1620 radial engine
**Performance:** maximum speed, 300 miles per hour; ceiling, 30,500 feet; maximum range, 950 miles
**Armament:** 4 × .50–caliber machine guns
**Service dates:** 1939–1942

The *Buffalo* was the U.S. Navy's first all-metal monoplane fighter. Advanced for its day, it was hopelessly outclassed in the early days of World War II by superior Japanese aircraft.

In 1936 the Brewster Aeronautical Corporation responded to a Navy contract for a new fighter plane by designing the Model 139. First flown in 1938, this single-wing craft was of all-metal construction and possessed fully retractable landing gear. Its performance was nimble, and that year the tubby fighter edged out Grumman's soon-to-be-famous XF4F to win a production order.

In 1939 54 *Buffalos* were delivered to the Navy. However, only 11 served onboard the carrier USS *Saratoga;* the remainder were shunted off to Finland, where they were immediately employed in the war against the Soviet Union, fighting with great distinction and producing several aces. The Navy subsequently acquired an additional 151 *Buffalos*, but it experienced difficulty in adopting the machines to the rigors of carrier operations. Furthermore, in order to bring the fighter up to European standards, additional armor and equipment were required. The added weight made considerable inroads into the F2A's otherwise fine performance, and the aircraft became regarded as something of a dud. Nonetheless, in the days prior to the war in the Pacific, a number of *Buffalos* were exported to Great Britain and the Netherlands for use at Singapore and the Dutch East Indies. Total production peaked at 509 units.

During the early days of World War II, *Buffalos* fought a valiant but unequal battle against superior and more modern Japanese aircraft, most notably the Mitsubishi A6M *Zero* fighter. The Americans felt its inadequacy at the June 1942 Battle of Midway when Marine Squadron VMF-121 lost 13 of its 20 F2As while scoring only a handful of hits. By September 1942, the surviving *Buffalos* were relegated to the junkyard. Ironically, the F2As in Finland fought effectively against the Red Air Force up through the end of World War II.

**Type:** Scout-Bomber

**Dimensions:** wingspan, 47 feet; length, 39 feet, 2 inches; height, 15 feet, 5 inches
**Weights:** empty, 9,924 pounds; gross, 14,289 pounds
**Power plant:** 1 × 1,700–horsepower Wright Cyclone R-2600 radial engine
**Performance:** maximum speed, 274 miles per hour; ceiling, 24,900 feet; maximum range, 1,675 miles
**Armament:** 2 × .50–caliber machine guns; 4 × .30–caliber machine guns; 1,000 pounds of bombs
**Service dates:** 1942–1945

Intended as a follow-up to the Brewster Model SBA, the *Buccaneer* was another mediocre design that was never committed to combat.

In 1939 the Brewster Aeronautical Corporation explored the possibility of enlarging and improving its SBA scout-bomber. The Navy displayed great interest, and in April 1939 it ordered a prototype of the new craft. The new Model 340 first flew in June 1941 and exhibited a radical redesign. It was fitted with an engine featuring twice the horsepower, a greatly enlarged fuselage to accommodate twice as many bombs, and a power turret at the rear of the cabin. The Navy was suitably impressed by the new craft, which it christened the SB2A *Buccaneer*, and it ordered 140 copies. The Netherlands and Great Britain also expressed interest and purchased an additional 162 and 750 machines respectively in 1940. However, when German forces occupied the Nether-

lands, the Dutch *Buccaneers* were seized by the Navy and assigned to the Marine Corps. The English SB2As, meanwhile, entered the Royal Air Force (RAF) as the *Bermuda*.

Despite its modern appearance, the SB2A was underpowered and overweight and lacked maneuverability. For this reason both the Navy and the RAF relegated it to second-line duties such as trainers and target tugs. This occurred despite the fact that later models featured folding wings and an arrester hook for carrier operations. There is no record of the *Buccaneers* or *Bermudas* ever being committed to combat, although the Marines used them while training their first night-fighter squadron, VMF (N)-531. A total of 771 *Buccaneers* was built by 1944, after which Brewster became one of few aviation companies to go out of business before World War II ended.

**Type:** Scout-Bomber

**Dimensions:** wingspan, 39 feet; length, 27 feet, 8 inches; height, 8 feet, 7 inches
**Weights:** empty, 4,017 pounds; gross, 6,759 pounds
**Power plant:** 1 × 950–horsepower Wright R-1820 radial engine
**Performance:** maximum speed, 254 miles per hour; ceiling, 28,300; maximum range, 1,015 miles
**Armament:** 1 × .30–caliber machine gun; 500 pounds of bombs
**Service dates:** 1940–1942

The Brewster Company, which had been established in 1810 to manufacture horse carriages, entered the aeronautical field in the early 1930s by assembling seaplane floats, wings, and tail units as a subcontractor. By 1934 the company was ready to market its own military designs, particularly as the Navy was undergoing an expansion of its carrier aviation arm. The fleet was in special need of new and longer-range scout-bombers to replace its aging biplanes. That year Brewster answered a bid for a new scout-bomber to equip two new carriers, the USS *Enterprise* and USS *Yorktown*, which were scheduled to be launched in 1936.

The XSBA-1 emerged as a very clean midwing monoplane, constructed almost entirely of metal and featuring retractable landing gear and an internal bomb bay. The crew of two occupied an elongated greenhouse canopy that provided good all-around vision. Brewster's prototype first flew in April 1936, and it was deemed to be underpowered. Refitted with a larger Wright radial engine in 1937, it achieved a relatively fast speed of 263 miles per hour during level flight. The Navy was sufficiently impressed to order 30 copies for evaluation in 1938, but Brewster lacked the facilities to handle such an order. Consequently, the SBA was built under license at the Naval Aircraft Factory in Philadelphia.

Delivery of the SBA, soon redesignated as the SBN, commenced in November 1940 and continued through March 1942. Like all Brewster products, this promising design was quickly overtaken by other, more modern aircraft and was relegated to second-line duties. After a brief stint with bombing squadron VT-8 onboard the carrier USS *Hornet*, the SBAs were assigned to serve as trainers. By 1943 all had been dropped from the inventory and scrapped.

**Type:** Light Bomber

**Dimensions:** wingspan, 35 feet, 10 inches; length, 29 feet, 3 inches; height, 8 feet, 10 inches
**Weights:** empty, 6,211 pounds; gross, 14,000 pounds
**Power plant:** $2 \times 2,850$–pound thrust General Electric J-85 turbojet engines
**Performance:** maximum speed, 507 miles per hour; ceiling, 41,700 feet; maximum range, 550 miles
**Armament:** $1 \times 7.62$mm minigun; up to 5,600 pounds of bombs or rockets
**Service dates:** 1968–1990

The *Dragonfly* was a lightweight counterinsurgency (COIN) aircraft first employed during the Vietnam era. It fought with distinction, and captured examples were subsequently employed by the North Vietnamese People's Air Force.

During the early 1960s, as American involvement in the guerrilla wars of Southeast Asia escalated, the Air Force began looking for a lightweight, inexpensive aircraft for use in COIN operations. Such a craft had to be fast, easy to operate, and heavily armed and possess considerable loiter time over the battlefield. In 1963 Cessna responded by modifying an existing T-37 trainer into a prototype named the YA-37A. This was the same airframe mounted with stronger engines and eight hardpoints on the wings to carry weapons. Like its forebear, the A-37 was delightful to fly, was simple to operate, and could perform well enough on one engine to complete its mission. The Air Force was sufficiently impressed to order the type into production, and in 1968 it entered the Vietnam War as the *Dragonfly*.

In combat the A-37A was a hard-hitting and effective COIN aircraft, and in 1968 alone it flew more than 10,000 missions. A total of 25 was turned over to the South Vietnamese Air Force, which employed them through the end of the war in 1975. Thereafter, several A-37s were impressed into service by the victorious North Vietnamese and saw service during the invasion of Cambodia in much the same role. Meanwhile, the Americans developed an improved version, the A-37B, of which 577 were built and deployed as light attack aircraft. However, its simplicity and firepower were much sought after by developing nations with homegrown guerrilla wars, and it was purchased by Paraguay, Uruguay, Chile, Peru, Ecuador, Guatemala, and Honduras. Several still fly in Air National Guard units as forward air control aircraft.

**Type:** Trainer; Transport

**Dimensions:** wingspan, 41 feet, 11 inches; length, 32 feet, 9 inches; height, 9 feet, 11 inches
**Weight:** empty, 3,500 pounds; gross, 5,700 pounds
**Power plant:** 2 × 245–horsepower Jacobs R-755 radial engines
**Performance:** maximum speed, 195 miles per hour; ceiling, 22,000 feet; maximum range, 750 miles
**Armament:** none
**Service dates:** 1941–1949

The *Bobcat* was a relatively common trainer/transport of World War II and derived from a successful commercial design.

In 1939 the Cessna Aircraft Company designed its first twin-engine aircraft to compete in the growing commercial field for multiengine aircraft. The Model T-50 was a low-wing monoplane with welded steel-tube construction, wooden wings and tail, and fabric covering. The aircraft was successfully flown, and its high performance and low price made it an ideal candidate as a military trainer or light personnel transport. Almost immediately it caught the attention of both the Army Air Corps and the Royal Canadian Air Force. The latter acquired 550 units in 1940 through the Lend-Lease program with the designation *Crane*, whereas the U.S. Army contracted for 33 aircraft under the name *Bobcat*.

The initial batch of *Bobcats* was employed as AT-8 transition trainers, but it was decided that they possessed too much power for inexperienced cadets. A subsequent model, the AT-17, was virtually identical but featured less powerful engines. As World War II progressed, a total of 673 airplanes of both versions was constructed. The Army also decided it needed a versatile light transport for pilot ferrying and other liaison duties, so it had Cessna design a new version, the UC-78, of which 1,287 were purchased. Of these, 67 were transferred to the Navy as JRCs. A further 2,133 UC-78As and UC-78Bs, which featured two-blade metallic propellers in place of wooden ones, were also acquired. *Bobcats* served throughout the war in a variety of functions and were affectionately known by their crews as *Bamboo Bombers*. A total of 4,522 had been constructed; all were declared surplus in 1949. Many ended up in civilian hands and are still flying today.

**Type:** Liaison

**Dimensions:** wingspan, 36 feet; length, 25 feet, 10 inches; height, 7 feet, 4 inches
**Weights:** empty, 1,614 pounds; gross, 2,400 pounds
**Power plant:** 1 × 210–horsepower Continental O-470 air-cooled engine
**Performance:** maximum speed, 135 miles per hour; ceiling, 18,500 feet; maximum range, 625 miles
**Armament:** 6 smoke rockets
**Service dates:** 1950–1974

The *Birddog* was the last in a long line of *Grasshoppers*, or light utility aircraft. It served with distinction in Korea and Vietnam before being replaced by faster, more heavily armed machines.

In 1950 the Army announced a competition to replace its aging fleet of World War II–vintage *Grasshoppers* with a more modern liaison craft. Cessna responded with its Model 305, a militarized version of the popular civilian Model 170. Like previous planes in this class, it was a braced high-wing cabin monoplane with fixed landing gear. After rigorous Army testing, Cessna was declared the winner; deliveries of the new plane, designated L-19 *Birddog*, commenced in 1951. Army aviators used it with distinction in Korea in the traditional roles of artillery spotting, communications work, and flying ambulance. The Marine Corps also received 60 examples that were put to similar use. Production ceased in 1963, by which time 3,431 L-19s had been manufactured.

In 1962 the Army revived the observation category for its aircraft, and thus the *Birddog* was given a new designation, the O-1E. The craft was then widely employed in the escalating Vietnam conflict as a forward air control (FAC) aircraft. In the FAC capacity, unarmed *Birddogs* would fly in support of military units under attack, spot enemy ambushes or formations, and mark them with smoke rockets. Immediately thereafter, jet aircraft circling the battlefield would saturate the marked zones with firepower, which usually resulted in heavy losses to communist units. However, the slow and unarmed O-1Es were also vulnerable to ground fire, and several were lost. By 1968 they had been supplanted in the FAC role by faster, better-defended aircraft like the OV-10 *Bronco* and O-2 *Skymaster*. During the American withdrawal from Vietnam, many O-1Es were turned over to the South Vietnamese Army, which used them up through the end of the war. *Birddogs* continued flying with National Guard units at home until 1974.

# Cessna O-2 *Skymaster*

**Type:** Reconnaissance

---

**Dimensions:** wingspan, 38 feet, 2 inches; length, 29 feet, 9 inches; height, 9 feet, 4 inches
**Weights:** empty, 2,848 pounds; gross, 5,400 pounds
**Power plant:** 2 × 210–horsepower Continental IO-360 air-cooled engines
**Performance:** maximum speed, 199 miles per hour; ceiling, 18,000 feet; maximum range, 755 miles
**Armament:** 1 × 7.62mm minigun; 4 smoke rockets
**Service dates:** 1967–

With its twin-engine layout and redundant fuel system, the O-2 was one of the safest military observation airplanes ever flown. It served many years in Vietnam, performing spotter and psychological warfare missions.

By 1966 the Air Force was seeking to replace its slow and vulnerable O-1E *Birddogs* for forward air control work in Vietnam, and Cessna demonstrated its civilian Model 337 as a logical replacement. This was a unique, twin-engine craft built around the principle of center-line thrust. It was a high-wing design with two rear booms, retractable landing gear, and a podded fuselage with an engine in front and rear. Because it flew and handled like a single-engine craft, no special rating was required to fly it. The Model 337 carried a pilot, an observer, and up to four passengers. The Air Force was impressed with the design, and in 1967 it started accepting deliveries of the new craft as the O-2A *Skymaster*.

The O-2A was a vast improvement over the old *Birddog* in combat situations. It was much faster and carried a lethal 7.62mm minigun pod for protection. Furthermore, it could lose an engine in combat and easily fly home on the remaining one, as the fuel tanks were interconnected. In 1970 a highly specialized version, the O-2B, was deployed. This craft was equipped for psychological warfare and possessed advanced communication systems, air-to-ground broadcasting, and leaflet dispensers. Both models were continuously employed until the American withdrawal in 1973; production ceased after 510 had been acquired. A number were also delivered to the air forces of Iran, Ecuador, and Venezuela for similar uses. Though retired from frontline service, several O-2s are still flown by the Air Force as light utility craft.

**Type:** Trainer

**Dimensions:** wingspan, 33 feet, 9 inches; length, 29 feet, 2 inches; height, 9 feet, 2 inches
**Weights:** empty, 3,870 pounds; gross, 6,600 pounds
**Power plant:** 2 × 1,025–pound thrust Teledyne CAE J69 turbojets
**Performance:** maximum speed, 426 miles per hour; ceiling, 35,100 feet; maximum range, 604 miles
**Armament:** none
**Service dates:** 1957–

The *Tweety Bird* was the first Air Force jet designed entirely as a trainer. It is still used to impart student pilots with the rudiments of aircraft handling, instruments, and formation flying.

In 1952 the Air Force decided it needed a primary jet trainer and announced a design competition. The following year, Cessna introduced its Model 318, which contained many novel features. It was a squat, straight-wing, all-metal design with wide-tract landing gear that placed it low to the ground. Furthermore, instead of the usual tandem arrangement, student and instructor sat side by side for more effective instruction. The prototype XT-37 first flew in 1954, and the type entered operational service three years later. Like all Cessna craft, the T-37A was responsive and forgiving to fly as well as strong and dependable. It was used to familiarize novices with the characteristics of jet aircraft before they moved on to the more demanding Northrop

T-38 *Talon*. Pilots took an immediate liking to the diminutive craft, giving it the unofficial name *Tweety Bird*. Cessna constructed 537 T-37As before introducing the more advanced T-37B. That machine featured stronger engines, redesigned instrument panels, and improved avionics. The Air Force eventually acquired a further 477 T-37Bs; the earlier A versions were slowly upgraded to B standards. At least 500 still remain in the Air Force inventory.

Another version developed by the Air Force in 1962 but never employed was the T-37C. This was an armed version built for export under the aegis of the Military Assistance Program, which provided cheap but effective warplanes to developing nations. The T-37C could be armed with bombs, rocket or gunpods, or four *Sidewinder* air-to-air missiles. A total of 252 was sold to and operated by Brazil, Portugal, Peru, Cambodia, Greece, Pakistan, and Thailand. It has since been replaced by more modern attack aircraft.

**Type:** Trainer

**Dimensions:** wingspan, 35 feet, 9 inches; length, 26 feet, 6 inches; height, 8 feet, 11 inches
**Weights:** empty, 1,255 pounds; gross, 2,400 pounds
**Power plant:** 1 × 210–horsepower Continental IO-360 air-cooled engine
**Performance:** maximum speed, 153 miles per hour; ceiling, 17,500 feet; maximum range, 600 miles
**Armament:** none
**Service dates:** 1965–

The *Mescalero* is based on the popular Cessna Model 172, the most widely produced aircraft in history. It serves as a primary trainer for cadets before they move on to more advanced types.

Cessna first introduced the Model 172 in 1955, and since then more than 36,000 have been constructed and flown. It can be seen in great numbers at airports across the United States and around the world. This craft is an all-metal, cabin monoplane with a braced high wing fitted for electric slotted flaps. The tricycle landing gear is fixed, and up to four occupants can be comfortably seated. By 1964 the Air Force felt an urgent need to acquire a new primary trainer that was both cheap and easy to fly. Because the Model 172 was on hand and well-suited for its needs, the Air Force purchased 204 machines as the T-41A. It intended for prospective cadet pilots to first complete 30 hours of training in T-41s before moving on to more challenging T-28s and T-34s. The

aircraft proved so successful as a trainer that in 1965 the Army ordered 255 T-41Bs for its own pilot program. It was also employed as a utility/light transport in support of Army bases. These differed from their Air Force counterparts in having a bigger engine, an enlarged, strengthened nosewheel for rough field operations, and more advanced avionics. The Army christened it the *Mescalero* in reference to a tribe within the Apache nation.

The Air Force was so pleased with the T-41s that in 1968 it purchased another 52 machines. However, they were fitted with a more powerful motor and used exclusively by cadets at the U.S. Air Force Academy in Colorado. Shortly thereafter, 299 examples of a more advanced version, the T-41D, were acquired, featuring corrosion proofing, reinforced ailerons, and wing-mounted pylons. This version has been exported abroad to several South American countries through the Military Assistance Program.

**Type:** Heavy Bomber

**Dimensions:** wingspan, 100 feet; length; 67 feet, 2 inches; height, 17 feet, 11 inches
**Weights:** empty, 36,500 pounds; gross, 56,000 pounds
**Power plant:** 4 × 1,200–horsepower Pratt and Whitney R-1830 supercharged radial engines
**Performance:** maximum speed, 303 miles per hour; ceiling, 28,000 feet; maximum range, 3,700 miles
**Armament:** 10 × .50–caliber machine guns; 8,000 pounds of bombs
**Service dates:** 1940–1950

The B-24 was the most numerous American bomber of World War II and saw action across the globe. Ungainly and slab-sided in appearance, it was often derided as "the crate the B-17 came in."

In 1939 the Army Air Corps decided to obtain a heavy bomber with greater range and payload than the existing B-17. Consolidated responded with its Model 32, unique with a tricycle landing gear arrangement and twin rudders. The aircraft was also fitted with a high–aspect ratio Davis wing, which was an efficient airfoil at cruising speed and gave the aircraft very long range. Furthermore, the deep, slab-sided fuselage was roomy and allowed for a bomb load of 8,000 pounds, two tons more than the B-17. The Army took delivery of the new bomber, christened the *Liberator*, in June 1940, and several were also delivered to the Royal Air Force for patrolling and transport duties.

During World War II B-24s rendered effective service in every theater, including the Pacific, the Mediterranean, and northern Europe. However, it is best remembered for Operation *Tidalwave*, the daring, low-altitude daylight assault on the oil refineries at Ploesti, Romania, in August 1943. Heavy damage was inflicted upon the installation, at a cost of 54 of the 177 aircraft committed. Ultimately, the B-24 equipped 45 bomber groups, which made daylight raids over Germany alongside B-17s and suffered heavy losses to enemy fighters and flak. In an attempt to discourage lethal head-on attacks by German aircraft, the B-24G, developed in 1944, was the first fitted with a power nose turret mounting two .50-caliber machine guns.

A number of B-24s were also converted to C-87 transports, F-7 reconnaissance, and PB4Y patrol bombers for the U.S. Navy. By war's end a total of 19,203 *Liberators* had been built, a greater number than any other warplane in history.

# ☆ Consolidated B-32 *Dominator*

**Type:** Heavy Bomber

---

**Dimensions:** wingspan, 135 feet; length, 83 feet, 1 inch; height, 32 feet, 9 inches
**Weights:** empty, 60,272 pounds; gross, 111,500 pounds
**Power plant:** 4 × 2,300–horsepower Wright Cyclone R-3350 radial engines
**Performance:** maximum speed, 365 miles per hour; ceiling, 35,000 feet; maximum range, 800 miles
**Armament:** 12 × .50–caliber machine guns
**Service dates:** 1944–1946

The *Dominator*, one of the biggest and most complicated aircraft of World War II, was a major disappointment. It flew only a handful of combat missions and was scrapped immediately after the war.

In 1939 Consolidated responded to an Army Air Corps request to obtain a so-called hemispheric defense weapon by designing a superheavy bomber based upon Consolidated's existing B-24 *Liberator*. The resulting prototype, in fact, looked like a scaled-up *Liberator*, but subsequent refinements gave the XB-32 a large single fin, a pressurized cabin arrangement, and five elaborate power turrets. It was intended to compete directly with Boeing's larger B-29 *Superfortress*, but prolonged teething problems delayed the prototype's maiden flight until September 1942. Nonetheless, the Army was sufficiently pleased by the craft to place an order for 1,713 airplanes in 1943.

Although an impressive airplane, the B-32 *Dominator* remained dogged by developmental and technical problems. At length it was decided to remove the pressurized cabin and power turrets and to restrict the B-32 to low-level operations. These modifications delayed deployment of the craft until December 1944, eight months after the B-29 had been committed to combat. At length, only 115 of the giant bombers were completed before the war ended. They flew a mere handful of missions over the Philippines and Taiwan before the war ended. However, one B-32 enjoys the distinction of flying the last combat mission of World War II. On August 18, 1945, a pair of *Dominators* from the 368th Bombardment Squadron flew to Tokyo on a photographic mission, where they were attacked and claimed two Japanese fighters shot down. Considering the time and expense invested in the B-32, it was still an embarrassing record. By 1946 all 115 B-32s, bomber and trainer versions alike, had been deactivated and sent to the smelter.

**Type:** Trainer

**Dimensions:** wingspan, 40 feet; length, 27 feet, 10 inches; height, 9 feet, 11 inches
**Weights:** empty, 1,801 pounds; gross, 2,627 pounds
**Power plant:** 1 × 220–horsepower Wright R-790 radial engine
**Performance:** maximum speed, 98 miles per hour; ceiling, 15,200 feet; maximum range, 300 miles
**Armament:** none
**Service dates:** 1926–1937

The NY was the Navy's first post–World War I trainer to be acquired in quantity. It possessed the same pleasant qualities as the Army's PT-1 and trained thousands of pilots during the interwar period.

By 1924 the Navy considered replacing its aging fleet of Curtiss JN-4 *Jennies* with a more modern trainer. The Navy observed the Army's success with the PT-1 *Trusty* and requested Consolidated to construct a version that could be used with floats or landing gear. That year a prototype emerged that differed from the PT-1 in having a 200-horsepower Wright R-790 engine, as well as provisions to attach floats to the fuselage and wingtips. Tail surfaces were also enlarged for better flying when configured as a seaplane. In 1925 the Navy ordered 25 machines as the NY-1; they became the first Consolidated aircraft developed for that service.

As a trainer, the NY-1 proved as docile as its Army counterparts, but with attached floats its high wing loading (the ratio of weight to wing area) made

it climb poorly. Consolidated countered by enlarging the wingspan to 40 feet and fitting a 220-horsepower Wright J-5 radial engine. The new craft, called the NY-2, possessed much better performance and handling characteristics, although it was slightly slower. Ultimately, the Navy acquired 186 of these machines; the earlier versions were subsequently retrofitted with new wings and engines. A final version, the NY-3, was also developed for reserve use; it differed mainly in possessing a 240-horsepower engine. A total of 302 of all models was built.

Like the PT-1, the NY series was the Navy's most numerous and popular trainer during the late 1920s through the mid-1930s. It was so stable that in September 1929 Lieutenant Jimmy Doolittle made his first demonstration of "blind flying" in a hooded NY-2. The type was gradually replaced by the Stearman NS-1s and Naval Aircraft Factory N3Ns by 1937, although a handful lingered into World War II.

# ✪ Consolidated P2Y *Ranger*

**Type:** Patrol-Bomber

---

**Dimensions:** wingspan, 100 feet; length, 61 feet, 9 inches; height, 19 feet, 1 inch
**Weights:** empty, 12,769 pounds; gross, 25,266 pounds
**Power plant:** 2 × 750–horsepower Wright R-1820 radial engines
**Performance:** maximum speed, 139 miles per hour; ceiling, 16,100 feet; maximum range, 1,180 miles
**Armament:** 3 × .30–caliber machine guns; 2,000 pounds of bombs
**Service dates:** 1934–1941

---

The *Ranger* was the Navy's first monoplane patrol aircraft. It enjoyed a long and productive service life and broke several world records for distance flying.

In 1928 the Navy contracted with Consolidated to design and build a monoplane flying boat to replace its aging Naval Aircraft Factory PN series. Consolidated built the XPY-1, a large parasol aircraft (a high-mounted wing on a single pylon) with a 100-foot wingspan and three engines. One engine was mounted above the wings in a nacelle, but it was subsequently deleted. However, owing to a lower bid from Martin, the Navy awarded it the construction contract in 1931, and nine were constructed as the P3M. Undeterred, Consolidated re-refined its existing design into a new aircraft, the XP2Y-1. It was a twin-engine sesquiplane, that is, a biplane with a shorter lower wing. The two engines were mounted on struts between the wings, and the cockpit was fully enclosed. The Navy was impressed with its performance and in 1933 authorized 23 machines produced as the P2Y-1 *Ranger*. These were followed by an additional 23 P2Y-3s, which sported stronger engines; the engine nacelles were faired directly into the wing's leading edge to reduce drag.

The *Ranger* proved itself to be a rugged and dependable aircraft, capable of oceanic flights. In September 1933 Lieutenant Commander Donald M. Carpenter of Patrol Squadron VP-5 made history by flying six P2Y-1s nonstop from Norfolk, Virginia, to Coco Solo Naval Air Station in the Panama Canal Zone, a distance of 2,059 miles. In January 1934 Lieutenant Commander Knefler McGinnis led six P2Y-1s of VP-10 from San Francisco 2,408 miles west to Hawaii, another world record. In each instance all aircraft performed up to expectations. The P2Ys remained actively employed in American service until 1941, when they went into storage. Ironically, one *Ranger* sold to Japan served as the basis for the Kawanishi H6K *Mavis* flying boat of World War II.

**Type:** Fighter

---

**Dimensions:** wingspan, 43 feet, 11 inches; length, 30 feet; height, 8 feet, 3 inches
**Weights:** empty, 4,306 pounds; gross, 5,643 pounds
**Power plant:** 1 × 700–horsepower Curtiss Conqueror V-1570 liquid-cooled engine
**Performance:** maximum speed, 274 miles per hour; ceiling, 28,000 feet; maximum range, 508 miles
**Armament:** 3 × .30–caliber machine guns; 125 pounds of bombs
**Service dates:** 1934–1941

The PB-2 was the only two-seat monoplane fighter operated by the Army Air Corps. Streamlined and fast, it nonetheless remained at a disadvantage against single-seat adversaries.

In 1931 the Army acquired the prototype Y1P-25 from Consolidated, a two-seat monoplane fighter. It crashed during testing in 1933, but preliminary results were impressive. At the Army's urging, Consolidated went back to the drawing board and produced a more refined version, the XP-30. It was an extremely clean machine, the first Army Air Corps design to feature hand-cranked, retractable landing gear, a constant-speed propeller, and a supercharged engine for better performance at high altitude. It sat a crew of two under a streamlined tandem canopy and sported split flaps to control landing speeds. The XP-30 also crashed during evaluation, but results were excellent, and 54 machines were ordered as the P-30. Shortly after entering service in 1934, the designation PB-2A, for "Pursuit, Bi-

plane," was applied. They were the only such fighters ever adopted by the U.S. Army.

For such a large aircraft, the PB-2A did evince lively performance, especially at high altitudes. However, the day of the two-seat fighter had passed, especially in view of heightened speed. Many pilots questioned the utility of a tail gunner, most of whom blacked out the instant sharp turns and dives commenced. Moreover, the penalties accrued by the added weight and lessened maneuverability simply outweighed the addition of a single gun. In 1936 Consolidated tried to address this problem by removing the gunner and the fairing over the canopy on a new prototype, but the competition was won by the very modern Seversky P-35. Consolidated also tried selling an attack version, the A-11, which deleted the supercharger and featured a higher bomb load. The Army, however, was losing interest in liquid-cooled engines, as radial designs were less vulnerable to ground fire. The last PB-2As were finally replaced in 1941.

# ⭐ Consolidated PB2Y *Coronado*

**Type:** Patrol-Bomber; Transport

**Dimensions:** wingspan, 115 feet; length, 79 feet, 3 inches; height, 27 feet, 6 inches
**Weights:** empty, 40,935 pounds; gross, 68,000 pounds
**Power plant:** 4 × 1,200–horsepower Pratt & Whitney R-1830 radial engines
**Performance:** maximum speed, 213 miles per hour; ceiling, 20,100 feet; maximum range, 1,490 miles
**Armament:** 8 × .50–caliber machine guns; 4,000 pounds of bombs externally, 8,000 pounds internally
**Service dates:** 1940–1945

Conceived as a long-range patrol-bomber, the *Coronado* spent most of World War II hauling cargo. Twice as heavy as and three times more expensive than the famous PBY *Catalina*, its lack of performance ensured a short service life.

In 1936 the Navy announced a competition to design a modern, four-engine flying boat. This was only three months after the PBY's maiden flight, and Consolidated responded with the Model 29, which incorporated many design features of its earlier plane. Like the *Catalina*, this new craft, christened the *Coronado*, was a high-wing design with floats that retracted into the wingtips. The prototype first flew in 1937, but instability problems resulted in major hull and tail modifications, including the adoption of twin rudders like the company's B-24 *Liberator* bomber. Accommodations were made for a crew of nine or ten. The Navy was sufficiently

pleased to place a preliminary order for six aircraft. They were delivered to Patrol Squadron VP-13 in 1940, where the need for additional armament, armor, and self-sealing fuel tanks became apparent.

During World War II 210 *Coronados* were delivered to the Navy in several minor variants. The most numerous, the PB2Y-4, could transport 44 fully equipped troops over long distances; a medical version, the PB2Y-5H, was outfitted for 25 casualty berths. Several of the later versions were also equipped with air-to-surface-vessel radar to enhance patrolling capabilities. Ten *Coronados* were also delivered to the Royal Air Force, which employed them for hauling freight over the North Atlantic. The PB2Ys performed capably in a variety of patrol, anti-submarine, and rescue functions but proved underpowered, difficult to fly, and expensive to operate. All were phased out of active duty by 1945.

**Type:** Patrol-Bomber

**Dimensions:** wingspan, 100 feet; length, 74 feet, 7 inches; height, 30 feet, 1 inch
**Weights:** empty, 37,485 pounds; gross, 65,000 pounds
**Power plant:** 4 × 1,350–horsepower Pratt & Whitney Twin Wasp R-1830 radial engines
**Performance:** maximum speed, 237 miles per hour; ceiling, 20,700 feet; maximum range, 2,800 miles
**Armament:** 12 × .50–caliber machine guns; 12,800 pounds of bombs
**Service dates:** 1944–1954

The *Privateer* was a navalized version of an already famous land bomber. It served briefly during World War II but managed to launch the first guided-missile attack in history.

Several months into World War II, the U.S. Navy had a pressing need for a land-based patrol-bomber to conduct long-range antishipping and antisubmarine missions. In August 1942 it accepted delivery of several modified B-24 *Liberators*, redesignated PB4Y-1 *Privateers*, but an airplane designed specifically for patrol work would better suit the Navy's needs. Accordingly, in 1943 Consolidated flew the first PB4Y-2 prototype. Although it shared a common wing and landing gear with the *Liberator*, the new craft was distinguished by a huge single stabilizer and a redesigned nose section lengthened by seven feet. Moreover, because the *Privateer* was destined to work mainly at low altitudes, the distinctive twin superchargers were removed from the engine cowlings. A total of 739

PB4Ys was delivered by 1945, with an additional 34 RY-3 transport versions.

Operationally, the *Privateers* saw duty during the closing months of World War II, patrolling the waters of the Western Pacific. On April 23, 1945, a PB4Y launched two guided BAT radar-directed bombs against Japanese ships in Balikpapan Harbor, Borneo, the first guided-missile attack in history. Other *Privateers* performed effective antishipping activities over Japan's home waters.

After the war the *Privateers* remained on active duty and were fitted with increasing amounts of electronic countermeasures and radar. Throughout the early Cold War they performed routine reconnaissance patrols around the Soviet Union, and in April 1950 a PB4Y was shot down by Russian fighters over the Baltic Sea. The type was phased out of active duty in 1954, although it served with the Brazilian and nationalist Chinese air forces for another decade. Several *Privateers* still perform fire-fighting duties.

# ⭐ Consolidated PBY *Catalina*

**Type:** Patrol-Bomber

---

**Dimensions:** wingspan, 104 feet; length, 63 feet, 11 inches; height, 18 feet, 10 inches
**Weights:** empty, 17,465 pounds; gross, 34,000 pounds
**Power plant:** 2 × 1,200–horsepower Pratt & Whitney Twin Wasp R-1830 radial engines
**Performance:** maximum speed, 196 miles per hour; ceiling, 18,200 feet; maximum range, 3,100 miles
**Armament:** 1 × .30–caliber machine gun; 2 × .50–caliber machine guns; 4,000 pounds of bombs
**Service dates:** 1936–1957

Slow and reliable, the stately PBY was built in greater numbers than any other flying boat. *Catalinas* were actively employed in every theater of World War II and continue flying in private service.

In 1933 Consolidated and Douglas competed in a Navy bid to provide a modern flying boat. The Consolidated design was an extremely clean monoplane with floats that folded up into the wingtips. The prototype first flew in 1935, with impressive speed and hydrodynamic performance, and the Navy placed an initial order for 30 PBYs, as they were called. In 1939 Consolidated introduced an amphibian version; retractable wheels allowed the craft to function on either water or land. Shortly before World War II, the air forces of Great Britain, Canada, and the Soviet Union all displayed interest in either purchasing or manufacturing the PBY under license. The Royal Air Force (RAF) christened the PBY with its popular name, *Catalina*.

During the war years the PBY established itself as a rugged and versatile patrol-bomber. In 1941 an RAF *Catalina* spotted the German battleship *Bismarck* and reported its location to a waiting British battle fleet. The PBY was also the most numerous American flying boat at the time of Pearl Harbor and saw extensive duty as a reconnaissance and rescue vehicle. In 1942 Patrol Squadron 12 started nighttime torpedo runs against Japanese shipping in the Solomon Islands, becoming the first of several "Black Cat" squadrons. The U.S. Army also operated 75 *Catalinas* as OV-10s, which rescued hundreds of downed Allied pilots. Though eventually supplanted in frontline service by the Martin PBM *Mariner*, more than 4,000 PBYs were constructed in the United States and abroad, more than any flying boat in aviation history. It was not withdrawn from Navy service until 1957, and many are still employed in fire-fighting operations.

**Type:** Trainer

**Dimensions:** wingspan, 34 feet, 5 inches; length, 27 feet, 9 inches; height, 9 feet, 10 inches
**Weights:** empty, 1,805 pounds; gross, 2,577 pounds
**Power plant:** 1 × 180–horsepower Wright E liquid-cooled engine
**Performance:** maximum speed, 92 miles per hour; ceiling, 14,000 feet; maximum range, 350 miles
**Armament:** none
**Service dates:** 1924–1936

The veritable PT-1 was the Army's first post–World War I trainer, the first military aircraft ordered in quantity. Deceptively easy to fly and virtually spin-proof, pilots affectionately referred to it as the *Trusty*.

After 1923 Consolidated Aircraft absorbed the Dayton-Wright Corporation, and it acquired the rights to the TW-3 civilian trainer. It was decided to modify it as a tandem two-seater and to sell it to the Army as a primary trainer to replace the vaunted Curtiss JN-4 *Jenny*. Despite its primitive appearance, the fabric-covered PT-1 was constructed of steel tubing and strongly built. The first models possessed a streamlined cowling reminiscent of the famous Fokker D-7, but subsequent production models left the engine exposed. In 1925 the Army purchased 221 machines, the largest aircraft order it had placed to date. During the next decade the PT-1 rendered excellent service as a primary trainer, introducing an entire generation of pilots to flying. In its first year alone the *Trusty* trained 531 cadets at Brooks Field, Texas, without mishap. In fact, its flying qualities were so tame that it bred overconfidence in trainees destined to handle more difficult aircraft.

In 1928 the PT-1s were retired into National Guard service by the PT-3. It was virtually an identical airframe but was powered by a stronger, 220-horsepower Wright R-970 radial engine. The Army eventually acquired 120 machines, which served until they were officially supplanted by the Stearman BT-13 in 1936. However, at least 34 remained in service through World War II. Concurrently, the Army developed a more militarized version of the PT-3, called the O-17, for training in gunnery and photography. This craft featured improved streamlining and oleo shock absorbers for landing on rough fields and was fitted with a .30-caliber rear-firing machine gun. Consolidated constructed 32 O-17s, all of which ended up in National Guard units. Production of all types totaled 469 aircraft.

# Convair B-36 *Peacemaker*

**Type:** Strategic Bomber

**Dimensions:** wingspan, 230 feet; length, 162 feet; height, 49 feet, 9 inches
**Weights:** empty, 179,000 pounds; gross, 410,000 pounds
**Power plant:** 6 × 3,500–horsepower Pratt & Whitney R-4360 radial engines; 4 × 5,200–pound thrust General Electric J-47 turbojet engines
**Performance:** maximum speed, 439 miles per hour; ceiling, 45,200 feet; maximum range, 7,500 miles
**Armament:** 12 × 20mm cannons; up to 72,000 pounds of bombs or 1 × Mark 17 hydrogen bomb
**Service dates:** 1948–1959

The awe-inspiring B-36 was the world's first inter-continental bomber, an aircraft so huge that it was dubbed the "Aluminum Overcast." It made the concept of nuclear deterrence a reality and helped guarantee peace at the height of the Cold War.

In 1941 the United States feared it would be drawn into World War II and would have to bomb Nazi-occupied Europe from bases in the United States. The Army Air Corps decided it needed an air-craft that could carry a minimum 10,000-pound bomb load for round-trip missions of at least 10,000 miles. Consolidated was then contracted to build its Model 37, which finally emerged in September 1945, one month after the war ended. It was a huge craft that sported no less than six pusher engines on a 230-foot wing featuring a swept-back leading edge. The fuse-lage was so large that pressurized fore and aft com-partments were joined by an 85-foot tunnel, through which crew members traveled on small trolleys.

The B-36 entered production in 1948 as the *Peacemaker*, which at the time was the Strategic Air Command's first intercontinental bomber and the world's largest warplane. A subsequent model, the B-36D, introduced four jet engines on outboard wingpods to increase speed and service ceiling. Al-though the *Peacemaker* could carry up to 72,000 pounds—36 tons—of bombs, it was intended to drop nuclear weapons on the Soviet Union. In this mode it could carry only one Mark 17 thermonu-clear weapon, which was 24 feet in length and weighed 21 tons. Fortunately, the B-36 lumbered on through the Cold War as a successful deterrent and never fired a shot in anger. The last of 382 *Peace-makers* retired from the Air Force in 1959.

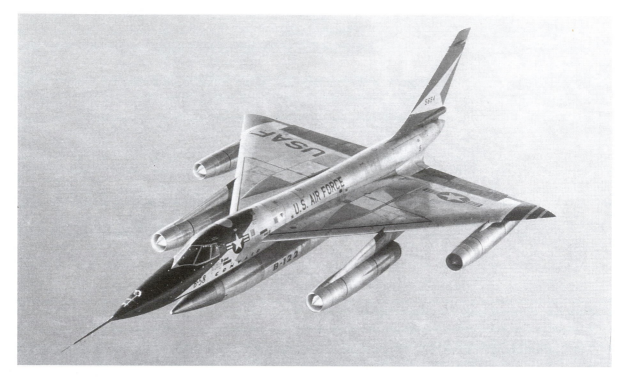

**Type:** Strategic Bomber

**Dimensions:** wingspan, 56 feet, 10 inches; length, 95 feet, 9 inches; height, 31 feet, 5 inches
**Weights:** empty, 56,560 pounds; gross, 177,000 pounds
**Power plant:** 4 × 15,600–pound thrust General Electric J79 turbojet engines
**Performance:** maximum speed, 1,385 miles per hour; ceiling, 64,000 feet; maximum range, 5,125 miles
**Armament:** 1 × 20mm Gatling gun; 4 nuclear weapons or 7,000 pounds of bombs
**Service dates:** 1960–1970

The sleek *Hustler* was the world's first supersonic bomber. In ten years it set 19 world records, more than any other warplane in history.

In 1948 Convair proposed building a strategic bomber that could reach supersonic speeds. The Air Force awarded Convair a contract, and a design was finalized by 1954. The prototype XB-58 emerged in 1956 as a large delta configuration with four podded engine nacelles slung underneath. Its unique honeycomb-sandwich skin was heat-resistant and enabled it to maintain Mach 2 flight for sustained periods. Despite its complexity, the *Hustler* was easy to fly, although its high landing speed necessitated a parachute brake for deceleration. The crew consisted of a pilot, a bombardier/navigator, and a systems operator, each equipped with a personal ejection capsule for survival. Speed was envisioned as its principal defense, although a 20mm cannon was fitted in the tail cone as a "stinger." However, the most radical feature of all was a large weapons pod carried beneath the belly that doubled as an external fuel tank. This contained fuel for the outward leg of the mission and was discarded once over the target. All told, the aircraft sported impressive supersonic performance, comparable to many fighter jets, and in 1960 it entered into service as the B-58 *Hustler*. A total of 116 was constructed, of which no less than 30 were collared for research purposes.

During the next decade, Strategic Air Command B-58s broke no less than 19 world speed and payload/altitude records. In 1963 one crew covered the 8,000-mile trip between Tokyo and London in only 8 hours, 35 minutes. However, the *Hustler*'s sterling performance carried an expensive price tag. Operating costs were prohibitive, and in 1970 the last of these impressive craft was retired for want of economy. They were replaced by the more cost-effective General Dynamics F-111 *Aardvark*.

# ✪ Convair C-131/R4Y *Samaritan*

**Type:** Transport

**Dimensions:** wingspan, 91 feet, 9 inches; length, 74 feet, 8 inches; height, 26 feet, 11 inches
**Weights:** empty, 29,248 pounds; gross, 50,417 pounds
**Power plant:** 2 × 2,500–horsepower Pratt & Whitney R-2800 radial engines
**Performance:** maximum speed, 262 miles per hour; ceiling, 25,500 feet; maximum range, 2,100 miles
**Armament:** none
**Service dates:** 1950–1985

Immediately after World War II there was a rush to develop a twin-engine commercial airliner to replace the venerable but still plentiful Douglas DC-3. In 1948 Convair began marketing its Model 240 as a more modern alternative. It was a sleek, low-wing design with tricycle landing gear, a pressurized cabin, and impressive performance. It was also one of the first civilian aircraft to feature reversible paddle-bladed propellers. A commercial success domestically, the Model 240 was also sold to airlines around the world.

In 1949 the Air Force approached Convair to produce a training version of the Model 240, and the following year it accepted deliveries of the first T-29s. In time more than 300 were acquired and employed for instructing student navigators and radar operators. The Air Force was pleased with the aircraft, so in 1954 it ordered 112 additional models as the C-131 *Samaritan*. This version could carry up to 44 passengers, 27 stretch-

ers, or 12,000 pounds of cargo. In addition to casualty evacuation, some examples performed special duties such as missile tracking and photographic survey work. Still others were fitted with comfortable interiors and served as staff transports for many years.

By 1952 the Navy grew interested in updating its transport fleet and adopted the *Samaritan* as the R4Y. That year the Navy accepted delivery of 36 machines as passenger cargo haulers. Like their Air Force counterparts, many R4Ys were fitted with numerous radomes and other electronic protuberances and served as special test aircraft. Some of the Air Force T-29s also found their way into Navy hands as flight trainers. Both services continually updated the engines and avionics of the *Samaritans*, which soldiered on into the early 1980s. C-131s remained in active service with the Air National Guard until 1985, when these reliable workhorses were finally put to pasture.

# Convair F-102 *Delta Dagger*

**Type:** Fighter

---

**Dimensions:** wingspan, 38 feet, 1 inch; length, 68 feet, 3 inches; height, 21 feet, 2 inches
**Weights:** empty, 19,350 pounds; gross, 28,150 pounds
**Power plant:** 1 × 16,000–pound thrust Pratt & Whitney J-57 turbojet engine
**Performance:** maximum speed, 780 miles per hour; ceiling, 51,800 feet; maximum range, 566 miles
**Armament:** 6 × Hughes AIM-4C radar-guided missiles; 24 × 2.75–inch unguided rockets
**Service dates:** 1956–1976

The *Delta Dagger* was the world's first supersonic interceptor and the first Air Force jet with a delta-wing configuration. It was also unique in being armed only with missiles and rockets, not guns.

In 1950 the Air Force, faced with the specter of Soviet bombers coming over the North Pole, announced a competition to build a supersonic all-weather interceptor. Two years earlier, Convair had already tested the XF-92, the world's first delta-wing jet aircraft, the design offering certain advantages at high speed. In 1954 a scaled-up version, the XF-102, was flown, although it failed to exceed the sound barrier, or Mach 1. Upon further investigation, engineer Richard Whitcomb hit upon the application of "area rule" to reduce drag along the fuselage. Henceforth, the XF-102 was fitted with a pinched waistline, which finally allowed the craft to reach almost 800 miles per hour. The Air Force was impressed, and in 1956 the aircraft went into production as the F-102

*Delta Dagger.* By 1958 1,100 fighter and trainer craft had been manufactured and deployed.

The F-102 thus became the world's first delta-wing supersonic interceptor; it was also highly automated. Once airborne, its advanced computers and telemetry would allow ground controllers to direct the craft precisely to an incoming target. When a radar lock was established, the sophisticated fire-control system would unleash numerous guided missiles or a cloud of unguided rockets at the intended target. Because guns were totally dispensed with, all missiles were stored in a weapons bay inside the belly. Ultimately, the Air Defense Command operated a total of 32 squadrons armed with the F-102. They remained in frontline service for two decades before being replaced by the faster McDonnell F-101 *Voodoo* and Convair F-106 *Delta Dart.* The aircraft was also operated in small numbers by Greece and Turkey.

# ⭐ Convair F-106 *Delta Dart*

**Type:** Fighter

**Dimensions:** wingspan, 38 feet, 3 inches; length, 70 feet, 8 inches; height, 20 feet, 3 inches
**Weights:** empty, 24,420 pounds; gross, 34,510 pounds
**Power plant:** 1 × 24,500–pound thrust Pratt & Whitney J-57 turbojet engine
**Performance:** maximum speed, 1,525 miles per hour; ceiling, 57,000 feet; maximum range, 1,800 miles
**Armament:** 1 × 20mm Gatling gun; 2 × AIM Falcon missiles; 1 × nuclear-tipped AIR-2 Genie missile
**Service dates:** 1959–1988

The *Delta Dart* guarded U.S. skies from Soviet bomber attacks for more than two decades. One of the most automated airplanes in history, its pilots did little more than direct takeoffs and landings.

The F-106 was originally a modification of the earlier F-102, but the changes proved so extensive that a new designation was warranted. Although it used the same wing, the fuselage was completely refined to incorporate a J-57 engine with twice the power, and the air ducts were moved further aft for increased efficiency. The prototype first flew in 1957 and set a world absolute speed record of 1,525 miles per hour—two-and-a-half times the speed of sound. Two more years of development were required before the F-106, christened the *Delta Dart*, was accepted into service. A total of 257 fighters and 63 two-seated

trainers was built; they equipped 14 Air Defense Command squadrons by 1961.

The F-106 was the most elaborately equipped fighter interceptor in history. Its MA-1 fire-control system was tied into the semiautomatic ground environment (SAGE) defense network; SAGE could quickly direct the F-106 to any threatened point within the United States. Once a target was identified, onboard computers would launch either radar-guided Falcon or nuclear-tipped Genie missiles before standing off. *Delta Dart* pilots had little to do but take off, monitor instruments, and land. This capable aircraft was continually updated over the years with new avionics and armaments, and it remained the frontline of American defense for 25 years. It then flew with Air National Guard squadrons before retiring in 1988; many ended their days as expendable QF-106 target drones.

**Type:** Liaison

**Dimensions:** wingspan, 40 feet, 6 inches; length, 31 feet, 9 inches; height, 7 feet, 2 inches
**Weights:** empty, 2,050 pounds; gross, 3,500 pounds
**Power plant:** 1 × 250–horsepower Franklin O-425 air-cooled engine
**Performance:** maximum speed, 115 miles per hour; ceiling, 15,000 feet; maximum range, 488 miles
**Armament:** none
**Service dates:** 1947–1955

Angular and ugly, the L-13 was a failed attempt by Convair to enter the liaison aircraft market. It was a capable and well-designed aircraft but proved more expensive than the planes it was supposed to replace.

In 1945 Consolidated-Vultee (Convair) designed a new craft as a follow-on to Stinson's L-5 *Grasshopper* after it had acquired that company. The resulting Model 105 was an all-metal, high-wing cabin plane with an angular front and a rather narrow, circular tail section. Although at first glimpse the model appeared to be a conventional light transport, the design incorporated several unique features. The wing was equipped with a slotted leading edge and slotted flaps for short takeoff performance, and it could clear a 50-foot obstacle after rolling only 230 feet. In contrast to the tandem seating arrangement found in most *Grasshoppers*, the Model 105 sat two pilots side by side, with room enough for four

additional passengers. Furthermore, for ease of storage and ground transport, the wings could be folded back along the fuselage and the tailplanes folded upward. The Army tested the Model 105 as a liaison candidate and rejected it as too novel, but in 1947 the Air Force ordered 300 copies as the L-13.

The L-13 flew for three years with Air Force units until the advent of the Korean War, when 43 of them were transferred to the Army for field use. The wing- and tail-folding features were deleted and standard communications equipment was added. However, all the L-13s remained stateside in order to free up more popular light aircraft for overseas service. The Army promptly returned the unwanted craft by 1954, although the Air Force went on to modify 28 L-13s with skis for Arctic use. The aircraft was declared surplus soon thereafter and replaced by the Cessna L19 *Birddog*, which did the same work at less expense.

## ✪ Convair R3Y *Tradewind*

**Type:** Transport; Tanker

---

**Dimensions:** wingspan, 145 feet, 9 inches; length, 139 feet, 8 inches; height, 51 feet, 5 inches
**Weights:** empty, 71,824 pounds; gross, 145,500 pounds
**Power plant:** 4 × 4,332–horsepower Allison T-40 turboprop engines
**Performance:** maximum speed, 388 miles per hour; ceiling, 39,700 feet; maximum range, 3,450 miles
**Armament:** none
**Service dates:** 1954–1958

Ostensibly the most beautiful flying boat ever built, the *Tradewind* was also the most balky. Constant problems with early turboprop engines limited its usefulness and ensured a brief service life.

In 1945 the Navy desired a new and more modern flying boat patrol craft to replace the Martin JRM *Mars* then in service. The Navy sought a craft that could operate from forward bases as well as perform air-sea rescue and antisubmarine duties. That year Convair conceived the Model 117, which was a sleek, high-wing design with fixed stabilizing floats and a large tail for stability. Moreover, it was the first flying boat outfitted with new turbojet engines, which drove six-bladed contrarotating propellers. The prototypes were completed in 1949, but difficulties in developing the Allison T-40 engines delayed its initial flight until 1950. By this time the Navy had reassigned the aircraft to transport duty, and it purchased five of the giant flying boats under the designation R3Y-2 *Tradewind*. In this configura-

tion it could carry 103 passengers or 92 stretchers and 12 medical attendants.

During its brief service life, the *Tradewind* set many flying boat records, many of which still stand. In October 1956 an R3Y crossed from California to Hawaii in only 6 hours, 45 minutes, beating a record previously held by the Martin *Mars*. However, the Navy became interested in developing an assault version of the *Tradewind*, the R3Y-2, which featured a hinged nose. This craft was intended to taxi up to a hostile beach, disgorge 103 fully armed troops, and withdraw before enemy defenses could react. Six of these craft were ordered in 1954, but soon thereafter they were converted into aerial tankers. In 1956 an R3Y-3 made aviation history by simultaneously refueling four Grumman F9F *Cougars* during one flight. However, recurring trouble with the Allison engines resulted in several costly crashes, and in 1958 the Navy ordered these magnificent seaplanes grounded and sold for scrap.

**Type:** Light Bomber; Reconnaissance

**Dimensions:** wingspan, 38 feet; length, 27 feet, 2 inches; height, 10 feet, 6 inches
**Weights:** empty, 2,875 pounds; gross, 4,476 pounds
**Power plant:** 1 × 435–horsepower Curtiss V-1150 liquid-cooled engine
**Performance:** maximum speed, 139 miles per hour; ceiling, 14,100 feet; maximum range, 628 miles
**Armament:** up to 6 × .30–caliber machine guns; 200 pounds of bombs
**Service dates:** 1927–1937

The *Falcon* was a reliable multimission observation and light bombardment machine. It was the first Army aircraft to bear the "A" designation for "Attack."

By 1924 the Army was struggling to replace its aging squadrons of leftover De Havilland DH-4s for light bombardment and observation work. A fly-off was arranged between competing Curtiss and Douglas designs, and the latter won. However, the following year the Curtiss XO-1 was refitted with a better Packard A-1500 engine, and it was selected for production instead. The new craft was a standard biplane in appearance but also unique in having sweepback on its broad upper wing and a fuselage constructed from aluminum tubing and steel-tie bracing. The crew of two sat in a tandem cockpit; the rear gunner was provided with twin Lewis machine guns for defense. However, when the Packard engine failed to live up to expectations, it was re-

placed on production models by the Curtiss D-12 engine. In 1927 the Army purchased ten O-1s followed by 27 improved O-1Bs. Subsequent modifications culminated in 37 O-1Es and 30 streamlined O-1Gs. The final 66 machines, known as the P-11, featured a Curtis Conqueror engine and a front cowling not unlike the P-6E *Hawk*.

By 1927 the Army wanted an existing design to fulfill its new designation of attack aircraft, and Curtiss answered with the A-3. This was basically a stock O-1B fitted with two additional machine guns under the wings. The Army acquired 66 A-3s and went on to purchase an additional 78 A-3Bs, which featured several refinements. Six A-3s were also modified with dual controls to function as advanced trainers. The various *Falcon* models served as the Army standard attack and observation craft for nearly a decade. They spent their last few years flying with National Guard units.

**Type:** Light Bomber

---

**Dimensions:** wingspan, 44 feet; length, 32 feet, 3 inches; height, 9 feet, 4 inches
**Weights:** empty, 3,898 pounds; gross, 5,900 pounds
**Power plant:** 1 × 690–horsepower Wright Cyclone R-1820 radial engine
**Performance:** maximum speed, 175 miles per hour; ceiling, 15,150 feet; maximum range, 140 miles
**Armament:** 5 × .30–caliber machine guns; 400 pounds of bombs
**Service dates:** 1932–1941

The *Shrike* was the first tactical monoplane constructed by Curtiss and possessed many technical innovations. When the Army began to de-emphasize inline engines for ground-attack machines, a radial-engine version was also produced.

By the late 1920s the Army sought to replace its Curtiss A-3 *Falcons* with a high-performance monoplane. In 1931, after competition between the General Aviation/Fokker XA-7 and the Curtiss XA-8, the latter was judged superior and ordered into production. The new craft thus became the first Curtiss monoplane sold to the Army and represented an advance in aerial technology. It was built entirely of metal and was the first Curtiss design to feature trailing-edge flaps, leading-edge slats, and fully enclosed cockpits. Pilot and gunner were widely separated, with the former controlling four machine guns, the latter, one. An unusual throwback was the use of external bracing on the main wing, which had not appeared on monoplanes since World War I. Nonetheless, the new craft was a big improvement over earlier planes, and in 1932 it entered production as the A-8 *Shrike*. The Army acquired 46 machines.

After a while the Army rejected inline liquid-cooled engines as too expensive and too vulnerable to ground fire; it turned to radial engines as cheaper, more rugged alternatives. Curtiss thereupon fitted a Wright R-1820 radial to an A-8 airframe and sold it to the Army under the designation A-12. It also differed by having open cockpits placed closer together. In 1934 a total of 34 A-12s was delivered; both versions served extensively with the Army Air Corps until 1936, when they began to be replaced by more modern Northrop A-17s. Nevertheless, a handful of A-12s were still present at Pearl Harbor in 1941; they spent their final days as mechanical trainers.

**Type:** Trainer

**Dimensions:** wingspan, 40 feet, 4 inches; length, 31 feet, 8 inches; height, 9 feet, 10 inches
**Weights:** empty, 4,600 pounds; gross, 6,000 pounds
**Power plant:** 2 × 295–horsepower Lycoming R-680 radial engines
**Performance:** maximum speed, 197 miles per hour; ceiling, 19,000 feet; range, 750 miles
**Armament:** none
**Service dates:** 1942–1944

The AT-9 was envisioned as an advanced transitional trainer for cadets destined to fly multi-engine attack bombers. It served briefly before being replaced by more versatile and effective training craft.

Prior to the U.S. entry into World War II, the Army Air Corps sought to intensify its training programs in anticipation of possible combat. Especially sought was an advanced trainer that closely mimicked the flight profile of the new, twin-engine attack bombers being deployed. It was hoped the new craft could quickly adjust new cadets from single-engine primary trainers to more demanding conditions. In 1941 Curtiss responded with its Model 25, a two-engine, low-wing monoplane constructed of a steel-tube fuselage structure and fabric covering. Being fast—and somewhat dicey to fly and land—it approximated the characteristics of a modern light bomber. This craft answered the Army's needs, and so it placed orders for 791 airplanes, which entered service as the AT-9 *Jeep*. Production models differed from the prototype by featuring stressed metallic skin instead of fabric.

By the summer of 1942 the *Jeep* was training pilots to handle the new generation of multiengine high-performance aircraft such as the Martin B-26 and the Lockheed P-38. And though the *Jeep* proved adequate for pilot instruction, the complexities of modern air war forced the Army Air Force to seek better trainers that allowed for full crew integration. This required an aircraft capable of simultaneous training in navigation, bombing, and gunnery to save time and to simulate combat conditions. The AT-9 was deemed inadequate for such purposes, and it was phased out of service by 1944 in favor of operational combat types such as the TB-25 and TB-26.

# ★ Curtiss B-2 *Condor*

**Type:** Heavy Bomber

---

**Dimensions:** wingspan, 90 feet; length, 47 feet, 4 inches; height, 16 feet, 4 inches
**Weights:** empty, 9,300 pounds; gross, 16,591 pounds
**Power plant:** 2 × 630–horsepower Curtiss Conqueror liquid-cooled engines
**Performance:** maximum speed, 132 miles per hour; ceiling, 17,500 feet; maximum range, 805 miles
**Armament:** 6 × .30–caliber machine guns; 2,500 pounds of bombs
**Service dates:** 1929–1936

The B-2 was descended from the earlier Martin MB-2 and possessed superior performance. However, its hefty price tag limited its production run in favor of the cheaper Keystone LB.

Curtiss acquired its first experience with heavy bombers when it contracted to build 50 Martin MB-2s in 1920. From this Curtiss developed the NBS-4 in 1924, which featured welded–steel tube construction in place of an all-wood fuselage. Curtis refined the design into the XB-2 with the addition of powerful Conqueror engines with radiators arrayed vertically above, a twin-rudder biplane tail, and a thicker airfoil. Another interesting feature was placement of gunners in the rear of the engine nacelles, imparting unobstructed fields of fire. Two additional machine guns were mounted in the nose.

In 1929 the XB-2 entered the Army's competition for a new heavy bomber in concert with Sikorsky, Atlantic-Fokker, and Keystone. The first two companies were quickly eliminated, and the Army

board wrangled over which bomber to build. The Curtiss design offered clear superiority in performance, but critics worried that it was larger than existing hangars and would pose maintenance problems. Ultimately, the deciding issue was price, and Keystone, whose LB bombers were much cheaper, gained the contract. As a concession to Curtiss, the Army also purchased 12 of the B-2s, which entered into service as the *Condor*.

Production models of the B-2 differed slightly from the prototype in having smaller radiators as well as three-bladed propellers. The B-2 was also the first large aircraft of its size to be fitted with a tail wheel instead of a tail skid. Skids traditionally had helped to brake aircraft upon landing but were also associated with structural failures. For many years the fabric-covered B-2s reliably served with the 11th and 96th Bomber Squadrons before being made obsolete by newer, all-metal monoplane bombers. These were finally struck off the service list in 1936.

**Type:** Transport; Light Bomber

**Dimensions:** wingspan, 82 feet; length, 49 feet, 1 inch; height, 16 feet, 4 inches
**Weights:** empty, 12,210 pounds; gross, 17,464 pounds
**Power plant:** 2 × 710–horsepower Wright R-1820 radial engines
**Performance:** maximum speed, 190 miles per hour; ceiling, 23,000 feet; maximum range, 715 miles
**Armament:** 5 × .30–caliber machine guns; 4,000 pounds of bombs
**Service dates:** 1934–1937

The *Condor* was the last biplane transport adopted for military service by the United States. It served only briefly but was actively employed by China during its war with Japan.

The Great Depression hit the U.S. aviation industry hard, and like many companies Curtiss scrambled to produce new and better machines for a shrinking domestic market. In 1933 Curtiss constructed the T-32 transport, a revolutionary aircraft in many respects. It was a big, nonstaggered biplane, the last of its kind designed in the United States. Construction was along traditional lines, being made of wood, metal tubing, and fabric covering. However, the T-32 featured several innovations. It was the first airliner with electrically retracted wheels, and the twin engines, located on the lower wings, possessed flexible mounts to reduce vibration. The power provided by two supercharged Cyclone motors pulled the big craft along at a spry 190 miles per hour. It was also the first commercial airliner capable of a two-ton payload. The T-32 was a limited commercial success, but as a biplane it was quickly superseded by all-metal monoplanes like the Douglas DC-2.

In 1935 the T-32 became the last biplane purchased by the Army Air Corps, and two examples went into service as the C-30. They conducted V. I. P. transport service around the United States before being replaced by the C-39, the military version of the DC-2. In 1937 the Navy also acquired two examples as the R4C, and both were operated by Marine Utility Squadron 7 as part of Admiral Richard E. Byrd's pioneering flights over the Antarctic. In 1941 both crashed and were abandoned there. However, the biggest user was the Nationalist Chinese government under General Chiang Kai-shek; it outfitted several examples with turrets and employed them as BT-32 bombers. A total of 45 T-32s was built.

# Curtiss C-46/R5C *Commando*

**Type:** Transport

**Dimensions:** wingspan, 108 feet, 1 inch; length, 76 feet, 4 inches; height, 21 feet, 9 inches
**Weights:** empty, 29,483 pounds; gross, 40,000 pounds
**Power plant:** 2 × 2,000–horsepower Pratt & Whitney Double Wasp R-2800 radial engines
**Performance:** maximum speed, 254 miles per hour; ceiling, 26,900 feet; maximum range, 1,500 miles
**Armament:** none
**Service dates:** 1941–1953

The C-46 was the largest twin-engine transport deployed by any air force during World War II. It performed valuable service on a variety of fronts, particularly in China, Burma, and India.

In 1936 the Curtiss-Wright Corporation decided to compete against Boeing and Douglas for the burgeoning civilian airliner market. Model CW-20 first flew in 1940 and featured a unique, double-bulged fuselage and stressed metal construction. The Army, looking to enhance the Air Transport Command, took immediate interest in the craft and ordered 25 copies. The C-46 *Commando*, as it was known, was the largest twin-engine transport ever operated by the Army Air Force. Its capacious fuselage could accommodate up to 40 fully equipped troops or more than 12,000 pounds of cargo. Initial deliveries arrived during the spring of 1941, just prior to U.S. entry into World War II.

The *Commando* saw service in every theater of operations, but it did particularly useful service flying the treacherous routes of China, Burma, and India. This sometimes entailed crossing the icy and turbulent "Hump," the name given to the Himalaya mountain system. Because the C-46 could carry more cargo and possessed superior high-altitude performance, it was preferred to the more famous and numerous Douglas C-47. It also flew in Europe toward the later phases of the war as a paratroop carrier and a glider tow. A total of 3,341 was built, including 160 R5Cs, which went to the Marine Corps.

The C-46 remained in service after 1945 and saw active duty during the Korean War. By 1953 the type was declared obsolete and gradually phased out, although some examples flew with Air Force Reserve units until the early 1960s. Several C-46s are still employed by airlines in Latin America to this day.

## ✪ Curtiss F-5L

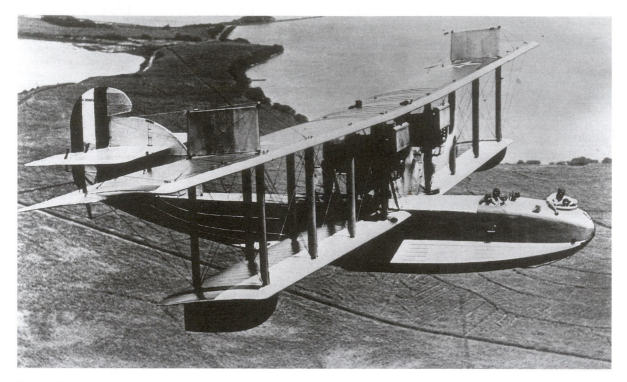

**Type:** Patrol-Bomber

**Dimensions:** wingspan, 103 feet, 9 inches; length, 49 feet, 3 inches; height, 18 feet, 9 inches
**Weights:** empty, 8,720 pounds; gross, 13,600 pounds
**Power plant:** 2 × 400–horsepower Liberty 12 liquid-cooled engines
**Performance:** maximum speed, 90 miles per hour; ceiling, 5,750 feet; maximum range, 830 miles
**Armament:** 6 × .30–caliber machine guns; 1,000 pounds of bombs
**Service dates:** 1918–1928

The F-5L flying boat was an American adaptation of a British design that in turn had originated with Curtiss. Produced too late to see effective service in World War I, the F-5L formed the mainstay of naval patrol aviation during the 1920s.

In 1915 the British acquired a number of Curtiss H-12s and H-16s, which they found unsatisfactory for use in the rough waters of the North Atlantic. Under the direction of Royal Navy Commander John C. Porte, the American planes were heavily modified with broader and more hydrodynamic hulls for better takeoffs and landings. However, the wings, engine mounts, and tail surfaces retained their original Curtiss design. This new craft, the Felixstowe F.5 series, subsequently made its way back to the United States in 1918, when the Navy began looking to replace its own H-16s. Impressed by its performance, the Navy decided to adopt the F.5 as the F-5L. Compared to the former craft from which it was derived, the F-5L featured longer wings, modified ailerons, and redesigned tail surfaces. By the time World War I ended, Curtiss had constructed 60 machines, the Naval Aircraft Factory 134, and Canadian Aeroplanes a further 30.

Despite its jumbled origins, the F-5L was a dramatic improvement over earlier Curtiss flying boats and distinguished itself during a decade of service. In 1919 an F-5L remained aloft for 24 hours, 19 minutes, establishing a new endurance record. The following year, a squadron of 12 F-5Ls lifted off from San Diego, California, and flew by stages to the Panama Canal Zone, 3,200 miles distant, without incident. During the summer of 1921 several of the giant craft participated in General William "Billy" Mitchell's controversial bombing exercises off the Virginia Capes, sinking several target vessels. By 1922 all F-5Ls received the designation PN-5, under which they flew for an additional six years.

# ⭐ Curtiss F6C/P-1 Hawk

**Type:** Fighter

**Dimensions:** wingspan, 31 feet; length, 22 feet, 6 inches; height, 8 feet, 6 inches
**Weights:** empty, 1,980 pounds; gross, 2,866 pounds
**Power plant:** 1 × 435–horsepower Curtiss V-1150 liquid-cooled engine
**Performance:** maximum speed, 160 miles per hour; ceiling, 22,000 feet; maximum range, 350 miles
**Armament:** 2 × .30–caliber machine guns; 232 pounds of bombs
**Service dates:** 1925–1930

The P-1 was the first Army aircraft to received the "P" for "Pursuit" designation. It was widely employed as a fighter and trainer and also served as a Navy dive-bomber.

In 1925 dissatisfaction with the PW-8 fighter prompted the Army to have Curtiss submit a more refined version. That year, Curtiss answered with the XP-1, which externally was very similar to the earlier craft. However, the XP-1 had a shorter lower wing and introduced a tapered upper wing. Because the new machine displayed somewhat better speed and handling characteristics than the predecessor, the Army ordered it into production as the P-1 *Hawk*, the first of a long fighter dynasty. Only ten of the P-1As were purchased, but they were followed by 83 B and C models, featuring longer fuselages and bigger tires. An additional 65 were acquired as AT-4 trainers, although these could readily be reconverted back to a fighter con-

figuration. Construction totaled 148 *Hawks* of all models.

The Navy also looked to the P-1 as a possible replacement for its Boeing FB-5s, and in 1926 it purchased nine aircraft as the F6C-1. They were nearly identical to the Army version and not suited for carrier use. But commencing with the F6C-2, arrester gear and a strengthened fuselage made the *Hawk* capable of dive-bombing operations. A total of 75 was produced. By 1927, however, the Navy decided that inline engines were too expensive and difficult to maintain at sea; it accordingly adopted cheaper, less complicated radial engines for Navy aircraft. Curtiss therefore fitted its final order of F6C-4s with the 1,200-horsepower Pratt & Whitney Wasp radial engine, but by 1930 the P-1 and F6C were being replaced by faster, newer aircraft. Throughout their career, modified *Hawks* also won several awards while competing in the National Air Races, 1926–1930.

**Type:** Fighter

**Dimensions:** wingspan, 32 feet, 8 inches; length, 22 feet, 2 inches; height, 10 feet, 4 inches
**Weights:** empty, 2,053 pounds; gross, 2,782 pounds
**Power plant:** 1 × 450–horsepower Pratt & Whitney R-1340 radial engine
**Performance:** maximum speed, 155 miles per hour; ceiling, 22,100 feet; maximum range, 355 miles
**Armament:** 2 × .30–caliber machine guns
**Service dates:** 1928–1933

The *Seahawk* was the first purposely designed Navy fighter built by Curtiss. However, it served in only limited numbers with the Marine Corps as a test vehicle.

By the late 1920s the Navy was no longer interested in adopting cast-off Army designs for its fighters and began seeking aircraft of its own. In 1927 Curtiss entered into a competition with Boeing for an aircraft that could be deployed either as a land-based fighter or float fighter capable of launching from battleships. To accomplish this, the desired aircraft would have to possess detachable landing gear and provisions for a central float and wingtip pontoons. Curtiss turned to its already established *Hawk* series as a starting point; the new Model 43 was a standard biplane configuration. It possessed an aluminum and steel-tubing fuselage structure and had fuel tanks built into the streamlined fairings where the lower wing joined. Another unusual aspect was an upper wing that employed a straight center section and outer panels that were swept back. The aircraft was fabric-covered throughout. The prototype also had a large streamlined spinner covering the radial engine, which was subsequently deleted. After extensive testing, the Boeing and Curtiss designs entered limited production as the F7C and the F3B, respectively.

Curtiss eventually built 18 F7C-1s for the Navy and christened it the *Seahawk*. However, because catapult fighters had been rendered obsolete by the advent of aircraft carriers, all the seaplane provisions were dropped. The *Seahawks* were consequently assigned to a Marine Corps squadron, VF-5M, at Quantico, Virginia, as land-based planes. There they spent their entire service life as test vehicles, experimenting with new forms of propellers, engine cowlings, and leading-edge slats. The F7Cs functioned in this useful, if unheralded, capacity until their retirement in 1933.

**Type:** Dive-Bomber

**Dimensions:** wingspan, 32 feet; length, 25 feet, 11 inches; height, 10 feet, 2 inches
**Weights:** empty, 2,506 pounds; gross, 3,728 pounds
**Power plant:** 1 × 450–horsepower Pratt & Whitney R-1340 radial engine
**Performance:** maximum speed, 137 miles per hour; ceiling, 19,800 feet; maximum range, 722 miles
**Armament:** 4 × .30–caliber machine guns; 1 × 500–pound bomb
**Service dates:** 1929–1937

The *Helldiver* was the first Navy aircraft specifically designed as a dive-bomber. Though somewhat slow, it rendered capable service—and was even featured in a Hollywood movie.

By 1927 the Marine Corps was eager to replace its World War I–vintage De Havilland DH-4s as tactical bombers. The Marines were also acutely interested in an aircraft capable of dive-bombing, a technique they had helped pioneer. When the earlier F8C/OC *Falcon* was tested and found better suited for reconnaissance work, the Marines turned to Curtiss for a new aircraft based upon the original design. The ensuing XF8C-2 had some similarities with the earlier prototype of the same name but had been heavily redesigned. Although possessing the trademark swept-back upper wing of the *Falcon* family, both wing and fuselage were shorter by several feet. Moreover, the forward part of the fuselage was formed by the external metal skin of the cheek tanks; the aft section remained fabric-covered.

Other changes included a cowled engine and relocation of machine guns from the lower to the upper wing. The Marines were impressed by the XF8C's ability to dive, and in 1929 they accepted an initial batch of 36 machines as F8C-4s *Helldivers*. This was the first Curtiss machine bearing that illustrious name.

In service the F8Cs were found to be capable dive-bombers, yet they were slower than the carrier fighters that by necessity escorted them. Thereafter it was decided to employ *Helldivers* as land-based aircraft. In 1931 a further 63 were manufactured as F8C-5s, an additional 30 as the O2C-1 reconnaissance craft. Subsequently, all *Helldivers* were designated O2Cs in light of their observation role. In 1931 several *Helldivers* also appeared in the Hollywood movie *Dive Bomber*, featuring Clark Gable and Wallace Beery. By 1937 the career of the O2Cs had ended, but several machines remained as the personal aircraft of high-ranking naval aviators.

**Type:** Reconnaissance

**Dimensions:** wingspan, 38 feet; length, 25 feet, 11 inches; height, 10 feet, 6 inches
**Weights:** empty, 2,440 pounds; gross, 3,918 pounds
**Power plant:** 1 × 432–horsepower Pratt & Whitney R-1340 radial engine
**Performance:** maximum speed, 129 miles per hour; ceiling, 17,300 feet; maximum range, 378 miles
**Armament:** 3 × .30–caliber machine guns; 4 × 100–pound bombs
**Service dates:** 1928–1935

The OC *Falcon* was one of few aircraft designed to meet a Marine Corps specification. Despite mediocre performance, the type saw active duty throughout the so-called Banana Republics in Central America.

As the United States found itself drawn into Caribbean affairs during the 1920s, the Marine Corps was increasingly landed on foreign soil to maintain order. Eventually, it was decided to acquire a land-based fighter-bomber/observation craft to support these operations. In 1927 Curtiss responded by fitting one of its Army O-1 *Falcons* with a radial engine preferred by the Navy. Like its predecessor, the new aircraft enjoyed a riveted, tubular fuselage covered by fabric. The wing was also typical of the family, consisting of a straight center section and swept-back outer panels. The pilot and gunner were seated in tandem, with the former controlling two .30-caliber machine guns firing through the cowling, the latter manning a similar weapon mounted on a scarf ring above the cockpit. Although it was hoped the craft would double as a two-seat fighter, the XF8C was clearly too sluggish, and that specification was dropped. Once preliminary testing was completed, the Marine Corps accepted six examples as the F8C *Falcon*.

In 1928 the new aircraft was hastily pressed into service with Marine detachments serving in China and Nicaragua, where they were redesignated OC-1s. Subsequently, Curtiss converted a number of its A-3 attack aircraft into OC-2s, of which an additional 21 were completed. They proved to be capable, if unspectacular, performers. It was found necessary to relocate the fuselage bomb racks to the outer wing panels so that the bombs would clear the landing gear when released. Ring cowlings were also eventually fitted to reduce engine drag. The *Falcon* soldiered on without fanfare as an observation and utility aircraft until it was finally retired in 1935.

# Curtiss F9C *Sparrowhawk*

**Type:** Fighter

**Dimensions:** wingspan, 25 feet, 6 inches; length, 20 feet, 1 inch; height, 10 feet, 7 inches
**Weights:** empty, 2,117 pounds; gross, 2,779 pounds
**Power plant:** 1 × 438–horsepower Wright Whirlwind R-975 radial engine
**Performance:** maximum speed, 176 miles per hour; ceiling, 19,200 feet; maximum range, 297 miles
**Armament:** 2 × .30–caliber machine guns
**Service dates:** 1932–1936

The diminutive *Sparrowhawk* holds a unique place in the annals of naval aviation. Designed as a parasite fighter, it successfully operated as a scout from giant airships.

Since World War I the Navy had entertained the idea of deploying giant dirigibles as distant early-warning systems. In 1928 it ordered construction of the *Akron* and *Macon*, which were 785 feet long and possessed a range of more than 9,000 miles. Because such airships would be helpless in the face of hostile aircraft, the Navy decided to defend them with tiny parasite fighters that were carried onboard. In 1930 the Navy announced competition for a lightweight aircraft, and the Curtiss entry beat out competing designs from Berliner-Joyce and General Aviation. Save for its small size, the XF9C was a conventional biplane with a metal fuselage and fabric-covered wings. The upper wing was formed into an inverted gull shape to improve pilot vision. The fighter was intended to fly up to the airship, latch on to a metal trapeze, and be brought aboard for storage. When the prototype proved itself to be inherently unstable, Curtiss redesigned it at company expense and finally obtained good results. Consequently, in 1931 the Navy ordered six additional aircraft as the F9C *Sparrowhawk*.

During a period of two years the F9Cs carried out 104 successful linkups with mother ships. When operating over vast expanses of water, it was found desirable to remove the landing gear and substitute a large drop tank for extra range. This also had the added effect of increasing the *Sparrowhawk*'s performance. After the *Akron* crashed at sea in April 1933, the six F9Cs were transferred to the *Macon*. They operated without incident until February 1935, when the *Macon* was also lost along with four F9Cs. The parasite-fighter program was then dropped, and the remaining two *Sparrowhawks* flew as squadron hacks before being retired in 1936. The sole surviving F9C can be seen at the National Air and Space Museum at the Smithsonian Institute.

# ✪ Curtiss F11C/BF2C *Goshawk*

**Type:** Fighter; Dive-Bomber

**Dimensions:** wingspan, 31 feet, 6 inches; length, 23 feet, 6 inches; height, 10 feet
**Weights:** empty, 3,100 pounds; gross, 5,086 pounds
**Power plant:** 1 × 750–horsepower Wright Cyclone R-1820 radial engine
**Performance:** maximum speed, 228 miles per hour; ceiling, 27,000 feet; maximum range, 797 miles
**Armament:** 2 × .30–caliber machine guns; 500 pounds of bombs
**Service dates:** 1933–1938

The *Goshawk* was the last Curtiss biplane fighter made for the Navy. Though procured in limited numbers, it found greater commercial success when exported abroad.

In 1931 the perfection of dive-bombing techniques prompted the Navy to seek a single-seat fighter capable of such work. The following year, Curtiss test-flew its XF11C, a radial-engine version of the successful P-6E *Hawk*. The new craft was of standard biplane configuration with fixed, single-strut landing gear and a semienclosed cockpit. As a dive-bomber, it was also fitted with a special crutch that swung down to prevent the bomb from hitting the propeller. Tests proved successful, and in 1933 the type entered production as the F11C *Goshawk*. A total of 28 was built and equipped a group onboard the carrier USS *Saratoga*.

By 1933 the appearance of the Grumman FF-1, which featured retractable landing gear, forced Curtiss to make similar modifications to the F11C. The

front of the fuselage was deepened and outfitted with wheels that were hand-cranked upward into two wells. A new, all-metal wing was also introduced. Thus configured, the new design could fly 25 miles per hour faster than earlier models. The Navy obtained 27 of these machines and berthed them aboard the carrier USS *Ranger*. In 1934 the Navy applied new designations to both versions, with the first becoming the BFC-2, the latter the BF2C to denote bomber status. Owing to vibration problems, BF2Cs served only briefly as dive-bombers, and all were scrapped by 1938.

In view of the small Navy orders, Curtiss lost no time developing an export version of the F11C, known simply as the *Hawk* I–IV. The first two had fixed wheels, whereas the latter two were retractable types. Its high performance led to 250 machines being sent overseas, mostly to China, but Turkey, Spain, Chile, Bolivia, and Colombia all purchased several machines.

**Type:** Patrol-Bomber

**Dimensions:** wingspan, 92 feet, 8 inches; length, 46 feet; height, 16 feet, 9 inches
**Weights:** empty, 5,800 pounds; gross, 7,989 pounds
**Power plant:** 2 × 330–horsepower Liberty 12 liquid-cooled engines
**Performance:** maximum speed, 85 miles per hour; ceiling, 10,800 feet; maximum range, 450 miles
**Armament:** 3 × .30–caliber machine guns; 2 × 236–pound bombs
**Service dates:** 1917–1921

Though designed for the Royal Navy, the H-12 was the first American-built warplane to shoot down a German aircraft during World War I. It was also a big improvement over previous flying boat designs.

In 1913 the *Daily Mail*, a British newspaper, offered 10,000 British pounds to the first person to cross the Atlantic in an airplane. Commander John C. Porte of the Royal Navy took up the challenge by resigning his commission and coming to America to work for Curtiss. There he helped design a modern flying boat, which he dubbed the *America*, but the onset of World War I prompted his return to England. Nonetheless, he convinced the admiralty to purchase 62 militarized versions of the *America*, which Curtiss designated the H-8. They proved underpowered and difficult to operate in choppy seas, so the Royal Navy requested Curtiss to construct a larger version.

In 1917 the Curtiss-Porte collaboration culminated in the H-12, dubbed the *Large America* on account of its origins. Thereafter, the H-8s still in service became known as *Small Americas*. Like its predecessor it possessed long, unstaggered wings and two engines in tractor configuration. It flew fine as an airplane but still possessed inadequate water performance. Nonetheless, the Royal Navy ordered 50 machines without waiting for a prototype. In May 1917 an H-12 became the first U.S.-manufactured aircraft to shoot down a German craft during World War I when it bagged a Zeppelin over the North Atlantic. A few days later another H-12 scored the first aerial victory over a submarine. Once the United States was drawn into the war, the U.S. Navy also expressed interest in the H-12 and acquired 20 machines. Because they were powered by the famous Liberty engine, they received the designation H-12L. Both versions remained in service until 1921.

**Type:** Patrol-Bomber

---

**Dimensions:** wingspan, 95 feet; length, 46 feet, 1 inch; height, 17 feet, 8 inches
**Weights:** empty, 7,400 pounds; gross, 10,900 pounds
**Power plant:** 2 × 400–horsepower Liberty liquid-cooled engines
**Performance:** maximum speed, 95 miles per hour; ceiling, 9,950 feet; maximum range, 378 miles
**Armament:** 5 × .30–caliber machine guns; 4 × 230–pound bombs
**Service dates:** 1918–1928

---

The hulkish H-16 was the best American flying boat of World War I. Heavily armed and enjoying good endurance, it helped suppress the German U-boat threat.

Wartime experience with the H-12 craft prompted the Royal Navy to ask Curtiss to design a slightly larger flying boat with better rough-water performance. In the spring of 1918 Curtiss constructed the H-16, which shared some similarities with the earlier craft but was an entirely new machine. The H-16 featured a two-step, boatlike hull, which afforded better hydrodynamic characteristics, along with an increased wingspan and a balanced rudder. Moreover, the bomb load had been increased over earlier versions; it also sported heavier defensive armament. The admiralty was suitably impressed by what they considered "the Big Boat" and placed an order for 110 machines. Curtiss constructed 184 H-16s; the Naval Aircraft Factory built an additional 150. Ultimately, the U.S. Navy acquired more than 200 H-16s, made in greater quantities than any other Curtiss twin-engine flying boat. The only difference between the British and American versions was that the former was powered by the Rolls-Royce Eagle VIII engine, the latter by the famous Liberty engine.

H-16s were actively employed at sea throughout the closing phases of World War I. They were part of the ongoing effort to suppress U-boat attacks against convoys, which was moderately successful. American seaplanes flew more than 4,000 patrols and initiated 27 attacks against German craft from the air. They sank no vessels but damaged several and discouraged their presence in the shipping lanes. Consequently, only three Allied ships were lost to submarines in areas patrolled by the Curtiss flying boats. The H-16 proved itself rugged and dependable and remained in British service up through 1921; the U.S. Navy maintained its fleet of H-16s until 1928.

# ✪ Curtiss HS

**Type:** Patrol-Bomber

**Dimensions:** wingspan, 74 feet; length, 39 feet; height, 14 feet, 7 inches
**Weights:** empty, 4,300 pounds; gross, 6,432 pounds
**Power plant:** 1 × 350–horsepower Liberty liquid-cooled engine
**Performance:** maximum speed, 82 miles per hour; ceiling, 5,200 feet; maximum range, 517 miles
**Armament:** 1 × .30–caliber machine gun; 2 × 230–pound bombs
**Service dates:** 1917–1926

The HS was one of few U.S.-built and -operated warplanes to see active service during World War I. Sturdy and dependable, it remained the Navy's standard patrol-bomber for more than a decade.

In 1917 Curtiss decided to downsize its unwieldy H series of flying boats by designing a single-engine craft. The resulting HS prototype was a wooden aircraft with unstaggered wings and a 200-horsepower Curtiss VXX engine mounted in pusher configuration. The new design was relatively fast and handled well on water, and production models became the first aircraft to mount the famous Liberty engine. It also carried a crew of three and was armed with a nose-mounted machine gun and two depth charges. The Navy initially ordered 664 from Curtiss, 250 from the Standard Airplane Corporation, 50 from the firm of Lowe, Willard, and Fowler, 50 from Gallaudet, 50 from Boeing, and a final 60 from Loughead (Lockheed).

The HS-1Ls were initially deployed along the Atlantic Coast, where they performed routine anti-submarine patrols. On July 21, 1918, an HS-1L carried out its first attack on a German submarine off Cape Cod, Massachusetts, but the bomb failed to explode. Throughout the summer, other HS-1Ls made their way to France, eventually operating from ten stations. However, experience demonstrated that the craft required a bigger bomb to reach submerged submarines, so Curtiss designed the HS-2L, which featured an additional six feet of wingspan and enlarged tail surfaces to compensate for the heavier load. Both versions served capably through the end of the war in November 1918.

HS boats continued their frontline service for nearly a decade after the war. Curtiss tried to extend their service life by designing the HS-3, which possessed a revised hull, but only six were completed before the Navy lost interest. The last HS boats left the service in 1926 following a construction run of 673 machines.

**Type:** Trainer

**Dimensions:** wingspan, 43 feet, 7 inches; length, 27 feet, 4 inches; height, 9 feet, 10 inches
**Weights:** empty, 1,467 pounds; gross, 2,017 pounds
**Power plant:** 1 × 150–horsepower Wright-Hispano liquid-cooled engine
**Performance:** maximum speed, 93 miles per hour; ceiling, 10,525 feet; maximum range, 268 miles
**Armament:** none
**Service dates:** 1915–1927

The *Jenny* was a legendary trainer from World War I. Afterward it continued with the military for many years, but it is best remembered as a barnstorming civilian craft.

By 1916 both the Army and Navy grew alarmed by the number of fatal crashes involving pusher-powered training planes; a more modern, tractor-type aircraft was needed. Because tractor propulsion was more advanced in Europe than in the United States, in 1915 Glenn Curtiss contracted with British engineer B. D. Thomas of Sopwith to design such a craft. Thomas submitted plans for what he called the Type J, which was built at the Curtiss plant in New York. Curtiss himself weighed in with a similar design, the Type N, which featured an improved airfoil. By 1915 it was decided to combine the best features of both to produce the legendary JN, or *Jenny*.

The JN was a standard biplane yet was unique in having all controls managed by a single cockpit stick. The Army was interested in the early JN-3 version, which in 1916 accompanied General John J.

Pershing's expedition into Mexico. Results were not entirely satisfactory, so Curtiss developed a stronger, more refined version, the JN-4. This aircraft performed well and was on hand in quantity when the United States entered World War I in 1917. Subsequently, almost 5,000 JN-4s were built and deployed by the Army Air Service, the Royal Flying Corps, and the Royal Canadian Air Force. Thousands of Allied pilots received their first exposure to aviation in the beloved *Jenny*, which was docile and forgiving yet also quite maneuverable. By war's end the U.S. Navy operated a fleet of 261 JN-4s, including some floatplane versions.

The *Jenny* remained in military service after the war, but several thousand passed into civilian hands. Piloted by some of America's legendary barnstormers, *Jennies* thrilled audiences at fairs and aircraft shows across the country. The JN thus became the first commercially successful aircraft in history, with 7,280 being constructed; military versions remained in service until 1927.

**Type:** Trainer

**Dimensions:** wingspan, 49 feet, 9 inches; length, 28 feet, 10 inches; height, 11 feet, 7 inches
**Weights:** empty, 1,850 pounds; gross, 2,488 pounds
**Power plant:** 1 × 100–horsepower Curtiss OXX liquid-cooled engine
**Performance:** maximum speed, 72 miles per hour; ceiling, 4,100 feet; maximum range, 345 miles
**Armament:** none
**Service dates:** 1918–1921

The MF was a refined version of Curtiss's original flying boat. After a brief stint with the Navy it was sold on the commercial market.

Curtiss had been experimenting with float-type seaplanes since 1911, and the following year a revolutionary craft, the Model F, was unveiled. This was the first true hull-type flying boat, which represented a major advance in marine aircraft design. The fuselage, though aerodynamic, possessed a streamlined boatlike shape for operations directly off water. For greater stabilization, the craft was also fitted with sponsons at the end of each wingtip. The Model F was powered by a single engine in the rearward-facing, or pusher, configuration that was conventional at that time. The Navy became intrigued by the new design and purchased five in 1914. One of these machines subsequently became the first aircraft to fly with the newly invented Sperry gyroscopic automatic pilot, which kept the aircraft in level flight. Ul-

timately, 144 Model Fs were acquired and employed as trainers during World War I.

As Curtiss gained additional expertise with large flying boats, the company resolved to refine the aging F-boat with new features. Thus was born the Modified F, or MF, of 1918. Though outwardly similar in appearance, the new craft incorporated a flat-sided hull and flared sponsons along the sides for greater buoyancy. The Navy placed an initial order for six machines, which was later expanded to 47. However, by the time World War I ended, only 16 had been delivered. During the postwar period the Naval Aircraft Factory was contracted to turn out an additional 80 MFs. One of these was experimentally converted into an amphibian ship by the addition of landing gear. The MFs remained in service until the early 1920s before being declared surplus. Many were then commercially marketed as the *Seagull*.

**Type:** Trainer

---

**Dimensions:** wingspan, 39 feet, 5 inches; length, 27 feet, 4 inches; height, 10 feet, 8 inches
**Weights:** empty, 2,138 pounds; gross, 2,960 pounds
**Power plant:** 1 × 240–horsepower Wright R-760 radial engine
**Performance:** maximum speed, 116 miles per hour; ceiling, 17,800 feet; maximum range, 384 miles
**Armament:** none
**Service dates:** 1928–1936

When it appeared, the N2C looked like a throwback to an earlier age. Its service career was undistinguished, although one machine became the first radio-controlled missile.

In response to a 1927 Navy competition for a new primary trainer, Curtiss constructed three prototypes of the XN2C-1. It went up against competing entries from Keystone and Boeing, beating both of them in the land plane and floatplane categories. Curiously, this "new" design appeared at first glance to be a relic from the World War I era. It was a two-bay biplane with staggered wings that were buttressed by a maze of struts and bracing wires. In fact, the XN2C-1 sported more struts and wires than the Curtiss JN *Jenny* it was supposed to replace. Nonetheless, the craft possessed forgiving flying qualities, and the Navy ordered 31 examples as the N2C *Fledgling*. The first machine delivered was altered by fitting shorter, single-bay wings, but subsequent models were restored to

their original format. Also, there were some minor variations in power plants. The three prototypes entered service with the 165-horsepower Curtiss Challenger engine and remained the only Navy airplanes thus powered. The bulk of N2Cs was supposed to utilize the tried and tested Wright J-5 radial engine, but when supplies ran out a new order of 20 machines was fitted with the newer, more powerful Wright R-760.

In service, the N2Cs received the orange-and-yellow paint scheme of training aircraft. Mostly they were assigned to Naval Reserve training units up through 1936. After they were retired, several *Fledglings* made history by being fitted with tricycle landing gear, an increased dihedral for better stability, and radio-control equipment. They functioned as pilotless target drones for antiaircraft gunners, but one apparently simulated a dive-bomb attack on a battleship. This feat is generally regarded as the first use of an air-to-surface missile in history.

**Type:** Trainer

---

**Dimensions:** wingspan, 53 feet, 3 inches; length, 30 feet, 10 inches; height, 10 feet, 8 inches
**Weights:** empty, 2,140 pounds; gross, 2,765 pounds
**Power plant:** 1 150–horsepower Hispano-Suiza A liquid-cooled engine
**Performance:** maximum speed, 80 miles per hour; ceiling, 9,850 feet; maximum range, 179 miles
**Armament:** none
**Service dates:** 1917–1926

The N-9 was the Navy's primary floatplane trainer throughout World War I. It was essentially a navalized version of the famous JN-4 *Jenny* and had an equally lengthy service life.

In 1916 the success of the JN-4 as an Army trainer induced the Navy to consider building a similar aircraft for float-training purposes. As a private venture, Curtiss first experimented with the N-8, which was similar to the JN-4 save for a different airfoil. This, in turn, gave way to the N-9, which was more heavily modified for its intended role. The new craft was outfitted with a single large float under the fuselage and stabilizing wingtip floats. It was also powered by the slightly more powerful OXX-6 engine. To compensate for the additional weight, the wingspan was increased an additional ten feet through use of a wider center panel. The tail surfaces were also enlarged on production models. Throughout the war, the Navy acquired

and operated 560 N-9s as its primary floatplane trainer.

The Army, which also conducted seaplane operations, considered the N-9 for its stable and purchased 14 machines. As good as they were as primary trainers, these machines proved underpowered for advanced bombing and gunnery training. Curtiss responded by fitting several N-9s with a more powerful, 150-horsepower Hispano-Suiza engine, resulting in the designation N-9H. They were instantly distinguished from earlier models by their flat propeller spinner.

Like the *Jenny*, the N-9 and its variants rendered valuable service during the war and the postwar period. Several were employed in the development of steam-powered catapults for launching aircraft at sea. Curiously, during the 1920s the Navy acquired 50 additional aircraft by assembling them from spare parts. N-9s remained in service as late as 1926 before being replaced by more advanced aircraft.

**Type:** Patrol-Bomber

---

**Dimensions:** wingspan, 126 feet; length, 68 feet, 3 inches; height, 24 feet, 6 inches
**Weights:** empty, 15,874 pounds; gross, 27,386 pounds
**Power plant:** 4 × 400–horsepower Liberty liquid-cooled engines
**Performance:** maximum speed, 85 miles per hour; ceiling, 4,500 feet; maximum range, 1,470 miles
**Armament:** 2 × .30–caliber machine guns
**Service dates:** 1918–1922

---

The historic NCs were the first aircraft to complete a transatlantic crossing. Despite their fame, they were outlasted in service by older H-16s and HS-2s.

When the United States entered World War I, the U.S. Navy was considered inadequate to defend Allied shipping against the German U-boat threat. Consequently, the Navy sought development of a large flying boat capable of being flown in stages to Europe and immediately conducting antisubmarine activities upon arrival. Because Curtiss was the only American firm with any experience building large flying boats, the Navy contracted with that company to build such a craft. In 1918 the design was finalized as the NC (for Navy-Curtiss). It was a large biplane with straight, unstaggered wings and three engines set in pusher-tractor arrangement. But unlike previous Curtiss flying boats, the new plane possessed a rather short fuselage, with the tail surfaces mounted on an outrigger structure. World War I ended before

the massive craft could be deployed, but in November 1918 NC-1 broke a world record by lifting off with 51 passengers. Soon after, the government decided to send four NCs on a historic mission across the Atlantic to Portugal.

On May 16, 1919, three NCs took off from Trepassy Bay, Newfoundland, and headed for the Azores. En route, NC-1 came down in heavy seas and had to be abandoned. NC-3 was also forced down in bad weather but was able to taxi 200 miles into Horta Harbor and safety. It fell upon NC-4, commanded by Commander Albert C. Read, to continue the voyage alone. On May 27 he finally landed at Lisbon—the first successful transatlantic flight. Four days later Read flew to Plymouth, England, where he was escorted by three British Felixstowe flying boats. Six additional NCs were then constructed; they performed routine patrol duty until being retired in 1922. The famous NC-4 remains on display at the Naval Air Museum in Pensacola, Florida.

**Type:** Reconnaissance

**Dimensions:** wingspan, 40 feet, 9 inches; length, 26 feet, 4 inches; height, 9 feet, 3 inches
**Weights:** empty, 4,231 pounds; gross, 5,364 pounds
**Power plant:** 1 × 600–horsepower Pratt & Whitney R-1340 radial engine
**Performance:** maximum speed, 220 miles per hour; ceiling, 21,000 feet; maximum range, 700 miles
**Armament:** 3 × .30–caliber machine guns
**Service dates:** 1940–1945

The *Owl* was the last design to receive the "O" designation for "Observation." It was a fine airplane but lacked a mission and was ultimately replaced by less expensive machines.

In 1939 the Army set forth specifications for a new two-seat observation aircraft. Curtiss responded with its Model 85, a radical departure from the biplanes of an earlier era. The new craft was a braced-parasol all-metal monoplane with retractable landing gear. The long greenhouse canopy housed a pilot and a gunner/observer who shared dual controls. Great care had been put into the plane's handling characteristics at slow speed, for the high wing possessed leading-edge slots and trailing-edge flaps that deployed automatically in concert. Actually, the Model 85 shared some design elements with other Curtiss aircraft, having obtained its collapsible rear turtledeck from the SOC *Seagull*. This feature gave the gunner unimpeded fields of fire for his machine gun. At the other end of the fuselage, the landing gear originated from the SBC *Helldiver* and retracted into wheel wells behind the engine. The design appeared so promising that in 1940 the Army purchased 203 machines as O-52 *Owls*. No prototype was flown.

In service the O-52 performed exactly as advertised, but its mission disappeared shortly after the commencement of World War II. Given recent advances in fighter and antiaircraft technology, the Army decided that long-range reconnaissance could best be handled by twin-engine bombers. Once outfitted with cameras, such machines could fly higher, faster, and farther than the plodding *Owl*. For short-term tactical reconnaissance, the new liaison class of aircraft such as the Piper L-3 *Grasshopper* was desirable based on economy, ease of maintenance, and ability to fly from improvised airfields. A handful of O-52s may have seen service overseas during the initial days of the war, but the majority remained stateside as training aircraft. Only three have survived to the present day.

## Curtiss P-6E *Hawk*

**Type:** Fighter

**Dimensions:** wingspan, 31 feet, 6 inches; length, 23 feet, 2 inches; height, 8 feet, 10 inches
**Weights:** empty, 2,699 pounds; gross, 3,392 pounds
**Power plant:** 1 × 600–horsepower Curtis Conqueror V-1570 liquid-cooled engine
**Performance:** maximum speed, 198 miles per hour; ceiling, 24,700 feet; maximum range, 570 miles
**Armament:** 2 × .30–caliber machine guns
**Service dates:** 1930–1937

The P-6E was the last biplane fighter built by Curtiss and the last acquired by the Army Air Corps. Though not as maneuverable as many contemporaries, it was fast and possibly the most beautiful biplane ever flown.

During the late 1920s both Army and Navy aircraft participated in the National Air Races, and technology developed for greater speed usually found military applications. In 1927 two P-1 fighters were converted into XP-6s by fitting them with experimental 600-horsepower Conqueror engines. During the National Air Race that year they placed first and second, with top speeds of 201 miles per hour. The Army was so impressed by the *Hawk* racers that it purchased nine YP-6s for evaluation, followed by an additional nine. As fighters they were fast, but the Army remained convinced that with proper streamlining the P-6 could go even faster. The problem revolved around placement of the radiator, which was invariably large and drag-producing. A partial solution was

hit upon with the invention of Prestone (ethylene glycol) as an engine coolant, which did not boil like water and allowed for smaller radiators. In 1932 all 18 were designated as P-6Ds and received turbosuperchargers for better performance at high altitude (they proved unreliable and were removed).

In 1933 the Army accepted delivery of the best of the family, the P-6E. Unlike earlier versions, this was a highly streamlined aircraft with single-strut landing gear and wheel fairings. The two machine guns had also been relocated from the top of the fuselage to the sides. Elegant in appearance, the latest *Hawk* was fast but not as maneuverable as competing Boeing fighters. Nevertheless, the Army acquired 46 of the speedy machines. Colorfully painted P-6Es served exclusively with the 1st and 8th Pursuit Groups in Michigan until 1937, when they were replaced by Boeing P-26s. They were the last biplanes accepted into Army Air Corps service and among the most distinctive.

# ⭐ Curtiss P-36 *Hawk*

**Type:** Fighter

---

**Dimensions:** wingspan, 37 feet, 4 inches; length, 28 feet, 6 inches; height, 9 feet, 6 inches
**Weights:** empty, 4,620 pounds; gross, 6,010 pounds
**Power plant:** 1 × 1,200–horsepower Pratt & Whitney Twin Wasp R-1830 radial engine
**Performance:** maximum speed, 311 miles per hour; ceiling, 33,700 feet; maximum range, 820 miles
**Armament:** 1 × .50–caliber and 3 × .30–caliber machine guns
**Service dates:** 1938–1942

---

The P-36 was the first Curtiss monoplane fighter built for the Army. During World War II it enjoyed the dubious distinction of having fought for both sides.

In 1935 the Army sponsored a competition to replace its aging Boeing P-26s with a new monoplane fighter. Curtiss submitted its Hawk 75, a streamlined, low-wing design featuring an enclosed canopy and retractable landing gear that rotated back 90 degrees into streamlined fairings. In 1936 Curtiss lost out to the Seversky XP-35, and the company subsequently fitted the craft with a stronger engine. Officials liked the increased performance, so in 1937 the Army contracted for 210 machines as the P-36A *Hawk*. This was the largest peacetime order placed for fighter craft since the Boeing MB-3 in 1922. Pilots enjoyed the strength and maneuverability of the P-36, but it was already marginally obsolete compared to the latest European aircraft.

Curtiss wasted no time exporting the Hawk 75 abroad, and almost 500 were sold to China, France, Norway, Siam, and the Dutch East Indies. When World War II broke out in September 1939, a French Hawk 75 claimed the first German plane shot down by a U.S.-built craft. After the fall of France, the Germans supplied many captured *Hawks* to ally Finland and to the Vichy French regime. They tangled briefly with Grumman F4F *Wildcats* during the November 1942 invasion of North Africa. Other Hawk 75s fought against the Japanese with both the British in Burma and the Chinese Air Force. During the air raid on Pearl Harbor in December 1941, P-36s were among the first American aircraft aloft, and they helped claim the first Japanese aircraft of the war. In view of their obsolescence, surviving *Hawks* were retained at home as advanced trainers. The P-36's greatest legacy was in being the direct ancestor of the more famous and capable P-40 *Warhawk*.

**Type:** Fighter

**Dimensions:** wingspan, 37 feet, 4 inches; length, 33 feet, 4 inches; height, 12 feet, 4 inches
**Weights:** empty, 6,550 pounds; gross, 8,850 pounds
**Power plant:** 1 × 1,360–horsepower Allison V-1710 liquid-cooled engine
**Performance:** maximum speed, 350 miles per hour; ceiling, 31,000 feet; maximum range, 360 miles
**Armament:** 6 × .50–caliber machine guns; 500 pounds of bombs
**Service dates:** 1939–1944

The famous *Warhawk* was America's most numerous fighter at the outbreak of World War II. Marginally obsolete, it was nonetheless fast, rugged, and produced a surprising number of aces.

In July 1937 the Army Air Corps attempted to improve the performance of its radial engined P-36 fighter by having Curtiss splice an inline, water-cooled Allison engine onto the existing airframe. The new craft was decidedly faster while retaining the pleasant flying characteristics of the P-36. Army officials were sufficiently impressed to place an order for 524 *Warhawks*, as the plane was called, in May 1939. Both the RAF and French Air Force also expressed interest and placed sizable orders.

In combat the P-40 proved something of a disappointment to the RAF, for it lacked the speed and altitude of the latest German fighters. The 1941 attack on Pearl Harbor plunged America into World War II, and the ensuing Philippines campaign also highlighted the

shortcomings of the P-40 in combat against more nimble Japanese adversaries. However, a legend was born when General Claire L. Chennault accepted 100 P-40Bs into his American Volunteer Group, the famous Flying Tigers. Capitalizing on the *Warhawk's* fast diving speed and ability to absorb damage, he instituted a campaign of brilliant hit-and-run tactics over Burma. Consequently, 286 Japanese aircraft were shot down at a cost of four *Warhawk* pilots. Back in Europe, both the RAF and the Army Air Corps used the P-40 as an effective fighter-bomber throughout the North African and Italian campaigns. In an attempt to improve the flying qualities of the P-40, the Model M was built with the high-powered Merlin engine, but results were marginal. Though by 1944 the P-40 had been phased out of frontline American service, a total of 13,700 *Warhawks* of all descriptions were built and flown by 28 air forces around the world. It was a classic American warplane.

**Type:** Fighter

**Dimensions:** wingspan, 32 feet, 9 inches; length, 23 feet, 1 inch; height, 9 feet, 1 inch
**Weights:** empty, 2,191 pounds; gross, 3,155 pounds
**Power plant:** 1 × 440–horsepower Curtiss D-12 liquid-cooled engine
**Performance:** maximum speed, 168 miles per hour; ceiling, 21,700 feet; maximum range, 544 miles
**Armament:** 2 × .30–caliber machine guns
**Service dates:** 1923–1926

The PW-8 was the first Army fighter in the "Pursuit" category. It was quickly overshadowed by contemporary designs, but it did serve as inspiration for the famous *Hawk* fighter series.

During the early 1920s Curtiss established an ascendancy in the design of racing aircraft. In 1922 the Curtiss R-6, a very streamlined craft powered by the successful D-12 engine, won the Pulitzer Race at a scorching 206 miles per hour. Curtiss was convinced it could make a fighter with similar performance to replace the balky Thomas Morse MB-3s. As a company venture, it went on to produce the prototype XPW-8, which shared the same lines as the R-6. It boasted a very clean airframe, two bays of wing struts, and metal-framed, fabric-covered tail surfaces. A very innovative touch was placement of surface radiators across the top of the wing. This feature, adapted from racers, dramatically reduced the drag associated with such devices. The Army purchased two prototypes,

and after extensive testing the craft went into production as the PW-8. It was the first such aircraft to receive the designation PW for "Pursuit, Water-cooled."

In service, PW-8s proved faster than the competing Boeing PW-9s, though less maneuverable. Furthermore, the novelty radiators were difficult to service and in combat would have been vulnerable to enemy fire. Nonetheless, the Army purchased 25 of the temperamental machines, probably through the instigation of General William "Billy" Mitchell, a vocal proponent of airpower. Apparently, Mitchell agreed to buy the craft if Curtiss would specially rig one for long-distance flying. Curtiss agreed, and on June 23, 1924, a PW-8 piloted by Lieutenant Russell Maughan dramatically flew the first dawn-to-dusk flight across the United States. The craft's remaining service was much less spectacular, but in 1925 a heavily modified PW-8 served as the XP-1 prototype, first in a long line of *Hawk* fighters.

**Type:** Reconnaissance; Torpedo-Bomber

**Dimensions:** wingspan, 57 feet; length, 33 feet, 5 inches; height, 14 feet, 2 inches
**Weights:** empty, 3,325 pounds; gross, 4,500 pounds
**Power plant:** 1 × 400–horsepower Liberty liquid-cooled engine
**Performance:** maximum speed, 88 miles per hour; ceiling, 11,000 feet; maximum range, 565 miles
**Armament:** 1 × 1,036–pound torpedo
**Service dates:** 1915–1926

The slow, sedate Curtiss R was a standard observation airplane that predated World War I. In 1919 it was updated to serve as the Navy's first torpedo-bomber.

In 1915 Curtiss sought to enlarge its existing Model J and Model N trainers by developing the Model R. This was a standard biplane configuration with staggered, two-bay wings and all wood-and-fabric construction. The prototype was fitted with a 160-horsepower Curtiss V-X liquid-cooled engine and possessed a single large cockpit to house both pilot and observer. Given the fragile nature of aircraft to date, it was customary to sit the observer in front of the pilot for, in his absence, the center of gravity would not be altered. The first production model was the R-1, of which the Army purchased two machines; the Royal Naval Air Service acquired 100 for patrol work. This model was followed up by the R-3, a floatplane for the Navy; the wingspan increased from 48 to 57 feet to absorb the additional weight. A total of 18 was produced. The next version was the R-4, with the original wingspan restored and a stronger, 200-horsepower Curtiss V-X-X installed. Several examples served along the Mexican border in 1916. An additional 12 R-4Ls with new Liberty engines followed in 1918. However, the most significant wartime purchase was that for 158 R-6 floatplanes by the Navy. They became the first U.S.-built warplanes to serve overseas during World War I when a squadron, based on the Azores, flew antisubmarine patrols.

Until that point the R series rendered solid, if unspectacular, service in both war and peace. In 1919 the Navy converted 40 R-6s into the R-9 by adding a powerful Liberty engine. They were subsequently fitted to drop torpedoes, thereby becoming the first American torpedo-bomber. Several R-9s functioned as such until retirement in 1926.

**Type:** Scout-Bomber

**Dimensions:** wingspan, 49 feet, 9 inches; length, 36 feet, 8 inches; height, 13 feet, 2 inches
**Weights:** empty, 10,547 pounds; gross, 16,616 pounds
**Power plant:** 1 × 1,900–horsepower Wright Cyclone R-2600 radial engine
**Performance:** maximum speed, 295 miles per hour; ceiling, 29,100 feet; maximum range, 1,165 miles
**Armament:** 2 × 20mm cannons; 2 × .30–caliber machine guns; 2,000 pounds of bombs
**Service dates:** 1943–1949

The *Helldiver* was the most produced dive-bomber in Navy history. Difficult to fly and maintain, it was unaffectionately known to pilots and repair crews as the "Beast."

In 1938 the Navy started looking into a new and more powerful scout-bomber to replace the Douglas SBDs then in service. Curtiss was awarded a design contract in competition with Brewster, and the Curtiss prototype XSB2C first flew in December 1940. It was a large, ham-fisted aircraft built around a powerful engine and possessed long wings with a short fuselage. It bore a remarkable resemblance to Brewster's competing entry, the SB2A *Buccaneer*. But unlike the earlier SBD, the bomb load was carried internally, with mounts for additional ordnance under the wings. The Navy liked the result and placed an order in November 1940, although the first models were not delivered until June 1942 due to technical difficulties. Christened *Helldiver*, the SB2C underwent prolonged periods of stability and other technical problems, which delayed its operational status until late 1943. However, by 1945 more than 7,200 had been produced.

The *Helldiver* proved something of a mixed blessing in combat. Heavy and unforgiving, it boasted a heavier bomb load than the easygoing *Dauntless* but was laborious to fly and repair. In fact, the SB2C was only marginally better than the aircraft it was designed to replace. However, the SB2C flew continuously in many significant carrier battles in the Pacific, and by war's end the "Beast" fully equipped all Navy dive-bomber squadrons. Earlier, the Army had expressed its interest in the SB2C and ordered 900 copies, known as the A-25, the folding wings and other naval equipment being deleted. When they failed to perform as anticipated, most were summarily turned over to the Marine Corps as training aircraft. This controversial aircraft, respected if unloved, remained in fleet service until 1949.

**Type:** Dive-Bomber

---

**Dimensions:** wingspan, 34 feet; length, 28 feet, 4 inches; height, 12 feet, 7 inches
**Weights:** empty, 4,841 pounds; gross, 7,632 pounds
**Power plant:** 1 × 950–horsepower Wright Cyclone R-1820 radial engine
**Performance:** maximum speed, 237 miles per hour; ceiling, 27,300 feet; maximum range, 590 miles
**Armament:** 2 × .30–caliber machine guns; 1,000 pounds of bombs
**Service dates:** 1937–1943

---

The *Helldiver* was the last biplane dive-bomber flown by the Navy. Ironically, it began its life as a monoplane fighter.

In 1932 the Navy desired a new monoplane fighter, and Curtiss responded by producing the XF12C-1, a barrel-chested aircraft sporting a parasol wing. When its inadequacy in this role became apparent, the Navy ordered it reconfigured as a two-seat scout/dive-bomber, but when the prototype crashed, Curtiss yanked the design for a complete overhaul. The final form emerged in 1936 as the XSBC-2, a standard all-metal biplane with retractable landing gear. The crew of two sat in tandem under a long canopy, which was faired directly into the aft fuselage. Its performance was impressive for the day, so the Navy ordered 83 machines. In 1937 the machines entered into service as the SBC-3 *Helldiver*, the second Curtiss design to bear that name.

In 1938 an improved version, the SBC-4, was developed, which featured a stronger Wright Cyclone engine. Because the bomb load had doubled to 1,000 pounds, the Navy agreed to purchase an additional 174 machines, which were deployed to the fleet in 1939. By that time biplanes were clearly obsolete, but in view of the deteriorating situation in Europe, France was assigned 50 SBC-4s directly out of the Navy's stocks. When France fell to Germany in 1940, the aircraft were diverted to Great Britain, which employed five of them as the *Cleveland*. However, they received no operational role. When the Japanese attacked Pearl harbor in December 1941, the Navy still possessed two squadrons of *Helldivers* onboard the carrier USS *Hornet*. However, they were quickly withdrawn and functioned stateside as mechanical trainers until 1943. Thus, the SBC-4, the last combat biplane in American history, never tested its mettle in battle.

**Type:** Scout

**Dimensions:** wingspan, 41 feet; length, 36 feet; height, 12 feet, 9 inches
**Weights:** empty, 6,320 pounds; gross, 9,000 pounds
**Power plant:** 1 × 1,350–horsepower Wright Cyclone R-1820 radial engine
**Performance:** maximum speed, 313 miles per hour; ceiling, 28,600 feet; maximum range, 625 miles
**Armament:** 2 × .50–caliber machine guns; 650 pounds of bombs
**Service dates:** 1944–1949

The SC was last in a long series of fleet-based scout aircraft. It was the best plane of its class to fly during World War II but was exposed to only brief combat operations.

By June 1942 the Navy needed to replace its Curtiss SO3C *Seamews* and Vought OS2U *Kingfishers* with a more modern aircraft. The new design had to be fast, heavily armed, and capable of operating from airfields, cruisers, or aircraft carriers. Curtiss entered the competition, and the following year the prototype XSC-1 first flew in February 1943. It was a low-wing monoplane of metal construction and could be fitted with wheels or floats depending upon intended use (either could be fixed to a common attachment point under the fuselage). The pilot was housed in a spacious bubble canopy allowing good all-around vision. Furthermore, the wings were hinged for storage at sea,

and the fuselage was spacious enough to carry an onboard stretcher for medical evacuation. The Navy found the craft desirable and immediately ordered an initial batch of 500 machines. Curtiss delivered the *Seahawks* as land planes; the Edo Company was contracted to manufacture the central and wingtip floats.

The SC began reaching the fleet during the fall of 1944 and was initially deployed aboard the cruiser USS *Guam*. The aircraft had its baptism of fire during a preinvasion bombardment of Borneo in June 1945 and performed well. The Navy placed a second contract for an additional 450 SCs, but only 66 were delivered before the war ended. An additional ten units of the SC-2, an improved model featuring a molded plastic canopy and revised tail surfaces, were also delivered. The *Seahawk* continued in fleet use until 1949.

**Type:** Trainer

**Dimensions:** wingspan, 35 feet; length, 26 feet, 6 inches; height, 7 feet, 6 inches
**Weights:** empty, 2,610 pounds; gross, 3,626 pounds
**Power plant:** 1 × 420–horsepower Wright Whirlwind R-975 radial engine
**Performance:** maximum speed, 201 miles per hour; ceiling, 21,900 feet; maximum range, 515 miles
**Armament:** 2 × .30–caliber machine guns
**Service dates:** 1941–1944

The SNC was developed from the CW-21 *Demon* as an interim trainer for the Navy. It had only a brief operational life before structural weakness restricted it to instrument training.

As the United States geared up for the possibility of war during 1940, the Navy started shopping for an advanced trainer to acquaint fledgling pilots with fighter tactics. The Navy turned initially to the Curtiss CW-21 *Demon*, which was light and relatively inexpensive and possessed high performance. The fuselage required extensive modifications to accommodate a cadet and an instructor, seated in tandem under a single glass canopy. Dual flight controls were also required so that the craft could be utilized for instrument flight training. However, the identical CW-21 wing and retractable landing gear were retained. The prototype CW-22 flew later that year as a low-wing monoplane of all-metal construction except for the ailerons, which were fabric-covered.

The Navy was pleased with the new airplane, christened the SNC *Falcon*, and placed an initial order for 150 in November 1940.

Through the early years of World War II, SNCs were employed as combat trainers; their maneuverability and pleasant flying characteristics imparted basic combat tactics to numerous cadets. However, the stress associated with this activity took its toll on the relatively lightly built fuselage, resulting in structural failures. The Navy ultimately procured a total of 305 *Falcons*, but toward the end of their service life they were deployed only as instrument trainers. However, the Netherlands acquired no less than 36 SNCs, configured as fighters, which were actively employed in the defense of the East Indies. An additional 50 were acquired by Turkey as military trainers. After the war several SNCs were licensed as civilian aircraft, and one or two examples are still flying today.

# ✪ Curtiss SO3C *Seamew*

**Type:** Scout

---

**Dimensions:** wingspan, 38 feet; length, 36 feet, 10 inches; height, 15 feet
**Weights:** empty, 4,284 pounds; gross, 5,729 pounds
**Power plant:** 1 × 660–horsepower Ranger SGV-770 liquid-cooled engine
**Performance:** maximum speed, 172 miles per hour; ceiling, 15,800 feet; maximum range, 1,150 miles
**Armament:** 1 × .30–caliber machine gun and 1 × .50–caliber machine gun; 200 pounds of bombs
**Service dates:** 1942–1944

In 1937 the Navy desired to replace its reliable but obsolete Curtiss SOC *Seagull* with a more modern, high-speed scout plane. Foremost among the Navy's requirements was a design that employed interchangeable floats and landing gear to accommodate water and land operations. Curtiss was awarded a contract to develop a prototype in 1938; the following year the XSO3C made its debut. This was a midwing monoplane of metal construction, save for fabric control surfaces, with detachable wheels and floats. The crew of two was housed in enclosed tandem cockpits. Flight trials highlighted instability problems, so production models were fitted with upswept wingtips and larger tail surfaces. The aircraft's performance was further eroded by the weight of additional naval equipment, but production of the SOC3 began in 1941. Ultimately, a total of 456 was manufactured; no less than 256 of

these were acquired by the Royal Navy under the Lend-Lease program, acquiring the name *Seamew*.

The SO3C enjoyed a brief, unhappy operational life with the U.S. Navy. Its inverted Ranger engine was a source of constant mechanical headaches, and performance-wise the type represented only a marginal improvement over the venerable SOC. The Royal Navy also expressed its dissatisfaction with the *Seamew*, and none were ever employed operationally. In fact, the most constant use for British SO3Cs was as expendable, unmanned radio-controlled target drones. American *Seamews* were finally withdrawn from frontline use in early 1944; the majority was subsequently employed as target aircraft. In an attempt to revive the design, Curtiss experimented with a reduced-weight version, the SO3C-3, but only 39 were manufactured, and production was not revived.

**Type:** Reconnaissance

**Dimensions:** wingspan, 36 feet; length, 26 feet, 6 inches; height, 14 feet, 9 inches
**Weights:** empty, 3,788 pounds; gross, 5,437 pounds
**Power plant:** 1 × 600–horsepower Pratt & Whitney Wasp R-1340 radial engine
**Performance:** maximum speed, 165 miles per hour; ceiling, 14,900 feet; maximum range, 675 miles
**Armament:** 2 × .30–caliber machine guns; 650 pounds of bombs
**Service dates:** 1935–1945

Slow but reliable, the *Seagull* actually replaced the aircraft designed to succeed it. It enjoyed a lengthy career and served onboard virtually every capital ship in the fleet.

By 1933 the Navy was seeking a replacement for its Vought O3U *Corsairs* to serve as a standard observation craft. The new design was therefore obliged to be a floatplane and capable of being catapulted off cruisers and battleships. Furthermore, it had to be readily convertible into a land plane through use of detachable floats. Curtiss, Douglas, and Vought all entered the competition, with the Curtiss model being declared the winner in 1934. The XSOC-1 was of standard biplane configuration and built of welded steel tubing with a covering of light alloy and fabric. The wings could be folded for shipboard storage; the crew of two was seated in tandem underneath a spacious greenhouse canopy. The prototype had been designed as an amphibian with wheels that retracted into the central float, but

that feature was abandoned on production models. The Navy was pleased with the results and in 1935 the craft began service as the SOC-1 *Seagull*. More than 300 were constructed in four slightly different models.

The *Seagull* became the Navy's standard scout/observation aircraft for many years and literally saw duty on every large ship in the fleet. Its strength, dependability, and ease of handling made it a favorite with pilots. The aged craft were actively employed throughout World War II, although by 1943 Curtiss was approached to provide an updated successor. Unfortunately, the new craft, the SO3C *Seamew*, proved a big disappointment, so the SOCs were immediately called out of retirement and resumed frontline duty on cruisers. Battleships, however, utilized the newer Vought O2SU *Kingfisher* in their place. The SOCs were finally phased out in 1945, concluding the final chapter of biplanes in the U.S. Navy.

**Type:** Fighter

**Dimensions:** wingspan, 25 feet; length, 22 feet; height, 8 feet
**Weights:** empty, 1,239 pounds; gross, 1,927 pounds
**Power plant:** 1 × 200–horsepower Lawrence J-1 radial engine
**Performance:** maximum speed, 131 miles per hour; ceiling, 14,400 feet; maximum range, 468 miles
**Armament:** 2 × .30–caliber machine guns
**Service dates:** 1923–1929

The diminutive TS-1 was the first aircraft designed for carrier use and the first to employ a radial engine. Slow and underpowered, it spent most of its career being launched overboard from battleships.

In 1920 the Navy took a giant step toward the future by converting the collier *Jupiter* into its first aircraft carrier, the USS *Langley*. However, the problem remained of securing viable fighter craft to operate off the ship. The existing Vought VE-7s were considered inadequate for shipboard use, so in 1921 the Naval Aircraft Factory (NAF) was authorized to design the Navy's first fighter aircraft. This new craft would also have to be convertible for water use through detachable floats. The resulting TS-1 appeared to be a conventional biplane but contained several unusual features. First, the all-wood fuselage was suspended midway between the two wings on struts. Next, the lower wing was actually longer than the top wing and employed a thickened center section as the fuel tank that could be jettisoned in an

emergency. Finally, the wings were joined by N-struts, thus avoiding use of bracing wires. The TS-1 proved itself an ugly aircraft, but it was functional. Furthermore, it confirmed the Navy officials' belief that radial engines, cheaper and less costly to maintain than complex liquid-cooled designs, were better suited to naval needs.

Because Curtiss underbid the NAF in its construction contract, it received an order to build 34 TS-1s in 1923. The craft flew reasonably well but was rapidly overtaken by newer, more imaginative designs from Boeing. After extensive testing with carriers, most TS-1s were fitted with floats and deployed onboard battleships as scouts. Catapults were not in widespread service at this date, so the standard launching practice was to lower the TS-1 overboard by crane and let it take off under its own power. All TS-1s were finally withdrawn in 1929, having demonstrated the practicality of carrier aviation.

**Type:** Fighter

**Dimensions:** wingspan, 35 feet; length, 27 feet, 2 inches; height, 8 feet, 11 inches
**Weights:** empty, 3,382 pounds; gross, 4,500 pounds
**Power plant:** 1 × 1,000–horsepower Wright R-1820 radial engine
**Performance:** maximum speed, 315 miles per hour; ceiling, 34,300 feet; maximum range, 630 miles
**Armament:** 2 × .30–caliber machine guns; 2 × .50–caliber machine guns
**Service dates:** 1940–1942

The *Demon* was an impressive little fighter built exclusively for export. However, it was totally outclassed by more modern Japanese designs and suffered heavy losses during the Battle of Java.

In 1938 the Curtiss-Wright plant in St. Louis, Missouri, sought to modify its unsuccessful CW-19 trainer into a lightweight fighter. The resulting prototype, the CW-21, was a low-wing monoplane of metal construction with landing gear that retracted rearward into clamshell fairings. The leading edge of the wings was also unique in being extremely swept back. Christened the *Demon*, the CW-21 first flew in January 1939 and exhibited sprightly performance, with impressive climbing and turning capabilities. It was also lightly armed and lacked armor protection for the pilot and fuel tank. However, when the Army Air Corps expressed no interest in lightweight fighters, Curtiss turned to the world market and offered the CW-21 for export.

In 1939 the nationalist Chinese government expressed interest in the *Demon* and placed an order for 35 examples. The order was filled the following year, although its record against equally nimble Japanese aircraft is unknown. In 1940 Curtiss began marketing an improved version, the CW-21B, which featured two additional wing-mounted machine guns and landing gear that retracted inward into the wing. The Netherlands ordered 24 examples of this new *Demon* and deployed them in defense of the Dutch East Indies. When the Pacific War broke out late in 1941 these aircraft were actively employed in the defense of Java but were totally outclassed by the Japanese A6M *Zero* fighters. After two days of combat, only five of the *Demons* survived. A final three CW-21Bs were assigned to assist the Flying Tigers under General Claire L. Chennault in Burma. However, on December 23, 1941, all three were lost in bad weather when they flew into a mountainside.

# ✪ De Havilland DH-4 *Liberty Plane*

**Type:** Light Bomber; Reconnaissance

---

**Dimensions:** wingspan, 42 feet, 5 inches; length, 29 feet, 11 inches; height, 9 feet, 8 inches
**Weights:** empty, 2,939 pounds; gross, 4,595 pounds
**Power plant:** 1 × 400–horsepower Liberty liquid-cooled engine
**Performance:** maximum speed, 123 miles per hour; ceiling, 14,000 feet; maximum range, 550 miles
**Armament:** 4 × .30–caliber machine guns; 322 pounds of bombs
**Service dates:** 1917–1932

Though derided with the nickname "Flaming Coffin," the venerable DH-4 was one of the most successful bombers to serve during World War I. It had an equally distinguished postwar career thanks to continual rebuilding programs.

In 1916 the British rolled out the first De Havilland DH-4, soon proclaimed as the best light bomber of World War I. It was a standard biplane in most respects, with extremely clean lines. However, the pilot and gunner were separated by a large fuel tank, which made communication difficult. Furthermore, the fuel tank's location exposed it to enemy fire, and the DH-4 gained a reputation for easily catching fire, thus the derogatory characterization as a flaming coffin. Nonetheless, when the United States entered the war in April 1917, it adopted the DH-4 for production purposes. The American version was powered by a 400-horsepower Liberty engine, and no less than 4,846 were constructed during 1918. These became the only U.S.-built warplanes to fly over German soil. By war's end they were flown in 150 missions and dropped 275,000 pounds of bombs.

After the war DH-4s formed the core of American bombardment aviation for nearly a decade. The marginally obsolete planes were continually rebuilt in programs that gave them stronger engines and metallic fuselages. Another significant modification was to exchange the pilot's seat with the fuel tank, bringing the crew closer together. In July 1923 an aging DH-4 demonstrated its utility by being the first aircraft to be refueled in the air—in this instance by a garden hose dangling from another DH-4! The following August, a DH-4 set a world endurance record by staying aloft for 37 hours thanks to 15 inflight refuelings. In 1925 the Marine Corps obtained the O2B-1 reconnaissance version, but by 1928 all DH-4s were finally replaced as bombing craft by the Curtiss A-3 *Falcon*. However, several lingered with training and communications units until 1932.

# De Havilland–Canada CV-2/C-7 *Caribou*

**Type:** Transport

**Dimensions:** wingspan, 95 feet, 7 inches; length, 77 feet, 3 inches; height, 28 feet, 7 inches
**Weights:** empty, 18,260 pounds; gross, 31,300 pounds
**Power plant:** 2 × 1,450–horsepower Pratt & Whitney R-2000 radial engines
**Performance:** maximum speed, 216 miles per hour; ceiling, 27,700 feet; maximum range, 1,400 miles
**Armament:** none
**Service dates:** 1960–1988

The *Caribou* was a capable light transport that did exceptional work throughout the Vietnam War. However, it became caught up in interservice rivalry and was consequently transferred to the Air Force under a different name.

During the mid-1950s De Havilland of Canada sought to improve upon the success of its L-20s and U-1 transports, many of which had been sold to the U.S. Army. By 1956 De Havilland resolved upon a totally new design, the DHC-4 *Caribou*, which was sold abroad in both military and civilian versions. This was a twin-engine, high-wing design fitted with a rear loading ramp that could easily accept up to four tons of cargo and be opened in flight for parachute operations. Moreover, it was specifically designed with short takeoff and landing capabilities and could operate from the roughest possible airfields. The Army, despite an agreement with the Air Force to limit its aircraft to less than 5,000 pounds,

took great interest in the new craft, and in 1960 it ordered 159 examples. The following year, the *Caribou* entered service under the designation CV-2.

The CV-2 was deployed to Vietnam in 1962 and successfully ferried men, equipment, and supplies to forward battle areas. In fact, the *Caribou* proved itself a godsend to isolated outposts in mountainous and jungle terrains. Rugged and easily maintained, it could carry 32 men, a three-ton truck, or two jeeps; land on rough landing strips; and then depart with medical evacuees. However, the sheer size of the craft violated the Army's own weight standards, and in 1967 it agreed to turn over all CV-2s to the Air Force Tactical Air Command, which monopolized large transport aircraft. The aircraft were then redesignated C-7s, although they continued serving with distinction until the American withdrawal from Vietnam in 1973. However, a handful remained with Army National Guard units until being retired in 1988.

# De Havilland–Canada L-20/U-6 *Beaver*

**Type:** Liaison; Transport

**Dimensions:** wingspan, 48 feet; length, 30 feet, 3 inches; height, 9 feet
**Weights:** empty, 2,850 pounds; gross, 5,100 pounds
**Power plant:** 1 × Pratt & Whitney R-985 Wasp, Jr., radial engine
**Performance:** maximum speed, 163 miles per hour; ceiling, 18,000 feet; maximum range, 455 miles
**Armament:** none
**Service dates:** 1952–

The rugged, dependable *Beaver* was operated in larger numbers by the U.S. Army than any other fixed-wing aircraft. It was the first in a distinguished line of Canadian bush planes employed by the United States.

In 1946 the Royal Canadian Air Force began looking for a new airplane to replace its aging Noorduyn *Norsemen* for use in the untamed bush country of northern Canada. Especially sought was an aircraft with short takeoff and landing characteristics to operate on unfinished airstrips. In 1947 De Havilland fielded its DHC-2 prototype, perhaps the most celebrated plane in Canadian history. It was an all-metal, high-wing cabin design that could be alternately fitted with skis or pontoons for use on snow or water. Its spacious fuselage could accommodate a crew of two and six fully armed troops or 1,000 pounds of cargo. Furthermore, a DHC-2 could lift off after rolling only 600 feet. The U.S. Army wanted to buy and evaluate the *Beaver*, but political opposition

against foreign-built aircraft thwarted the idea. It was not until the Korean War emergency that Congress allowed the Army to evaluate the *Beaver* in 1950, and the first of 763 machines was delivered in 1952 as the L-20. An additional 212 were acquired by the Air Force.

The Army wasted no time employing the new aircraft in Korea, and it distinguished itself in a number of capacities. Foremost among those was hauling high-ranking generals, including Dwight D. Eisenhower, on battlefield inspections, and the *Beaver* became popularly known as the "General's Jeep." In 1962 the L-20 designation was dropped in favor of U-6, and the *Beaver* was sent overseas to Vietnam. Again, it proved an unqualified success both as a transport and courier vehicle; one version, the RU-6A, was outfitted for psychological warfare. This dependable craft was slowly phased out during the 1970s, although some U-6s still operate with Army National Guard units.

# ⭐ De Havilland–Canada U-1 *Otter*

**Type:** Transport

**Dimensions:** wingspan, 58 feet; length, 41 feet, 10 inches; height, 12 feet, 7 inches
**Weights:** empty, 4,168 pounds; gross, 8,000 pounds
**Power plant:** 1 × 600–horsepower Pratt & Whitney R-1340 radial engine
**Performance:** maximum speed, 160 miles per hour; ceiling, 18,800 feet; maximum range, 960 miles
**Armament:** none
**Service dates:** 1956–1974

Regarded as an "airborne, one-ton truck," the U-1 *Otter* was designed as a big brother to the earlier and very successful U-6 *Beaver*. It was actively involved in Vietnam and also saw extensive use in the Antarctic.

The commercial success of the earlier DHC-2 *Beaver* prompted De Havilland of Canada to explore a scaled-up version with greater carrying capacity. By 1951 the company introduced the DHC-3 *Otter* utility aircraft, which was offered in both civilian and military models. Like the *Beaver*, the new plane was designed with short takeoff and landing capability, although it could carry twice the load. The U.S. Army evaluated a single example in 1953 during Operation Skydrop, which pitted small, fixed-wing aircraft against the newer helicopters. It was impressed by the aircraft's ability to carry nine fully equipped combat troops or 3,000 pounds of cargo while operating from unprepared forward airfields. In 1956 a production order was placed for 184 of the rugged Canadian machines, which entered U.S. service as the U-1 *Otter*. At that time it was also the largest single-engine transport operating in the world.

The Army applied the *Otter*'s many strengths to good use throughout the Vietnam War, where it flew generals, casualties, and supplies to virtually every theater of that conflict. Additionally, several were fitted for electronic warfare and flown under the designation UB-1. The wonderful takeoff abilities of the *Otter* also impressed the Navy, and in 1956 it purchased four to serve as the air arm with Operation Deep Freeze in the Antarctic. There, U-1s were fitted with a variety of skis and pontoon floats for winter/water operations. Following this success, another 14 were acquired and sent south to supplement them. The U-1 was finally retired from frontline service in 1974, one of the most rugged bush planes of all time. A handful continue operating with the Army National Guard.

# ⭐ Douglas A3D *Skywarrior*

**Type:** Bomber

**Dimensions:** wingspan, 72 feet; length, 76 feet; height, 23 feet, 6 inches
**Weights:** empty, 39,409 pounds; gross, 82,000 pounds
**Power plant:** 2 × 12,400–pound thrust Pratt & Whitney J57 turbojet engines
**Performance:** maximum speed, 610 miles per hour; ceiling, 43,000 feet; maximum range, 2,000 miles
**Armament:** 2 × 20mm cannons; 12,000 pounds of conventional or nuclear bombs
**Service dates:** 1956–1993

The *Skywarrior* was the largest jet ever catapulted from a carrier deck. Its sheer size earned it the nickname the "Whale."

In 1947 the Navy sought to harness the power of the jet engine to produce a strategic (i.e., nuclear) bomber capable of operating from aircraft carriers. The existing North American AJ *Savage* was prop-driven and considered too slow for that role. By 1949 Douglas finalized the design for such a craft and was authorized to construct a prototype. It emerged in 1953 as the XA3D, a swept-back high-wing design with twin podded engines and landing gear that retracted into the fuselage. To facilitate carrier storage, the outer wings and the vertical tail could be folded. The crew of three was housed in a pressurized forward cabin and defended itself with a radar-controlled 20mm cannon array in the tail. Production of the A3D commenced soon after, and it en-

tered fleet service in 1956 as the *Skywarrior.* An imposing aircraft, it broke several speed records and was the largest craft of its kind ever launched from a carrier deck. A total of 280 was constructed.

When the United States became confronted with low-intensity guerrilla wars, such as that in Vietnam, the A3D's role as a nuclear bomber had much less relevance. Fortunately, the plane proved remarkably adaptable, and it spent the war years as a tanker, the KA-3B, and as a photo reconnaissance craft, the RA3B. A more specialized version, the EA-3B, was also deployed as an electronic countermeasures aircraft during the later stages of the war. This model featured a completely pressurized fuselage that housed additional crew members in the bomb bay section. The venerable *Skywarrior* remained in service with Navy Reserve squadrons until 1993.

# ✪ Douglas A-4 *Skyhawk*

**Type:** Light Bomber

---

**Dimensions:** wingspan, 27 feet, 6 inches; length, 40 feet, 3 inches; height, 15 feet
**Weights:** empty, 10,465 pounds; gross, 27,420 pounds
**Power plant:** 1 × 8,000–pound thrust Pratt & Whitney J52 turbojet engine
**Performance:** maximum speed, 670 miles per hour; ceiling, 49,000 feet; maximum range, 920 miles
**Armament:** 2 × 20mm cannons; 9,155 pounds of bombs, rockets, or nuclear weapons
**Service dates:** 1956–1990

---

Douglas attained distinction for building both the largest and smallest attack bombers ever launched from a carrier deck. The diminutive A-4 was small, tough, and heavily armed, going by the affectionate nickname "Scooter."

In 1950 the Navy sought a jet-powered replacement for its prop-driven AD *Skyraiders* and put out specifications for an aircraft weighing in excess of 30,000 pounds. The Army was surprised yet pleased when Ed Heinemann of Douglas designed a compact attack bomber weighing half that amount. The prototype XA-4 emerged in 1954 as a delta-wing configuration, its small size precluding the need for folding wings. It went into production in 1955 as the A-4 *Skyhawk* and served with Navy and Marine Corps attack squadrons for the next 25 years.

In combat the *Skyhawk* was legendary for its speed, maneuverability, and heavy payloads. Pilots were also grateful that the Scooter could absorb great amounts of damage and keep flying. During the Vietnam War, A-4s formed the backbone of Naval attack aviation, flew most of the missions, and took heavy losses. But overall, the *Skyhawk* performed superbly and established itself as the best light attack aircraft of its day. By 1969 the A-4s were being phased out in favor of the more advanced Vought A-7 *Corsair.* A total of 2,960 had been constructed by 1979.

The low cost and high performance of the *Skyhawk* made it a popular export aircraft, and several hundred were purchased and deployed by Israel, Argentina, New Zealand, Australia, and Kuwait. These versions performed well against England during the 1981 Falklands War as well as during the 1991 invasion of Iraq. Furthermore, they served on the Navy's *Blue Angels* flight demonstration team from 1974 to 1986, longer than any other plane. A handful flew as Marine Corps TA-4J trainers until 1990; foreign models are expected to serve well into the 21st century.

# ⭐ Douglas A-20 *Havoc*

**Type:** Light Bomber

---

**Dimensions:** wingspan, 61 feet, 4 inches; length, 45 feet, 11 inches; height, 17 feet, 7 inches
**Weights:** empty, 11,400 pounds; gross, 27,200 pounds
**Power plant:** 2 × 1,700–horsepower Wright Double Cyclone GR-2600 radial engines
**Performance:** maximum speed, 351 miles per hour; ceiling, 25,300 feet; maximum range, 1,000 miles
**Armament:** up to 8 × .50–caliber machine guns; 4,000 pounds of bombs
**Service dates:** 1940–1945

The *Havoc* was the most widely produced attack aircraft operated by the Army Air Force. It was also the first aircraft to be flown by American crews in the European theater.

The A-20 was designed in 1937 to meet an Army specification for a new light bomber. It emerged as a twin-engine, shoulder-wing monoplane with retractable bicycle landing gear and a crew of three. As a bomber the A-20 proved fast, was solidly built to withstand punishment, and possessed pleasant handling characteristics. The prototype first flew in 1938, and the French government immediately placed an order for 105 craft. Known as DB-7s, these bombers served with distinction with the Armée de l'Air during the German invasion in May 1940. When France fell, numerous DB-7s were turned over to the British, who christened them *Bostons* and deployed them in North Africa against the German Afrika Korps. In August 1942 several American crews flying borrowed British planes participated in the first American raid over Europe.

The Army Air Corps acquired an initial batch of 206 A-20s in 1940, and several were present during the Japanese attack on Pearl Harbor. As the war progressed, the versatile A-20 was deployed in numerous attack versions. Foremost among them was the numerous Model G, which featured a solid nose housing six machine guns for strafing work. A-20s in the southwestern Pacific also pioneered the art of low-level skip-bombing against Japanese shipping with great effect. Another important design was the P-70, the first American night fighter.

By war's end, no less than 7,385 *Havocs* had been manufactured. Of these, no less than 3,125 were given to the Soviet Union, with others serving in the air forces of Australia, Brazil, the Netherlands, and South Africa. The aircraft proved to be an outstanding light bomber of World War II.

# ★ Douglas A/B-26 *Invader*

**Type:** Light Bomber

---

**Dimensions:** wingspan, 70 feet; length, 50 feet; height, 18 feet, 6 inches
**Weights:** empty, 22,370 pounds; gross, 32,000 pounds
**Power plant:** 2 × 2,000–horsepower Pratt & Whitney R-2800 Double Wasp radial engines
**Performance:** maximum speed, 355 miles per hour; ceiling, 22,100 feet; maximum range, 1,400 miles
**Armament:** up to 18 × .50–caliber machine guns; 6,000 pounds of bombs
**Service dates:** 1944–1969

---

The *Invader* was the fastest and deadliest ground-attack bomber of World War II. It combined high speed with fantastic armament and rendered effective service up through the Korean and Vietnam Wars.

Conceived as a replacement for the North American B-25 and Martin B-26, the prototype XA-26 first flew in July 1942. It was a shoulder-winged, twin-engine design with tricycle landing gear, much like the A-20 *Havoc*, but it was also larger and more capable. The A-26 carried twice its required bomb load at high speed and could be fitted with lethal arrays of machine guns and rockets. The Army was delighted with the results and purchased 2,502 of the new craft, named the *Invader*. A-26s were initially deployed in Europe and the Pacific during the late fall of 1944; they earned a tremendous reputation as strafers and suffered the lowest loss rate of any American bomber.

After the war and despite the development of jet aircraft, the new U.S. Air Force maintained its *Invader* bomber force, redesignating them B-26s in July 1948. When the Korean War broke out in June 1950, B-26s flew routinely from bases in Japan as night intruders against communist supply lines. In July 1953 *Invaders* from the 3rd Bomber Wing made the final raid of that war, only 30 minutes before the armistice began. The B-26 was slowly phased out until 1964, when the conflict in Vietnam meant that they would be pressed back into service. A new model, the B-26K, was manufactured as a counterinsurgency bomber and saw active service along the Ho Chi Minh Trail until finally withdrawn in 1969. Many B-26s continued flying with Latin American air forces through the 1970s, demonstrating the soundness of the original design.

# Douglas AD/A-1 *Skyraider*

**Type:** Light Bomber

**Dimensions:** wingspan, 50 feet; length, 38 feet, 2 inches; height, 15 feet, 8 inches
**Weights:** empty, 12,313 pounds; gross, 25,000 pounds
**Power plant:** 1 × 3,025–horsepower Wright Cyclone R-3350 radial engine
**Performance:** maximum speed, 366 miles per hour; ceiling, 32,000 feet; maximum range, 3,000 miles
**Armament:** 4 × 20mm cannons; 8,000 pounds of bombs, rockets, torpedoes, mines, or napalm
**Service dates:** 1946–1974

The legendary *Skyraider* served with distinction during two wars in Asia and performed a bewildering variety of roles. Incredibly strong, it could absorb tremendous amounts of damage yet invariably return home.

In 1944 the Navy laid out requirements for a carrier-based single-seat dive-bomber/torpedo-bomber to replace the Curtiss SB2C *Helldiver* then in service. In 1945 Douglas fielded the prototype XBTD-1, a large, low-wing monoplane designed by Ed Heinemann. Amazingly, its 15 wing and fuselage hardpoints carried an 8,000-pound payload, greater than the famous B-17 *Flying Fortress!* In 1946 the Douglas design squeezed past the even bigger Martin AM-1 *Mauler* and entered into production as the AD *Skyraider*. During the Korean War (1950–1953) the *Skyraider* formed the backbone of Navy attack aviation, establishing itself as the world's greatest ground-support aircraft. It could unload so much ordnance on a target that it

was commonly referred to as the "Dump Truck." After the war, the *Skyraider* continued in naval service, and a number of specialized attack, search, and transport versions were developed. A total of 3,180 was constructed.

The Air Force acquired *Skyraiders* from the Navy during the Vietnam War, flying them as the A-1. These specialized not only in ground attack but also in search and rescue of downed pilots behind enemy lines. The A-1s renewed their reputation for smothering firepower, incredible loiter time (14 hours!), and ruggedness under fire. A number were eventually transferred to the fledgling South Vietnamese Air Force. The Navy also employed *Skyraiders* in similar roles, and these accounted for the only two MiG-17 jets shot down by propeller-driven aircraft. The last of the Air Force A-1 units was finally disbanded in 1974 following a legendary career. The *Skyraider* remains one of the greatest combat aircraft ever built.

**Type:** Heavy Bomber

**Dimensions:** wingspan, 89 feet, 6 inches; length, 57 feet, 10 inches; height, 15 feet, 2 inches
**Weights:** empty, 16,321 pounds; gross, 27,673 pounds
**Power plant:** 2 × 1,000–horsepower Wright Cyclone R-1820 radial engines
**Performance:** maximum speed, 215 miles per hour; ceiling, 23, 900; maximum range, 1,200 miles
**Armament:** 3 × .30–caliber machine guns; 6,500 pounds of bombs
**Service dates:** 1937–1944

The B-18 was the most numerous bomber in the Army Air Corps at the start of World War II. Hopelessly obsolete in a combat role, it was pressed into service for antisubmarine patrols.

In 1934 the Army Air Corps decided to seek a replacement for its newly arrived Martin B-10 bombers and announced a competition for a new aircraft that would carry twice as many bombs twice as far. In 1935 Douglas responded by fielding its DB-1, which was based on the successful DC-2 commercial transport. The B-18, as it came to be called, was a midwing, twin-engine, all-metal design with good range, payload, and speed for its day. More importantly, it could be had for one-third less than its closest competitor, Boeing's XB-17, a clearly superior craft. The Army chose to go with quantity, and in 1936 it awarded Douglas a contract for 133 B-18s. In 1937 this was followed up by an order for 217 improved B-18As, which featured a totally redesigned nose that gave it an unmistakable sharklike profile.

By the advent of World War II, the B-18, unofficially known as the *Bolo*, was America's most numerous bombardment aircraft. Several had been caught on the ground and destroyed at Pearl Harbor in 1941 and saw no part in operations against the Japanese. The Army Air Force realized the futility of pressing the *Bolos* into frontline service, so 122 of the surviving aircraft were modified as B-18Bs, the first aircraft to be fitted with magnetic anomaly detection (MAD) equipment. They were dispatched to the Caribbean Sea in 1942 and managed to sink two German U-boats before being replaced by the far superior B-24 *Liberators*. The B-18 served out its final days as a transport and training aircraft before being retired in 1944.

# Douglas B-23 *Dragon*

**Type:** Medium Bomber

---

**Dimensions:** wingspan, 92 feet; length, 58 feet, 4 inches; height, 18 feet, 6 inches
**Weights:** empty, 19,059 pounds; gross, 30,475 pounds
**Power plant:** 2 × 1,600–horsepower Wright Cyclone R-2600 radial engines
**Performance:** maximum speed, 282 miles per hour; ceiling, 31,600 feet; maximum range, 1,455 miles
**Armament:** 1 × .50–caliber machine gun; 3 × .30–caliber machine guns; 4,000 pounds of bombs
**Service dates:** 1940–1945

---

The B-23 was a vast improvement over the earlier B-18 and was the first American bomber to be equipped with a manned tail gun. However, it was rapidly overtaken by more modern designs and enjoyed only a brief service life.

In 1938 Douglas sought to improve its existing B-18 by offering the Army Air Force a drastically modified form. The new craft featured a longer wing, a smaller fuselage cross-section to reduce drag, and more powerful engines. The prototype flew for the first time in July 1939, and its performance was promising enough for the Army to order 38 production copies for evaluation. They passed into service as the B-23 *Dragon* and displayed a marked improvement in performance over the older *Bolos*, being 66 miles per hour faster and possessing a longer range. This was also the first American design to incorporate a manned tail-gun position to defend against stern attacks.

Unfortunately, the B-23 had no sooner been deployed than the military decided it had fallen behind prevailing European designs in terms of speed, armament, and performance. It was also markedly inferior to the North American B-25, the Martin B-26, and Boeing's new B-17E, which was the first combat-ready model of that famous bomber. When the United States entered World War II in December 1941, the B-23s were pressed into service as patrol-bombers and did useful work off the Pacific Coast. Within months, however, they were withdrawn and assigned to training duties. A total of 18 B-23s was also reconfigured as C-67 transports and glider tugs. After the war the surviving B-23s were put up for sale, and many found a new lease on life as corporate airliners. Several continue flying in that capacity.

# ☆ Douglas B-66 *Destroyer*

**Type:** Bomber; Reconnaissance; Electronic Warfare

---

**Dimensions:** wingspan, 72 feet, 6 inches; length, 75 feet, 2 inches; height, 23 feet, 6 inches
**Weights:** empty, 42,369 pounds; gross, 83,000 pounds
**Power plant:** 2 × 10,000–pound thrust Allison J71 turbojet engines
**Performance:** maximum speed, 610 miles per hour; ceiling, 43,000 feet; maximum range, 2,000 miles
**Armament:** 2 × 20mm cannons; 15,000 pounds of bombs
**Service dates:** 1956–1982

The *Destroyer* was the last tactical bomber constructed for the Air Force, although it was deployed in many other roles. Expensive to maintain and operate, it was never as fully successful as its Navy counterpart.

During the early 1950s the Air Force sought to replace its aging North American B-45 *Tornados* with a new tactical bomber. The Air Force turned to the Navy, which had begun deploying A3D *Skywarriors* with considerable success. Thus, the new craft, christened the B-66 *Destroyer*, had no prototype but was rather a totally rebuilt version of an existing design. In addition to the elimination of naval equipment such as the arrester hook, folding wings, and reinforced landing gear, the new craft had an entirely new airfoil and new engines. By 1956 both the RB-66 photoreconnaissance model and the B-66 bomber model were received by the Tactical Air Command and deployed in Europe. For many years they patrolled the tense border between NATO and the communist Warsaw Pact nations, and several were shot down.

By the mid-1960s the bomber role for the B-66 was redundant, so a new version, the RB-66C, was extensively refitted as an electronic countermeasures (ECM) aircraft. These saw intense duty throughout the air war against North Vietnam. As an ECM platform, the RB-66C would fly in ahead of the main strike force to record and evaluate the radar environment. On the basis of this information, enemy antiaircraft and missile radars could be tricked with chaff or jammed electronically, which in turn reduced losses. A final version, the WB-66, was dedicated to gathering weather information over prospective strike areas. However, the RB-66 utilized very intricate equipment that was often expensive to operate and difficult to maintain. For this reason, the B-66 was phased out in 1982 by the more modern General Dynamics EF-111 *Raven*. A total of 209 was built.

# ★ Douglas BTD *Destroyer*

**Type:** Torpedo-Bomber/Dive-Bomber

**Dimensions:** wingspan, 45 feet; length, 38 feet, 7 inches; height, 13 feet, 7 inches
**Weights:** empty, 11,561 pounds; gross, 19,000 pounds
**Power plant:** 1 × 2,300–horsepower Wright Cyclone R-3350 radial engine
**Performance:** maximum speed, 344 miles per hour; ceiling, 23,600 feet; maximum range, 1,480 miles
**Armament:** 2 × 20mm cannons; 3,200 pounds of bombs or torpedoes
**Service dates:** 1944–1945

Designed as an all-purpose attack craft, the BTD was quickly made obsolete by more modern designs. It nonetheless served as the forerunner of the successful AD *Skyraider* series.

In June 1941 the Navy sought a more advanced replacement for its existing Douglas SDB *Dauntless* and the SB2C *Helldiver* then under development. Douglas responded to the competition with the XSB2D-1, which was intended to combine both dive- and torpedo-bombing functions into a single airframe. It was a large, two-man design with inverted gull wings that utilized a laminar low-drag airfoil. It was also the first carrier-based Navy plane with both tricycle landing gear and remote-controlled turrets. In April 1943 the XSB2D-1 was successfully test-flown, but by that time the Navy decided it wanted a single-seat bomber instead. Douglas went back to the drawing board and produced the XTBD-1, the turrets and rear gunner position being deleted. It was also fitted with air brakes in the fuselage and two wing-mounted 20mm cannons. Furthermore, the internal bomb bay was enlarged to accommodate either two aerial torpedoes or 3,200 pounds of bombs. The Navy approved the new design and in August 1943 contracted Douglas to build 358 machines under the name *Destroyer*.

The first BTDs began arriving in June 1944, when they were found to be underpowered and slower than expected. Their performance was quickly eclipsed by new designs that had been originally conceived as single-seaters. By the time World War II ended only 28 *Destroyers* had been delivered; the rest of the contract was canceled. The BTD saw no active service with Navy units but redeemed itself when two examples became prototypes for the new and highly successful AD *Skyraider*.

**Type:** Transport

**Dimensions:** wingspan, 60 feet; length, 36 feet; height, 14 feet
**Weights:** empty, 3,900 pounds; gross, 7,412 pounds
**Power plant:** 1 × 420–horsepower Liberty liquid-cooled engine
**Performance:** maximum speed, 121 miles per hour; ceiling, 15,950 feet; maximum range, 750 miles
**Armament:** none
**Service dates:** 1925–1929

The C-1 was the Army's first purposely designed cargo craft. It was also one of the first airplanes to transfer fuel to another in midair.

In 1925 the Army contracted with Douglas to build its first large cargo plane, which was also intended to serve as the first personnel transport. Douglas modified an existing O-2 observation airplane fuselage, enlarging the girth. The two-cockpit system was dropped in favor of a single cockpit forward of the wings in which pilot and copilot sat side by side. In construction, the new craft utilized the Douglas World Cruiser method, which employed welded steel tubing and covered the forward engine compartment with aluminum. Wings were made of wood, and the balance of the aircraft was fabric-covered. Up to six passengers could be carried on seats, although for cargo hauling the seats were removed. Curiously, cargo was loaded and unloaded through a large door mounted in the floor.

After initial testing, the Army approved the design, and in 1926 nine C-1s were built and would become the first planes assigned the "C" designation for "Cargo." In 1926 an improved version, the C-1C, appeared; it featured increased wingspan, a lengthened fuselage, redesigned tail surfaces, and modified landing gear. Another improvement was the installation of metal flooring instead of wood. In 1927 the Army purchased 17 of these machines.

The ponderous C-1s gave a good account of themselves over the years, although they were deployed individually to airfields rather than used as a unified transport squadron. The high point occurred on December 17, 1928, when a C-1 functioned as an aerial tanker in the first successful transfer of fuel to a waiting Fokker C-2. Beginning in 1929 the C-1s were slowly phased out in favor of more modern and capable designs.

**Type:** Transport

**Dimensions:** wingspan, 85 feet; length, 61 feet, 6 inches; height, 19 feet, 7 inches
**Weights:** empty, 14,729 pounds; gross, 21,000 pounds
**Power plant:** 2 × 975–horsepower Wright R-1820 radial engines
**Performance:** maximum speed, 202 miles per hour; ceiling, 20,600 feet; maximum range, 900 miles
**Armament:** none
**Service dates:** 1939–1945

The C-39 was a composite forerunner of the famous C-47 *Skytrain*. It shared many of the traits associated with its more famous counterpart and rendered useful service as an Army transport.

In 1933 Douglas responded to a plea from Trans-World Airlines (TWA) for a new modern transport, and two weeks later it drew up plans for the revolutionary DC-1. This craft heralded a revolution in aerial transportation, for it combined high speed with greater payloads. The prototype, a low-wing, all-metal monoplane, went into production the following year as the DC-2 and enjoyed great commercial success. Naturally, such a high-performance design caught the military's attention, and in 1934 the Navy obtained the first of five R2Ds. Two years later the Army followed suit, obtaining a single XC-32 for evaluation, followed by 18 C-33s. These aircraft flew 50 miles per hour faster than other transports then in service. In 1937 a single C-32 was fitted with the tail unit of a DC-3 and

was called the C-38. This design underwent additional modifications, which included combining the fuselage of a DC-3 with the wings of a DC-2 and the landing gear of the B-18 *Bolo* bomber, to emerge in 1939 as the C-39. That same year, the Army purchased 35 examples for its transport service.

During the early years of World War II the C-39s were actively engaged in transport duties. Faced with the impending U.S. defeat in the Philippines, C-39s evacuated military staff and other personnel during a heroic, if hectic, journey to Australia. Another C-39 distinguished itself by establishing the air route from Maine to Gander, Newfoundland. This subsequently became the first leg of the all-important aerial lifeline to England. Eventually, the C-39s were joined by 24 civilian DC-2s, which had been impressed into service as C-32As. After serving many months alongside the more famous C-47, all were either retired or scrapped by 1945.

# ⭐ Douglas C-47/R4D *Skytrain*

**Type:** Transport; Gunship

**Dimensions:** wingspan, 95 feet; length, 64 feet, 2 inches; height, 16 feet, 11 inches
**Weights:** empty, 16,970 pounds; gross, 26,000 pounds
**Power plant:** 2 × 1,200–horsepower Pratt & Whitney Twin Wasp R-1830 radial engines
**Performance:** maximum speed, 229 miles per hour; ceiling, 23,200 feet; maximum range, 1,500 miles
**Armament:** none
**Service dates:** 1940–1976

The most famous transport plane of all time, the C-47 saw service in every theater of just about every war since 1941. Its simple design, easy flying characteristics, and great reliability endeared it to a generation of pilots and crews.

The famous DC-3 airliner first flew in 1936, but it was not until 1940 that the Army placed an order for several as C-47 transports. It was a low-wing, streamlined, twin-engine craft that was outstandingly tough yet forgiving to fly. Known affectionately to its crews as the "Gooney Bird," this venerable aircraft formed the backbone of the Army Air Force transport service. Ultimately, more than 10,000 were procured for the Army, with 568 destined for the Navy as R4Ds. During World War II they flew in every theater and functioned as cargo carriers, medical evacuation aircraft, glider tugs, and troop carriers. On D day, the invasion of Europe in June 1944, C-47s dropped two American airborne divisions and one British airborne division—nearly 20,000 men—

behind German lines. In concert with the lesser-known C-46 *Commando*, the *Skytrain* also flew supplies over the treacherous "Hump"—the Himalayan mountain system. Prewar licensing agreements also allowed the C-47 to be built by Japan and the Soviet Union in considerable quantities.

After the war the C-47 continued to serve the U.S. Air Force as a useful cargo hauler. They performed with distinction during the Korean War and evacuated 4,700 casualties from Chosin in only five days. Many C-47s were then refitted with rapid-fire miniguns for use in Vietnam. Nicknamed "Puff the Magic Dragon," the AC-47 gunship could blanket an entire football field with 20mm cannon shells in only three seconds. The C-47s were finally retired from United States service in 1976, but several hundred continue flying in Latin American and Asian air forces. A truly beloved machine, the C-47 will be remembered as one of America's great airplanes.

# ✪ Douglas C-54/R5D *Skymaster*

**Type:** Transport

**Dimensions:** wingspan, 117 feet, 6 inches; length, 93 feet, 10 inches; height, 27 feet, 6 inches
**Weights:** empty, 37,000 pounds; gross, 62,000 pounds
**Power plant:** 4 × 1,290–horsepower Pratt & Whitney R-2000 radial engines
**Performance:** maximum speed, 265 miles per hour; ceiling, 22,000 feet; maximum range, 3,900 miles
**Armament:** none
**Service dates:** 1942–1974

The *Skymaster* was the Army Air Force's first four-engine transport. Though never intended for military service, it performed superbly for some 30 years by hauling troops and cargo around the world.

In 1938 Douglas joined five leading companies to produce a functional, transatlantic airliner, called the DC-4. Rejected as too big and costly, the prototype was sold to Japan while a new model, the DC-4A, was developed. It was an advanced, four-engine design featuring all-metal construction, a pressurized cabin, and a cargo load of 32,500 pounds or 50 passengers. Douglas was in the process of delivering the first 24 models when World War II broke out and the Army pressed them into service as C-54 *Skymasters*.

Like its stablemate, the C-47, the C-54 was rugged, reliable, and easy to fly and maintain. The Army Air Force acquired more than 1,000 machines; an additional 183 were accepted by the Navy as R5Ds. *Skymasters* flew all over the world during the war, from Europe to Alaska to Burma, and achieved outstanding safety records: In completing no less than 79,642 transatlantic crossings to England, only three C-54s were lost. The aircraft became a natural choice for many high-ranking officials, and U.S. President Franklin D. Roosevelt, British Prime Minister Winston Churchill, and U.S. General Douglas MacArthur all traveled in personalized C-54s.

After the war the C-54 remained the prime cargo hauler in the new U.S. Air Force. Its finest hour came in 1948 during Operation Vittles, a massive, around-the-clock airlift that broke the Soviet blockade of Berlin. Upon the outbreak of the Korean War, June 25, 1950, a C-54 parked at Kimpo Airfield was the first American aircraft destroyed by North Korean Yak fighters. The *Skymasters*, though aging, remained in active service with the Air Force and Navy and continued functioning until 1974. Only Lockheed's C-130 *Hercules* has compiled such a lengthy and distinguished record.

**Type:** Transport

**Dimensions:** wingspan, 173 feet, 3 inches; length, 124 feet, 2 inches; height, 43 feet, 9 inches
**Weights:** empty, 86,172 pounds; gross, 165,000 pounds
**Power plant:** 4 × 3,000–horsepower Pratt & Whitney R-4360 radial engines
**Performance:** maximum speed, 328 miles per hour; ceiling, 21,300 feet; maximum range, 7,250 miles
**Armament:** none
**Service dates:** 1945–1955

At the time of its appearance, the *Globemaster I* was the world's largest transport plane. It possessed many novel features but was quickly overtaken by more advanced designs.

When the United States entered World War II in December 1941, the Army Air Force lacked a truly long-range heavy transport plane. The following spring, Douglas advanced the idea of a very large, four-engine aircraft with transoceanic range to be scaled up from its existing C-54. When the Army expressed interest, a prototype XC-74 was constructed and flown in October 1945, too late to participate in the war. Only 14 had been delivered by 1947, when production ceased.

By the standards of its day, the *Globemaster I* was a true giant and carried many unusual features for an aircraft in its class. It was one of the first transports fitted with an A-12 autopilot to assist long-distance flights, and the wings, utilizing a high-lift, low-drag, laminar design, helped give the C-74

tremendous range—more than 7,000 miles. With only two refueling stops it could circle the globe, and in 1949 it became the first aircraft to carry more than 100 passengers across the Atlantic. To facilitate cargo handling, it was fitted with two onboard cranes capable of lifting 8,000 pounds each. The lower part of the fuselage, just aft the wings' trailing edges, also doubled as an electric cargo lift and could handle 30-ton loads. Up to 125 troops or 41,150 pounds of cargo could be carried over great distances.

The most distinctive feature of the C-74, however, was its unusual twin bubble canopies. This was intended to give both pilot and copilot unobstructed vision, but in practice it separated the men and interfered with their ability to cooperate. Eventually, all 14 planes were retrofitted with a more conventional cabin arrangement. These giants were retired in 1955 and replaced by the C-124 *Globemaster II.*

# ★ Douglas C-118/R6D *Liftmaster*

**Type:** Transport

---

**Dimensions:** wingspan, 117 feet, 6 inches; length, 106 feet, 10 inches; height, 28 feet, 9 inches
**Weights:** empty, 55,130 pounds; gross, 108,000 pounds
**Power plant:** 4 × 2,500–horsepower Pratt & Whitney R-2800 radial engines
**Performance:** maximum speed, 300 miles per hour; ceiling, 21,900 feet; maximum range, 3,765 miles
**Armament:** none
**Service dates:** 1947–1984

The *Liftmaster* was a militarized version of the very successful Douglas DC-6 commercial airliner. It had a service life of some 35 years and gained a reputation for dependability and safety.

Even before World War II ended, U.S. airplane manufacturers began thinking about the next generation of commercial airliners. They would incorporate all the latest technology developed during wartime, including pressurized cabins for better comfort at high altitudes. Douglas decided to capitalize on its existing DC-4 by enlarging and improving it. The new prototype first flew in 1946 as the XDC-6 and was immediately purchased by two airlines. However, the Air Force also expressed interest in the craft, so in 1946 Douglas modified a DC-6 with upgraded engines, an extended fuselage, and large cargo doors to produce the XC-118. As a transport it could haul 76 soldiers or 27,000 pounds of cargo. The following year, the Air Force accepted deliveries of the first *Liftmasters;* 101 were ulti-

mately purchased. President Harry S. Truman was so impressed that he authorized a C-118 to serve as his personal airplane and christened it *Independence,* after his Missouri hometown. This craft differed from military versions by carrying 25 passengers in relative comfort and was equipped with a plush executive stateroom.

The Navy did not adopt the new aircraft until the Korean War highlighted deficiencies in its air transport capacity. Starting in 1951 the Navy accepted delivery of 61 *Liftmasters* as R6Ds, virtually identical to the Air Force machines save for naval avionics and communications gear. In 1961 an agreement was reached with the Air Force by which 38 R6Ds would be transferred over to the Military Airlift Command. However, within five years, growing Navy involvement in the Vietnam War resulted in these aircraft being returned to the Navy. The Air Force phased out its C-118s in 1965, but the Navy continually updated them until final retirement in 1984.

# ★ Douglas C-124 *Globemaster II*

**Type:** Transport

---

**Dimensions:** wingspan, 174 feet; length, 130 feet, 5 inches; height, 48 feet, 3 inches
**Weights:** empty, 101,165 pounds; gross, 194,500 pounds
**Power plant:** 4 × 3,500–horsepower Pratt & Whitney radial engines
**Performance:** maximum speed, 304 miles per hour; ceiling, 21,800 feet; maximum range, 6,820 miles
**Armament:** none
**Service dates:** 1950–1974

---

The C-124, better known as "Old Shaky," was the Air Force's first strategic cargo plane. It could carry men and equipment to virtually any point in the globe and served for nearly 25 years.

Following World War II the United States became saddled with global military responsibilities. Because the Air Force desired better equipment to meet its tasks, it asked Douglas to improve upon the already impressive C-74 *Globemaster.* By 1949 a new craft, the XC-124, was ready for flight. It retained the wings, tail, and engines of the old C-74 but possessed a new fuselage with nearly twice the volume. The front end consisted of hinged, clamshell doors and a strong ramp that enabled tanks and other vehicles to roll in and out under their own power. The XC-124 also retained the electric cargo ramp of its predecessor, although total lifting power had nearly doubled to 74,000 pounds. In 1950 it went into production as the C-124A *Globemaster II.*

The C-124A's appearance was timely, for the Korean War had erupted, and this aircraft proved to be the only one capable of flying army equipment across the Pacific. As a troop transport, it also carried 220 fully armed soldiers and could evacuate 136 casualties on stretchers. All told, the *Globemaster II* acquitted itself well and endowed the Military Air Transport Service a global reach it never before possessed.

In 1951 the C-124C was introduced, incorporating a distinct radar dome on the nose and wingtip heaters for the cabin and wing leading edges. These features were subsequently retrofitted to all C-124As. By 1955 a total of 447 *Globemasters* had been constructed. They served the Air Force well during the initial stages of the Vietnam War in 1965 before being rendered obsolete by the jet-powered Lockheed C-141 *Starlifter.* C-124s flew on reserve status for many years until being phased out in 1974.

# ⭐ Douglas C-133 *Cargomaster*

**Type:** Transport

**Dimensions:** wingspan, 179 feet, 8 inches; length, 157 feet, 6 inches; height, 48 feet, 3 inches
**Weights:** empty, 120,263 pounds; gross, 286,000 pounds
**Power plant:** 4 × 7,000–horsepower Pratt & Whitney T-34 turboprop engines
**Performance:** maximum speed, 359 miles per hour; ceiling, 29,950 feet; maximum range, 4,300 miles
**Armament:** none
**Service dates:** 1957–1980

The *Cargomaster* was the largest turboprop transport ever operated by the Air Force. It was designed specifically for carrying intercontinental ballistic missiles (ICBMs) but could haul virtually any piece of Army equipment.

By 1953 the Air Force foresaw the need for a new, strategic transport capable of transporting the new ICBMs then under production. They turned to Douglas, an established leader in cargo-plane design, requesting that it modify the existing C-124 *Globemaster*. The resulting aircraft, the C-133, was accepted without a prototype and owed very little to its predecessor. It was a sleek, shoulder-winged giant with a completely pressurized fuselage and four powerful turboprop engines. For landing it required two tandem sets of main wheels housed in nacelles on either side of the fuselage. Furthermore, its cargo hold was cavernous and could accommodate 96 percent of all Army equipment through its rear-loading doors. The new plane went into production as the C-133 *Cargomaster* in 1956, and two years later it broke a world record by hauling a payload of 117,900 pounds up to 10,000 feet. The Air Force eventually acquired a total of 49 of these giants.

The principal task of the *Cargomaster* was to transport the new *Atlas*, *Thor*, *Titan*, and *Jupiter* rockets from factories to launching silos. Despite the size and weight of these ICBMs, the C-133s carried them easily, without disassembly. This mode of transport was cheaper, faster, and infinitely less dangerous than driving ICBMs by tractor-trailer. The giant aircraft was also a capable troop transport and could transfer 200 troops and all their equipment from the United States to Europe nonstop. They remained the superstars of the Military Airlift Command until withdrawn from active service and replaced by another giant, Lockheed's C-5A *Galaxy*, in 1980. Three still fly as civilian cargo haulers.

**Type:** Torpedo-Bomber

**Dimensions:** wingspan, 50 feet; length, 34 feet, 2 inches; height, 13 feet, 7 inches
**Weights:** empty, 3,737 pounds; gross, 6,502 pounds
**Power plant:** 1 × 400–horsepower Liberty liquid-cooled engine
**Performance:** maximum speed, 101 miles per hour; ceiling, 7,800 feet; maximum range, 293 miles
**Armament:** 1 × 1,835–pound torpedo
**Service dates:** 1921–1928

The DT was the first Douglas aircraft delivered to the Navy and helped establish a long working relationship. However, four Army versions gained fame by becoming the first aircraft to circumnavigate the world.

In 1921 Donald Douglas modified the commercial *Cloudster* into a single-seat torpedo-bomber and offered it to the Navy. It was a large, angular craft with a steel-tubing fuselage, fabric covering, and unstaggered wooden wings. The wings could be folded for onboard storage; the landing gear could also be interchanged for pontoon floats. The Navy purchased one DT-1 that same year and later acquired two more DT-2s, which differed only in seating an observer. The DTs then underwent rigorous testing and proved to be excellent aircraft, so in 1922 the Navy acquired an additional 64 machines. They were distributed at torpedo stations around the country, but the type also performed reconnaissance and communications work. Exposure to saltwater badly deteriorated its wooden parts, however, and by 1926 the DT had been supplanted by the Curtiss R-6 and the Naval Aircraft Factory PT.

Despite a short service life, the DT gained immortality in 1924 as part of an Army-sponsored flight around the world. Four modified aircraft were delivered as DWCs (Douglas World Cruisers), being stripped of military equipment in favor of dual controls and radio direction finding. On March 17, 1924, the four DWCs, christened *Seattle*, *Boston*, *Chicago*, and *New Orleans*, lifted off from Seattle with stops at Japan, India, the Middle East, Europe, England, and Ireland. En route, *Seattle* crashed in Alaska and *Boston* ditched in the North Atlantic, but *Seattle* and *New Orleans* continued on to Nova Scotia. They returned to Seattle on September 28, 1924, having covered 28,000 miles, 175 days, and 371 actual flying hours. The Army was so impressed with the DWCs that it ordered an additional five as O-5 observation craft. *Chicago* remains on display at the National Air and Space Museum at the Smithsonian Institute.

## ⭐ Douglas F3D *Skyknight*

**Type:** Night Fighter

**Dimensions:** wingspan, 50 feet; length, 45 feet, 6 inches; height, 16 feet, 1 inch
**Weights:** empty, 14,313 pounds; gross, 21,500 pounds
**Power plant:** 2 × 3,400–pound thrust Westinghouse J34 turbojet engines
**Performance:** maximum speed, 535 miles per hour; ceiling, 33,000 feet; maximum range, 1,297 miles
**Armament:** 4 × 20mm cannons; 4 × AAM *Sparrow* missiles
**Service dates:** 1951–1971

The *Skyknight* was the Navy's first all-weather interceptor and was the first jet to shoot down another jet at night. Though it suffered a lack of engine thrust, it enjoyed impressive longevity and served in Korea and Vietnam.

Shortly before World War II ended, the Navy issued specifications for a new jet-powered night fighter. It required a craft that could reach at least 500 miles per hour, be combat-capable at night, and be able to detect enemy craft 125 miles away. Douglas answered by developing its XF3D in 1948, a rather conventional straight-wing early jet. Designer Ed Heinemann conceived it as a compact, heavy craft, big enough to fit a Westinghouse APQ-35 radar system. Its two engines were located on the bottom of the fuselage. The airplane was also equipped with a unique escape tunnel for the two crew members. This feature passed down from the cockpit and enabled the crew to literally slide out from a ventral escape hatch, even at high speed. Like all Heine-

mann designs, the craft was easy to fly and delightfully responsive. In 1948 the Navy placed an initial order for 28 F3Ds, which went into service as the *Skyknight*. In view of its plump appearance, the ship was affectionately dubbed "Willie the Whale." Only 268 were produced.

The F3D was on hand in several Marine squadrons when the Korean War broke out in 1950, and in November 1952 a *Skyknight* scored the first nighttime kill of a MiG-15 jet. A total of six nighttime kills was registered altogether, scoring more than any other Navy type. The F3D, unfortunately, was somewhat slow by jet standards, owing to the weakness of its engines, and it spent the next decade serving as an experimental missile launcher and an electronic countermeasures aircraft. In 1962 F3Ds were committed to the Vietnam War, and they flew several years sounding out communist radar defenses. The venerable *Skyknight* was finally discharged from service in 1971.

**Type:** Fighter

**Dimensions:** wingspan, 33 feet, 6 inches; length, 45 feet, 8 inches; height, 13 feet
**Weights:** empty, 16,030 pounds; gross, 27,000 pounds
**Power plant:** 1 × 16,000–pound thrust Pratt & Whitney J57 turbojet engine
**Performance:** maximum speed, 725 miles per hour; ceiling, 55,000 feet; maximum range, 950 miles
**Armament:** 4 × 20mm cannons; 4,000 pounds of bombs or missiles
**Service dates:** 1956–1964

The *Skyray* was the first Navy jet to exceed the sound barrier (Mach 1) in level flight. Popular with pilots and highly maneuverable, it received the unlikely nickname "Ford" on account of its reliability.

In 1947 the Naval Bureau of Aeronautics approached Douglas to build a jet-powered interceptor with a delta-wing configuration. The Douglas design, based on the work of German scientist Dr. Alex Lippisch, promised better performance at high altitude than did conventional layouts. The following year, a team of engineers under designer Ed Heinemann proposed the XF4D, a stubby, tailless fighter with the largest wing area ever given to a Navy fighter. The delta wing was surprisingly thick for an airplane aiming at supersonic speed and was also unusual in possessing rounded wingtips. The prototype emerged in 1953, powered by a weak Allison J35 jet engine, but it still established a world speed record of 753 miles per hour.

This was the first such distinction for a Navy fighter. Even better performance was anticipated once the more powerful Pratt & Whitney J57 engine became available, and so the Navy authorized its construction. The F4D entered into service in 1956 as the *Skyray*, so named because its shape closely resembled that of a manta ray. Production ceased in 1958 at 420 machines.

Once deployed, the F4D was an immediate hit with pilots. Fast and maneuverable, it quickly set five additional rate-of-climb records. It was also ruggedly built, could carry bombs, and made a decent attack fighter. However, owing to its original design specifications, the F4D was short-legged, lacking range, and its already cramped fuselage could not easily accommodate the latest electronic equipment and radar. Within eight years the speedy *Skyray* was being replaced by the bigger, more capable McDonnell-Douglas F-4 *Phantom*.

# ★ Douglas O-2, O-25, O-38

**Type:** Reconnaissance

**Dimensions:** wingspan, 40 feet; length, 30 feet; height, 10 feet, 6 inches
**Weights:** empty, 3,072 pounds; gross, 4,458 pounds
**Power plant:** 1 × 525–horsepower Pratt & Whitney Hornet R-1690 radial engine
**Performance:** maximum speed, 149 miles per hour; ceiling, 20,700 feet; maximum range, 300 miles
**Armament:** 2 × .30–caliber machine guns; 400 pounds of bombs
**Service dates:** 1925–1941

The O-2 gave rise to a complex family of long-lived observation aircraft. After 18 years of service, many versions were still flying by the advent of World War II.

In 1924 Douglas answered the Army's call for a new photoreconnaissance plane to replace its aging fleet of World War I–vintage De Havilland DH-4s. It selected a design based upon the Navy's DT torpedo-bomber. The new XO-2 was a standard biplane layout constructed from welded steel tubing, wooden wings, and fabric covering. Fuel tanks were uniquely located in the thickened center-section stubs of the lower wing; the chosen power plant was the famous Liberty liquid-cooled engine. The craft was offered in both short- and long-wing versions, but the Army chose the latter, and in 1925 it entered service as the O-2. A total of 46 was built before 18 additional O-2As, equipped for night flying, were also obtained. These were followed by 32 O-2Cs,

with minor revisions, and 132 heavily redesigned O-2Hs, featuring staggered wings, streamlined cowlings, and new landing gear.

The next important model was the 1930 O-25A, which was powered by a Curtiss Conqueror engine and fitted with a revised nose section. After receiving 25 machines, the Army ordered development of the O-25B, which featured dual controls. The final variant was the O-38A, which was also the last Douglas observation biplane. These 46 machines were the first to be fitted with Pratt & Whitney radial engines and a distinct engine cowling. Next came 63 O-38Bs, sporting additional refinements. The final 37 machines, the O-38E, were deployed almost exclusively with National Guard units. By this time the heyday of the observation biplane had long passed, but the basic ruggedness of the Douglas O-2 family kept the line active up through World War II as trainers and target tows. A total of 649 was built.

**Type:** Reconnaissance

**Dimensions:** wingspan, 45 feet, 9 inches; length, 34 feet, 6 inches; height, 10 feet, 8 inches
**Weights:** empty, 4,776 pounds; gross, 6,639 pounds
**Power plant:** 1 × 725–horsepower Pratt & Whitney Wasp Junior R-1535 radial engine
**Performance:** maximum speed, 200 miles per hour; ceiling, 24,150 feet; maximum range, 435 miles
**Armament:** 2 × .30–caliber machine guns
**Service dates:** 1930–1941

The second family of Douglas observation aircraft was also the company's first monoplane design. Like the earlier O-2, it served with distinction up through the early years of World War II.

In 1930 Douglas, which had a near-monopoly on Army observation aircraft, decided to field its first monoplane. The ensuing XO-31 was a complete departure from previous designs, with an overhead gull wing and all-metal construction. The two-seat fuselage also possessed a sliding enclosed cockpit. The prototype was built in similar fashion to the earlier Thomas-Morse O-19, which made extensive use of corrugated duraluminum. Power was obtained from a liquid-cooled Curtiss Conqueror engine. In 1931 the Army ordered five test models as Y1O-31As, although they were heavily modified, as the fuselage was covered with sheet metal; they entered service as the O-31A. Five additional Y1O-31Cs were also obtained, which differed by possessing single land-

ing struts and what would become the trademark parasol-mounted elliptical wing. At length, 24 of these machines went into production as the O-43A.

The final model of this family was also the most numerous. A standard O-43A, it was fitted with a Pratt & Whitney Wasp Junior radial engine and a long-chord cowling. The ugly fuselage-mounted cabane-and-wire bracing system was eliminated in favor of wing struts. The fuselage was also revised by fairing the canopy directly into the aft section for an extremely streamlined effect. In 1935 the Army purchased 90 of these handsome machines as the O-46A, and they served in frontline units for almost six years. Most were delivered to the National Guard by 1941, but a handful were serving in the Philippines with the 2nd Observation Squadron when the Japanese attacked. Thereafter, their tactical mission was fulfilled by the smaller, less expensive, Liaison-class *Grasshoppers*.

# ★ Douglas OA-4/RD *Dolphin*

**Type:** Transport

**Dimensions:** wingspan, 60 feet; length, 45 feet, 1 inch; height, 14 feet
**Weights:** empty, 7,000 pounds; gross, 9,530 pounds
**Power plant:** 2 × 450–horsepower Pratt & Whitney Wasp R-1340 Radial engines
**Performance:** maximum speed, 156 miles per hour; ceiling, 17,000 feet; maximum range, 720 miles
**Armament:** none
**Service dates:** 1931–1945

The *Dolphin* saw extensive service with the Army, Navy, and Coast Guard during a period of nearly 15 years. It was called upon to provide service as a cargo plane, a transport, and a rescue craft.

In 1930 Douglas introduced a twin-engine commercial amphibian, which it called the *Dolphin*. It possessed an all-metal, boatlike hull and a single high-mounted wooden wing sporting two engine nacelles. A brace joining the two engines also acted as an airfoil. Easy to fly and operate, the *Dolphin* possessed good range and could accommodate up to eight passengers. It so happened that the military was seeking to replace its aging Loeing OAs and OLs with a more modern craft, and the Douglas craft received close scrutiny. The first service to obtain one was the Coast Guard, which in 1931 obtained three machines as RDs. Also that year, the Navy bought and evaluated four RD-1s, which featured slightly larger engines. Testing and service trials were com-

pleted successfully, so in 1934 the Coast Guard acquired ten more RDs, and the Navy, six.

In 1932 the Army ordered six Douglas craft as Y1C21s, which led to additional orders for 14 more as C-26s. They were configured as cargo planes, and in 1934 two were given better engines and redesignated C-29s. That same year, however, the Army employed them as observation amphibians under the designation OA and rebuilt them with metal wings. One machine was also experimentally fitted with tricycle landing gear, a configuration not seen since World War I. Consequently, Douglas adopted such a landing arrangement on the giant new C-54 transport.

Despite their age, *Dolphins* of every variety were actively employed throughout World War II. They ably performed transport, patrol, and rescue missions and remained in frontline service until 1945. Thereafter, several made their way back to the commercial market.

# ☆ Douglas P-70 *Night Havoc*

**Type:** Night Fighter

**Dimensions:** wingspan, 61 feet, 4 inches; length, 47 feet, 7 inches; height, 17 feet, 7 inches
**Weights:** empty, 16,031 pounds; gross, 20,984 pounds
**Power plant:** 2 × 1,600–horsepower Wright Cyclone R-2600 radial engines
**Performance:** maximum speed, 329 miles per hour; ceiling, 28,250 feet; maximum range, 1,460 miles
**Armament:** 4 × 20mm cannons
**Service dates:** 1942–1944

Intended as a stopgap measure, the P-70 suffered from poor performance at high altitude and was only moderately successful. However, it was the first radar-equipped night fighter in American history.

After the Battle of Britain, the Royal Air Force had to cope with numerous German intruders who raided the country at night. Faced with a shortage of fighter aircraft, the British converted some French DB-7 bombers in their possession into night fighters. They did this by installing the latest British airborne radar and a solid nose sporting four .303-inch machine guns. It was hastily pressed into service with minor success but successfully held the line until night-fighter variants of the De Havilland *Mosquito* could be deployed.

The United States watched these developments with alarm, as it, too, lacked a specialized night-fighting aircraft in 1941. Until Northrop's promising P-61 *Black Widow* was ready, the Army

Air Corps decided the follow the British example and converted several A-20 *Havocs*. These machines were outfitted with radar developed at the Massachusetts Institute of Technology and armed with an underbelly pod housing four 20mm cannons. However, the engines were not equipped with superchargers as planned, owing to acute shortages, and the plane suffered in terms of high-altitude performance. A total of 269 was built.

The new P-70s, as they were designated, were hastily deployed at Guadalcanal in the Pacific in an attempt to halt Japanese nighttime attacks on U.S. installations. Owing to their lack of superchargers, the P-70s could not intercept raiders flying above 25,000 feet, although some kills were made at lower altitudes. Despite this inadequacy, the *Night Havoc* held the line until 1944, when they were withdrawn and replaced by the more effective P-61. Thereafter they served as night-fighting trainers.

## ⭐ Douglas PD-1

**Type:** Patrol-Bomber

---

**Dimensions:** wingspan, 72 feet, 10 inches; length, 49 feet, 2 inches; height, 16 feet, 4 inches
**Weights:** empty, 7,453 pounds; gross, 14,122 pounds
**Power plant:** 2 × 575–horsepower Wright Cyclone R-1750 radial engines
**Performance:** maximum speed, 121 miles per hour; ceiling, 10,900 feet; maximum range, 1,309 miles
**Armament:** 1 × .30–caliber machine gun; 2,000 pounds of bombs
**Service dates:** 1929–1938

The PD-1 was based on the proven PN-12 design and served for nearly a decade. It was also the first flying boat assembled on the West Coast since World War I.

Throughout the 1920s the Navy's aging fleet of Curtiss H-16s and F-5Ls was in dire need of replacement. During this period the Naval Aircraft Factory (NAF) was responsible for the design of new flying boats, and a breakthrough occurred following introduction of the powerful Wright R-1750 Cyclone engine. This power plant weighed much less than contemporary liquid-cooled engines and was far easier to maintain. The Navy decided to produce a new craft that utilized these engines, based on the NAF's proven, metal-hulled PN-12. In 1929 Douglas of San Francisco was elected to construct 25 flying boats, the first time since World War I that a West Coast manufacturer had worked on seaplanes.

Douglas engineers gave the PN-12's blueprints a thorough going-over and decided that they were good, yet certain improvements were necessary.

Wings and tails remained fabric-covered, but to reduce drag Douglas engineers streamlined the canted wing struts and bracing wires. Next, the nacelles housing the Wright radial engines underwent a similar process, and they were flattened into distinct, horizontal knife edges. Modern three-bladed metal propellers were also utilized. Finally, the Douglas craft was outfitted with an array of sophisticated instruments, including a gyroscopically stabilized autopilot, electric engine starters, and improved communications gear.

The PD-1s were initially delivered in July 1929 and ultimately equipped Patrol Squadrons VP-1, VP-4, VP-6, and VP-7. While in service they were updated with more powerful Wright R-1820 Cyclone engines. The PD-1s proved to be robust craft with excellent endurance, but by 1937 they were rendered obsolete by Consolidated's P2Y *Ranger*. After two years as advanced trainers in Pensacola, Florida, the PD-1s were finally withdrawn in 1938.

# ☆ Douglas SBD *Dauntless*

**Type:** Scout-Bomber

**Dimensions:** wingspan, 41 feet, 6 inches; length, 33 feet; height, 12 feet, 11 inches
**Weights:** empty, 6,535 pounds; gross, 9,519 pounds
**Power plant:** 1 × 1,200–horsepower Wright Cyclone R-1820 radial engine
**Performance:** maximum speed, 252 miles per hour; ceiling, 24,300 feet; maximum range, 456 miles
**Armament:** 2 × .50–caliber machine guns; 2 × .30–caliber machine guns; 1,200 pounds of bombs
**Service dates:** 1940–1945

During World War II the SBD sank 300,000 tons of Japanese shipping, more than any other Allied aircraft. Slow and cumbersome to fly when fully loaded, it was referred to by crew members as the "Barge."

In 1938 the Northrop Corporation became a subsidiary of Douglas, which took over development of the BT-1 dive-bomber. This was extensively modified into the BT-2, a low-wing monoplane with fully retracting landing gear and perforated flaps to slow the aircraft when diving, giving it increased time to track its target. The Navy was suitably impressed by the new craft and in 1940 accepted it into service as the SBD-1 *Dauntless*. Subsequent models introduced armor, self-sealing tanks, and heavier, forward-firing armament. The Army also expressed interest and acquired several A-24s, which were nearly identical save for deletion of the tail hook and other naval gear.

During the early days of World War II the SBD formed America's first line of defense. Several A-24s were committed to the defense of Java as early as February 1942, but they were found to be slow and inadequately armed. After that the 834 Army versions saw little action. However, Navy SBDs performed brilliantly during the Battle of the Coral Sea and the Battle of Midway during May and June 1942, sinking five Japanese aircraft carriers. They accounted for a sixth carrier off Guadalcanal that September. Though somewhat slow, the *Dauntless* was toughly built and could absorb damage. Of 5,936 produced, only some 100 were lost in action, giving it the lowest loss rate of any American aircraft. A replacement bomber, the Curtiss SB2C *Helldiver*, was only marginally better; consequently, the aging Douglas design remained in frontline service until late 1944. The following year, all were declared surplus, although the French flew SBDs against communists in Vietnam as late as 1949.

# ✪ Douglas T2D/P2D

**Type:** Torpedo-Bomber; Patrol-Bomber

---

**Dimensions:** wingspan, 57 feet; length, 44 feet; height, 14 feet, 7 inches
**Weights:** empty, 6,011 pounds; gross, 10,890 pounds
**Power plant:** 2 × 525–horsepower Wright Cyclone R-1820 radial engines
**Performance:** maximum speed, 124 miles per hour; ceiling, 13,830 feet; maximum range, 422 miles
**Armament:** 2 × .30–caliber machine guns; 1 × 1,618–pound torpedo
**Service dates:** 1927–1937

---

The T2D was the Navy's first twin-engine torpedo-bomber and the first twin-engine aircraft to operate from a carrier. However, political pressure from the Army kept it mainly employed as a float-plane.

By 1925 the Navy was looking for torpedo-bombers with better performance than existing Douglas DTs and Martin T3Ms. That year the Naval Aircraft Factory built a twin-engine prototype christened the XTN-1, a radical departure from existing aircraft. The new design was a twin-engine biplane with unstaggered, equal-length wings and a slab-sided fuselage. It could be fitted either with landing gear for land operations or dual floats for operating off water. To facilitate carrier storage, the wings could also be folded aft. The crew of four, including two gunners, was seated in tandem. The new craft appeared promising, and a production contract was awarded to Douglas to build 12 examples. They arrived in 1927 as the T2D, which was both faster than previous torpedo-bombers and had a longer range. That year several made history by becoming the first twin-engine aircraft to operate off the carrier USS *Langley*.

The T2D was well-liked for its speed and the good vision it afforded pilots for carrier landings. It would have also made a capable land-based medium bomber, but the Army jealously reserved such weapons to its service alone. After complaints were made to the War Department, the T2Ds were thereafter almost exclusively employed as floatplanes attached to the seaplane tender USS *Aroostook*. In 1930 the Navy acquired an additional 18 aircraft as P2Ds, which differed only in having twin rudders. Furthermore, to mute Army criticism, they were all equipped as floatplanes and deployed for patrolling purposes only. The majority outfitted Patrol Squadron VP-3 at Coco Solo in the Panama Canal Zone until 1937, when they were replaced by Consolidated PBY *Catalinas*.

# ✪ Douglas TBD *Devastator*

**Type:** Torpedo-Bomber

---

**Dimensions:** wingspan, 50 feet; length, 35 feet; height, 15 feet, 1 inch
**Weights:** empty, 6,182 pounds; gross, 10,194 pounds
**Power plant:** 1 × 850–horsepower Pratt & Whitney R-1830 radial engine
**Performance:** maximum speed, 206 miles per hour; ceiling, 19,700 feet; maximum range, 416 miles
**Armament:** 1 × .50–caliber machine gun; 1 × .30–caliber machine gun; 1 × 1,000–pound torpedo or bomb
**Service dates:** 1937–1942

---

At the time of its deployment, the TBD was the world's most advanced torpedo-bomber. By World War II, however, it was hopelessly outclassed and suffered heavy losses in battle.

In 1934 the Navy announced a competition to build the next generation of torpedo-bombers to equip its latest carriers. Douglas conceived an all-metal, low-wing monoplane equipped with novel features like retractable landing gear and folding wings to assist storage. The crew of three was housed in a long, high-visibility greenhouse cockpit. The prototype XTBD-1 first flew in April 1935 and handily defeated its nearest competitor, a biplane manufactured by Great Lakes. The following year, Douglas was contracted to build 129 TBD *Devastators*, which were the first carrier-based monoplane aircraft acquired by the Navy. At that time they were also the most advanced torpedo-bombers in the world and eventually outfitted squadrons on the new carriers *Saratoga*, *Lexington*, *Yorktown*, *Enterprise*, and *Ranger*.

By the time of the Japanese attack on Pearl Harbor in December 1941, the *Devastator* was obsolete yet still in frontline operational service. Throughout the spring of 1942 they performed capably during numerous raids on the Marshall and Gilbert Islands, sinking several ships. They also scored significant hits during the Battle of the Coral Sea in May. However, technology caught up with the TBDs during the decisive American victory at Midway Island on June 4, 1942. Clawing their way through sheets of well-directed Japanese antiaircraft fire and waves of Mitsubishi A6M *Zero* fighters, no less than 35 were shot down without scoring a single hit. Thereafter, the Navy decided to immediately retire the aging *Devastators* in favor of a new and more modern aircraft, the Grumman TBM *Avenger*.

# ✪ Fairchild A-10 *Thunderbolt II*

**Type:** Close Support

**Dimensions:** wingspan, 57 feet, 6 inches; length, 53 feet, 4 inches; height, 14 feet, 8 inches
**Weights:** empty, 21,519 pounds; gross, 50,000 pounds
**Power plant:** 2 × 9,065–pound thrust General Electric TF34 turbofan engines
**Performance:** maximum speed, 423 miles per hour; ceiling, 45,000 feet; maximum range, 620 miles
**Armament:** 1 × 30mm GAU cannon; 16,000 pounds of bombs and rockets
**Service dates:** 1975–1995

Grotesque in appearance, the A-10 was the first Air Force jet expressly designed for low-altitude close-support work. Heavily armed and armored, it could operate in extremely hostile airspace and survive.

Drawing upon experiences from the Vietnam War, the Air Force in 1970 set specifications for a new jet aircraft dedicated to low-level attack missions in support of ground troops. Because modern jet airplanes traveled too fast and were too vulnerable to ground fire to be accurate, the new craft was envisioned as deliberately slow, heavily armored, and carrying a variety of weapons. Fairchild responded in 1972 with its prototype XA-10, which was pitted against the Northrop XA-9. The XA-10 was a low-wing design, its unconventional layout maximizing strength and attack over speed. Everything came in pairs to enhance survivability: two tail fins, two engines, and redundant flight-control systems. The fuselage was built around a 4,000-round-per-minute GAU 30mm multi-barrel Gatling gun, whose milk bottle–sized, depleted uranium shells penetrated any known armor. Moreover, the entire cockpit consists of a titanium "bathtub" designed to withstand hits from 23mm antiaircraft shells. Fairchild beat Northrop in the fly-off, and in 1975 the Air Force ordered 721 A-10s. Though the A-10 was officially christened *Thunderbolt II* in honor of the Republic P-47, pilots affectionately referred to their ugly craft as the "Warthog."

Slow but highly maneuverable, the A-10's principal mission was to defeat enemy armor. During the 1991 Gulf War, *Warthogs* flew 8,100 missions and destroyed several hundred Iraqi tanks, personnel carriers, and other vehicles. Losses amounted to only five planes despite intense curtains of modern, radar-directed antiaircraft fire. The A-10s have since been phased out of active duty in favor of the General Dynamics F-16. However, several aircraft have been reconfigured to fly forward air control missions with the Air National Guard.

**Type:** Trainer

**Dimensions:** wingspan, 52 feet, 8 inches; length, 38 feet; height, 13 feet, 1 inch
**Weights:** empty, 8,654 pounds; gross, 11,288 pounds
**Power plant:** 2 × 520–horsepower Ranger V-770 liquid-cooled engines
**Performance:** maximum speed, 225 miles per hour; ceiling, 22,150 feet; maximum range, 910 miles
**Armament:** 3 × .30–caliber machine guns
**Service dates:** 1943–1944

The AT-21 was the only U.S. aircraft of World War II designed for the purpose of teaching aerial gunnery. However, production problems delayed its debut until late in the war, and thus it served but briefly.

The onset of World War II in 1939 revolutionized aircraft design from the standpoint of defensive armament. Bombers, in particular, began sprouting multigun power turrets for defense against heavily armed fighters. By 1940 the Army Air Corps realized it totally lacked aircraft and facilities for proper instruction of modern aerial gunnery, and it announced a competition to acquire such trainers. In March 1941 Fairchild responded with its Model 77, a midwing twin-engine design that could perform both gunnery and bombing instruction. More important from a military standpoint, it was constructed almost entirely of Duramold, a plastic-bonded plywood. This, in turn, freed up scarce metal alloys for use in fighters and bombers. The Army authorized two prototypes to be built under the designations XA-13 and XA-14, for bombing and gunnery training, respectively. Both flew for the first time in 1942, but the Army ordered only the gunnery version into construction under the designation AT-21 *Gunner.* As such it was designed with a .30-caliber machine gun in the nose and twin .30-caliber guns in a dorsal power turret.

Unfortunately for Fairchild, the all-wood design presented production problems to workers accustomed to working with metal. Extensive retraining and retooling were required, and by 1943 only two AT-21s had been delivered. Ultimately, 179 were delivered; they equipped no less than seven specialized gunnery schools across the nation. By 1944, however, there were sufficient B-25 and B-26 bombers around to shunt them directly into the training process, and the AT-21's role quickly faded. Two were flown as experimental XBQ-3 radio-controlled flying bombs, but the remaining aircraft were quickly scrapped by war's end.

# ⭐ Fairchild C-82 *Packet*

**Type:** Transport

**Dimensions:** wingspan, 106 feet, 6 inches; length, 77 feet, 1 inch; height, 26 feet, 4 inches
**Weights:** empty, 29,700 pounds; gross, 54,000 pounds
**Power plant:** $2 \times 2{,}100$–horsepower Pratt & Whitney R-2800 radial engines
**Performance:** maximum speed, 248 miles per hour; ceiling, 21,200 feet; maximum range, 2,140 miles
**Armament:** none
**Service dates:** 1946–1954

When it appeared, the C-82 was a radical departure in transport design. It was used to pioneer new and better cargo procedures for the next generation of cargo aircraft.

In 1941 the Army Air Force decided to reevaluate its ability to transport large amounts of military supplies by air. Because most Army transports were basically civilian craft minus the seating, the Army decided to acquire a new design specifically laid out for military supplies. That year Fairchild engineer Armand Thieblot came up with an unusual configuration. He called for a central fuselage pod with a high wing and twin booms. This arrangement freed up the rear of the aircraft so that it could be fitted with large clamshell doors. The cargo deck, in turn, was mounted at truck-bed level for ease of moving cargo. Given the spaciousness of the hull, a number of standard Army vehicles could be driven on and off the ramp under their own power. Moreover, as a troop carrier, the XC-82 could handle 44 fully equipped paratroopers or 34 stretchers. The Army liked the proposal and authorized construction of a prototype, which was tested in 1944; permission to construct 220 aircraft was granted. In early 1946 they entered service as the C-82 *Packet*.

Given its capacity for quickly disgorging cargo, the *Packet* was used to pioneer new methods of loading and deploying military loads. For example, large equipment could be air-dropped by parachute using a small drogue chute that dragged the load out of the plane before opening up the main chute. Much practical experience was gained when *Packets* were called upon to fly duty during the 1948 blockade of Berlin. They performed well there and in the ensuing Korean conflict. However, all C-82s were declared obsolete in 1954 and were replaced by the bigger and more capable C-119 *Flying Boxcar*.

**Type:** Transport; Gunship

**Dimensions:** wingspan, 109 feet, 3 inches; length, 86 feet, 6 inches; height, 26 feet, 6 inches
**Weights:** empty, 37,691 pounds; gross, 77,000 pounds
**Power plant:** $2 \times 3,350$–horsepower Wright R-3350 radial engines
**Performance:** maximum speed, 250 miles per hour; ceiling, 24,000 feet; maximum range, 1,900 miles
**Armament:** up to $2 \times 20$mm cannons and $4 \times 7.62$mm miniguns
**Service dates:** 1949–1975

The *Flying Boxcar* was the most famous cargo plane designed specifically for military use. It served with distinction in Korea as a transport and again in Vietnam as a gunship.

By 1947 the Air Force sought to improve upon the C-82 *Packets* then in service with a new generation of transports. That year, Fairchild revealed its prototype XC-119, which was an enlarged, updated version of the early design. The biggest difference was that the flight deck was moved from above the cargo compartment to the front of it, which greatly improved pilot vision. Furthermore, the wings and motors were strengthened for better performance with heavier weights. The Air Force approved the changes and in 1949 received the first deliveries of the C-119 *Flying Boxcar.* Crew members, however, informally referred to the hulking craft as the "Dollar Nineteen" (for 119). A total of 1,112 was built, including 99 that went to the Marine Corps as R4Qs.

The new aircraft was to perform brilliantly during the Korean War. During the Marine Corps retreat from Chosin, C-119s kept troops supplied with food and ammunition and flew out a steady stream of casualties and frostbite victims. Furthermore, C-119s lifted and air-dropped, piece by piece, a 32-ton bridge for crossing the Hungnam Gorge. As operations with the Far East Air Force progressed, *Flying Boxcars* carried an estimated 250,000 passengers, disgorged 30,000 paratroopers and 18,000 tons of cargo, and airlifted 5,500 casualties. In March 1951 C-119s made history by dropping the entire 187th Regimental Combat Team behind enemy lines to rescue American prisoners of war.

*Flying Boxcars* returned to combat in Vietnam as AC-119 "Spooky" gunships. They were armed with a battery of 20mm Gatling guns, 7.62mm miniguns, and infrared equipment for detecting Vietcong nighttime operations. They were particularly successful along the Ho Chi Minh Trail before the war ended. The last few of the *Flying Boxcars* were finally retired in 1975.

# Fairchild C-123 *Provider*

**Type:** Transport

**Dimensions:** wingspan, 110 feet; length, 75 feet, 3 inches; height, 34 feet, 1 inch
**Weights:** empty, 31,058 pounds; gross, 60,000 pounds
**Power plant:** 2 × 2,300–horsepower Pratt & Whitney R-2800 radial engines
**Performance:** maximum speed, 245 miles per hour; ceiling, 25,000 feet; maximum range, 1,470 miles
**Armament:** none
**Service dates:** 1955–1976

The *Provider* was a versatile cargo plane originally designed as a glider. It performed yeoman service in Vietnam, including aerial spraying, animal transport, and night interdiction.

In 1949 Russian-born engineer Michael Stroukoff designed the XC-20 for Chase Aircraft of New Jersey. It was a large, all-metal glider that could carry 60 combat troops, but the Air Force had ceased operations with such craft. Therefore, Chase fitted two Pratt & Whitney R-2800 engines to the design and offered it to the Air Force as the XC-122 *Aviatruck*. When Chase was acquired by the Kaiser-Frazer Company in 1953, it remodified the design, now called the C-123 *Provider*, and the Air Force contracted for 310 machines. However, Air Force dissatisfaction with the company led to a new contract being awarded to Fairchild for the same plane.

The C-123 represented the new class of assault transports, designed to operate from unfinished airstrips close to the front. It was a high-wing twin-engine design with a large cargo door along the aft fuselage and could carry 60 troops, 50 litters, or 15,000 pounds of cargo. Designed for easy maintenance, its engines were simply bolted to the wings, and fuel was carried in underneath tanks. A variant, the C-123B, was equipped with two jet engines on the outboard wings and a set of skis for service in the Arctic. It was a simple, rugged piece of equipment, capable of performing a variety of tasks.

*Providers* did legendary work throughout the Vietnam War. They carried everything from combat troops to food to livestock in all theaters of the conflict. Perhaps its most notorious role was in spraying the defoliant Agent Orange along Vietcong infiltration routes. Two C-123s were also fitted with a battery of miniguns and infrared detectors for nighttime interdiction work. After the war, *Providers* served in various Air National Guard units until retirement in 1976.

**Type:** Trainer

**Dimensions:** wingspan, 36 feet; length, 27 feet, 8 inches; height, 7 feet, 7 inches
**Weights:** empty, 2,022 pounds; gross, 2,736 pounds
**Power plant:** 1 × 200–horsepower Ranger L-440 liquid-cooled engine
**Performance:** maximum speed, 122 miles per hour; ceiling, 13,200 feet; maximum range, 400 miles
**Armament:** none
**Service dates:** 1940–1948

During World War II more Allied pilots received primary flight instruction in PT-19s and variants than in any other trainer. It was deliberately less stable than biplane trainers to better acquaint cadets with modern fighter craft.

Shortly after World War II broke out in Europe, the Army Air Corps was authorized to greatly expand the yearly number of cadet pilots it graduated. In 1939 a competition was held for a new primary trainer to replace the popular Stearman PT-17, a gentle, forgiving aircraft. The new trainer would be less stable than the faithful PT-17 to better acquaint young pilots with the characteristics of modern aircraft. Fairchild entered a modified version of their civilian M-32 trainer and beat out 16 other competitors. In 1940 the Army ordered no less than 270 of the new aircraft with the designation PT-19. It had been the largest contract secured by Fairchild to date; the company was hard-pressed to fulfill it in time.

When the United States entered World War II in 1941, the Army's pilot training program was drastically and immediately expanded. The PT-19 was needed in such droves that Fairchild had to license production to two rival firms, Aeronca and St. Louis. Because available quantities of Ranger engines were insufficient, a number of trainers were constructed with the readily available Continental R-670 radial engine and called the PT-23. A final variant was constructed in Canada as the PT-26 *Cornell*; it was identical to the PT-19 but, owing to cold Canadian weather, it was outfitted with an enclosed glass canopy. Ultimately, 7,250 of the Fairchild trainers were built and deployed in the United States, with another 1,150 from Canada. They were flown by air forces around the world and retired from U.S. service in 1948.

# Fairchild UC-61 *Forwarder*

**Type:** Transport

---

**Dimensions:** wingspan, 36 feet, 4 inches; length, 23 feet, 9 inches; length, 7 feet, 7 inches
**Weights:** empty, 1,613 pounds; gross, 2,562 pounds
**Power plant:** 1 × 165–horsepower Warner Super Scarab R-500 radial
**Performance:** maximum speed, 132 miles per hour; ceiling, 15,700 feet; maximum range, 640 miles
**Armament:** none
**Service dates:** 1942–1948

---

The *Forwarder* was another popular civilian aircraft pressed into military service. However, the bulk of its service was performed for the British.

In 1933 the Fairchild Aircraft Corporation of Hagerstown, Maryland, introduced its Model 24 to the civilian market. This was a high-wing cabin plane and powered by either a Ranger inline engine or a Warner radial engine. It could seat up to four passengers and was also fitted with dual controls. Both models exhibited excellent flight characteristics, being stable and easy to take off and land. Despite the Depression-era economy, the Model 24 was commercially successful and built in several versions depending upon the power plant chosen.

When World War II broke out the U.S. government acquired several hundred Model 24s either through purchase or temporary confiscation. In 1942 the Army Air Force obtained 163 radial-engine Model 24Ws, which entered the service as the UC-61 (for "Utility, Cargo") *Forwarder*. However, there being a glut of light transports available, most were turned over to the Royal Air Force as the *Argus I*. They were assigned to the Air Transport Auxiliary for conveying ferry pilots in England, the Middle East, and India. Shortly after, the UC-61A was introduced with a 24-volt electrical system, and of 509 constructed, 364 were also requisitioned by the Royal Air Force as *Argus IIs*. A final, Ranger-powered version, the UC-61K, was also built, and all 306 were delivered to England as *Argus IIIs*.

As early as 1936 the Navy acquired two Ranger-powered Model 24Rs as J2K-1s; an additional two ended up in Coast Guard hands as the J2K-2. By 1942 the Navy was also operating 13 UC-61As for instrument training and personnel transport under the designation GK-1. In 1948 all Model 24s had been restored to previous owners or been declared surplus and put on the commercial market. A total of 961 UC-61s had been produced.

# Fokker C-2/RA Trimotor

**Type:** Transport

**Dimensions:** wingspan, 74 feet, 10 inches; length, 48 feet, 9 inches; height, 13 feet
**Weights:** empty, 7,033 pounds; gross, 11,026 pounds
**Power plant:** 3 × 330–horsepower Wright R-975 radial engines
**Performance:** maximum speed, 136 miles per hour; ceiling, 18,500 feet; maximum range, 296 miles
**Armament:** none
**Service dates:** 1926–1932

The C-2/RA series was the American military's first trimotor transport. Big and ungainly, it nonetheless established many world records and performed several historic deeds.

In 1925 the Army, then looking for a new multi-engine transport, evaluated the Dutch Fokker F-VIIA trimotor. Because of bad publicity surrounding Anthony Fokker's association with Germany in World War I, his American subsidiary went under the label Atlantic Aircraft Corporation. The trimotors were large, high-wing monoplanes with a steel-tube fuselage and wood-covered wings. Tests were successfully concluded, and in 1926 three were purchased as C-2s, being only the second aircraft to bear the "C" designation. During its relatively short career, the type established a number of historic firsts. On May 9, 1926, an Army C-2 lent to Commander Richard E. Byrd of the Navy made the first crossing of the North Pole from Greenland. On June 28, 1927, an Air Corps C-2 named "Bird of Paradise" completed the first nonstop flight from Oakland,

California, to Hawaii, a distance of 2,400 miles, in only 24 hours, 49 minutes. That feat was upstaged during January 1–7, 1929, when a C-2 named "Question Mark" flew for an entire week, being refueled in the air by a Douglas C-1 tanker. Pilots Carl Spaatz, Ira C. Eaker, and Elwood Quesada later went on to become famous World War II generals. The Army ultimately acquired 11 C-2s and six improved models called C-7s.

In 1926 the Navy also tested the C-2 and purchased three examples as the TA-1. They were later redesignated RA-1 to avoid confusion with Navy planes already utilizing the "T" prefix for "Torpedo." These aircraft were used exclusively by the Marine Corps, which was then waging a relentless guerrilla war in Nicaragua. The RA-1s proved useful in shuttling supplies and casualties back and forth between bases. Despite complaints about the machine's instability, the Navy purchased three RA-2s with an increased wingspan. Both the Army and Navy versions had all been retired by 1932.

# ★ Fokker T-2

**Type:** Transport

---

**Dimensions:** wingspan, 79 feet, 8 inches; length, 49 feet, 1 inch; height, 12 feet, 7 inches
**Weights:** empty, 7,933 pounds; gross, 10,800 pounds
**Power plant:** 1 × 420–horsepower Liberty liquid-cooled engine
**Performance:** maximum speed, 95 miles per hour; ceiling, 10,700 feet; maximum range, 2,900 miles
**Armament:** none
**Service dates:** 1922–1923

---

The ugly T-2 premiered as one of the largest commercial aircraft in the world. It gained fame by becoming the first aircraft to fly nonstop across the United States.

After World War I, noted aircraft designer Anthony Fokker diversified from military aircraft and began manufacturing civilian designs. In 1922 he unveiled the T-2, a high-wing monoplane made of steel tubing, wooden wings, and fabric covering. This ungainly, angular craft was also an efficient transport capable of carrying 10 passengers, and it was the largest plane of its class in the world. Around this time the United States Army Air Service was seeking to pioneer long-distance aircraft with both military and commercial applications. In June 1922 the Air Service purchased two of the giant Fokker craft. One of them entered the service as the A-2 and was used as an ambulance aircraft. The other, simply known as the T-2, became the focus of the nation's first nonstop cross-country flight.

Before embarking on its historic voyage, the T-2 was subject to certain modifications to ensure success. Extra fuel tanks were fitted to the wing's upper section and the fuselage to increase range. Because two pilots were on the flight, a second set of controls was installed to maintain control of the craft while exchanging places. During October 5–6, 1922, Lieutenant John Macready and Oakley Kelly broke the world record for endurance by staying aloft for 35 hours, 19 minutes. However, two west-to-east cross-country flights failed as anticipated, and on May 2, 1923, a third attempt, east to west, was readied. Macready and Kelly lifted off from Roosevelt Field, New York, and landed at Rockwell Field, San Diego, California, having covered 2,520 miles in 26 hours, 50 minutes. This success demonstrated the practicality of long-distance flying and earned both men the prestigious Mackay Trophy for that year. The famous T-2 currently resides at the National Air and Space Museum, Smithsonian Institute.

**Type:** Transport

**Dimensions:** wingspan, 77 feet, 10 inches; length, 50 feet, 3 inches; height, 13 feet, 6 inches
**Weights:** empty, 8,149 pounds; gross, 13,499 pounds
**Power plant:** 3 × 450–horsepower Pratt & Whitney R-1340 radial engines
**Performance:** maximum speed, 135 miles per hour; ceiling, 18,000 feet; maximum range, 505 miles
**Armament:** none
**Service dates:** 1928–1935

The Ford trimotor was a famous civilian airplane adopted for military use. It was also the first all-metal monoplane aircraft to be flown by the Navy.

In 1927 the Ford Motor Company of Detroit, Michigan, had adapted the all-metal Stout transport with three Wright radial engines. When this proved unsuccessful, a refined version powered by three Pratt & Whitney Wasp motors was introduced in 1928 and became an instant commercial success. The new craft had one engine installed in the nose and two more placed in nacelles under the wings. A three-man crew sat in an elevated cockpit, and up to ten passengers could be carried. This was also the largest all-metal aircraft built in the United States to that time, and, owing to strong construction, it could be looped, rolled, and stalled in complete safety. The Ford trimotor was purchased by many commercial airlines, both at home and abroad, and proved instrumental in blazing new air routes along the Northern Hemisphere.

In 1927 the Navy contracted with Ford to obtain a single example of the trimotor, which they inventoried as the JR. Soon after, designations were changed to RR. The Navy acquired nine examples, in various versions, and assigned several to the Marine Corps. These were among the first all-metal monoplanes acquired by that service. One was fitted with pontoons and tested as an experimental torpedo-bomber, and on November 28, 1928, an RR under Admiral Richard E. Byrd made the first crossing of the South Pole. In 1928 the Army also expressed interest in the trimotor and purchased 13 machines, with minor modifications, as the C-3, C-4, and C-9. After eight years of useful service, all military trimotors were phased out in 1935 by more modern designs. Several of these amazing aircraft remain in flying condition.

# General Dynamics EF-111 *Raven*

**Type:** Electronic Warfare

**Dimensions:** extended wingspan, 63 feet; length, 76 feet; height, 20 feet
**Weights:** empty, 54,425 pounds; gross, 89,000 pounds
**Power plant:** $2 \times 21,000$–pound thrust Pratt & Whitney TF-30 turbofan engines
**Performance:** maximum speed, 1,659 miles per hour; ceiling, 50,000 feet; maximum range, 2,000 miles
**Armament:** none
**Service dates:** 1981–

The *Raven* is currently the most combat-capable tactical jamming craft in the world. Developed from the earlier F-111A, it combines a high-performance flight profile with highly automated electronic equipment.

The lessons of the Vietnam War underscored the Air Force's need for a new and better electronic countermeasures (ECM) aircraft to replace the aging Douglas EB-66 *Destroyer*. By the mid-1970s the only available ECM platform was the Navy's EA-6B *Prowler*, which the Air Force rejected as too slow and, with four crew members, too costly. Therefore, in 1975 the Air Force contracted Grumman to convert two aging F-111A *Aardvarks* into dedicated ECM aircraft. The prototype EF-111 debuted in 1977 with a greatly redesigned airframe. The nose had been extended four feet to accommodate new equipment, and a large, canoe-shaped antenna protruded along the bottom fuselage. Furthermore, the tip of the tail fin now sported a large radome, or "football." The craft's principal computer

is the AN/ALQ-99E jamming subsystem, which is a modified version of equipment already used in the EA-6B. However, because this has been extensively automated, it can function with only one operator. Thus the EF-111's crew remains at two members, half the size of the earlier Grumman craft. A total of 42 aircraft was built and deployed in 1981 as the *Raven*. However, in view of its highly electronic nature, crews referred to it as the "Spark-vark."

The EF-111 is a much more formidable warplane. It retained the high-speed, low-altitude penetration characteristics inherent in its bomber ancestry and can actually escort F-111s on combat missions. The *Raven* also has very long loiter times over a battlefield and can accurately assess and neutralize a vast array of enemy radar systems. During the 1991 Gulf War against Iraq, EF-111s flew more than 1,300 sorties with the loss of only one plane. With constant upgrades and modifications, the *Raven* will be the Air Force's principal ECM craft for the next two decades.

# ✪ General Dynamics F-16 *Fighting Falcon*

**Type:** Fighter; Fighter-Bomber

---

**Dimensions:** wingspan, 31 feet; length, 49 feet, 4 inches; height, 16 feet
**Weights:** empty, 18,238 pounds; gross, 42,300 pounds
**Power plant:** 1 × 28,900–pound thrust Pratt & Whitney F110 turbojet engine
**Performance:** maximum speed, 1,500 miles per hour; ceiling, 60,000 feet; maximum range, 1,575 miles
**Armament:** 1 × 20mm cannon; 20,540 pounds of missiles or bombs
**Service dates:** 1980–

Conceived as a lightweight air-superiority fighter, the F-16 has matured into a capable multirole aircraft. It remains one of the world's most maneuverable jets and is used by 15 nations around the world.

Facing the prospect of Soviet numerical superiority, the Air Force sponsored a lightweight fighter (LTF) competition during the mid-1970s. The goal was to supplement the superb but expensive F-15 *Eagle* with vast numbers of cheaper but equally capable aircraft. In 1974 General Dynamics fielded the prototype XF-16, which defeated a contender from Northrop, the XF-17. The XF-16 was a small, compact fighter with stubby wings and a large bubble canopy. It was the first fighter to be flown entirely on a fly-by-wire basis, which links an onboard computer to all exterior control surfaces. Because the sheer thrust of the engine equals the weight of the aircraft, it enjoys phenomenal acceleration. The aircraft can sustain turns of up to nine Gs (nine times

the force of gravity), which is so hard on the pilot that his seat reclines 30 degrees to help him remain conscious. The Air Force was clearly delighted by such amazing performance, and in 1980 the F-16 went into operation as the *Fighting Falcon*.

The F-16 is currently operated by the United States and 15 other air forces around the world with brilliant success. In 1981 Israeli pilots shot down 44 Syrian MiGs without loss, and Pakistani F-16s also claimed several Russian MiGs during the Soviet invasion of Afghanistan. However, the greatest combat record occurred during the 1991 Gulf War against Iraq. F-16s flew 13,500 sorties with tremendous success and only four losses. To date more than 4,000 *Fighting Falcons* have been jointly constructed and flown by the United States, Belgium, Norway, the Netherlands, and Denmark. More than 2,400 serve in the U.S. inventory alone and will remain potent fighter-bombers well into the 21st century.

**Type:** Bomber; Strategic Bomber

**Dimensions:** extended wingspan, 63 feet; length, 73 feet, 6 inches; height, 17 feet
**Weights:** empty, 50,000 pounds; gross, 114,300 pounds
**Power plant:** 2 × 25,000–pound thrust Pratt & Whitney TF30 turbofan engines
**Performance:** maximum speed, 1,320 miles per hour; ceiling, 60,000 feet; maximum range, 2,925 miles
**Armament:** 31,500 pounds of bombs or missiles
**Service dates:** 1968–1996

The F-111 was the first combat aircraft manufactured with a swing wing. It weathered a controversial debut while serving in Vietnam but has since served capably in a variety of functions.

In 1960 the Department of Defense announced its Advanced Tactical Fighter (TFX) project, intended to build an aircraft that could be used as a bomber by the Air Force and a fighter by the Navy. In 1964 General Dynamics flew the prototype XF-111, a large aircraft with a most conspicuous feature—the swing wing. The wings could be lengthened at will by the pilot, moving them forward for slow landing speeds and completely back for supersonic flight. It was the first combat aircraft so equipped. The two crew members sat side by side in a unique cockpit that could be jettisoned as an escape capsule. Another advanced feature was terrain-following radar (TFR), which enabled the aircraft to fly at high speeds in darkness or bad weather only 200 feet above ground to avoid enemy radar. The

Navy rejected the craft as too heavy and underpowered for carrier operations, but the Air Force accepted it as the F-111. Crews immediately nicknamed the bomber the *Aardvark* on account of its extended nose. Another version, the FB-111, was a strategic bomber specializing in deep-penetration nuclear attacks.

The F-111's combat debut in Vietnam proved troubling: Of six aircraft deployed, three mysteriously crashed. Defects in the TFR were suspected, and the Air Force ceased operations until modifications were made. Within months, large numbers of F-111s resumed air raids from Thailand and established the machines as effective all-weather bombers. In 1981 F-111s conducted an extremely long-range raid from England against Libya with excellent results. Ten years later the *Aardvark* excelled in night raids during the Gulf War against Iraq, flying 4,000 sorties without a single loss. This outstanding attack aircraft was finally retired in 1996.

**Type:** Dive-Bomber

**Dimensions:** wingspan, 36 feet; length, 28 feet, 9 inches; height, 11 feet
**Weights:** empty, 3,903 pounds; gross, 6,347 pounds
**Power plant:** 1 × 750–horsepower Pratt & Whitney R-1535 radial engine
**Performance:** maximum speed, 188 miles per hour; ceiling, 20,100 feet; maximum range, 549 miles
**Armament:** 2 × .30–caliber machine guns; 1 × 1,000–pound bomb
**Service dates:** 1934–1940

The BG-1 was the only aircraft manufactured by Great Lakes for the Navy. A capable design, it lasted in service for several years after the company went out of business.

In 1928 the Glenn Martin Aircraft Corporation relocated from Cleveland, Ohio, to Baltimore, Maryland. Before doing so, it sold its aircraft facilities to the Great Lakes Aircraft Corporation. That firm had previously sold sport planes to the civilian market as well as several innovative prototypes, which were offered to the Navy. Great Lakes now acquired the rights to build Martin's T4M bomber under its own designation, TG-1, and became better acquainted with naval aircraft manufacturing. In 1932 the Navy issued specifications for a new dive-bomber capable of carrying a 1,000-pound bomb, and Great Lakes entered an original design in competition with the Consolidated XB2Y-1. However, the XBG-1, a standard biplane with fixed landing gear and an enclosed canopy, was judged to be the superior entry. In 1933 a contract was signed to build 60 machines

as the BG-1, which achieved operational status the following year.

Shortly after delivery, the first BG-1s were fitted with a new, controllable-pitch propeller and were finally judged ready for service. They initially served with Bombing Squadron VB-3B onboard the carrier USS *Ranger* before equipping Marine Corps Bombing Squadrons VB-4M and VB-6M. However, Great Lakes failed to secure further contracts from the Navy for new aircraft, and it went out of business in 1936. Repair and spare-part responsibilities were then acquired by the newly formed Bell Aircraft Corporation of Buffalo, New York. Meanwhile, the three squadrons of BG-1s performed admirably for several more years before being phased out by Northrop BT-1s and Vought SB2U *Vindicators* in 1938. The last operational Marine squadron, VMO-1, finally relinquished its BG-1s in 1940. Several surviving aircraft were then employed as radio-controlled target drones throughout 1943.

# Grumman A-6 Intruder

**Type:** Bomber

**Dimensions:** wingspan, 53 feet; length, 54 feet; height, 16 feet, 2 inches
**Weights:** empty, 26,850 pounds; gross, 60,400 pounds
**Power plant:** 2 × 9,300–pound thrust Pratt & Whitney J52 turbojet engines
**Performance:** maximum speed, 643 miles per hour; ceiling, 42,420 feet; maximum range, 1,012 miles
**Armament:** 18,000 pounds of bombs or missiles
**Service dates:** 1963–

The *Intruder* was the world's first all-weather attack bomber and displayed uncanny abilities to ferret out targets in the worse possible weather. It is still in use after 35 years of distinguished service.

The Korean War highlighted the Navy's need for an all-weather carrier aircraft that could successfully engage targets under all weather conditions. In 1957 it announced specifications for such a craft, and a design proposed by Grumman emerged as the winner. The prototype first flew as the XA2F in 1960, a squat aircraft with a bulbous nose housing the huge radar antenna essential to its mission. The two engines were mounted in pods along the bottom sides, contributing to the tadpole-shaped fuselage. A crew of two, seated side by side, was encased in a spacious canopy that allowed excellent vision. But despite its rather drab, conventional appearance, the XA2F was one of the most computerized aircraft in the world. Its digital integrated attack and naviga-

tion equipment enabled the craft to locate and accurately strike targets in weather that would ground most aircraft. The Navy was pleased with the results, and in 1963 the new bomber went into service as the A-6 *Intruder*. A tanker version, the KA-6, was introduced in 1966. All told, more than 700 A-6s of various models have been built.

Throughout the Vietnam War, the slow and ungainly A-6 formed the backbone of Navy and Marine Corps attack aviation, flying some 35,000 sorties. The aircraft sometimes achieved pinpoint accuracy under terrible operating conditions and established itself as the world's best carrier attack plane. Constant upgrades of engines and avionics have extended the *Intruder*'s service life to three decades, and it rendered conspicuous service in the 1981 raid against Tripoli and the 1991 Gulf War against Iraq. By the turn of the century, this veteran warrior will be replaced by the more modern F/A-18E *Super Hornet*.

**Type:** Antisubmarine

**Dimensions:** wingspan, 60 feet, 8 inches; length, 43 feet, 4 inches; height, 16 feet, 2 inches
**Weights:** empty, 14,580 pounds; gross, 25,500 pounds
**Power plant:** 1 × 2,400–horsepower Pratt & Whitney R-2800 radial engine
**Performance:** maximum speed, 317 miles per hour; ceiling, 32,500 feet; maximum range, 1,500 miles
**Armament:** 2 × 20mm cannons; 5,000 pounds of rockets, bombs, torpedoes, or depth charges
**Service dates:** 1950–1957

The *Guardian* was the largest single-engine carrier aircraft of its day. Fighting in teams of two, it could successfully locate and neutralize enemy submarines under daytime or nighttime conditions.

By 1944 the Navy was seeking to replace its highly successful TBF *Avenger* with a newer design capable of engaging in antisubmarine warfare (ASW). The following year Grumman fielded its XTB3F, a large, midwing design like the *Avenger* but equipped with a Westinghouse jet in the tail for speedy escapes. After much testing, it was decided to delete the jet from production models, and in 1950 the craft began service as the AF *Guardian*.

Unlike the earlier TBF, the *Guardian* was built in two distinct versions that formed a hunter/killer pair. The AF-2W possessed a large, protruding radome on its belly and a crew of four, including two radar operators seated in the fuselage. Its mission was to detect and identify the location of submarines operating underwater. When a target was found the information would be relayed to a nearby AF-2S, manned by three crew members. This craft pinpointed the target location with sonobuoys before attacking with homing torpedoes or depth charges. For night attacks on surface targets, a powerful searchlight and several 5-inch high-velocity aircraft rockets could also be carried. Once deployed to the fleet in 1950, the two versions became known as the "Guppy" and "Scrapper," respectively.

The *Guardians* first saw active duty during the Korean War, providing the American fleet with effective submarine protection. By 1954, however, they were slowly phased out in favor of a more integrated aircraft, the Grumman S2F *Tracker*, which combined both hunter and killer functions. The last AFs flew with the Naval Reserve until 1957. A total of 386 had been constructed.

# ⊛ Grumman C-2 *Greyhound*

**Type:** Transport

**Dimensions:** wingspan, 80 feet, 7 inches; length, 56 feet, 10 inches; height, 16 feet, 5 inches
**Weights:** empty, 36,346 pounds; gross, 54,354 pounds
**Power plant:** 2 × 5,250–horsepower Allison T56 turboprop engines
**Performance:** maximum speed, 357 miles per hour; ceiling, 33,500 feet; maximum range, 1,200 miles
**Armament:** none
**Service dates:** 1966–

Developed from the E-2 *Hawkeye*, the *Greyhound* is the Navy's current carrier onboard delivery (COD) aircraft. It is used to carry everything from mail to nuclear weapons for use by the fleet.

During the early 1960s the Navy considered replacing its aging fleet of TF-1 *Traders* with a more modern aircraft for COD work. As with the earlier plane, it turned to Grumman with suggestions to develop the E-2 *Hawkeye* into a transport. This was accomplished by giving the fuselage a wider cross-section for greater storage and equipping the aft section with an upswept cargo door to permit on- and off-loading of bulk items. The new design retained the four rudders of the original plane, although with the huge radome removed the pronounced tailplane dihedral was eliminated. The nosewheel, greatly strengthened, was adopted from the A-6 *Intruder* to permit takeoffs and landings at greater operating

weights. Provisions were also made to carry up to 39 passengers, 20 stretcher cases, or a payload of 18,000 pounds. Finally, both the wings and tail could be folded to facilitate carrier storage. In 1966 the Navy purchased 19 of these new machines as the C-2 *Greyhound*. It is the largest transport craft ever catapulted off a carrier deck.

The C-2 proved useful in hauling a wide assortment of men and materiel needed by the fleet. In 1989 delivery of 39 improved models, the C-2A, was completed. They differed from earlier versions by having upgraded engines, better avionics, and improved corrosion treatment to prevent rust. Throughout the 1991 Gulf War against Iraq, C-2As were deployed on every carrier and flew innumerable missions to support fleet operations. *Greyhounds* will remain the mainstay of COD operations well into the next century.

**Type:** Airborne Early Warning

**Dimensions:** wingspan, 72 feet, 7 inches; length, 43 feet, 6 inches; height, 16 feet, 7 inches
**Weights:** empty, 19,033 feet; gross, 26,867 feet
**Power plant:** $2 \times 1,525$–horsepower Wright R-11820 radial engines
**Performance:** maximum speed, 253 miles per hour; ceiling, 22,000 feet; maximum range, 1,150 miles
**Armament:** none
**Service dates:** 1960–1977

The *Tracer* was the first airborne early warning (AEW) system aircraft to launch from a carrier deck. The massive radome gave it an unmistakable profile and actually contributed to overall lift.

In 1954 the Navy began seeking an airborne early warning system to protect its vital carrier fleets. Such a craft would be responsible for detecting the approach of hostile forces and be able to vector in fighters using airborne intercept control. The original aircraft chosen for the role, the S-2 *Tracker*, was deemed unsuitable for a variety of technical reasons, so Grumman experimented with a design derived from the dependable TF-1 *Trader*.

The new craft flew for the first time in 1957 with a massive dish-type radome astride its back. This structure housed a 17-foot-diameter radar dish inside that constantly rotated six times per minute, scanning the horizon. To accommodate its size, the aircraft was fitted with a twin-rudder configuration on a short center pylon. The dish also required the folding wings to swing aft, instead of vertically, for carrier storage. To better house the four-person crew (pilot, tactical officer, and two radar operators), the fuselage was extended an additional 20 inches. After technical problems with the radar had been resolved, the type entered into service in 1960 as the WF-2 *Tracer*, which gave rise to the nickname "Willie Fudd." For obvious reasons, it was also known as the "only aircraft with its own umbrella." The Navy accepted delivery of 88 aircraft.

The WF-2 (subsequently redesignated E-1) was deployed as an interim aircraft until the more advanced E-2 *Hawkeye* could be debugged. Nonetheless, it was a quantum leap over shipborne radar in terms of providing early warning to the fleet. They could also be used to direct S-2 *Trackers* on antisubmarine flights to ensure precise search patterns. *Tracers* were finally phased out of service in 1977.

# ★ Grumman E-2 *Hawkeye*

**Type:** Airborne Early Warning

---

**Dimensions:** wingspan, 80 feet, 7 inches; length, 57 feet, 6 inches; height, 18 feet, 3 inches
**Weights:** empty, 37,945 pounds; gross, 51,817 pounds
**Power plant:** 2 × 5,250–horsepower Allison T56 turboprop engines
**Performance:** maximum speed, 374 miles per hour; ceiling, 30,800 feet; maximum range, 1,525 miles
**Armament:** none
**Service dates:** 1964–

The *Hawkeye* was the first aircraft designed specifically as an airborne early warning (AEW) platform. It currently supplies vitally important command-and-control functions to carrier battle groups in any type of weather.

Great advances in computer and radar technology made the possibility of an AEW platform feasible by the late 1950s. Because Grumman's E-1 *Tracer* was considered an interim aircraft, that company went on to design the world's first AEW aircraft in 1961. The E-2 was a high-wing, twin-turboprop monoplane, much larger than the aircraft it replaced. This was principally because nearly one-quarter of its weight consisted of computer and radar equipment. Its most distinctive feature was a 24-foot-diameter rotodome, a radar antenna possessing an aerodynamic shape. This obviates the need to place the device in a fixed radome. Considerable ingenuity was also expended on the tail section, the four rudders carefully placed to lay below the antenna's horizon line. Despite its size, the E-2 was highly maneuverable and ruggedly constructed for catapult launches. The type entered fleet service in 1964 as the E-2 *Hawkeye*, its name being adopted from the sharpshooting frontier hero of James Fenimore Cooper's novels.

As a radar platform and information processor, the E-2 has few equals. Tasked with providing early warning to the fleet of enemy attack, from an altitude of 30,000 feet it can look down upon 3 million cubic feet of space, roughly an area from Boston to Washington, D.C. Moreover, its onboard computers can track no less than 600 targets individually and relay the information to at least 40 waiting fighters. The E-2 served in Vietnam with distinction, and during the 1991 Gulf War against Iraq, 27 airplanes completed 1,183 sorties without loss. This valuable craft has also been acquired by Israel, Japan, and Singapore for similar purposes. With constant electronics upgrades, the *Hawkeye* will provide fleet security for several decades to come.

**Type:** Electronic Warfare

**Dimensions:** wingspan, 53 feet; length, 59 feet, 10 inches; height, 16 feet, 3 inches
**Weights:** empty, 32,162 pounds; gross, 65,000 pounds
**Power plant:** 2 × 11,200–pound thrust Pratt & Whitney J52 turbojet engines
**Performance:** maximum speed, 610 miles per hour; ceiling, 38,000 feet; maximum range, 2,085 miles
**Armament:** none
**Service dates:** 1971–

The *Prowler* is one of the most sophisticated electronic-warfare airplanes in existence. It remains the only Navy warplane specifically designed for such a mission.

Because modern air warfare began assuming a decidedly electronic nature by the early 1960s, the Navy began investigating new and better aircraft to replace its aging F3D *Skyknights* and EA3D *Skywarriors*. It outfitted the tried and tested A-6 *Intruder* as an electronic countermeasures (ECM) platform and deployed it over Vietnam as the EA-6A with both Navy and Marine squadrons. The 28 aircraft constructed were strikingly successful, so it was decided to adopt aircraft entirely dedicated to electronic warfare.

The new craft, the EA-6B, was revealed in 1968 as the *Prowler*. Although possessing an airframe based on the earlier jet, it had been radically redesigned for ECM activities. The most notable development was the fuselage, which was extended by four feet to accommodate additional crew and equipment. Unlike the A-6, the new airplane seats four crew members: a pilot, an ECM officer, and two radar operators. Their purpose is to accompany airstrikes, all the while evaluating the electronic environment. Once enemy radars have been scanned and analyzed, the EA-6B uses its six powerful jamming pods, slung underwing, to jam them along with radio communications. The craft is also capable of performing electronic surveillance and antiship missile defense for the fleet. Those EA-6Bs deployed to Vietnam in 1971 were also successfully employed, and the Navy currently maintains nine entire squadrons devoted solely to ECM warfare.

Since Vietnam, the *Prowler* has been continually upgraded with stronger engines and better electronics capabilities. During the 1991 Gulf War, Navy and Marine EA-6s flew 1,626 missions without loss. These craft will most likely remain at the forefront of Navy ECM warfare for several decades.

# ★ Grumman F2F

**Type:** Fighter

**Dimensions:** wingspan, 28 feet; length, 21 feet, 5 inches; height, 10 feet, 6 inches
**Weights:** empty, 2,580 pounds; gross, 3,539 pounds
**Power plant:** 1 × 700–horsepower Pratt & Whitney R-1535 radial engine
**Performance:** maximum speed, 231 miles per hour; ceiling, 27,100 feet; maximum range, 985 miles
**Armament:** 2 × .30–caliber machine guns; 2 × 116–pound bombs
**Service dates:** 1935–1940

The tubby F2F was Grumman's first single-seat fighter and an improvement over the FF-1. Its trademark squat appearance ultimately characterized an entire series of famous Navy aircraft.

In 1932 the success of Grumman's revolutionary FF-1 prompted the company to refine the existing design into that of a single-seat fighter. A prototype was constructed and flown the following year, again with startling success. The new craft was a single-bay biplane with a distinct rotund outline. This was on account of the retractable undercarriage, which, as in its predecessor, was hand-cranked into the forward fuselage. The all-metal fuselage sported a completely enclosed canopy, and only the wings and control surfaces were fabric-covered. A highly streamlined cowling snuggled close to the powerful twin-row radial engine, so that the craft appeared simultaneously sleek and squat.

Despite appearances, the XF2F could climb like a rocket and maneuver like a dream. The Navy was delighted with the aircraft's all-around excellence, and in 1935 the Navy accepted it into service as the F2F. Because the prototype suffered from a degree of longitudinal instability, however, it was found necessary to extend the fuselage on production models by several inches. A total of 55 was constructed.

Navy pilots immediately dubbed the F2F the "Flying Barrel" on account of its appearance, but it quickly replaced the legendary Boeing F4B as a frontline fighter. They equipped Fighting Squadrons VF-2B on the carrier USS *Lexington* and VF-3B on the USS *Ranger* for the next five years. F2Fs remained in service until 1940, when they were withdrawn to function as gunnery and training aircraft. However, the groundwork had been laid for a succession of tubby fighters, which culminated in the F4F *Wildcat* and F6F *Hellcat* of World War II.

**Type:** Fighter

**Dimensions:** wingspan, 32 feet; length, 23 feet, 2 inches; height, 9 feet, 4 inches
**Weights:** empty, 3,285 pounds; gross, 4,795 pounds
**Power plant:** 1 × 950–horsepower Wright R-1820 radial engine
**Performance:** maximum speed, 264 miles per hour; ceiling, 33,200 feet; maximum range, 980 miles
**Armament:** 2 × .30–caliber machine guns; 2 × 116–pound bombs
**Service dates:** 1936–1943

An era ended with the passing of the F3F, the Navy's last biplane fighter. In service it was fast and maneuverable, but it could not compete against modern monoplane designs.

Because the successful F2F's performance was somewhat marred by instability, in 1934 Grumman modified one to serve as the prototype XF3F. This was accomplished by extending the fuselage one foot and the wings by four feet. The resulting aircraft was much easier to handle than its predecessor and even more maneuverable. However, during dive-testing in March 1935 the prototype crashed, killing the pilot. A second prototype, somewhat strengthened, was then constructed, but it too was lost the following May. Undeterred, the Navy decided to go ahead with the new plane and in 1936 purchased 54 machines as the F3F-1. They were deployed with Fighting Squadrons VF-5B on the carrier USS *Ranger* and VF-6B of the USS *Saratoga* with great success.

In 1937 Grumman attempted to upgrade the F3F's performance by fitting it with an 850-horsepower supercharged Wright radial engine. The prototype displayed marked improvement in high-altitude performance, and the Navy acquired another 81 examples as the F3F-2. This constituted the largest single order Grumman had received to date. By that time, however, it was clear that monoplane fighters were the wave of the future, and so even the superb F3F was inherently obsolete. Nonetheless, the Navy tried salvaging its pride with a final version, the F3F-3. This featured a streamlined cowling, a three-bladed propeller, and a modified canopy. The 27 machines that were purchased exhibited better performance but were also the last biplane fighters designed for Navy use. In a bow to the inevitable, the F3Fs were finally phased out by more modern Grumman F4F *Wildcats* and Brewster F2A *Buffalos* in 1940. Several remained employed as training craft until 1943, but by then the age of biplane fighters was but a memory.

# ☆ Grumman F4F *Wildcat*

**Type:** Fighter

**Dimensions:** Wingspan, 38 feet; length, 28 feet, 9 inches; height, 11 feet, 11 inches
**Weights:** empty, 4,694 pounds; gross, 5,876 pounds
**Power plant:** 1 × 1,200–horsepower Wright Cyclone R-1830 radial engine
**Performance:** maximum speed, 318 miles per hour; ceiling, 35,000 feet; maximum range, 900 miles
**Armament:** 6 × .50–caliber machine guns; 500 pounds of bombs
**Service dates:** 1940–1944

The F4F was the first successful American fighter of World War II. Although outclassed as a dogfighter by nimble Japanese aircraft, rugged design and clever tactics accounted for a nearly 7:1 kill ratio.

In 1935 the F4F began life as a biplane project but was changed to a monoplane in response to a Navy competition for new carrier fighters. However, when the prototype lost out to Brewster's F2A *Buffalo*, Grumman engineers went back and refitted the craft with a more powerful engine. The revisions were successful, and in 1939 the Navy placed an initial order for 54 machines. True to its Grumman heritage, the *Wildcat* (as it was named) was a squat aircraft with squared wings and tail surfaces. The landing gear was manually cranked into the fuselage, but it was also delightful to fly. The French government ordered 100 copies before being overrun by the Germans in May 1940. Those aircraft passed into British service as the *Martlet* and served well in carrier operations.

The F4F became the mainstay of American carrier strength after the bombing of Pearl Harbor, and in December 1941 it drew first blood by shooting down Japanese bombers and sinking a destroyer near Wake Island. For the next 18 months the *Wildcat* remained the first line of defense against the nimble Japanese A6M *Zero* fighters. Because of the F4F's inferiority as a dogfighter, Navy Commander Jimmy Thatch invented a maneuver known as the Thatch Weave, whereby two F4Fs would cover each other's tail and shoot down any Japanese craft attempting a stern shot. This expedient, coupled with the Wildcat's robust design, resulted in a 6.9:1 kill ratio by the time the F4F was phased out in favor of its bigger brother, the F6F *Hellcat*. A total of 7,251 *Wildcats* was constructed by Grumman and Eastern Aircraft by 1944, the same year it was phased out of active duty.

**Type:** Fighter

**Dimensions:** wingspan, 42 feet, 10 inches; length, 33 feet, 7 inches; height, 13 feet, 1 inch
**Weights:** empty, 9,042 pounds; gross, 12,186 pounds
**Power plant:** 1 × 2,000–horsepower Pratt & Whitney Double Wasp R-2800 radial engine
**Performance:** maximum speed, 376 miles per hour; ceiling, 37,500 feet; maximum range, 1,090 miles
**Armament:** 6 × .50–caliber machine guns; 2,000 pounds of bombs
**Service dates:** 1943–1950

The *Hellcat* enjoyed the highest kill ratio of any American fighter plane during World War II. Fast, robust, and maneuverable, it wrested control of the sky away from the famous A6M *Zero*.

Grumman began work on a new fighter to replace the F4F *Wildcat* in 1941, several months before World War II began. It was clearly an outgrowth of the earlier craft, although much bigger, stouter, and better powered. The resulting XF6F first flew in June 1942 and was distinctly superior to the superbly maneuverable Japanese aircraft of the day. It could outclimb and outrun the famous Mitsubishi A6M *Zero* fighter, and, being ruggedly constructed, could absorb much more damage and keep flying. The Navy rushed the new craft immediately into production, and the *Hellcat*'s first combat missions occurred during the fall of 1943.

From the onset the *Hellcat* established its superiority over existing Japanese aircraft, and it retained that superiority through the remainder of the war. The Navy's leading ace, David McCampbell, flew a *Hellcat* and scored 34 times. By 1945 the F6F had established a staggering 19:1 kill ratio, making it one of the most successful fighter designs ever. No less than 4,947 of the 6,477 enemy aircraft claimed by the Navy were shot down by *Hellcats*. An important version, the F6F-5N, was also the Navy's first night fighter, and it, too, produced numerous aces. Production ended in 1945 at 12,275 units. During the war, the mighty Grumman fighter was in such demand that it rolled off assembly lines at the amazing rate of one per minute!

After the war, the F6F was retained in service as an advanced flight trainer. Commencing in 1950, several fought in the Korean War as radio-controlled, explosive-laden drones, which were directed against communist targets.

# ✪ Grumman F7F *Tigercat*

**Type:** Fighter; Night Fighter

**Dimensions:** wingspan, 51 feet, 6 inches; length, 45 feet, 4 inches; height, 16 feet, 7 inches
**Weights:** empty, 16,270 pounds; gross, 25,720 pounds
**Power plant:** 2 × 2,100–horsepower Pratt & Whitney R-2800 Double Wasp radial engines
**Performance:** maximum speed, 435 miles per hour; ceiling, 40,700 feet; maximum range, 1,200 miles
**Armament:** 4 × .50–caliber machine guns; 4 × 20mm cannons; 1 × 2,000–pound torpedo
**Service dates:** 1944–1954

The mighty *Tigercat* was the Navy's first twin-engine fighter. It arrived too late to see service during World War II, and it accrued only a brief record in Korea before being replaced by jets.

In 1941 the Navy sought to develop a fighter of unprecedented firepower and speed. Grumman responded by proposing the XF7F, a radical departure from carrier fighters of the day. This was the first twin-engine design of its class as well as the first such craft equipped with tricycle landing gear. It was very heavily armed by standards of the day, carrying no less than four machine guns in the nose and four cannons in the wing roots. The Navy was intrigued by having it serve as a ground-attack aircraft for the Marine Corps, and in 1943 the prototype successfully flew. It went into production the following year as the F7F *Tigercat*, and by 1945 several squadrons had been deployed in the Pacific. However, World War II ended before the powerful fighter saw real combat. A total of 346 had been built by 1946.

Of several variants built, the F7F-2 was unusual in serving as a two-seat night fighter. In this variant, the nose armament was dropped in favor of radar, and the rear gas tanks were eliminated in favor of a second crew member. As good as the *Tigercat* was, however, it was hopelessly outclassed by the new jet fighters then under development. When the Korean War broke out in 1950 several squadrons were on hand in Japan, and they fought extremely well in support of ground operations. The night-fighting F7F-2s also scored kills against a difficult target, the slow North Korean PO-2 biplanes, which harassed Allied troops at night. After the war the F7F continued flying with reserve units until 1954. A handful continue serving as civilian firefighters.

**Type:** Fighter

**Dimensions:** wingspan, 35 feet, 10 inches; length, 28 feet, 3 inches; height, 13 feet, 10 inches
**Weights:** empty, 7,070 pounds; gross, 12,947 pounds
**Power plant:** 1 × 2,400–horsepower Pratt & Whitney Double Wasp R-2800 radial engine
**Performance:** maximum speed, 421 miles per hour; ceiling, 40,000 feet; maximum range, 1,105 miles
**Armament:** 4 × .50–caliber machine guns or 4 × 20mm cannons; 2,000 pounds of bombs
**Service dates:** 1945–1953

Arguably the finest piston-powered fighter of all time, the *Bearcat* combined superb maneuverability with an outstanding rate of climb. It arrived too late to see combat during World War II but subsequently made a name for itself fighting for the French in Indochina.

By 1943 the Navy was looking for a lightweight fighter that could outfly the latest Japanese fighters yet be small enough to operate off the smallest escort carriers in the fleet. Grumman took a standard R-2800 engine, the same engine that powered Grumman's F6F *Hellcat*, and designed the smallest possible airframe around it. The resulting XF8F first flew in 1944 and bore a marked resemblance to other fighters in the family save for its size. It was a squat, low-wing design with wide-tract landing gear, folding wings, and a bubble canopy. The new plane was also extremely light, which gave it exceptional maneuverability and a rate of climb clocked at 4,500 feet per minute. Armament had been reduced to only four machine guns, but provisions were made to allow two 1,000-pound bombs under the wings. The Navy was delighted with the aircraft; in 1944 it went into production as the F8F *Bearcat*. A total of 1,266 was ultimately constructed.

World War II ended before the *Bearcat* saw combat, but it served several years as a frontline naval fighter. However, it had the misfortune of competing against the new jet fighters and was immediately rendered obsolete. When the Korean War broke out in 1950 the Navy decided against committing F8Fs to combat, as the F4U *Corsair* possessed greater range and carried more bombs. However, France and Thailand expressed interest in the design, and the former flew *Bearcats* for many years against communist insurgents in Vietnam. The Navy phased out its last *Bearcats* in 1953, but many continue to fly as racing planes to this day.

**Type:** Fighter

**Dimensions:** wingspan, 36 feet, 5 inches; length, 41 feet, 7 inches; height, 15 feet
**Weights:** empty, 13,000 pounds; gross, 20,000 pounds
**Power plant:** 1 × 7,250–pound thrust Pratt & Whitney J48 turbojet engine
**Performance:** maximum speed, 690 miles per hour; ceiling, 40,000 feet; maximum range, 1,000 miles
**Armament:** 4 × 20mm cannons; 2,000 pounds of bombs
**Service dates:** 1952–1960

The rakish *Cougar* was the last of the F9F series and the first swept-wing jet to perform carrier service. It offered significant advantages over earlier straight-wing machines.

The Navy's experience in fighting the swept-wing MiG-15 during the Korean War prompted it to develop similar aircraft for its own use. Grumman modified one of its straight-wing F9F *Panthers* with a 35-degree sweep and flew it successfully in September 1951. To enhance slow-speed character-istics, essential to carrier landings, the broad wing was also fitted with trailing-edge flaps, leading-edge slots, wing fences, and spoilers. Furthermore, the trademark wingtip tanks were deleted. The new aircraft displayed marked improvements in speed with no negative effects upon handling, so the following year it went into production as the F9F *Cougar*. In service it proved itself a highly ma-neuverable dogfighter and a stable gun platform at all speeds. During the next eight years 1,988 F9Fs were constructed.

Once deployed, the *Cougar* established a num-ber of aviation firsts. It was the Navy's first swept-wing aircraft committed to carrier service, whereas another version, the F9F-8T, also became its first swept-wing training plane. In 1955 it also became the first swept-wing plane to serve with the Navy's *Blue Angels* demonstration team. During 1956–1957 the F9Fs of VA-46 aboard the carrier USS *Randolph* became the first American unit to deploy at sea while armed with the new AIM-9 *Sidewinder* antiaircraft missile. By mid-decade the *Cougar* was the most numerous Navy fighter, but it was rapidly being overtaken by new de-signs like the F11F-1 *Tiger* and the F-8 *Crusader*. It was finally phased out of frontline service by 1960, al-though some training aircraft served in Vietnam as forward air control aircraft. Others ended their days as radio-controlled target drones.

**Type:** Fighter

**Dimensions:** wingspan, 38 feet; length, 38 feet, 10 inches; height, 12 feet, 3 inches
**Weights:** empty, 10,147 pounds; gross, 18,721 pounds
**Power plant:** 1 × 6,250–pound thrust Pratt & Whitney J48 turbojet engine
**Performance:** maximum speed, 579 miles per hour; ceiling, 42,800 feet; maximum range, 1,300 miles
**Armament:** 4 × 20mm cannons; 2,000 pounds of rockets or bombs
**Service dates:** 1949–1957

The rugged *Panther* was the first Navy jet committed to combat in Korea. It distinguished itself as a fighter-bomber and even shot down an advanced MiG-15 fighter.

In 1946 Grumman submitted a proposal to the Navy to construct its first jet-powered fighter. The original design consisted of four low-powered engines in a relatively thick wing, but by 1947 this was discarded in favor of a more conventional single-engine approach. In November of that year the prototype XF9F was successfully flown as a midwing design with unswept wings. Jet intakes were mounted at the wing roots, and the exhaust passed through a single tailpipe under the rudder. It was highly maneuverable and relatively fast for the time, so in 1949 it became operational as the F9F. Consistent with the Grumman tradition for endowing its fighters with feline names, the craft was dubbed *Panther*.

Actually, two versions were built. The F9F-2 was powered by a troublesome but high-powered British Rolls-Royce Nene engine, whereas the F9F-3 had a lower-thrust Allison J33. When the bugs were finally worked out of the Nene engine, it was clearly the better performer; all F9F-3s were then retrofitted with the British engine. In service, the *Panther* had fine characteristics for carrier operations, for it could take off in only 800 feet, and landing speeds were less than 100 miles per hour. In 1949 it also became the first jet to equip the famous *Blue Angels* flying team. Ultimately, the Navy accepted 1,382 of these machines.

When the Korean War commenced in 1950, F9Fs became the first Navy jet committed to combat. Flying from the carrier USS *Philippine Sea* that August, they commenced a distinguished career as hard-hitting fighter-bombers. On November 9, 1951, an F9F shot down a superior Soviet-built MiG-15 fighter while dogfighting. The *Panther* continued rendering excellent service until 1957, when it gave rise to the new, swept-wing F9F *Cougar*.

# ⭐ Grumman F11F *Tiger*

**Type:** Fighter

**Dimensions:** wingspan, 31 feet, 7 inches; length, 46 feet, 11 inches; height, 13 feet, 2 inches
**Weights:** empty, 13,428 pounds; gross, 22,160 pounds
**Power plant:** 1 × 7,450–pound thrust Wright J65 turbojet engine
**Performance:** maximum speed, 750 miles per hour; ceiling, 41,900 feet; maximum range, 1,270 miles
**Armament:** 4 × 20mm cannons; 4 × AIM-9 *Sidewinder* missiles
**Service dates:** 1957–1968

One of the most beautiful jets ever conceived, the *Tiger* was the Navy's first supersonic fighter. However, it was rapidly overtaken by more advanced machines and spent most of its career as a trainer and stunt plane.

As a result of the Korean War, the Navy sought to acquire jet fighters with supersonic capabilities. In 1953 Grumman was authorized to develop the existing F9F *Cougar* to its maximum potential. The prototype emerged in July 1954 with so many changes that it received a new designation, XF11F. The new craft had longer, thinner wings than its predecessor and a pinched-in "wasp" waist governed by new area-rule principles. Consequently, the XF11F reached supersonic speed once it was fitted with an afterburner in 1955. The new jet was also very maneuverable and delightful to fly, so in 1957 it entered production as the F11F *Tiger*. After a preliminary batch of 47 short-nosed machines, 157 more were constructed with the characteristic long nose. A total of 201 *Tigers* was deployed.

For all its good looks and handling, the F11F was underpowered and slower than other designs that were also being deployed. The J65 engine was a constant source of trouble, so two F11Fs were fitted with a powerful General Electric J79 engine with nearly twice the thrust. These new *Super Tigers* easily reached Mach 2 (twice the speed of sound) but lacked range and were considered too heavy for carrier operations. By 1959 the standard-powered F11Fs were being replaced in frontline units by the much faster F-8 *Crusader* and the F-4 *Phantom II*. However, once the *Tiger* was adopted by the *Blue Angels* demonstration team in 1958, its fine flying characteristics were put to spectacular use. The *Blue Angels* operated the *Tiger* for a decade, longer than any other craft to that time. The remaining F11Fs subsequently served as advanced trainers before being withdrawn in 1968.

**Type:** Fighter

**Dimensions:** extended wingspan, 64 feet, 1 inch; length, 62 feet, 8 inches; height, 16 feet
**Weights:** empty, 39,762 pounds; gross, 74,348 pounds
**Power plant:** 2 × 20,900–pound thrust Pratt & Whitney TF-30 turbofan engines
**Performance:** maximum speed, 1,544 miles per hour; ceiling, 56,000 feet, maximum range, 2,000 miles
**Armament:** 1 × 20mm Gatling gun; 6 × AIM-54 *Phoenix* missiles; 2 × AIM-9 *Sidewinder* missiles
**Service dates:** 1972–

The capable *Tomcat* has been America's premier long-range interceptor for more than two decades. Continual engine, avionics, and weapons upgrades promise to make this excellent fighter even more formidable.

With the failure of the General Dynamics F-111 to adapt to naval service in 1968, Grumman took the lessons of swing-wing technology and commenced designing an entirely new aircraft. When the prototype XF-14 first flew in 1970, it was a much more capable fighter. Like the F-111, it employed a variable-geometry wing, although here the sweep is computer-controlled for maximum maneuverability while dogfighting. The fuselage itself was also carefully designed as a lifting body. But the heart of the plane is the complex Hughes AWG-9 radar, which enables 24 targets to be tracked simultaneously. Furthermore, it carries a battery of six advanced AIM-54 *Phoenix* missiles with a range of more than

100 miles. A *Vulcan* Gatling gun and *Sidewinder* missiles are also employed for medium- to close-range encounters. This formidable aircraft went into service in 1972 as the F-14 *Tomcat*. Its debut ushered in a new era in long-range fighter interception, and it remains one of the greatest warplanes ever designed and flown. More than 700 have been built.

The F-14 was initially deployed during the final phases of the Vietnam War but saw no action. However, a decade later it was conspicuously employed during confrontations with Libya and shot down two Sukhoi-22s and two MiG-23s without loss. During the 1991 Gulf War against Iraq, *Tomcats* completed 3,401 sorties, more than any other Navy airplane. A new version with updated engines and electronics, the F-14D, is under consideration and will afford carrier groups efficient protection well into the next century. Failing this, it will be supplanted by the F/A-18E *Super Hornet*.

# Grumman FF/SF

**Type:** Fighter

**Dimensions:** wingspan, 34 feet, 6 inches; length, 24 feet, 6 inches; height, 11 feet, 1 inch
**Weights:** empty, 3,250 pounds; gross, 4,828 pounds
**Power plant:** 1 × 700–horsepower Wright Cyclone R-1820 radial engine
**Performance:** maximum speed, 207 miles per hour; ceiling, 21,000 feet; maximum range, 921 miles
**Armament:** 3 × .30–caliber machine guns
**Service dates:** 1933–1940

The "FiFi" was the first in a long line of Grumman fighters and the first Navy fighter to possess a retractable undercarriage. It set a long-term trend in naval fighter design.

The Grumman Aviation Engineering Corporation had been established in 1929 at Bethpage, Long Island, for the purpose of manufacturing pontoon floats for naval aircraft. In 1931 it acquired a contract to produce a new two-seat fighter with several innovative features. The ensuing XFF-1 was the first Navy fighter equipped with retractable landing gear, the placement of which accounted for the very deep, potbellied appearance of the fuselage. The fuselage itself was entirely made of metal and sported one of the first fully enclosed canopies. The aircraft, powered by the new and powerful Wright Cyclone engine, easily exceeded 200 miles per hour during test flights, a speed that far exceeded contemporary fighters then in service. The Navy was impressed by

the results and in 1932 placed an order for 27 machines under the designation FF-1. Pilots, who initially questioned the many innovations, came to regard it affectionately as "FiFi."

In 1933 FF-1s equipped Squadron VF-5B on the carrier USS *Lexington* for two years, until being replaced by F2Fs in 1935. They quickly passed into the reserves and were fitted with dual controls to become FF-2 trainers. Grumman, meanwhile, sought to capitalize on its success by designing a scout version. This differed from the FF-1 only in that it carried observation equipment and a slightly revised engine. The Navy remained impressed by its high speed and in 1933 ordered 33 as SF-1s. An additional 57 machines were also completed by the Canadian Car & Foundry Company, which sold 15 FF-1s to the Royal Canadian Air Force as the *Goblin I*. Several others ended up serving in Spain, Nicaragua, and Japan. A handful of FF-2s remained in service as late as 1943.

**Type:** Transport

**Dimensions:** wingspan, 39 feet; length, 34 feet; height, 13 feet, 11 inches
**Weights:** empty, 4,400 pounds; gross, 7,700 pounds
**Power plant:** 1 × 900–horsepower Wright Cyclone R-1820 radial engine
**Performance:** maximum speed, 190 miles per hour; ceiling, 25,000 feet; maximum range, 750 miles
**Armament:** 2 × .30–caliber machine guns; 2 × 325–pound depth charges
**Service dates:** 1936–1948

The gangly *Duck* was one of the most versatile and beloved multipurpose aircraft ever built. Throughout a long service life it was employed in photographic-survey, reconnaissance, patrol, rescue, and target-towing missions.

Leroy Grumman had previously worked for Loeing and inherited considerable interest in amphibian aircraft. In 1932 he approached the Navy with a new design proposal and was contracted to build the prototype. The new XJF-1 was in most respects a conventional biplane reminiscent of the Loeing OL series but contained several refinements. The large pontoon was now a streamlined, integral part of the all-metal fuselage, which also sported a fully enclosed canopy. Most importantly, the plane employed typical Grumman landing gear that retracted into the pontoon section. The entire craft was aerodynamically clean and, when fitted with a powerful engine, performed dramatically better than the old OL-9. The Navy liked the design and in 1934 purchased an initial batch of 27 machines as

the JF-1. Given its awkward appearance on land, crew members affectionately referred to it as the *Duck*.

The JF series rendered such excellent service that in 1937 Grumman was authorized to introduce greater refinements. The new J2F series featured greater streamlining and provisions for carrier and catapult launching. After World War II commenced, many *Ducks* were outfitted with machine guns and bomb racks for patrol work. They provided particularly good service in the Pacific and rescued hundreds of downed pilots. Others were employed for general utility work such as transportation, reconnaissance, and target towing. When Grumman was forced to concentrate more on fighters and bombers, production of J2Fs shifted to the nearby Columbia Aircraft Corporation. Thus, the lowly *Duck* became the only biplane manufactured during the war. In 1946 several examples were turned over to the Army Air Force as OA-12s and flew for several more years. A total of 645 *Ducks* was constructed.

# Grumman J4F/OA-14 *Widgeon*

**Type:** Transport

**Dimensions:** wingspan, 40 feet; length, 31 feet, 1 inch; height, 11 feet, 5 inches
**Weights:** empty, 3,189 pounds; gross, 4,500 pounds
**Power plant:** 2 × 200–horsepower Ranger L-440C liquid-cooled engines
**Performance:** maximum speed, 153 miles per hour; ceiling, 14,600 feet; maximum range, 920 miles
**Armament:** 1 × 325–pound depth charge
**Service dates:** 1941–1949

The *Widgeon* was the second light amphibious transport designed by Grumman and was a smaller version of the already successful *Goose*. It was responsible for the first sinking of a German U-boat by the U.S. Coast Guard.

Buoyed by the commercial success of its G-21 *Goose*, Grumman in 1939 set about designing a smaller, less expensive amphibious transport. The result was the G-44, a high-wing, five-seat craft that was partly fabric-covered. Like the *Goose*, it sported landing gear that retracted into the fuselage, but this new plane was restricted to carrying only five passengers. The prototype first flew in June 1940, and 11 were ordered by the Portuguese Navy. These, however, were confiscated by the Army Air Force as OA-14s shortly following U.S. entry into World War II; they then received the name *Widgeon*.

As the war progressed, a second order of 25 *Widgeons* was acquired for the U.S. Coast Guard.

Because the J4F lacked the power and altitude of the original *Goose*, it was mainly relegated to anti-submarine patrolling. On August 1, 1942, a *Widgeon* from Coast Guard Squadron 212 bombed and sank the U-boat *U-166* in the Gulf of Mexico off the coast of Mississippi. This was the first enemy submarine ever sunk by that branch of the armed forces. Eventually, 136 additional examples were delivered to the Navy, who employed the craft as a utility transport and coastal patrol duties. Fifteen examples were also turned over to the Royal Navy, where they received the designation *Gosling*.

After the war the majority of J4Fs was declared surplus and offered for sale in the civilian market. However, the Navy accepted delivery of an improved model, the G-44A, which sported a redesigned hull for better water performance. These soldiered on well into the 1950s before being replaced by helicopters. Many *Widgeons* continue flying today in private hands.

**Type:** Transport

**Dimensions:** wingspan, 49 feet; length, 38 feet, 6 inches; height, 16 feet, 2 inches
**Weights:** empty, 5,425 pounds; gross, 8,000 pounds
**Power plant:** 2 × 450–horsepower Pratt & Whitney R-985 radial engines
**Performance:** maximum speed, 201 miles per hour; ceiling, 21,300 feet; maximum range, 640 miles
**Armament:** 2 × 250–pound bombs or depth charges
**Service dates:** 1939–1945

The *Goose* was the first in a long line of Grumman's small amphibious transports. It served well in a military capacity but found its real niche in the civilian sector.

The JRF was conceived in 1936 as the G-21, a general-purpose utility transport intended for the commercial market. The prototype first flew in 1937, and during the following year the Navy acquired a single example for evaluation. The G-21 was a high-wing, twin-engine design with landing gear that retracted into the fuselage and provisions for seven passengers. It employed a two-step hull to enhance water performance and was stabilized by fixed floats near the wingtips. In 1939 the Navy placed an order for 20 units, designated as JRF, which could be outfitted with bombs or depth charges. The Army was also impressed with the craft and purchased 31 as OA-9s.

During World War II numerous JRFs were exported to England and Canada, where they acquired the name *Goose*. Like all Grumman aircraft, it was rugged and versatile, being employed for search-and-rescue operations, antisubmarine patrols, target towing, and photographic surveys. One version, the JRF-3, was supplied to the Coast Guard for work in northern waters and was equipped with an autopilot as well as anti-icing equipment. Ultimately, 345 were built.

After the war the *Goose* was quickly retired from frontline service yet found additional work overseas. The French employed a squadron of JRFs until 1959, and the Portuguese Navy also operated them for several decades. The JRF's simplicity, versatility, and ease of maintenance also made it attractive to the civilian sector, and many surplus machines continue flying in various Caribbean airlines.

# ✪ Grumman OV-1 *Mohawk*

**Type:** Reconnaissance

**Dimensions:** wingspan, 47 feet, 10 inches; length, 43 feet; height, 12 feet, 8 inches
**Weights:** empty, 12,054 pounds; gross, 18,109 pounds
**Power plant:** 2 × 1,400–horsepower Lycoming T53 turboprop engines
**Performance:** maximum speed, 289 miles per hour; ceiling, 25,000 feet; maximum range, 1,200 miles
**Armament:** none
**Service dates:** 1962–

The *Mohawk* remains the only fixed-wing aircraft expressly designed to meet Army aviation requirements. Bristling with radar and other sensors, it projects "eyes and ears" over the battlefield.

In 1957 Grumman responded to a joint Army–Marine Corps requirement to build an advanced battlefield surveillance platform. In 1959 the prototype YOV-1A was completed and flown. It was a unique-looking aircraft with outstanding short takeoff and landing capability. It was a midwing design with two high-mounted turboprop engines and three rudders for stability at low speed. Turboprops were deliberately chosen due to their reliability and ease of maintenance over piston engines. Furthermore, the two pilots sit side by side in a bulged canopy that provides good visibility while they operate various radar and sensing equipment. The Marines withdrew from the program before the first aircraft was deployed, but in 1962 the OV-1A *Mohawk* entered Army service. A total of 375 was delivered.

The *Mohawk* was an excellent low-altitude aircraft and could operate easily from rough landing strips close to the battlefield. However, four successive models carried a variety of photographic and electronic equipment used to monitor enemy movements at night and under foggy conditions. OVs served with distinction throughout the Vietnam War, where they observed and reported on Vietcong activities with considerable success. Pinpointing the location of communist bases deep in the jungle, they were essential in forwarding coordinates for B-52 strikes. No less than 27 *Mohawks* had been lost in action, but the Army considered their contributions so essential to battlefield intelligence that they were retained after the war. The latest model, the OV-1D, can be fitted with an advanced side-looking aerial radar pod, which monitors radio transmissions and heat emissions from enemy forces. At least 110 *Mohawks* remain in the Army inventory, and they will provide advanced battlefield reconnaissance for years to come.

# ✪ Grumman S2F *Tracker*

**Type:** Antisubmarine

**Dimensions:** wingspan, 72 feet, 7 inches; length, 43 feet, 6 inches; height, 16 feet, 7 inches
**Weights:** empty, 18,750 pounds; gross, 29,150 pounds
**Power plant:** 2 × 1,525–horsepower Wright Cyclone R-1820 radial engines
**Performance:** maximum speed, 267 miles per hour; ceiling, 23,000 feet; maximum range, 1,300 miles
**Armament:** 2 × Mk.46 homing torpedoes; 2 × Mk.101 depth charges
**Service dates:** 1954–1976

Slow but dependable, the *Tracker* was the Navy's first effective antisubmarine warfare (ASW) hunter/killer aircraft. It owed its longevity in service to simplicity of design and the ability to accept new equipment.

By 1950 the advent of missile-armed nuclear submarines prompted the Navy to improve its ASW capabilities. To accomplish this it blended the hunter/killer roles shared by aircraft like the TBF *Avenger* and AF *Guardian* into a single airframe. In 1952 Gruman test-flew the prototype XS-2. It was a twin-engine, high-wing monoplane; its long wing, slotted flaps, and fixed slots on the outer leading edges ensured the low speed necessary for landing on small escort carriers. It carried a crew of four, including a pilot, a copilot/navigator, and two radar operators. To fulfill its mission, the plane carried a magnetic anomaly detector (MAD) boom, which could be extended behind the craft while in flight,

along with provisions for several sonobuoys. Once contact with an enemy submarine was established, a variety of conventional or nuclear devices could be delivered. In 1954 the plane went into production as the S2F *Tracker*, although crew members dubbed it the "Stoof." Over the next 20 years, the Navy acquired 1,281 of these machines.

For all its conventional appearance, the *Tracker* was an effective weapon in the role it was designed for. Constant electronics upgrades endowed it with modern ASW capacities despite an obsolete airframe and piston-powered engines. The basic design proved so successful that it gave rise to two other workhorses, the C-1 *Trader* and the E-1 *Tracer*. Relatively cheap and cost-effective, the S2F was also purchased in large numbers by Japan, Canada, Australia, and Argentina. It was finally replaced in 1976 by the Lockheed S-3 *Viking*, but several examples continue flying as fire-fighting aircraft.

# ⭐ Grumman SA-16/UF-1 *Albatross*

**Type:** Transport/Rescue

**Dimensions:** wingspan, 96 feet, 8 inches; length, 62 feet, 10 inches; height, 25 feet, 10 inches
**Weights:** empty, 22,883 pounds; gross, 37,500 pounds
**Power plant:** 2 × 1,425–horsepower Wright R-1820 radial engines
**Performance:** maximum speed, 236 miles per hour; ceiling, 25,000 feet; maximum range, 2,850 miles
**Armament:** none
**Service dates:** 1949–1976

Though originally designed as a Navy plane, the versatile *Albatross* was delivered in greater numbers to the Air Force than any other amphibian. For many decades it formed the backbone of search-and-rescue operations.

In 1944 Grumman proposed a new and enlarged replacement for its JRF *Goose* to the Navy, then was authorized to construct the prototype G-64, flown in 1947. The new craft was a twin-engine, high-wing monoplane with a two-step hull, retractable landing gear, and fixed outboard pontoons. The plane boasted impressive water-handling characteristics, and provisions were made to carry 20 passengers or 12 stretchers onboard. The Navy expressed mild interest, and in 1949 it purchased six as the UF-1 *Albatross*. However, the Air Force sorely needed to replace its OA-10 *Catalinas* as search-and-rescue craft, so it placed an order for 395 as the SA-16. The Coast Guard also operated 34 UF-1s.

The *Albatross* proved worthy during the Korean War, when it rescued more than 900 troops and downed Allied pilots. In 1955 Grumman marketed an improved version, the SA-16B, which sported a 16-foot increase in wingspan and larger control surfaces. The Navy, which ultimately obtained 94 UF-1s, also retroactively refitted its *Albatrosses* up to SA-16B standards at that time. This version also distinguished itself throughout the Vietnam War, flying numerous and hazardous rescues behind enemy lines. On occasion, the rugged seaplanes would taxi through miles of water rather than hazard a takeoff in rough weather.

During its long career, the *Albatross* broke no less than seven payload, distance, and altitude records for amphibian craft. The *Albatross* was also purchased and employed by the navies of Germany, Japan, Canada, Indonesia, and several Latin American countries. This dependable craft was finally phased out from both services in 1976.

**Type:** Torpedo-Bomber

---

**Dimensions:** wingspan, 54 feet, 2 inches; length, 40 feet; height, 16 feet, 5 inches
**Weights:** empty, 10,100 pounds; gross, 15,905 pounds
**Power plant:** 1 × 1,700–horsepower Wright Cyclone R-2600 radial engine
**Performance:** maximum speed, 278 miles per hour; ceiling, 23,400 feet; maximum range, 1,215 miles
**Armament:** 3 × .50–caliber machine guns; 1 × .30–caliber machine gun; 1 × 2,000–pound torpedo
**Service dates:** 1942–1954

The *Avenger* was the second leading aircraft of World War II in the Pacific. In concert with the Douglas SBD *Dauntless*, it helped destroy Japanese sea power.

In 1939 Grumman responded to a Navy competition to replace its Douglas TBD *Devastator* with a more modern aircraft. The company, which up to that point had only constructed naval fighters, responded with a large, robust design. Like most Grumman products, the prototype sported the trademark rotund fuselage and squared wings of earlier designs. Among its innovative features were rearward folding wings, a powered ball turret, and a fully enclosed bomb bay. The crew consisted of three; the pilot and gunner were housed in a long greenhouse canopy, and the radio operator was seated to the bottom-rear. After a successful testing in August 1941, the Navy ordered the plane into production as the TBF *Avenger*.

In time the *Avenger* would constitute a major part of the naval air arm, but its debut during World War II was inauspicious. Six were committed without air cover during the June 4, 1942, Battle of Midway, and five were shot down by marauding Japanese *Zeros*. After that, TBFs compiled an outstanding record as a torpedo-bomber and sank thousands of tons of Japanese vessels. Among its victims were the battleships *Yamato* and *Muashi*, the world's largest. In the Atlantic, 31 German U-boats were also dispatched. Ultimately, a total of 9,842 *Avengers* was manufactured, with those built by Eastern Aircraft receiving the designation TBM.

After the war most *Avengers* were declared surplus and scrapped, but a new version, the TBM-3W, with bulging antisubmarine radar domes on its belly, was delivered. They remained in U.S. service through 1954, but the navies of Canada, Japan, and the Netherlands flew them into the early 1960s.

# ⭐ Grumman TF-1/C-1 *Trader*

**Type:** Transport

**Dimensions:** wingspan, 69 feet, 8 inches; length, 42 feet; height, 16 feet, 3 inches
**Weights:** empty, 16,631 pounds; gross, 24,600 pounds
**Power plant:** 2 × 1,525–horsepower Wright R-1820 radial engines
**Performance:** maximum speed, 280 miles per hour; ceiling, 24,800 feet; maximum range, 1,110 miles
**Armament:** none
**Service dates:** 1955–1988

The *Trader* was a successful and long-serving Navy cargo plane. It was the last piston-powered airplane to operate from U.S. carriers.

By 1950 the Navy was seeking to replace its single-engine TBF *Avengers* and AD-1 *Skyraiders* as carrier onboard delivery (COD) transports. It turned to Grumman to modify the existing S2F *Tracker* into a more capable cargo plane that was large enough to carry such essentials to the fleet as jet engines and nuclear weapons. A prototype first flew in 1955 with the identical wing and engines of the S2F, but it featured an enlarged fuselage capable of carrying up to nine passengers. The result was an easily maintained and pleasant-flying aircraft that greatly enhanced the quantity and types of cargo delivered to the fleet at sea. In 1955 the type entered the service as the TF-1 *Trader*. A total of 82 was acquired and generally known, by their function, as the "Cod."

Over the years TF-1s were a common sight on carrier flight lines. They could haul mail, personnel, spare parts—anything deemed useful to fleet operations. Throughout the war in Southeast Asia, *Traders* constantly shuttled between Subic Bay in the Philippines and Da Nang in South Vietnam. However, a dependence on aviation gasoline (avgas) for their reciprocating engines eventually meant obsolescence. When carriers ceased dispensing avgas during the 1970s the *Traders* were restricted to flying from naval bases where they could be refueled. They were gradually supplanted in this function in 1988 by the turbine-powered Grumman C-2 *Greyhound.*

An unusual subtype of the *Trader* was the WF *Tracer*, of which four were built. This featured a large radome over the canopy and the additional electronic equipment for electronic warfare. In 1962 both types were redesignated C-1 and EC-1.

**Type:** Patrol-Bomber

**Dimensions:** wingspan, 72 feet, 10 inches; length, 51 feet; height, 19 feet, 10 inches
**Weights:** empty, 9,614 pounds; gross, 17,679 pounds
**Power plant:** 2 × 750–horsepower Wright Cyclone R-1820 radial engines
**Performance:** maximum speed, 159 miles per hour; ceiling, 21,350 feet; maximum range, 1,937 miles
**Armament:** 1,000 pounds of depth charges
**Service dates:** 1932–1943

The PH was the last of the Navy's biplane flying boats. A handful saw service with the Coast Guard during World War II before closing a glorious chapter in naval aviation history.

From the early 1920s to the early 1930s, most American flying boats were patterned after designs originating with the Naval Aircraft Factory (NAF) in Philadelphia. It became standard practice for companies to build aircraft based upon an existing NAF prototype. In 1927 the Hall Aluminum Company was authorized to construct a new seaplane based closely upon the existing PN-11. It emerged that year as a typical biplane design, with a stepped hull, unstaggered wings of equal length, and two motor nacelles placed midway between the wings. However, the Hall machine was characterized by a tapered hull, wide at the bottom and narrow at the top, which made no use of the flared sponsons along the sides. Service tests revealed it to possess exceptional short-takeoff performance, and it handled

well in rough water. In 1930 the Navy ordered nine PH-1s, which differed from the prototype by having enclosed canopies and a single rudder. These machines equipped Patrol Squadron VP-8 until 1937, when they were replaced by Consolidated PBY *Catalinas*.

In 1936 the Coast Guard also became attracted to the PH for its water handling, and it ordered seven PH-2s with stronger engines and greater range. These machines could rescue up to 20 people at a time and remained in service until 1940. The year previously, the Coast Guard had ordered seven more examples of an improved design, the PH-3, which employed streamlined, long-chord cowlings on the motors and cockpits that were faired directly into the fuselage. This model remained active during World War II and was fitted with depth charges for antisubmarine work. When they were replaced by more modern craft in 1943, the era of biplane flying boats had come to an end.

# Helio U-10 *Super Courier*

**Type:** STOL Transport

**Dimensions:** wingspan, 39 feet; length, 31 feet; height, 8 feet, 10 inches
**Weights:** empty, 2,095 pounds; gross, 3,600 pounds
**Power plant:** 1 × 295–horsepower Lycoming GO-480 air-cooled engine
**Performance:** maximum speed, 185 miles per hour; ceiling, 20,500 feet; maximum range, 710 miles
**Armament:** none
**Service dates:** 1953–1985

Adopted from a successful civilian design, the *Super Courier* was the military's first true short takeoff and landing (STOL) aircraft. It served throughout the Vietnam War and in a variety of roles.

In 1949 Dr. Otto Koppen and Lynn Bollinger started designing a light aircraft with unsurpassed STOL capability. Commencing with a modified Piper *Vagabond*, they continually refined their product until a totally new airplane, the Helio *Super Courier*, was flown in 1950. This was an all-metal, high-wing, cabin monoplane with a unique high-lift flap system and full-span leading-edge slats that gave it remarkable STOL performance. Though fully loaded with four passengers, it could nonetheless lift off in less space than a football field. The *Super Courier* could also fly at incredibly slow speeds (down to 25 miles per hour) without stalling, which made it useful for visual reconnaissance.

Such an aircraft naturally appealed to the Army, and in 1952 it acquired a single *Super Courier* for evaluation. The following year it purchased three aircraft under the designation L-28, and in 1958 the Air Force acquired an additional 28. In 1962 both services changed the designation to U-10A. The Army ultimately obtained another 20 aircraft, and the Air Force went on to acquire an additional 57 U-10Bs and 36 U-10Ds. This last model was fitted with a stronger engine and paratroop doors and enjoyed an operating endurance of ten hours. Both branches actively employed these machines during the Vietnam War, mostly in support of special forces operations. This versatile design also saw service doing liaison, cargo, supply drop, leaflet, forward air control, and reconnaissance missions. After the war the U-10 remained in American service for similar purposes but was slowly replaced by more modern fixed-wing and rotary aircraft. It was finally phased out of reserve status in 1985.

**Type:** Reconnaissance Helicopter

**Dimensions:** rotor span, 35 feet, 5 inches; length, 28 feet, 6 inches; height, 9 feet, 9 inches
**Weights:** empty, 1,759 pounds; gross, 2,800 pounds
**Power plant:** 1 × 340–horsepower Lycoming VO-540 air-cooled engine
**Performance:** maximum speed, 96 miles per hour; ceiling, 16,207 feet; maximum range, 420 miles
**Armament:** none
**Service dates:** 1950–1971

Although one of the first military helicopters, the *Raven* enjoyed a long service life by dint of good performance and mechanical reliability. It fought during two wars and functioned in a variety of missions.

In 1948 Stanley Hiller perfected his Model 360 helicopter and offered it to the commercial market. It featured his unique "Rotor-Matic" control system, consisting of small servo rotors installed below the main rotor as counterbalancing weights. This innovation provided excellent directional stability and permitted the first "hands off" flight by helicopters. Furthermore, it was an extremely simple, elegant craft, with a thin fuselage boom sporting an anti-torque tail rotor on the right side. A crew of two and one passenger could be housed in the distinctive slanted cockpit. In 1949 the Model 360 made the first transcontinental flight across the United States by a commercial helicopter. The Army was impressed by this machine and obtained several examples for

evaluation. In October 1950 it placed an order for 100 examples as the H-23 *Raven*, its largest helicopter purchase to date. The Navy, then in need of a light, inexpensive helicopter, also purchased 16 Model 360s as the HTE-1. Ultimately, more than 2,000 machines were constructed and sold worldwide, with 1,800 going to the Army.

Both Army and Navy *Ravens* served during the Korean War, where they won praise for ease of maintenance and were actively employed in liaison and reconnaissance work. For medical evacuation, two stretchers could also be lashed to either side of the ship. Over the years Hiller continually refined the basic design, and in 1955 the H-23D was introduced, featuring a goldfish-bowl canopy, for enhanced visibility, and a better transmission. This version performed similar work in Vietnam before being phased out to reserve and National Guard units in 1971. The *Raven* is still employed by many African and South American air forces.

# ✪ Hughes 500MD *Defender*/AH-6 *Little Bird*

**Type:** Helicopter Gunship

**Dimensions:** rotor span, 26 feet, 4 inches; length, 30 feet, 10 inches; height, 8 feet, 8 inches
**Weights:** empty, 1,976 pounds; gross, 3,550 pounds
**Power plant:** 1 × 650–horsepower Allison 250 turboshaft engine
**Performance:** maximum speed, 155 miles per hour; ceiling, 15,800 feet; maximum range, 380 miles
**Armament:** either 2 × 7.62mm gunpods or 4 × TOW antitank missiles or 2 × Mk.46 homing torpedoes
**Service dates:** 1976–

Developed from the earlier OH-6 *Cayuse*, the *Little Bird* is a highly classified special operations helicopter incorporating many stealth characteristics. Quiet, fast, and heavily armed, it is a formidable war machine.

During the mid-1960s Hughes took an existing OH-6 airframe and fitted it with a more powerful Allison 250 turboshaft engine. Thus was born the Model 500M for commercial export, although the design could also be adapted to military applications. The *Defender* light attack version featured self-sealing fuel tanks, fuselage hardpoints for carrying heavy ordnance, a new T-tail, and exhaust suppression systems to defeat heat-seeking missiles. Furthermore, the new craft acquired a slow-turning, four-bladed tail rotor to reduce noise and a mast-mounted sight for viewing targets while hovering close to the ground. Heavily armed for its size, *Defenders* can be outfitted with heavy tube-launched optically tracked wire-guided (TOW) missiles for tank-killing missions or Mk.46 homing torpedoes for antisubmarine warfare. Since 1968 *Defenders* have been sold to air forces around the world, whereas South Korea, Italy, and Japan also manufacture them under license.

A lesser-known version is the AH-6 *Little Bird*, a highly classified stealth helicopter utilized exclusively by the U.S. Army since 1981. This craft has been fitted with a five-bladed main rotor for increased performance and lessened noise; the latest versions lack tail rotors altogether, replaced by a small, variable-pitch fan at the end of the tail boom that counteracts torque by expelling hot engine gases. This new craft is probably the most quiet helicopter ever flown. At least 50 are assigned to the 160th Aviation Battalion at Fort Campbell, Kentucky, a special operations support unit. Reportedly, *Little Birds* obtained their baptism of fire by landing Green Berets behind enemy lines during the 1991 Gulf War. Their latest activities and equipment remain closely guarded secrets.

**Type:** Helicopter Gunship

**Dimensions:** rotor span, 48 feet; length, 49 feet, 5 inches; height, 12 feet, 6 inches
**Weights:** empty, 10,268 pounds; gross, 17,650 pounds
**Power plant:** 2 × 1,536–horsepower General Electric T700 turboshaft engines
**Performance:** maximum speed, 232 miles per hour; ceiling, 20,500 feet; maximum range, 380 miles
**Armament:** 1 × 30mm chain gun; 16 × *Hellfire* antitank missiles or 76 × 2.75–inch unguided rockets
**Service dates:** 1985–

The *Apache* is the most advanced combat helicopter in the world. Fast, heavily armed, and armored, it can detect, stalk, and destroy targets under all weather conditions.

During the mid-1970s, mounting concern over Soviet tank superiority prompted the U.S. Army to announce specifications for the world's first dedicated attack helicopter. The craft envisaged would be large, heavily armed, and capable of destroying targets at night and in any kind of weather. In 1976 the Hughes YA-64 prototype edged out a similar machine from Bell and was declared the winning design. It was a rather large and purposeful-looking machine, distinguished by grotesque bumps and protuberances in the nose section. In fact, the YAH-64 was designed to fight and survive in hostile airspace. It is heavily armored and can withstand direct hits from 23mm cannons. Furthermore, it is the most automated helicopter in history and boasts a target acquisition and designation sight, a

forward-looking infrared laser range finder, and a futuristic integrated helmet and display sight system. This last feature allows the pilot to aim weapons at a target merely by looking at it. After a long and problem-plagued gestation, the new machine joined the Army arsenal in 1985 as the AH-64 *Apache.*

Questions had been raised as to how such a large, expensive machine would hold up to the rigors of combat. These were partially answered in 1989, when six *Apaches* fought in the invasion of Panama, mostly at night, with good results. However, the big test occurred two years later, during the 1991 Gulf War. Commencing with a successful attack upon enemy radar sites in southern Iraq, *Apaches* flew countless sorties against Republican Guard tanks, destroying several hundred. No AH-64s were lost. An even more capable version, the AH-64D *Apache Longbow,* with advanced fire-and-forget missiles, began deploying in 1997.

# ★ Hughes H-55 *Osage*

**Type:** Helicopter Trainer

**Dimensions:** rotor span, 25 feet, 3 inches; length, 28 feet, 11 inches; height, 8 feet, 3 inches
**Weights:** empty, 1,008 pounds; gross, 1,850 pounds
**Power plant:** 1 × 180–horsepower Lycoming HIO air-cooled engine
**Performance:** maximum speed, 86 miles per hour; ceiling, 11,900 feet; maximum range, 204 miles
**Armament:** none
**Service dates:** 1964–1988

In 1955 Hughes undertook development of its Model 269 light helicopter for the commercial market. It was a piston-powered design and almost primitive in appearance. The craft consisted of a large, bug-eyed cabin for good all-around vision, to which was attached a welded steel-tube fuselage. It also had a fully articulated three-blade main rotor and a two-blade antitorque rotor. In practice, the Model 269 proved strong, reliable, and easily maintained, traits that drew it to the Army's attention in 1958. That year, five models were evaluated at Fort Rucker, Alabama, as a possible training helicopter. Tests were successful, but several modifications were suggested, including encasing the open rear boom in metal sheathing and adding wheels to the front of the twin landing skids for better ground handling. Unfortunately, the Army's budget for the next several years did not allow for purchasing new

trainers, so Hughes went ahead and continued selling the Model 269 on the commercial market as planned. The helicopter was completely successful, and by 1964 the Army had acquired sufficient funding to order 792 machines as the H-55 *Osage*.

In service the H-55 was used to train an entire generation of Army helicopter pilots. Their routine was aided by the *Osage's* mild flight characteristics and spacious canopy, which provide a good learning environment for students and instructors. Despite its seemingly frail appearance, the craft was strongly built and, being equipped with shock-absorbing skids, could withstand the stress of repeated hard landings. They remained in frontline service until being replaced by the Bell UH-1 *Iroquois* in 1988. Several hundred were also supplied to Algeria, Brazil, Ghana, and India. It was also built under license in Italy.

**Type:** Reconnaissance Helicopter

**Dimensions:** rotor span, 26 feet, 4 inches; length, 30 feet, 3 inches; height, 8 feet, 1 inch
**Weights:** empty, 1,229 pounds; gross, 2,700 pounds
**Power plant:** 1 × 317–horsepower Allison T63 turboshaft engine
**Performance:** maximum speed, 150 miles per hour; ceiling, 15,800 feet; maximum range, 1,560 miles
**Armament:** up to 2 × 7.62mm machine gun packs or 2 × 40mm grenade launchers
**Service dates:** 1966–1984

The egg-shaped "Loach" was a common sight over the skies of South Vietnam. Fast and maneuverable, it was the best reconnaissance helicopter of the war.

In 1960 the Army announced specifications for a new light observation helicopter (LOH) that was turbine-powered, easy to maintain, and very cost-effective. Twelve companies responded with various designs, and in 1965 the Hughes YOH-6 defeated Bell and Hiller entrants in a difficult fly-off. The winner was a unique craft from a company with little prior experience building helicopters. Based on a civilian model, it was a streamlined, egg-shaped machine with a four-blade rotor, an articulated rotor system, and a slender tail boom with an antitorque rotor on the left side. The turbine was fed through inlets on the cabin roof, and the exhaust shot directly out the rear of the fuselage, adding to thrust. The YOH-6 held a crew of two and could also carry four fully armed soldiers. The Army was clearly pleased with this fast, attractive helicopter, and in 1966 it began serving as the OH-6 *Cayuse*. In view of its designation as an LOH, pilots affectionately referred to it as the "Loach."

In 1968 the OH-6 was deployed in Vietnam, where it gained a reputation for ruggedness and dependability under trying field conditions. During the next five years it accumulated more than 2 million combat hours while flying reconnaissance and artillery-spotting missions. To better protect themselves at treetop level, crews sometimes strapped 7.62mm machine gunpods or 40mm grenade launchers to the fuselage for flak suppression. After the war, the *Cayuse* was rapidly replaced in Army units by the Bell OH-58 *Kiowa;* by 1984 most were transferred to reserve and National Guard units. At least 300 still fly in that capacity.

# Interstate L-6 *Cadet*

**Type:** Liaison

**Dimensions:** wingspan, 35 feet, 6 inches; length, 23 feet, 5 inches; height, 7 feet
**Weights:** empty, 1,103 pounds; gross, 1,650 pounds
**Power plant:** 1 × 102–horsepower Franklin air-cooled engine
**Performance:** maximum speed, 114 miles per hour; ceiling, 16,500 feet; maximum range, 540 miles
**Armament:** none
**Service dates:** 1941–1945

The L-6 was a popular civilian light plane and the least acquired *Grasshopper* of World War II. It nonetheless served well in a variety of liaison capacities.

In 1940 the Army began searching for a light liaison and observation aircraft to use with armed forces in the field; it turned to the civilian sector for existing machines. At that time the Interstate Aircraft and Engineering Corporation had just entered the market with an original design, the S-1 *Cadet*. Interstate was no stranger to military contracts, having produced bomb shackles and hydraulics systems for other military aircraft. The Army chose the *Cadet*, along with numerous other small-cabin airplanes, for evaluation. The S-1 was a high-wing design with tandem seating and fixed landing gear; it received the designation XO-63. It was the last airplane to be categorized as an observation craft. The trials were deemed successful, and the Army placed an order for 250 machines, although they differed from civilian versions by having an extended transparent canopy for better all-around vision. The *Cadet* then joined comparable designs from Aeronca, Piper, Stinson, and Taylorcraft with the universal title *Grasshopper*. However, this proved to be the only order received, and Interstate remained the least numerous craft of its class.

In 1942 the *Cadet* received the updated designation L-6 and was pressed into service as a utility and liaison aircraft. As such, it served as an artillery spotter, a courier craft, a flying ambulance, and a reconnaissance platform. Throughout World War II, *Grasshoppers* of every variety gained renown for their seeming ability to land and take off from any field, no matter how small or rough. The L-6 served on battlefields around the globe and, like most of its contemporaries, was put on sale as surplus immediately after the war. A number are still flying under civilian ownership.

**Type:** Transport Helicopter; Rescue Helicopter

**Dimensions:** rotor span, 51 feet, 6 inches; length, 25 feet; height, 15 feet, 6 inches
**Weights:** empty, 4,469 pounds; gross, 8,800 pounds
**Power plant:** 1 × 860–horsepower Lycoming T53 turboshaft engine
**Performance:** maximum speed, 120 miles per hour; ceiling, 25,700 feet; maximum range, 235 miles
**Armament:** none
**Service dates:** 1958–1979

The *Huskie* was the world's first fire-fighting and rescue helicopter. Despite an unorthodox design, it was fast and stable, and downwash from the rotors actually helped to save trapped victims.

After World War II the Kaman Aircraft Corporation was formed to design and build helicopters employing a dual, intermeshing rotor configuration popularly known as "eggbeaters." In 1950 the Model 600 evolved to win a Navy competition for an observation/utility helicopter. Distinctly alien in appearance, the new craft possessed a squat fuselage, twin booms, and triple rudders. A single piston-powered engine drove two roof-mounted propellers that intermeshed at high speeds. A crew of two as well as five passengers could be carried. In flight, the Model 600 was a steady, capable craft, so in 1956 the Marine Corps received 81 machines as the HOK-1; the Navy took delivery of 24 HUK-1s. About this time, the Air Force decided it needed a stable platform to serve as a fire-fighting aircraft, and it also evaluated

the Kaman craft. The machine demonstrated impressive hovering characteristics, and the Air Force ordered 18 examples as the H-43A *Huskie*. In 1959 the H-53B version was introduced, which featured a turbine engine and a rear-facing exhaust tube. Because of increased power and saved space, this craft could carry up to 10 passengers.

In time, the H-43 gained renown as a rescue aircraft. Stationed at almost every air base, *Huskies* on crash alert could be launched within 60 seconds and often reached burning wrecks ahead of the fire trucks. Hovering overhead, they doused burning wrecks with foam and carbon dioxide while downwash from the giant propellers created a path through the flames, enabling workers to rescue trapped survivors. During the Vietnam War, H-43s were also used to retrieve downed airmen. The *Huskie* was finally retired in 1979; a total of 254 was delivered to the Air Force. It was also operated by Thailand, Burma, Colombia, Pakistan, and Iran.

# ⭐ Kaman SH-2 *Seasprite*

**Type:** Transport Helicopter; Antisubmarine Helicopter

**Dimensions:** rotor span, 44 feet; length, 52 feet, 7 inches; height, 15 feet, 6 inches
**Weights:** empty, 7,040 pounds; gross, 12,800 pounds
**Power plant:** 2 × 1,350–horsepower General Electric T58 turboshaft engines
**Performance:** maximum speed, 165 miles per hour; ceiling, 22,500 feet; maximum range, 422 miles
**Armament:** 2 × Mk.46 homing torpedoes
**Service dates:** 1962–

The *Seasprite* was the Navy's first turbine-powered all-weather helicopter. Fast and reliable, it has been in continuous use since 1962 and currently functions as an antisubmarine warfare (ASW) aircraft.

In 1956 the Navy put forth specifications for a fast multipurpose helicopter that was turbine-powered. Such a craft would also have to be small enough to operate from the decks of frigates, destroyers, and cruisers. Kaman was announced the winner, and in 1959 it test-flew the prototype XHU2K-1 for the first time. It was an extremely clean, single-engine machine with a four-bladed main rotor, retractable landing gear, and a sealed, watertight hull. It carried a crew of two in the forward cabin and could transport up to 11 passengers in the main hold. In 1961 the Navy placed orders for 191 machines, which entered the service as UH-2s. During the initial phases of the Vietnam War they were employed as search-and-rescue machines, but

several were successfully converted into an armored gunship, the HH-2. Commencing in 1967, all *Seasprites* were reconfigured to mount two General Electric T58 turboshaft engines, with impressive gains in performance. A handful of UH-2s was also acquired by the Army for testing purposes as the *Tomahawk*. One aircraft was experimentally mounted with a J85 jet pod and established a speed record of 225 miles per hour.

In 1972 the Navy decided to overhaul its entire fleet of UH-2s into ASW aircraft. This entailed fitting extensive radar and sonar arrays, a towed magnetic anomaly detector (MAD) boom, and expendable sonobuoys. For armament, two Mk.46 homing torpedoes can be carried. The Navy was so pleased by the conversion of SH-2 *Seasprites* into its light airborne multipurpose program that in 1980 it purchased an additional 88, followed by 18 more in 1982. This flexible, reliable machine is expected to serve the Navy well into the 21st century.

**Type:** Light Bomber

**Dimensions:** wingspan, 74 feet, 9 inches; length, 48 feet, 10 inches; height, 17 feet, 2 inches
**Weights:** empty, 8,037 pounds; gross, 13,374 pounds
**Power plant:** 2 × 575–horsepower Pratt & Whitney R-1860 radial engines
**Performance:** maximum speed, 121 miles per hour; ceiling, 14,100 feet; maximum range, 855 miles
**Armament:** 3 × .30–caliber machine guns; 2,500 pounds of bombs
**Service dates:** 1928–1935

Commencing in 1926, Keystone dominated American bomber design for nearly a decade. The basic aircraft underwent no less than 14 revisions and served longer than any other bomber to that date.

In 1925 the Huff-Daland Company (which eventually changed its name to Keystone) built the XLB-1, a large, single-engine biplane bomber. Performance was excellent, but the Army wanted bombers with two engines with better range and safety, so the XLB-1 was fitted accordingly and became the XLB-3. It was a standard biplane configuration with two unstaggered wings of equal length and twin rudders. With better engines it entered production in 1928 as the LB-5. Over the years a succession of new designs emerged, all based upon the basic airframe but with minor adjustments to the engines and rudders. The various types were alternately known as *Pirates* or *Panthers*, but these were strictly company designations and never formally adopted. Numerically, the most important version Keystone designed was the LB-10 of 1930, of which 63 were constructed. That same year the Army stopped differentiating between "Light Bomber" (LB) and "Bomber" (B) categories and denoted all bombardment aircraft with the single prefix. Thus, the LB-10 became known as the B-3A. In 1932 the Army purchased 39 of the final version, designated the B-6A.

Though obsolete in appearance, the Keystone series was rugged, reliable, and much safer to operate than similar bombardment aircraft of World War I. Almost 200 of all versions were constructed, with roughly half remaining stateside and the remainder serving in such distant posts as Hawaii and the Philippines. They constituted the bulk of Army Air Corps bombardment strength until the advent of all-metal monoplane craft, like the Martin B-10 and Boeing B-17, during the early 1930s. A handful were still in service at the commencement of World War II but saw no action.

# Lockheed A-28/PBO *Hudson*

**Type:** Patrol-Bomber

---

**Dimensions:** wingspan, 65 feet, 6 inches; length, 44 feet, 4 inches; height, 11 feet, 10 inches
**Weights:** empty, 12,000 pounds; gross, 18,500 pounds
**Power plant:** 2 × 1,200–horsepower Pratt & Whitney R-1830 radial engines
**Performance:** maximum speed, 246 miles per hour; ceiling, 24,500 feet; maximum range, 1,960 miles
**Armament:** 7 × .303–inch machine guns
**Service dates:** 1939–1944

---

The *Hudson* was the most significant foreign aircraft acquired by the Royal Air Force during World War II, one of few originally based upon a civilian design. It also accounted for the first U-boat kill by the U.S. Navy.

In 1938 the British Purchasing Commission approached Lockheed for a new patrol-bomber, as the British aviation industry could not keep pace with defense needs. The company responded with Model 214, a militarized version of its successful Model 14 transport. The British approved of the design and ordered 250 before the prototype could be built. That flew in December 1938, and deliveries commenced in February 1939. The aircraft, known in the United States as the A-28, was christened the *Hudson* in British service. Fortunately, the Royal Air Force (RAF) Coastal Command had several *Hudson* squadrons up and running by the time World War II erupted in September 1939. On October 8, 1939, a *Hudson* claimed one of the first German planes shot down by a U.S.-built warplane. Sturdy and reliable, *Hudsons* were also capable patrol-bombers and sank several U-boats in the North Atlantic. Many were subsequently supplied to the Royal Australian Air Force and saw action against the Japanese.

In October 1941 the Navy requisitioned 20 RAF *Hudsons* and incorporated them into the service as PBO-1s. These flew with Patrol Squadron PV-82 out of Argentia, Newfoundland, and on March 1, 1942, a PBO sank the first U-boat claimed by the Navy. Two weeks later a PBO claimed a second victory. *Hudsons* were also supplied to the Army Air Force as A-28s; a trainer version, the AT-18, was also developed. *Hudsons* on both sides of the Atlantic proved reliable, versatile aircraft, and they served well as patrol-bombers, transports, and photographic aircraft until their gradual replacement in 1944. A total of 2,822 was constructed.

**Type:** Gunship

**Dimensions:** wingspan, 132 feet, 7 inches; length, 97 feet, 9 inches; height, 38 feet, 3 inches
**Weights:** empty, 79,469 pounds; gross, 175,000 pounds
**Power plant:** 4 × 4,508–horsepower Allison T56 turboprop engines
**Performance:** maximum speed, 345 miles per hour; ceiling, 33,000 feet; maximum range, 2,356 miles
**Armament:** 1 × 105mm howitzer; 1 × 40mm cannon; 2 × 20mm Gatling guns
**Service dates:** 1968–

Currently the world's largest aerial gun platform, the *Specter* is jammed full of weapons and sensor arrays. It proved particularly deadly in Vietnam and has fought in every American conflict since.

The guerrilla war in Vietnam highlighted the Air Force's need for specialized aircraft to counter the nighttime infiltration tactics of the Vietcong. At first, it experimented with several AC-47s and AC-119s, better known as "Spooky" gunships, which were heavily armed transports. By 1968 the Air Force decided to convert several C-130 *Hercules* transports to the role, as they were larger and could carry more sensors, ammunition, and fuel. Four versions were fitted with infrared heat-sensing equipment, a battery of four 20mm cannons, and two 7.62mm miniguns. Impressive results were achieved in the interdiction role, and consequently 11 more aircraft were converted to AC-130A standards. In 1973 they were upgraded as the AC-130H, with bet-

ter engines, a 105mm howitzer, and two 40mm cannons. It is estimated that over six years *Specters* destroyed at least 10,000 trucks and other vehicles along the Ho Chi Minh Trail.

Since Vietnam, advances in night-sensing radar and other nocturnal equipment prompted the Air Force to continually improve and update its small fleet of 28 *Specters*. The latest model, the C-130U, retains the usual heavy armament, but the miniguns have been replaced by even faster-firing 25mm Gatling guns. These spew out 3,500 rounds per minute, enough to saturate a football field with one burst. All weapons and sensors are linked centrally in a battle-management center for accurate target detection and fire delivery. Thus equipped, this latest generation of gunships rendered critically useful fire-support missions to U.S. forces fighting in Grenada, Panama, and Kuwait. They are operated entirely by one active and one reserve special operations squadron.

# Lockheed C-5 *Galaxy*

**Type:** Transport

**Dimensions:** wingspan, 222 feet, 8 inches; length, 247 feet, 10 inches; height, 65 feet, 2 inches
**Weights:** empty, 374,000 pounds; gross, 837,000 pounds
**Power plant:** 4 × 43,000–pound thrust General Electric TF39 turbofan engines
**Performance:** maximum speed, 571 miles per hour; ceiling, 35,750 feet; maximum range, 3,434 miles
**Armament:** none
**Service dates:** 1969–

A machine so vast it could almost fill a football stadium, the *Galaxy* held the title of world's biggest aircraft for more than 15 years. It can carry virtually any piece of Army equipment available and provided impressive service during the 1991 Gulf War.

In 1963 a design study by the Military Airlift Command called for the creation of a very large strategic transport weighing in excess of 700,000 pounds fully loaded. Two years later Lockheed won a contract to build the prototype of such an imposing craft, and in 1968 the XC-5 flew for the first time. This gigantic airplane is a shoulder-wing, four-engine design with a high-mounted tail section. Being equipped with a hinged front end and spacious rear doors, it can simultaneously load and unload cargo in one stop. The spacious hull, which is fully pressurized and air-conditioned, can accommodate 345 fully armed troops, or two M-1 tanks, or three C-47 *Chi-*nook helicopters, or almost 100 jeeps and trucks. Up to 291,000 pounds of cargo can be carried. In flight, the craft is monitored by more than 800 sensors for potential malfunctions, but it is light and very responsive to all controls. In 1969 the Air Force accepted delivery of 81 C-5As, appropriately christened the *Galaxy*, and an additional 50 C-5Bs in 1987.

As a transport, the *Galaxy* broke virtually all records for aircraft in that class. In June 1989 alone one C-5B air-dropped four M-551 *Sheridan* tanks and 73 paratroopers on a single outing. Throughout the 1991 Gulf War, *Galaxies* proved their worth by flying 3,800 sorties that delivered 87,850 passengers and 230,600 tons of cargo. Only one plane crashed due to an accident. By 1990 the *Galaxy* lost its title as world's biggest airplane to the Antonov AN-124 *Condor*, a similar design with six engines. The C-5 is slated to be phased out of frontline service by the new and ultramodern C-17 *Globemaster III*.

**Type:** Transport

**Dimensions:** wingspan, 65 feet, 6 inches; length, 49 feet, 10 inches; height, 11 feet, 1 inch
**Weights:** empty, 11,650 pounds; gross, 17,500 pounds
**Power plant:** 2 × 1,200–horsepower Wright R-1820 radial engines
**Performance:** maximum speed, 253 miles per hour; ceiling, 23,300 feet; maximum range, 1,600 miles
**Armament:** none
**Service dates:** 1941–1945

The C-56 was a popular transport derived from a successful civilian version. Although not flown in great numbers, it was actively employed as a cargo plane, a glider tug, and a VIP transport for high-ranking officers.

In 1940 Lockheed developed its Model 18 passenger transport from the earlier and very successful Model 14. Like its predecessor, this was a midwing, twin-engine, twin-rudder design, among the fastest transports of its class in the world. It was flown by a two-member crew and could seat up to 15 passengers. That same year, the Navy expressed interest in this capable craft and purchased three examples as R5Os for evaluation. In May 1941 the Army followed suit, obtaining a single example, christened the C-56 *Lodestar.* Three more were ordered with more powerful motors and received the designation C-57. A total of 13 was ultimately bought.

When the United States entered World War II the military commandeered numerous civilian *Lode-*stars and pressed more than 100 of them into service under the designations C-59 and C-60, depending upon motors and other internal arrangements. An additional 346 C-60s were constructed for the Army Air Force, which employed them in a variety of capacities including transport, paratroop carrier, and glider tug. Its long range and large payload made it especially popular as a staff transport for high-ranking officers. The Navy, Marine Corps, and Coast Guard also requisitioned numerous *Lodestars* as R5Os. In time, the Royal Air Force received 10 C-59s and 15 C-60s, which it employed throughout the Middle East as air ambulances and general transports. Twenty additional aircraft were supplied to the Royal Netherlands Indies Army Air Corps for service in the Pacific.

After the war, *Lodestars* of all descriptions were either returned to their original owners or declared surplus and sold to private operators. A handful are still in operation today.

# ✪ Lockheed C-69/R7O *Constellation*

**Type:** Transport

**Dimensions:** wingspan, 123 feet; length, 95 feet, 2 inches; height, 23 feet, 8 inches
**Weights:** empty, 50,500 pounds; gross, 72,000 pounds
**Power plant:** 4 × 2,200–horsepower Wright Cyclone R-3350 radial engines
**Performance:** maximum speed, 330 miles per hour; ceiling, 25,000 feet; maximum range, 2,400 miles
**Armament:** none
**Service dates:** 1944–1945

The graceful *Constellation* was the largest and fastest transport plane operated by the Army Air Force during World War II. It set several world records before being returned to the civilian sector.

Lockheed was developing a new passenger aircraft for Trans-World Airlines (TWA) and Pan American immediately before U.S. involvement in World War II. Specifications called for a pressurized cabin and sufficient range to fly across the United States nonstop. Work began in 1940, and the Model 049 prototype successfully flew in January 1943. At that time, the Army Air Force was in great need of high-speed transports, so it confiscated the aircraft while they were still on the assembly lines. Christened the C-69 *Constellation*, its was an enormous, four-engine design with a graceful "turtle back" fuselage, tricycle landing gear, and a distinct, triple-rudder tail. It could also seat up to 65 troops.

No sooner had the C-69 been deployed than it set several world records for distance and payload. In April 1944 millionaire financier and TWA president Howard Hughes flew a *Constellation* on a record-breaking flight from Burbank, California, to Washington, D.C., in just 6 hours, 58 minutes. In January 1945 the first nonstop *Constellation* flight to Paris was accomplished in a record 14 hours, 12 minutes. At that time, 22 C-69s of the 180 ordered had been acquired by the Army and were employed by the Air Transport Command in every theater. The Navy also acquired a handful of R7Os. By war's end the *Constellations* were declared surplus and sold or released to their original owners. In civilian hands, these elegant giants symbolized the romance of modern air travel as well as American domination of that field for years to come.

**Type:** Transport; Electronic Warfare

**Dimensions:** wingspan, 123 feet; length, 124 feet, 8 inches; height, 24 feet, 8 inches
**Weights:** empty, 72,815 pounds; gross, 145,000 pounds
**Power plant:** 4 × 3,250–horsepower Wright R-3350 radial engines
**Performance:** maximum speed, 368 miles per hour; ceiling, 22,300 feet; maximum range, 2,100 miles
**Armament:** none
**Service dates:** 1948–1979

The *Super Constellation* was an important aircraft throughout the Cold War period, and it flew in a variety of configurations.

In 1948 the U.S. Air Force decided to place *Constellations* back in the inventory after a three-year absence. It purchased 10 aircraft, which functioned as long-range troop transports. However, several were converted into staff couriers for Generals Dwight D. Eisenhower and Douglas MacArthur. Another aircraft was delivered to President Harry S. Truman to serve as Air Force One. By 1951 demand for the "Connies," as they were known, had increased, so the Air Force acquired an additional 33 of the newest L-1049 models. These aircraft, known as C-121s, were improved versions of the earlier C-69 and lengthened by 20 feet. The Navy also purchased 32 *Super Constellations* for its own use as the R7V.

The mounting intensity of the Cold War, and the threat of a surprise Soviet attack upon the United States, resulted in the development of radar picket planes. The prototype EC-121 flew in 1954 and was distinct from other *Super Constellations* by the addition of giant radomes above and below the fuselage. These housed six tons of radar equipment for early-warning or surveillance functions. That same year, the Navy deployed radar picket *Super Constellations*, called the WV-2 *Warning Star*, which required 33 crew members to operate. A total of 142 was acquired.

The EC-121s and WV-2s were often on the frontlines of the Cold War. In October 1967 a *Super Constellation* flying over the Gulf of Tonkin successfully guided a U.S. fighter on the first-ever radar-directed intercept of a MiG-21. On April 14, 1969, however, a WV-2 was shot down by North Korean aircraft with the loss of all 31 crew members. The reliable planes were finally retired from service in 1979.

**Type:** Transport

**Dimensions:** wingspan, 132 feet, 7 inches; length, 97 feet, 9 inches; height, 38 feet, 3 inches
**Weights:** empty, 76,469 pounds; gross, 175,000 pounds
**Power plant:** 4 × 4,591–horsepower Allison T56 turboprop engines
**Performance:** maximum speed, 374 miles per hour; ceiling, 33,000 feet; maximum range, 4,894 miles
**Armament:** none
**Service dates:** 1956–

The *Hercules* is one of the most famous, most versatile aircraft ever built and flown. It has compiled four decades of distinguished service—and its best years are yet to come.

By 1952 the Air Force was seeking to update its tactical airlift capabilities by adopting its first turboprop-powered transport. Lockheed was awarded a contract, and the prototype XC-130 rolled out in 1955. It represented a radical departure in transport design by possessing a shoulder-mounted wing and an inclined cargo door at the rear of the fuselage. The capacious cargo hold was also completely pressurized and air-conditioned for ease of work. Moreover, the new craft was fully capable of landing on rough, unprepared landing strips under battlefield conditions. Despite the new plane's size, pilots reported that it was "built like a truck and handled like a Cadillac." It went into service with the Air Force as the C-130 *Hercules* in 1956; since then more than

2,000 have been built. In every respect the aircraft has lived up to its legendary name.

The variety of tasks assigned to the *Hercules* is staggering. It can haul passengers or paratroopers, perform aerial refueling, search-and-rescue, electronic warfare, and communications work. It was both the first large transport to be equipped with skis for work in the Antarctic and also the first four-engine plane to both land on and take off from a carrier deck. Naturally, this capable craft was sought out by the Navy, Marine Corps, and Coast Guard, each of which operates hundreds of its own specialized versions. Furthermore, the *Hercules* has been widely exported abroad and is operated by no less than 24 different countries. With continuous engine and avionics upgrades, the mighty C-130 will be a prime tactical transport for several more decades. One of the greatest aircraft ever.

# Lockheed C-141 *StarLifter*

**Type:** Transport

**Dimensions:** wingspan, 159 feet, 11 inches; length, 168 feet, 3 inches; height, 39 feet, 2 inches
**Weights:** empty, 144,492 pounds; gross, 343,000 pounds
**Power plant:** 4 × 21,000–pound thrust Pratt & Whitney TF33 turbofan engines
**Performance:** maximum speed, 566 miles per hour; ceiling, 41,600 feet; maximum range, 6,140 miles
**Armament:** none
**Service dates:** 1965–

The *StarLifter* was the world's first all-jet transport aircraft. It has served with distinction for more than 30 years and has set many international payload records.

Faced with the prospect of aging, propeller-driven aircraft, the Military Air Transport Service in 1960 began looking for a jet-powered design to increase and modernize its global capacities. Such a craft would have to carry at least 60,000 pounds for a distance of 4,045 miles. Lockheed won the ensuing design competition, and in 1963 the prototype XC-141 emerged. Like the successful C-130 *Hercules*, the new aircraft possessed a high wing to promote unobstructed use of the cargo hold. The landing gear was stowed in pods on either side of the lower fuselage for the same reason. It also had large rear cargo doors on the upswept aft fuselage and a vertical stabilizer mounted high atop the rudder. The Air Force liked the design, and in 1965 it received its

first deliveries of C-141A *StarLifters*. The 284 aircraft constructed endowed the United States with truly strategic transport capacity.

C-141As operated capably throughout the Vietnam War, where they broke many aviation records for distance and payload. However, a constant problem was that the plane filled up with cargo long before its maximum weight had been reached. In 1987 Lockheed designed the C-141B, which stretched the fuselage by 23 feet with the addition of two plug-in sections. This modification enabled the plane to accommodate up to 200 combat troops or loads of up to 94,508 pounds. The Air Force purchased 80 of these new planes and has since retrofitted all earlier *StarLifters* up to C-141B standards. During the 1991 Gulf War against Iraq, C-141s flew 8,470 missions without mishap and carried 91,000 passengers and 159,600 tons of cargo. They are currently assigned to operate with Air Force Reserve and National Guard units.

# ⭐ Lockheed F-80 *Shooting Star*

**Type:** Fighter

**Dimensions:** wingspan, 39 feet, 11 inches; length, 34 feet, 6 inches; height, 11 feet, 4 inches
**Weights:** empty, 7,920 pounds; gross, 16,856 pounds
**Power plant:** 1 × 4,600–pound thrust Allison J33 turbojet engine
**Performance:** maximum speed, 580 miles per hour; ceiling, 42,750 feet; maximum range, 1,380 miles
**Armament:** 6 × .50–caliber machine guns; 2,000 pounds of bombs
**Service dates:** 1946–1956

The *Shooting Star* was the first mass-produced jet fighter in American history and the first to exceed 500 miles per hour in level flight. It later fought well in Korea and won the first jet-to-jet battle in history.

With the failure of Bell's P-59 *Airacomet* to perform as expected, the Army Air Force approached Lockheed to design a new aircraft around the British H-1 turbojet engine. A team led by Clarence "Kelly" Johnson completed the task in only 143 days, and the prototype XP-80 first flew in January 1944. The new craft was a streamlined, low-wing monoplane with retractable landing gear and a bubble canopy. It exceeded 500 miles per hour on its first flight, and the Army authorized a production order for 5,000 machines as quickly as possible. However, World War II ended before the P-80 could be committed to battle, and orders were scaled back to only 917 planes. Nonetheless, the *Shooting Star*

was America's introduction to the jet age, and during the next five years it became the most numerous fighter in the newly created U.S. Air Force. A total of 1,714 was built.

In 1948 the Air Force dropped the designation "P" for "Pursuit" in favor of "F" for "Fighter." When the Korean War broke out in 1950, F-80s were on hand in Japan and rushed to the scene of combat. On June 27, 1950, a *Shooting Star* of the 35th Fighter Squadron scored the first American jet victory by downing two IL-10 bombers over South Korea. Then, on November 8, 1950, an F-80 engaged and shot down a Russian-built MiG-15 in the first clash between rival jet fighters. However, as the F-80s were badly outclassed by swept-wing aircraft, they were eventually withdrawn from frontline service and served as fighter-bombers. After the war they were gradually replaced by more modern types.

# Lockheed F-94 *Starfire*

**Type:** Fighter; Night Fighter

---

**Dimensions:** wingspan, 42 feet, 5 inches; length, 44 feet, 6 inches; height, 14 feet, 11 inches
**Weights:** empty, 12,700 pounds; gross, 24,200 pounds
**Power plant:** 1 × 8,750–pound thrust Allison J48 turbojet engine
**Performance:** maximum speed, 585 miles per hour; ceiling, 51,400 feet; maximum range, 1,275 miles
**Armament:** 24 × 2.75–inch *Mighty Mouse* rockets
**Service dates:** 1950–1959

The *Starfire* was the first American jet to be equipped with an afterburner and the first interceptor armed entirely with rockets. It saw service in Korea but spent most of its operational career defending the continental United States.

When the Soviet Union exploded its first atomic bomb in 1949, the Air Force resolved to update its bomber-interceptor capacities—and quickly. It turned to the Lockheed T-33 jet trainer for an airframe, as it was a proven design. The XF-94 was flown soon thereafter with satisfactory results, and it rushed into production as the F-94A *Starfire*. Like its ancestor, this was a low, straight-wing monoplane with retractable landing gear and a two-member crew seated tandem under a long canopy. The armament originally consisted of four .50-caliber machine guns. The plane was also unique in being the first American jet to be equipped with an afterburner. This device dumped raw jet fuel into the rear of the jet engine for an added boost in performance. Over short distances, the F-94 could hit 600 miles per hour, making it extremely fast for its day. The F-94As were first deployed in 1950 as radar-equipped all-weather interceptors and night fighters.

Soon thereafter, the F-94B was introduced, which featured large wing tanks and other modifications. However, the final version, the F-94C, introduced a longer, thinner wing for better performance; redesigned tail surfaces; and a reconfigured nose. Machine guns were dispensed with in favor of 24 unguided *Mighty Mouse* rockets, which were housed around the radar dome and in midwing pods. It was the first jet aircraft so armed. *Starfires* served briefly in Korea, where they scored a few nighttime kills, but they spent the bulk of their service guarding American skies. F-94s were withdrawn in 1959 after 854 of all models had been built.

# Lockheed F-104 *Starfighter*

**Type:** Fighter

**Dimensions:** wingspan, 21 feet, 11 inches; length, 54 feet, 9 inches; height, 13 feet, 6 inches
**Weights:** empty, 21,690 pounds; gross, 28,779 pounds
**Power plant:** 1 × 15,800–pound thrust General Electric J79 turbojet engine
**Performance:** maximum speed, 1,450 miles per hour; ceiling, 58,000 feet; maximum range, 775 miles
**Armament:** 1 × 20mm cannon; 4 × AIM-9 *Sidewinder* missiles; 7,500 pounds of bombs
**Service dates:** 1958–1975

The *Starfighter* began its life as a high-speed high-altitude interceptor and ended it as a ground attack aircraft. It was the first Air Force jet to hold simultaneous speed and altitude records.

The Korean War experience prompted the Air Force to develop aircraft that placed a premium on high-speed performance, even at the expense of range and maneuverability. In 1952 a Lockheed design team headed by Clarence "Kelly" Johnson conceived an aircraft that was literally a "missile with a man in it." The prototype XF-104 emerged two years later as a relatively lengthy jet fighter with a seemingly impossibly small wingspan and a high tail. The pilot flew from a cockpit that was placed well forward and gave him excellent all-around vision. The pilot would need it, as the F-104 proved itself a very "hot" and unforgiving aircraft. Curiously, the plane was equipped with a downward-firing ejection seat. It was first deployed in 1958 as the F-104A *Starfighter* and went on to simultaneously set several speed and altitude records. However, F-104s never overcame range limitations and were never popular with pilots. After 1960 it was slowly transferred to Air National Guard units and replaced by more flexible aircraft. Some 300 were built and operated before being retired in 1975.

Ironically, the F-104's saving grace was its capability as a ground fighter. Lockheed strengthened the fuselage and wings, added several hardpoints, and exported 400 abroad as the F-104G. An additional 1,600 were manufactured under license in Germany, Japan, Belgium, Italy, and the Netherlands, where they remained in frontline service through the 1980s. The final version, the F-104S, was built by Aeritalia and is still flown by Turkey.

# ⭐ Lockheed F-117A *Nighthawk*

**Type:** Stealth Fighter

**Dimensions:** wingspan, 43 feet, 7 inches; length, 65 feet, 11 inches; height, 12 feet, 5 inches
**Weights:** empty, 29,000 pounds; gross, 52,500 pounds
**Performance:** maximum speed, 645 miles per hour; ceiling, 45,000 feet; maximum range, 691 miles
**Power plant:** 2 × 11,000–pound thrust General Electric F404 turbofan engines
**Armament:** 5,000 pounds of precision-guided rockets or bombs
**Service dates:** 1983–

Looking more like a malevolent pizza slice than a warplane, the *Nighthawk* was the world's first operational stealth aircraft. It has the radar cross-section of a small bird and is virtually undetectable at night.

During the early 1970s the Central Intelligence Agency obtained and translated a profound, top-secret Soviet study about making warplanes nearly invisible to enemy radar. Thus was born the American stealth-fighter program. Capitalizing upon this hypothesis, American scientists and engineers in 1981 constructed a working prototype unlike anything ever flown. It is deliberately triangular in shape and covered with radar-absorbent materials to either defeat or deflect hostile radar signals away from the craft. The two biggest sources of radar reflections, the engine turbines and the pilot canopy, were placed above the wings and angularly shaped to reduce electronic signatures. Furthermore, the two engines are carefully

screened from the rear and eject the hot efflux in sheets to dissipate any infrared signature. Naturally, a design this unaerodynamic could never fly on its own, so the pilot is assisted by four onboard computers to stabilize the craft in flight. It is capable of carrying and delivering several tons of precision-guided munitions against high-priority targets. Christened the F-117 *Nighthawk*, 64 were constructed and deployed through 1990.

The F-117 first saw action during the 1989 ouster of Panamanian dictator Manuel Noriega when two aircraft bombed an army barracks. However, during the 1991 Gulf War against Iraq, 42 *Nighthawks* were committed to battle. They flew 1,299 sorties against strategic targets, scoring 1,664 recorded direct hits. None were lost in action. This state-of-the-art fighter has demonstrated the validity of stealth technology and will remain in the frontline of American defense for years to come.

# ⭐ Lockheed P2V *Neptune*

**Type:** Patrol-Bomber

---

**Dimensions:** wingspan, 102 feet; length, 81 feet, 7 inches; height, 28 feet, 1 inch
**Weights:** empty, 41,754 pounds; gross, 76,152 pounds
**Power plant:** 2 × 3,250–horsepower Wright R-3350 radial engines
**Performance:** maximum speed, 341 miles per hour; ceiling, 29,000 feet; maximum range, 4,750 miles
**Armament:** 6 × .50–caliber machine guns or 20mm cannons; 8,000 pounds of bombs, mines, or torpedoes
**Service dates:** 1947–1970

---

The *Neptune* was the most famous and widely used Navy patrol-bomber of the postwar era. It set several records for range and successfully fulfilled various duties throughout a long service life.

In 1941 the Lockheed Company concluded that the Navy needed a land-based patrol-bomber with greater range and payload than existing models provided. Work began on such a craft as a private venture, but World War II delayed the prototype's rollout until 1945. The new aircraft was a large, twin-engine design that weighed more than most four-engine Army bombers. In 1947 a preproduction model named *Truculent Turtle* demonstrated its range by flying 11,236 miles nonstop from Perth, Australia, to Columbus, Ohio, in 55 hours, 17 minutes. This record for propeller-driven aircraft stood for 16 years. The bomber went into production that same year as the P2V *Neptune* and was assigned to various patrol squadrons. More than 1,000 were built, with 838 being delivered to the Navy.

During the next 15 years, the P2V was continuously modified for various missions. The canopy was enlarged and bulged, a lengthy magnetic anomaly detector boom was installed in the rear, and the last version, the P2V-7, had two 3,400-pound thrust Westinghouse J34 turbojet engines mounted under the wings. *Neptunes* were basically employed for antisubmarine warfare and could carry a number of torpedoes, bombs, and nuclear depth charges. Curiously, by the Vietnam War they were employed as electronic warfare aircraft for dropping sound sensors deep into Laos to detect truck convoys. The Air Force also employed a reconnaissance version called the RB-69A. The last P2Vs were phased out of American service by the Lockheed P-3 *Orion* in 1970, but the Japanese continued flying them until 1995.

# ✪ Lockheed P-3 *Orion*

**Type:** Patrol-Bomber

---

**Dimensions:** wingspan, 99 feet, 8 inches; length, 116 feet, 10 inches; height, 33 feet, 8 inches
**Weights:** empty, 61,491 pounds; gross, 142,000 pounds
**Power plant:** 4 × 4,910–horsepower Allison T56 turboprop engines
**Performance:** maximum speed, 574 miles per hour; ceiling, 28,300 feet; maximum range, 5,562 miles
**Armament:** up to 19,000 pounds of homing torpedoes, bombs, mines, or rockets
**Service dates:** 1962–

The complex, expensive *Orion* remains the Navy's frontline antisubmarine aircraft. It is also capable of reconnaissance, maritime patrol, and interdiction at sea.

In 1957 the Navy announced a competition to replace its aging P2V *Neptunes* as a standard antisubmarine patrol aircraft. To curtail costs, it was suggested that an existing civilian plane be utilized. Lockheed responded by modifying its L-188 *Electra* turboprop passenger liners, and in 1958 it was announced as the winner. This aircraft is a graceful, low-wing, four-engine design outfitted with a bomb bay and a lengthy magnetic anomaly detection (MAD) boom that trails from the fuselage. To prevent fatigue on extended maritime patrols, it seated a crew of ten in relative air-conditioned comfort. The original *Electra* wing was retained, but it was fitted with ten external stations for weapons. The entire plane is highly automated and features several advanced computing and sensor arrays, linked to sonobuoys, which are dropped to pinpoint hostile submarines at great distances.

The first model, the P-3A, entered into squadron service in 1962 as the *Orion* (named after the mythical hunter) and was followed by the P-3B, featuring more powerful engines. Both versions performed duty during the Vietnam War. However, by 1968 the definitive version, the P-3C, was first flown; it has served as the standard Navy antisubmarine warfare craft for more than 30 years. During the 1991 Gulf War *Orions* helped pinpoint 105 Iraqi naval targets and vectored in airstrikes to sink them. They successfully completed 369 combat sorties without loss. Constant upgrades in equipment will keep the P-3Cs operational well into the next century. The *Orion* has also been widely exported abroad and serves maritime forces in Japan, Canada, New Zealand, the Netherlands, Australia, Norway, and Spain. More than 549 have been constructed.

# Lockheed P-38 *Lightning*

**Type:** Fighter

**Dimensions:** wingspan, 52 feet; length, 37 feet, 10 inches; height, 12 feet
**Weights:** empty, 12,800 pounds; gross, 17,500 pounds
**Power plant:** 2 × 1,475–horsepower Allison V-1710 liquid-cooled engines
**Performance:** maximum speed, 414 miles per hour; ceiling, 40,000 feet; maximum range, 1,100 miles
**Armament:** 4 × .50–caliber machine guns; 1 × 20mm cannon; 4,000 pounds of bombs
**Service dates:** 1940–1949

Fast and heavily armed, the P-38 was the largest single-seat aircraft of World War II. Although not as maneuverable as other fighters, it shot down more Japanese craft than any other airplane.

In 1937 the Army Air Corps sponsored a design competition for a new long-range interceptor. Lockheed, which had never manufactured warplanes before, responded with a radical twin-engine, twin-boom design that placed pilot and heavy armament in a central pod. With a wingspan of more than 50 feet, it was the largest and heaviest single-seat fighter plane built to that date. The prototype first flew in February 1938 and established a transcontinental speed record of 420 miles per hour. The Army was delighted with the results and ordered the P-38, dubbed the *Lightning* by the British, into production. Ironically, the Royal Air Force tested the craft for possible service, without supercharged engines, and rejected it on account of poor high-altitude performance.

During World War II the P-38 saw extensive service in all theaters and established itself as a versatile fighter and attack craft. Although it could not roll as readily as its single-engine adversaries, it was still formidable in a contest of diving and zooming, and the Germans dubbed it *der Gabelschwanz Teufel*, or the "Fork-tailed Devil." However, the *Lightning* went on to score brilliantly in the Pacific, where its two engines were a welcome safety factor while operating over large bodies of water. A flight of P-38s operating from Guadalcanal in August 1943 ambushed and shot down Japanese Admiral Isoroku Yamamoto's transport over Bougainville, killing him. More significantly, the two leading American aces of the war, Richard I. Bong and Thomas B. McGuire, both flew *Lightnings*. A photo version, the F-5, was also the most widely used reconnaissance aircraft of the war. Nearly 10,000 P-38s of all variants were built, and the photo versions remained in service until 1949.

**Type:** Patrol-Bomber

**Dimensions:** wingspan, 65 feet, 6 inches; length, 51 feet, 5 inches; height, 13 feet, 2 inches
**Weights:** empty, 19,373 pounds; gross, 31,077 pounds
**Power plant:** 2 × 2,000–horsepower Pratt & Whitney Double Wasp R-2800 radial engines
**Performance:** maximum speed, 300 miles per hour; ceiling, 26,300 feet; maximum range, 900 miles
**Armament:** 4 × .50–caliber machine guns; 2 × .30–caliber machine guns; 3,000 pounds of bombs
**Service dates:** 1941–1945

The *Ventura* was an enlarged version of the earlier *Hudson*, although it never enjoyed the former's popularity. The craft was nonetheless widely employed in Europe and over the Pacific.

Encouraged by the success of the A-28 *Hudson*, the British Purchasing Commission in 1940 approached the Lockheed subsidiary Vega for a new bomber based on the company's Model 18 transport. The new aircraft, christened the *Ventura*, appeared to be a more powerful version of the *Hudson* with stronger engines, a lengthened fuselage, and greater armament. Furthermore, it was the first bomber to feature control surfaces made entirely of metal instead of being fabric-covered. The *Ventura* entered British service in 1941, and it was found to be unsuitable as a daylight bomber. Thereafter, it was restricted to maritime reconnaissance and antishipping duties, where it functioned capably.

In 1942 the Army requisitioned 200 *Venturas* for use as the B-34 *Lexington*. They were intended as coastal patrol-bombers but were ultimately employed as navigational trainers. However, the Navy acquired 1,600 *Venturas*, which it called PV-1s, for use in the Pacific. As flying boats were too slow and vulnerable to patrol certain areas, faster and more heavily armed PV-1s were employed instead. They could carry a wide assortment of rockets, torpedoes, and depth charges. Many squadrons were stationed on the Aleutian Islands, from where they began raiding the northernmost Japanese islands in 1943. PV-1s also equipped the first Marine Corps night-fighter squadron, VMF (N)–531, in the Solomon Islands. Production ended in May 1944, when a total of 3,350 *Venturas* was built and deployed, mostly by the Navy and Royal Air Force. Most were phased out from active duty after the war, but a handful served with South Africa's navy until the 1970s.

# Lockheed PV-2 *Harpoon*

**Type:** Patrol-Bomber

---

**Dimensions:** wingspan, 74 feet, 11 inches; length, 52 feet; height, 11 feet, 11 inches
**Weights:** empty, 21,028 pounds; gross, 36,000 pounds
**Power plant:** 2 × 2,000–horsepower Pratt & Whitney R-2800 radial engines
**Performance:** maximum speed, 282 miles per hour; ceiling, 23,900 feet; maximum range, 1,790 miles
**Armament:** 7 × .50–caliber machine guns; 6,000 pounds of bombs
**Service dates:** 1945–1948

---

The *Harpoon* was a final attempt to improve upon the tested *Hudson* design. Fuel leaks delayed its appearance until the final months of World War II, but the airplane proved to be a capable craft.

In June 1943 the Navy sought to improve the performance of its existing PV-1 *Ventura* bombers by requesting a new, heavily modified version. Vega, a subsidiary of Lockheed, responded by making the requested changes, although the engines and general configuration of the earlier design remained. It enlarged the wingspan by six feet, thereby increasing fuel capacity and range. To enhance stability, the twin rudders were enlarged, and the improved armament now consisted of up to seven .50-caliber machine guns. More dramatically, the bombardier's position was eliminated in favor of a solid nose. The Navy ordered 500 of the new airplanes, which they named the PV-2 *Harpoon*, accepting deliveries beginning in March 1944. Unfortunately, a persistent problem with leaking wing tanks delayed its opera-

tional deployment for several months. The first 30 aircraft were accordingly withdrawn from service and, once their wing tanks were sealed off, gained employment as trainers. Once the problem was corrected, deliveries of *Harpoons* resumed, and they were deployed as patrol-bombers during the final stages of the Pacific War.

In service, the *Harpoon* registered decreases in operational ceiling and overall speed compared to its predecessor, but it enjoyed commensurate improvements in range and takeoff performance. It was employed only briefly during the final months of the war, becoming a popular and reliable airplane. After the war PV-2s were withdrawn from frontline service, although they equipped 11 Navy Reserve squadrons until 1948. However, *Harpoons* continued serving with the Italian, Japanese, Netherlands, Peruvian, French, and Portuguese navies up through the 1960s, being replaced by Grumman S2F *Trackers*.

# Lockheed S-3 *Viking*

**Type:** Antisubmarine Warfare

**Dimensions:** wingspan, 68 feet, 8 inches; length, 53 feet, 4 inches; height, 22 feet, 9 inches
**Weights:** empty, 26,650 pounds; gross, 52,540 pounds
**Power plant:** 2 × 9,275–pound thrust General Electric TF34 turbofan engines
**Performance:** maximum speed, 506 miles per hour; ceiling, 35,000 feet; maximum range, 2,303 miles
**Armament:** 4 depth charges, bombs, or torpedoes; 2 × AGM-84 *Harpoon* antiship missiles
**Service dates:** 1974–

Compact and stubby, the *Viking* is currently the world's most advanced carrier-based antisubmarine warfare (ASW) aircraft. It is literally packed with ultramodern sensors, sonars, computers, and a variety of weapons.

By 1968 the Navy was seeking a modern ASW aircraft to replace the venerable Grumman S2F *Tracker*. Lockheed won the competition, and in 1972 the prototype XS-3 first flew. It was a high-wing, twin-engine design seating all four crew members in the front of the fuselage. Yet it is so relatively small that the wings literally fold over each other for carrier storage. The prominent rudder is also collapsible. Inside, the craft is crammed with a variety of the latest ASW and avionics technology. No less than 60 sensitive sonobuoys are stored in launch tubes toward the rear of the fuselage. They are wired into a retractable magnetic anomaly detector boom for locating underwater targets. The plane also sports a forward-looking infrared scanner to assist the navigation and search radars. Furthermore, the long bomb bay can carry an assortment of weapons including bombs, nuclear depth charges, homing torpedoes, and mines. Thus arrayed, the new aircraft is not only faster than the old S2F but also has a longer range and is infinitely more sophisticated.

In 1974 the S-3A entered service as the *Viking;* 187 were constructed. The electronics were considered so advanced that the Royal Canadian Navy chose to rig its P-3 *Orions* with the APS-137 radar instead of the arrays normally assigned to that capable craft. A new version, the S-3B, was developed and deployed in 1980. In addition to enhanced electronics, it also has the ability to carry AGM-84 *Harpoon* antiship missiles. During the 1991 Gulf War, *Vikings* flew 1,674 sorties without loss. They will remain the Navy's standard ASW aircraft for the next several decades.

# ★ Lockheed SR-71 *Blackbird*

**Type:** Reconnaissance

**Dimensions:** wingspan, 55 feet, 7 inches; length, 107 feet, 5 inches; height, 18 feet, 6 inches
**Weights:** empty, 60,000 pounds; gross, 172,000 pounds
**Power plant:** 2 × 32,500–pound thrust Pratt & Whitney J58 turbojet engines
**Performance:** maximum speed, 2,300 miles per hour; ceiling, 80,000 feet; maximum range, 3,000 miles
**Armament:** none
**Service dates:** 1964–

The legendary *Blackbird* remains the world's most advanced strategic reconnaissance aircraft. Part jet, part spaceship, it holds several absolute speed and altitude records.

In 1959 the Air Force and Central Intelligence Agency began looking for a follow-on aircraft to Lockheed's successful U-2. This need was underscored in 1960 when Gary Francis Powers was shot down over Russia by a missile. Lockheed's Clarence "Kelly" Johnson proposed building a craft capable of sustained speeds in excess of three times the speed of sound (Mach 3—faster than a bullet!) at altitudes of 80,000 feet. To accomplish this, new generations of metals, engines, and electronics were constructed to withstand the rigors posed by extremely high temperatures. In 1962 the prototype SR-71 was rolled out, marking a revolution in aerodynamic design. It was built mostly of heat-resistant titanium and covered with special black paint to deflect heat away from the craft. The engines—part turbojet,

part ramjet—run on a special kerosene fuel that also absorbs additional heat from the airframe. Despite these precautions, at Mach 3 surface temperatures as high as 1,000 degrees are not uncommon. In fact, the fuselage is designed to stretch 11 inches to allow for metal expansion. This ultrasecret spy plane went into operation in 1964, and at least 30 were constructed and deployed.

Each SR-71 mission is planned with all the precision of a spaceflight, and the two pilots wear astronaut suits while flying. From 80,000 feet, the *Blackbird* can survey 100,000 square miles of the earth's surface with a variety of photographic, radar, and infrared equipment. For 25 years it was sent on routine flights over the Soviet Union and Red China without meeting resistance. In 1991 all SR-71s were retired from service on account of high operating costs and the collapse of the Soviet Union. However, three aircraft were reactivated in 1995 and continue flying reconnaissance missions around the globe.

# ★ Lockheed T-33/T2V *Sea Star*

**Type:** Trainer

**Dimensions:** wingspan, 38 feet, 10 inches; length, 37 feet, 9 inches; height, 11 feet, 7 inches
**Weights:** empty, 8,084 pounds; gross, 12,000 pounds
**Power plant:** 1 × 5,400–pound thrust Allison J33 turbojet engine
**Performance:** maximum speed, 525 miles per hour; ceiling, 47,500 feet; maximum range, 1,275 miles
**Armament:** 2 × .50–caliber machine guns
**Service dates:** 1948–1987

The venerable "Tee-bird" was the world's first jet trainer. Thousands of Air Force and Navy pilots earned their wings flying it during the 1950s, and several countries still operate updated versions.

In 1948 Lockheed undertook a private venture to develop its F-80 *Shooting Star* fighter into a training craft. This was accomplished by extending the fuselage and canopy by three feet to accommodate an extra pilot. The new aircraft retained all the delightfully responsive characteristics of the fighter, and in 1948 it went into production as the T-33. Over the next decade 5,781 were built, which makes it the most-constructed jet in American history. Throughout the 1950s, an entire generation of cadets gained aerial proficiency in the front seat of a T-33.

The Navy, then beginning to experiment with early jets, also expressed an interest in the T-33 and in 1948 accepted 150 machines as the T2V. However,

because of its relatively high landing speed, the craft was judged unsuitable for carrier landings, and Lockheed developed a new version. Christened the T2V-1 *Sea Star*, this model had a higher backseat that resulted in an ungainly hump along the top-rear of the fuselage. It was also equipped with leading- and trailing-edge flaps, for lower landing speeds, and an arrester hook. These modifications had the desired effect, and in 1958 the Navy accepted the first of 700 T2V-1s.

The T-33 enjoyed an equally distinguished service record overseas. It was imported in numbers by France, Greece, Italy, the Philippines, Portugal, Spain, Taiwan, Thailand, Turkey, and West Germany. Canada also produced 210 of a version named the CL-30 *Silver Star*. The last T-33s were retired from the Air National Guard in 1987, although several Latin American countries still operate them as reconnaissance and light attack craft.

# ★ Lockheed U-2/TR-1

**Type:** Reconnaissance

---

**Dimensions:** wingspan, 103 feet; length, 62 feet, 9 inches; height, 16 feet, 1 inch
**Weights:** empty, 14,990 pounds; gross, 41,000 pounds
**Power plant:** 1 × 17,000–pound thrust Pratt & Whitney J75 turbojet engine
**Performance:** maximum speed, 510 miles per hour; ceiling, 90,000 feet; maximum range, 3,500 miles
**Armament:** none
**Service dates:** 1956–

---

Dubbed the "Black Lady of Espionage" by the Russians, the U-2 is the most famous spy plane of all time. This 40-year-old design still provides continuous strategic reconnaissance, day or night, in any weather.

The debut of the Russian hydrogen bomb in 1953 prompted the Air Force and the Central Intelligence Agency to seek dramatically new reconnaissance aircraft, planes able to fly so high that they could escape detection. At Lockheed, it fell upon Clarence "Kelly" Johnson to design such a craft, which first flew in 1955. Basically, the U-2 was a large, jet-propelled glider with a thin fuselage and long, high-lift wings. To save weight, the two landing gear were placed in tandem in the fuselage, and the wingtips sported outrigger wheels that were jettisoned upon takeoff. The aircraft could reach a staggering 80,000 feet, which required the pilot to wear a pressurized spacesuit to survive. However, the U-2 was difficult to fly and nearly impossible to maneuver except in a straight line. Furthermore, its light structure made it highly susceptible to crosswinds and extremely tricky to land. The U-2 nonetheless entered service in 1956 as a closely guarded secret and overflew the Soviet Union for the next four years. However, when a Russian SA-2 missile successfully shot down Gary Francis Powers's U-2 in May 1960, clandestine overflights were assigned to satellites and the forthcoming SR-71 *Blackbird*.

Despite this setback, the U-2 remained an active player in the international intelligence-gathering game. In 1981 the Air Force developed a tactical reconnaissance version for European battlefields called the TR-1. This was basically a U-2 airframe fitted with new and highly advanced avionics in two massive "superpods" set midwing. It is also capable of electronic intelligence and communications intelligence work. At least 32 U-2/TR-1s remain operational to this day under the combined designation U-2R.

**Type:** Air Supremacy Fighter

**Dimensions:** wingspan, 44 feet, 6 inches; length, 62 feet, 1 inch; height, 16 feet, 5 inches
**Weights:** empty, 34,000 pounds; gross, 62,000 pounds
**Power plant:** 2 × 35,000–pound thrust Pratt & Whitney F119 turbofan engines
**Performance:** maximum speed, 1,500 miles per hour; ceiling, 65,000 feet, maximum range, 1,000 miles
**Armament:** 1 × 20mm cannon; 4 × AIM-120 missiles; 2 × AIM-9 *Sidewinder* missiles
**Service dates:** 2005–

The futuristic *Lightning II* will be the standard American fighter during the early 21st century. It is the first military aircraft designed for air dominance and achieves it through a combination of speed and stealth.

No sooner had the superb McDonnell-Douglas F-15 *Eagle* been deployed during the mid-1970s than the Air Force began considering a new advanced tactical fighter (ATF) to replace it. Based upon projections of Soviet technology at the turn of the century, the new ATF would have to combine traditional fighter qualities such as speed and maneuverability with a new quality—stealth—to survive. The specifications were finally issued in 1985, and five years later a competition developed between the Lockheed YF-22 and Northrop's YF-23. The Lockheed design edged out its rival, and the Air Force ordered 339 of the craft, due to become operational in 2005.

The F-22 appears somewhat conventional, but it has been carefully engineered to reduce radar signatures to almost nothing. It is also designed to fly for hours at supersonic speeds without use of a heat-generating afterburner, a condition known as supercruise. Finally, it places great emphasis on being able to outmaneuver enemy aircraft in combat. The F-22 is fitted with engines whose vectoring nozzles can swing 20 degrees up or down to increase turn rates. However, the onboard computers controlling the craft are carefully programmed not to allow the pilot to damage it through excessively violent maneuvers and actually alert him to that fact. Thus, man and machine are closely linked in the quest for total air supremacy over an enemy force.

The F-22 will cost some $80 million per plane and will not be deployed before the year 2005. After that, American control of the skies in wartime will be difficult to challenge.

# Loeing M-8

**Type:** Fighter

**Dimensions:** wingspan, 32 feet, 9 inches; length, 24 feet; height, 6 feet, 7 inches
**Weights:** empty, 1,623 pounds; gross, 2,068 pounds
**Power plant:** 1 × 300–horsepower Hispano-Suiza liquid-cooled engine
**Performance:** maximum speed, 145 miles per hour; ceiling, 22,000 feet; maximum range, 240 miles
**Armament:** 2 × .30–caliber machine guns
**Service dates:** 1918–1922

The M-8 was the first American monoplane fighter to reach production. Performance was excellent, but the prevailing prejudice in favor of biplanes worked against its acceptance.

In 1918 Grover C. Loeing's young company was given the daunting task of creating a two-seat fighter with better performance than the British Bristol F.2B, itself a formidable aircraft. Soon he responded with the M-8, one of the most innovative warplanes to emerge during that period. Instead of a traditional biplane, Loeing's creation was a shoulder-mounted monoplane that sported a number of advanced features. Foremost among these was placement of the drag-producing radiator deep inside the fuselage, which was fed cold air by use of a tunnel beneath the propeller. Furthermore, the conspicuous struts bracing the wings were given airfoil cross-sections, thereby contributing to overall lift. Finally, both pilot and gunner had excellent, unobstructed views of the airspace around them. The prototype exhib-

ited fast speed and good maneuverability, so the Army placed an order for 5,000 machines. However, when World War I concluded several months later, the contracts were summarily canceled.

Fortunately for Loeing, the Navy also expressed interest in his M-8 prototype as a possible submarine-launched fighter. The Navy purchased several examples as M-8-1 *Kittens* and in 1919 authorized the Naval Aircraft Factory to construct 54 machines. They were deployed as observation scouts, and several were also outfitted as twin-float seaplanes. However, the sheer speed of the aircraft could not be ignored, and in 1920 a modified M-8-1 was entered into the Pulitzer Air Race. The craft, piloted by Marine Lieutenant B. G. Bradley, had pulled ahead of the pack and was on the verge of winning when a radiator leak suddenly forced him to abort. Thereafter, a deep-seated military prejudice in favor of less radical biplanes exerted itself, and monoplane designs remained quiescent in America until the mid-1930s.

**Type:** Reconnaissance

**Dimensions:** wingspan, 45 feet; length, 34 feet, 9 inches; height, 12 feet, 9 inches
**Weights:** empty, 3,649 pounds; gross, 5,404 pounds
**Power plant:** 1 × 450–horsepower Pratt & Whitney R-1340 radial engine
**Performance:** maximum speed, 122 miles per hour; ceiling, 14,300 feet; maximum range, 625 miles
**Armament:** none
**Service dates:** 1923–1937

By melding the features of land planes to seaplanes, the "Flying Shoehorn" introduced a number of innovations to aviation. It was also the first aircraft acquired by the U.S. Coast Guard.

Following the successful debut of his M-8 monoplane fighter, Grover C. Loeing returned to a consuming passion—the flying boat. In 1923 he offered the Navy a new amphibian design based upon his civilian luxury "Air Yacht." The craft employed what the designer called a "unitary hull," whereby a large pontoon was directly merged into the aircraft's fuselage. This arrangement greatly reduced the drag associated with more conventional floats and struts. A set of functioning, hand-cranked retractable wheels was also employed, which made the aircraft a true amphibian. However, based on his earlier experience with military bureaucracies, Loeing deliberately designed it as a biplane to placate conservative-minded critics. The prototype flew extremely well, and in 1923 the Army ordered several OA-1s and subsequent models as they were produced. The

Navy also looked favorably upon the new design and purchased more than 100 examples as the OL. In 1926 three OL-5s became the first aircraft acquired by the U.S. Coast Guard. The final variant, the OL-9, was fitted with a high-powered radial engine.

Despite its frail appearance, the OA/OL series was robust and extremely functional. In 1925 three Navy OL-2s, borrowed from the Army, accompanied the 1925 summer expedition to the Arctic. Braving horrific flying conditions, they successfully surveyed 30,000 square miles of Greenland without mishap. Between December 1926 and May 1927, five Army OA-1s, named *New York*, *San Antonio*, *San Francisco*, *Detroit*, and *St. Louis*, were dispatched on a goodwill tour of South America. Two OA-1s were lost in a collision over Buenos Aires, but the survivors returned intact, having covered 22,000 miles. The *San Francisco* is preserved at the National Air and Space Museum, Smithsonian Institute. After 1936 the Loeing amphibians were slowly superseded by the Grumman JF-1 *Duck*.

# ❂ Martin A-22 *Maryland*

**Type:** Light Bomber

---

**Dimensions:** wingspan, 61 feet, 4 inches; length, 46 feet, 8 inches; height, 14 feet, 11 inches
**Weights:** empty, 11,213 pounds; gross, 16,809 pounds
**Power plant:** 2 × 1,000–horesepower Pratt & Whitney Twin Wasp R-1830 radial engines
**Performance:** maximum speed, 304 miles per hour; ceiling, 29,500 feet; maximum range, 1,300 miles
**Armament:** 6 × .303–inch machine guns; 2,000 pounds of bombs
**Service dates:** 1940–1944

The *Maryland* was an excellent light reconnaissance bomber designed for the export market. It enjoys the dubious distinction of having served on both sides during World War II.

The Martin Model 167 was built for a 1938 Army Air Corps competition for a new light bomber. The prototype was a low-wing, streamlined affair sporting an exceptionally narrow fuselage. It first flew in February 1939 and exhibited excellent low-altitude performance, but the contract went to Douglas and its A-20 *Havoc*. Seeking to recoup its losses, Martin turned to the export market and found a willing partner in France, then eager to bolster its aging bomber fleet with more modern weapons. A contract for 115 machines was signed, followed by orders for an additional 100 Model 167s that October. By the time of the German invasion of France in May 1940, the French Armée de l'Air possessed 140 Model 167s, which sustained the lowest loss rate of any French bomber. After the country

was overrun, several of the surviving aircraft continued to serve with the Vichy French regime; the British Royal Air Force picked up the balance of the undelivered aircraft.

In British service the aircraft became known as the *Maryland I*, and it was exclusively used as a reconnaissance bomber at Malta and throughout the Western Desert. Ultimately, two British and four South African squadrons employed the craft for several years, often against Vichy machines operating out of Morocco and Syria. It was a *Maryland* that did the preliminary scouting work over the Italian fleet at Taranto prior to the devastating British raid of November 1940. In combat the *Maryland* proved fast, strong, and very reliable, but it was no match for modern fighters. By 1943 it was replaced in front-line service by the newer Martin *Baltimore* bombers and spent the remainder of the war as a target tow and long-range reconnaissance craft. A total of 400 was constructed.

**Type:** Light Bomber

**Dimensions:** wingspan, 61 feet, 4 inches; length, 48 feet, 5 inches; height, 17 feet, 9 inches
**Weights:** empty, 15,460 pounds; gross, 22,600 pounds
**Power plant:** 2 × 1,660–horsepower Wright Cyclone GR-2600 radial engines
**Performance:** maximum speed, 325 miles per hour; ceiling, 23,300 feet; maximum range, 1,082 miles
**Armament:** 8 × .303–inch machine guns; 2,000 pounds of bombs
**Service dates:** 1941–1945

The *Baltimore* was another fine aircraft that never saw service with U.S. forces. It was employed exclusively by the British in North Africa and Italy with good results.

In 1940 the British Purchasing Commission sought additional light bombers and approached Martin for an improved version of its Model 167 *Maryland.* The new Model 187 was similar in appearance to its predecessor but possessed a greatly deepened fuselage; a pointed, glazed nose; and four crew members. It was also equipped with self-sealing fuel tanks and 211 pounds of armor for the crew. The prototype first flew in June 1941, whereupon the Royal Air Force (RAF) placed an order for 400 aircraft, pronouncing it the *Baltimore.* For export purposes the Army Air Force designated it the A-30, although it would never serve with American forces.

Commencing in January 1942 the *Baltimore* was committed to action in North Africa. It performed sterling service during the El Alamein and Italian campaigns despite suffering heavy losses for want of fighter escorts. Otherwise, the craft proved itself to be a fast and well-constructed airplane capable of bombing, close support, reconnaissance, and a host of other functions. Ultimately, many squadrons—ten British, three South African, two Australian, one Greek, and one Free French—were equipped with the *Baltimore.* By 1944 the type was being phased out of frontline service in favor of the B-26 *Marauder,* and many *Baltimores* ended up in the hands of the newly authorized Co-Belligerent Italian Air Force. They rendered additional service in the Balkans. A total of 71 was also transferred to Turkey in an attempt to induce that country to join the Allies. After the war, several *Baltimores* ended up with an RAF squadron in Kenya, where they spent their final years combating locusts. A total of 1,575 was constructed.

# Martin AM-1 *Mauler*

**Type:** Torpedo-Bomber/Dive-Bomber

**Dimensions:** wingspan, 50 feet; length, 41 feet, 2 inches; height, 16 feet, 10 inches
**Weights:** empty, 14,500 pounds; gross, 23,386 pounds
**Power plant:** 1 × 2,975–horsepower Pratt & Whitney R-3350 Cyclone radial engine
**Performance:** maximum speed, 367 miles per hour; ceiling, 30,500 feet; maximum range, 1,800 miles
**Armament:** 4 × 20mm cannons; 4,500 pounds of bombs, rockets, or torpedoes
**Service dates:** 1948–1953

The powerful, impressive *Mauler* set several lifting records but was difficult to fly and maintain. Too big for its own good, it enjoyed only a brief, undistinguished service life.

Midway through World War II the Navy optimized its combat experience with aircraft by combining dive-bombers and torpedo planes into a single-seat design. It decided that a fast machine could dispense with defensive armaments and rely solely upon speed to escape. A heavy weapons load was also required, externally mounted so as not to restrict the types of ordnance carried. Martin responded to the competition in August 1944 with the XBTM-1, a large, low-wing monoplane built around the largest engine then available, the 28-cylinder Pratt & Whitney XR-4360. The Navy requested 750 machines in January 1945, but the end of the war meant only 150 were purchased. Because of the craft's sheer size and bulk, it was deemed necessary to install a complicated hy-draulics-assisted system to help the pilot fly. Additional work was also required to modify the propeller spinner, wing dihedral, and rudder. After continuous testing, the aircraft was redesignated the AM-1 and entered service as the *Mauler* in 1948.

The AM-1 was an impressive lifting platform, and in April 1949 a *Mauler* established a payload record of 10,648 pounds by lifting three torpedoes, 12 bombs, and 800 rounds of ammunition. However, its very size made it poorly situated for carrier operations, and pilots referred to it as the "Awful Monster." All had been assigned to Naval Reserve squadrons. For a brief time, the Navy also operated a number of AM-1Qs, which were rigged for electronic warfare and carried a radar operator in a compartment behind the pilot. All AM-1s were finally retired in 1953 so that the Navy could concentrate on production of the smaller and more manageable Douglas AD *Skyraider*.

**Type:** Light Bomber

**Dimensions:** wingspan, 70 feet, 6 inches; length, 44 feet, 9 inches; height, 15 feet, 5 inches
**Weights:** empty, 9,681 pounds; gross, 16,400 pounds
**Power plant:** 2 × 775–horsepower Wright Cyclone R-1820 engines
**Performance:** maximum speed, 213 miles per hour; ceiling, 24,400 feet; maximum range, 1,240 miles
**Armament:** 3 × .30–caliber machine guns; 2,260 pounds of bombs
**Service dates:** 1933–1940

The B-10 was the first modern bomber and the first American aircraft equipped with a gun turret. A revolutionary design, it flew faster than contemporary fighters.

In 1930 Martin undertook a privately funded venture to build an advanced bomber for the Army. The prototype Model 123 emerged in 1932 as a sleek design with open cockpits, and it achieved an impressive speed of 197 miles per hour. However, Martin decided that the craft could be further modified, and a greatly altered prototype was tested again the following year. The new design was no less than revolutionary in outlook and performance. It was an all-metal, midwing monoplane with retractable landing gear, enclosed cockpits, variable propellers, and an internal bomb bay. Furthermore, it was defended by a powered nose turret, a first for an American bomber. During testing, the Model 123 reached 206 miles per hour, outpacing biplane bombers and fighters alike. The Army was delighted with the new

craft, and in 1933 it entered production as the B-10. Ultimately, 152 were built in versions that differed only in the engines mounted. B-10s rendered excellent service through the late 1930s, when they were replaced by even more advanced Boeing B-17s and Douglas B-18s.

As an indication of the Army Air Corps's faith in the B-10, in 1934 Colonel Henry "Hap" Arnold led ten on a round-trip from Washington, D.C., to Fairbanks, Alaska, and back. His 7,360-mile flight was almost flawless and demonstrated the practicality of strategic bombing.

Not surprisingly, this high-performance aircraft was successfully exported abroad. No less than 190 were sold to Argentina, China, Siam, and the Dutch East Indies. By the beginning of World War II, most surviving American B-10s were employed as target tows. However, Dutch B-10s fought actively in the defense of the East Indies, sustaining heavy losses from Japanese fighters.

# ☆ Martin B-26 *Marauder*

**Type:** Medium Bomber

**Dimensions:** wingspan, 71 feet; length, 58 feet, 6 inches; height, 20 feet, 3 inches
**Weights:** empty, 24,000 pounds; gross, 37,000 pounds
**Power plant:** 2 × 2,000–horsepower Pratt & Whitney R-2800 radial engines
**Performance:** maximum speed, 285 miles per hour; ceiling, 19,800 feet; maximum range, 1,100 miles
**Armament:** up to 12 × .50–caliber machine guns; 4,000 pounds of bombs
**Service dates:** 1941–1946

Despite its early reputation as a "widowmaker," the B-26 suffered the lowest loss ratio of any American bomber in World War II. It was also the only Army aircraft rigged to drop torpedoes.

In 1939 the Martin Company responded to the Army's medium-bomber competition with its Model 179. The military was so impressed that it ordered 201 B-26s off the drawing board without a prototype being built. Martin selected a high-speed design and the resulting aircraft, delivered in 1941, was simultaneously rotund but sleek. However, it was a "hot," unforgiving plane to handle for inexperienced pilots. Several training accidents occurred, owing to the B-26's high landing speed; the plane acquired an unsavory reputation as a killer. In 1942 six feet of wingspan were added in an attempt to improve landing characteristics, and the *Marauders*, so named by the British, went on to a distinguished career.

In spring 1942 the B-26 was among the first American medium bombers committed to combat, being deployed in Australia. In combat over New Guinea it proved to be a rugged and fast attack craft. Outfitted with torpedo racks, four B-26s took part in the Battle of Midway. However, by fall 1942 the *Marauders* had been withdrawn to Europe in favor of the more easily maintained B-25 *Mitchell*. For the rest of the war B-26 units staged numerous low-level raids over heavily defended German positions and took surprisingly few casualties to flak and enemy fighters. The craft was also successfully employed by the Royal Air Force and South African Air Force with similar results. By war's end, 5,157 of the speedy *Marauders* had been built, with an additional 272 serving in the Navy as JM target tugs. This outstanding bomber was declared surplus and removed from operational status in 1946.

**Type:** Light Bomber

**Dimensions:** wingspan, 64 feet; length, 65 feet, 6 inches; height, 15 feet, 7 inches
**Weights:** empty, 49,000 pounds; gross, 55,000 pounds
**Power plant:** 2 × 7,200–pound thrust Wright J65 turbojet engines
**Performance:** maximum speed, 580 miles per hour; ceiling, 45,000 feet; range, 2,300 miles
**Armament:** 4 × 20mm cannons or 4 × .50–caliber machine guns; 6,000 pounds of bombs or rockets
**Service dates:** 1953–1982

The *Intruder* was one of few European aircraft adopted by the U.S. Air Force following World War II. It began as a tactical bomber but was developed into a high-altitude reconnaissance craft.

During the Korean War, the Air Force wanted to replace its aging fleet of B-26 *Invaders* with a jet-powered tactical bomber. As it was deemed impractical to transform the North American B-45 *Tornado* for this purpose, the Air Force turned to a promising British design. In 1951 two English Electric *Canberra* bombers arrived at Baltimore, Maryland, for evaluation. The *Canberra* was a two-engine, midwing design that sat very low to the ground and exhibited excellent speed and maneuverability. Air Force representatives decided to manufacture it under license, and in 1953 the first B-57A *Intruder* was deployed. Externally, it looked identical to the British version, especially with the bowl canopy. However, the next model,

the B-57B, had a standard teardrop canopy with tandem seating, along with rotary bomb-bay doors and hardpoints on the wings for additional ordnance. They served exclusively with the Tactical Air Command.

Because the *Intruder* exhibited excellent high-altitude performance, it was decided to develop a reconnaissance version for the Strategic Air Command. That plane, the RB-57D, retained the standard *Intruder* fuselage but had outsized wings extending to 106 feet. A subsequent model, the RB-57F, carried the practice to extremes by mounting a broadened, 120-foot wing with oversized engine nacelles; it could reportedly operate at 90,000 feet. A final variant, the B-57G, was a night attack bomber that saw extensive service during the Vietnam War. *Intruders* were finally released from frontline duty in 1974; they flew with Air National Guard units until 1982. A total of 403 had been produced.

**Type:** Dive-Bomber

**Dimensions:** wingspan, 41 feet; length, 28 feet, 9 inches; height, 12 feet, 4 inches
**Weights:** empty, 3,662 pounds; gross, 6,218 pounds
**Power plant:** 1 × 625–horsepower Pratt & Whitney R-1690 radial engine
**Performance:** maximum speed, 146 miles per hour; ceiling, 16,800 feet; maximum range, 413 miles
**Armament:** 2 × .30–caliber machine guns; 1 × 1,000–pound bomb
**Service dates:** 1932–1938

The BM was the Navy's first purposely designed dive-bomber. Though produced in limited quantities, it successfully demonstrated the viability of the new aerial tactic of dive-bombing.

In 1926 fliers from the Navy and Marine Corps began to experiment with dive-bombing tactics against rebels in Nicaragua. Results were encouraging, because in dive-bombing the pilot aims the bomb, thereby dispensing with a need for bombardiers. However, the airplanes employed for this tactic were structurally weak and less than satisfactory. Consequently, in 1928 the Naval Bureau of Aeronautics announced competition for its first official dive-bomber. Specifications were stringent: The new design was not only required to carry a 1,000-pound bomb but also had to survive the stress of a 6,000-foot dive and pull up with the bomb still attached! At length the Naval Aircraft Factory and Martin put forth competing designs, and in 1930 Martin's Model 125 was declared the winner. The new craft was a traditional biplane in appearance but was unique in possessing an all-metal fuselage. The wing was also made of metal, with the top being slightly swept back and covered with fabric. Pilot and gunner sat tandem in open cockpits. In 1931 this design was accepted into service as the BM-1, and 17 were manufactured. Initial models were equipped with racy-looking cowls and wheel spats, but these features were eventually deleted.

Dive-bombing was dangerous work, and the BM-1, though adept, sustained its share of accidents. In an attempt to improve the basic design, Martin strengthened parts of the wings and fuselage and called the new plane the BM-2. The Navy subsequently purchased 17 of these craft, which served alongside BM-1s on the carrier USS *Lexington* as part of Torpedo Squadron One. Soon thereafter, this unit was revised as the famous Bombing Squadron VB-1. Martin dive-bombers functioned well for several years until being gradually replaced by more modern Vought SB2U *Vindicators* in 1938.

**Type:** Transport

**Dimensions:** wingspan, 200 feet; length, 117 feet, 3 inches; height, 38 feet, 5 inches
**Weights:** empty, 75,373 pounds; gross; 165,000 pounds
**Power plant:** 4 × 2,200–horsepower Wright Duplex Cyclone R-3350 radial engines
**Performance:** maximum speed, 221 miles per hour; ceiling, 14,600 feet; maximum range, 4,945 miles
**Armament:** none
**Service dates:** 1943–1956

The *Mars* was the largest military flying boat operated by the U.S. Navy. It served with distinction for 13 years, setting many range and payload records.

Martin developed its giant Model 170 to meet a 1938 Navy specification for a long-range patrol-bomber. The prototype, designated XPB2M, boasted a 200-foot wingspan, 2 miles of internal piping, and 7.5 miles of wiring. It was unveiled as the world's largest flying boat and first flew in July 1943. On its first actual trial flight in December 1943, the "Old Lady" carried 13,000 pounds of cargo from Patuxent River Naval Air Station, Maryland, to Natal, Brazil—a distance of 4,375 miles. Early the following year, it carried a 20,500-pound load 4,700 miles from California to Hawaii. By the time the "Old Lady" was retired in March 1945, it had transported 3 million pounds of cargo throughout the Pacific without mishap. The Navy was sufficiently impressed to

order 20 additional machines, but by that time the aircraft's mission had been changed from patrol-bomber to transport.

By war's end only five JRM-1 and one JRM-2 *Mars* flying boats had been completed, and the remainder was canceled. These planes differed from the prototype in sporting a single tailfin, for greater stability, and more powerful engines. One craft, the *Caroline Mars*, crashed only two weeks after being delivered, but the remaining five plied the important cargo routes of the Pacific with Navy Transport Squadron VR-2. A second JRM, the *Marshall Mars*, was lost to fire in April 1950, but the four surviving machines rendered distinguished service until retirement in 1956. It is estimated that the *Mars* transported some 200,000 passengers more than 12 million miles. In July 1959 they were sold to Canada as fire-fighting aircraft and were outfitted with tanks that could hold 7,000 gallons of water. Two of these craft are still in service.

**Type:** Heavy Bomber

---

**Dimensions:** wingspan, 74 feet; length, 42 feet, 8 inches; height, 14 feet, 8 inches
**Weights:** empty, 7,269 pounds; gross, 12,064 pounds
**Power plant:** 2 × 420–horsepower Liberty 18A liquid-cooled engines
**Performance:** maximum speed, 99 miles per hour; ceiling, 8,500 feet; maximum range, 558 miles
**Armament:** 4 × .30–caliber machine guns; 3,000 pounds of bombs
**Service dates:** 1920–1928

The MB was America's first heavy bomber and became famous thanks to the exploits of General William "Billy" Mitchell. Together with the successful Keystone series, it formed the backbone of Army Air Corps bombardment strength throughout the 1920s.

In 1917 Glenn L. Martin started his aircraft company in Cleveland, Ohio. The following year, the government invited him to design a heavy bombardment craft superior to the British-designed Handley-Page 0/400. Martin came up with the MB-1, which for its time was an excellent bombing platform. It enjoyed a conventional biplane layout with straight, unstaggered wings, but it was also very fast and long-ranged. Testing began in August 1918, and the Army ordered 22 as the MB-1; the Navy and Marine Corps received several MBT-1s as torpedo-bombers. World War I ended soon thereafter, and thus the MB-1 never entered operational service. However, by 1920 the government expressed interest in an improved version, and Martin soon rolled out the MB-2. It featured longer wings, fewer landing gear, and stronger engines mounted on the lower wing. Because the new craft was intended as a night bomber, the speed and range of the MB-1 were sacrificed for greater bomb loads. During the next few years the Army acquired 120 examples as the NBS-1.

Martin bombers formed the core of American bombardment aviation until 1925, when they were joined by the Keystone series. However, in 1921 the MBs gained lasting fame as part of Billy Mitchell's bombing demonstrations off the Virginia Capes. Mitchell felt that airpower had made Navy ships vulnerable to attack, and in a carefully staged demonstration his bombers sank several surplus warships. Among them was the captured German battleship *Ostfriesland*, alleged to be unsinkable. Hence, Mitchell proved beyond all doubt the utility of large bombing aircraft. The remainder of the MB's career was less spectacular, and they were finally replaced by Keystones and Curtiss B-2 *Condors* in 1928.

**Type:** Reconnaissance

**Dimensions:** wingspan, 53 feet, 1 inch; length, 38 feet, 1 inch; height, 12 feet, 11 inches
**Weights:** empty, 3,526 pounds; gross, 4,642 pounds
**Power plant:** 1 × 435–horsepower Curtiss D-12 liquid-cooled engine
**Performance:** maximum speed, 104 miles per hour; ceiling, 10,000 feet; range, 482 miles
**Armament:** 1 × .30–caliber machine gun
**Service dates:** 1924–1926

In contrast with the splendid MB-1 heavy bomber, Martin's MO-1 was a conspicuous failure. This was less the company's fault than it was the Navy's insistence on unrealistic specifications.

By the end of World War I most American capital ships (e.g., battleships and cruisers) had become equipped with a pair of floatplanes for observation purposes. Typically, these planes would be shot off the stern using steam-driven catapults and then hauled aboard by crane. In 1921 the Navy Bureau of Aeronautics had been established to provide new aircraft for the fleet, as well as to help advance the state of the art. One of its first quests was for an all-metal, three-seat "spotter" plane that could be launched at sea. The following year, Martin issued a design plan for the Model 57, which appeared to approximate what the Navy wanted. It was a high-wing monoplane constructed entirely of metal and powered by the new Curtiss D-12 engine. Impetus for the

design came from Dr. George H. Nadelung, formerly of the German firm Junkers, who had designed similar land planes during World War I. The new craft sported an all-metal fuselage and wings of aluminum alloy. Wood was only employed in the engine mount to help absorb vibrations. With some satisfaction, the Bureau of Aeronautics contracted with Martin to build 36 examples, and in 1924 they entered service as the MO-1.

Unfortunately, the MO-1, though promising, far outstripped the technology of its day to meet expectations. Heavy and underpowered, it was even more sluggish when fitted with two large pontoons for water operations. Moreover, the early generation of steam catapults lacked the power to successfully launch such a hefty craft at sea, so MO-1s were fitted with wheels and restricted to shore stations. After several months of mediocre service, the ungainly aircraft were finally replaced by better machines in 1926.

# Martin P4M *Mercator*

**Type:** Patrol-Bomber

---

**Dimensions:** wingspan, 114 feet; length, 85 feet, 3 inches; height, 29 feet, 9 inches
**Weights:** empty, 43,240 pounds; gross, 83,378 pounds
**Power plant:** 2 × 3,250–horsepower Pratt & Whitney R-4360 Wasp Major radial engines;
  2 × 4,600–pound thrust Allison J33 turbojet engines
**Performance:** maximum speed, 411 miles per hour; ceiling, 36,000 feet; maximum range, 3,100 miles
**Armament:** 2 × .50–caliber machine guns; 4 × 20mm cannons; 16,000 pounds of bombs
**Service dates:** 1950–1960

---

The *Mercator* was one of the first aircraft to incorporate piston- and jet-engine technology into a single design. A large and complicated machine, it served principally as a spy plane.

The advent of jet propulsion during World War II prompted the Navy to meld it to a piston-engine craft for increased speed. In 1944 it approached Martin to design a hybrid patrol-bomber and thus was born the XP4M. It was a large, midwing aircraft displaying extremely handsome lines. The bulged canopy was ahead of its time and afforded an excellent side and bottom visibility for a bomber. Moreover, each of the two nacelles housed a regular piston engine and a jet engine below and behind it. After a prolonged development period, the first prototype flew in 1946. It was one-third larger than its closest competitor, the Lockheed P2V *Neptune*, and nearly 100 miles per hour faster with the jets engaged. How-ever, the *Neptune* was a cheaper, less complicated craft, and the Navy chose it as a regular patrol plane. Nevertheless, in 1949 18 P4Ms were ordered; they became operational the following year as the *Mercator*.

The only squadron to operate P4Ms was Patrol Squadron VP-21, based at Patuxent River, Maryland. They performed routine service until 1953, when most aircraft were modified as P4M-1Q ELINT (electronic intelligence) aircraft. Heavily loaded with secret sensing devices, the *Mercators* skirted the borders of the Soviet Union, eavesdropping on radar and radio signals. This duty was attended by considerable hazard, and in August 1956 a P4M was shot down with the loss of 14 crew members near Wenchow, China. Similar close calls were also recorded in the Balkans. With better spy planes available by the end of the decade, the P4Ms were finally retired from service in 1960.

**Type:** Patrol-Bomber

**Dimensions:** wingspan, 118 feet, 2 inches; length, 101 feet, 1 inch; height, 32 feet, 8 inches
**Weights:** empty, 50,485 pounds; gross, 85,000 pounds
**Power plant:** 2 × 3,700–horsepower Wright R-3350 radial engines
**Performance:** maximum speed, 251 miles per hour; ceiling, 24,000 feet; maximum range, 3,600 miles
**Armament:** 2 × 20mm cannons; 8,000 pounds of bombs or depth charges
**Service dates:** 1952–1967

The *Marlin* was the last in a long line of flying boats. Its retirement concluded five decades of continuous seaplane operations by the Navy.

In 1944 Martin proposed to the Navy that it redesign the already successful PBM *Mariner* flying boat. Permission was granted, and in 1948 the XP5M-1 first flew. The new craft employed the same wing as its predecessor but enjoyed a totally lengthened, redesigned hull and a mammoth single tail. The prototype was also heavily armed with nose and tail turrets sporting two 20mm cannons. On production models the nose turret was deleted in favor of a powerful APS-80 search radar housed in what became the characteristic nose dome. These machines were also equipped with a magnetic anomaly detector for antisubmarine warfare, along with "Julie and Jezebel" droppable sonobuoys. In 1949 the Navy ordered 167 P5M-1s, and in 1952 they entered service as the *Marlin*.

In 1954 the Navy ordered an additional 119 P5M-2s, which differed from earlier versions by having a distinct, high-set "T" tail and a lower hull line to deflect water from the engines upon landing. The Coast Guard acquired seven *Marlins* for search-and-rescue work, but it found the craft too difficult and expensive to operate, and they were returned. In 1959 the French Navy also operated 12 P5Ms under a lend-lease program for a period of five years. Commencing in 1964, three squadrons of *Marlins* patrolled North Vietnam's Gulf of Tonkin while serviced by tenders anchored in Camh Ranh Bay. They were occasionally employed in attacking small surface vessels but otherwise saw little combat. That same year, a P5M was fitted with a jet engine in the tail to boost performance, but the scheme was not adopted. A *Marlin* concluded the last flight of a Navy flying boat on November 6, 1967, whereupon the remainder were laid up and sold for scrap. A total of 287 had been constructed.

# ☆ Martin P6M *Seamaster*

**Type:** Flying Patrol Boat

---

**Dimensions:** wingspan, 102 feet, 7 inches; length, 134 feet, 4 inches; height, 31 feet
**Weights:** empty, 84,000 pounds; gross, 160,000 pounds
**Power plant:** 4 × 15,800–pound thrust Allison J75 turbojet engines
**Performance:** maximum speed, 646 miles per hour; ceiling, 43,900 feet; maximum range, 1,600 miles
**Armament:** 2 × 20mm cannons; 30,000 pounds of bombs or mines
**Service dates:** 1959

---

The radical and short-lived *Seamaster* was the most sophisticated flying boat ever conceived. It had the performance of a land-based bomber and could be refueled and rearmed at sea.

During the early 1950s the Navy decided to apply jet technology to the concept of patrol planes. It wanted a craft that was fast and amphibious and could deploy mines. In 1952 Martin beat out Convair with its Model 275 and was authorized to construct two prototypes. They emerged in 1955 as large, swept-wing craft with a long hull and a high "T" tail. They were powered by four jet engines placed on the top of the wings and canted outward. The main wing also featured a pronounced drooping dihedral with fixed wingtip floats. To deliver ordnance, a watertight rotary bomb bay was fitted on the midbottom of the fuselage. The XP6M-1s first flew in 1955 with surprisingly good results both in water and air. However,

both prototypes crashed soon after, and an extensive redesign of control mechanisms was undertaken. The additional delay only added to expenses, and in 1958 the Navy was forced to restrict its purchase to only 24 aircraft.

At the time of its debut, the P6M *Seamaster* was one of the world's most advanced and capable aircraft. Fast and strong, it rivaled Boeing's famous B-52 *Stratofortress* in overall performance. During wartime the Navy intended to deploy them individually or in small groups for mining and reconnaissance purposes. Landing at sea, they could be refueled and rearmed by submarines in open ocean! Because the long development period greatly increased overall costs, the Navy opted for only six preproduction YP6Ms and three P6M-2s in a single squadron. However, the era of the flying boat had passed, and by August 1959 the costly, complicated *Seamasters* were scrapped.

**Type:** Patrol-Bomber

**Dimensions:** wingspan, 118 feet; length, 79 feet, 10 inches; height, 27 feet, 6 inches
**Weights:** empty, 33,175 pounds; gross, 58,000 pounds
**Power plant:** 2 × 1,900–horsepower Wright Cyclone R-2600 radial engines
**Performance:** maximum speed, 211 miles per hour; ceiling, 19,800 feet; maximum range, 2,240 miles
**Armament:** 8 × .50–caliber machine guns; 8,000 pounds of bombs or depth charges
**Service dates:** 1940–1956

The *Mariner* was the second-most important American flying boat of World War II, even though it offered better performance than the older PBY *Catalina*.

In 1937 Martin designed its Model 162 to compete with the successful Consolidated PBY *Catalina*. The new craft was envisioned as a deep-hull, high–gull wing design with retractable floats and numerous gun turrets for defense. The two nacelles housing the engines were elongated to accommodate a supply of bombs or depth charges. The Navy expressed interest in the proposal and ordered 20 machines for evaluation. Martin's design was also unique in possessing twin rudders with a pronounced dihedral. The prototype first flew in 1939, and the balance was delivered and in service as PBM *Mariners* when the United States entered World War II. The Martin boats proved to be fast, rugged, and seaworthy, so the Navy placed continual orders for more.

The first PBMs could carry twice as much ordnance as the PBY and possessed twice the range, and Martin continually refined them as the war progressed. Later models featured strut-braced stabilizing floats; one variant, the PBM-3C, was an unarmed transport that could carry 20 passengers. The next version, the PBM-3D, introduced a large radar dome behind the canopy to help find submarines and surface vessels. The final wartime version, the PBM-S, was designed specifically for antisubmarine duty. It featured fewer guns and armor but greater fuel capacity for extended range.

By the time production ceased in April 1949, a total of 1,366 aircraft had been manufactured and deployed. The PBM was actively employed during the Korean War but was finally phased out of service in 1956 by the larger P5M *Marlin*. It served other navies around the world through the 1960s.

**Type:** Patrol-Bomber

**Dimensions:** wingspan, 72 feet, 10 inches; length, 49 feet, 3 inches; height, 16 feet, 4 inches
**Weights:** empty, 8,680 pounds; gross, 15,835 pounds
**Power plant:** 2 × 575–horsepower Wright Cyclone R-1820 radial engines
**Performance:** maximum speed, 120 miles per hour; ceiling, 9,600 feet; maximum range, 1,240 miles
**Armament:** 4 × .30–caliber machine guns; 4 × 230–pound bombs
**Service dates:** 1930–1938

The PM-1 was Martin's first flying boat and yet the latest variation of the PN-12. Slow but solid, it gave an excellent account of itself during a relatively short service life.

When the United States entered World War I, the Navy possessed only six flying boats. Within 18 months the number swelled to 1,172, mostly Curtiss H-16s, F-5Ls, and HS-2Ls. They were fine, wood-hull machines, but in the budget-cutting that followed, the Navy received little funding to replace them. Consequently, they served long past their expected replacement dates. By 1929 only a handful were still in service, so the Navy began seeking bids to produce the excellent Naval Aircraft Factory PN-12. The first contract was awarded to Douglas to build PD-1s, but when Martin managed to underbid Douglas, it was authorized to build 27 machines as PM-1s.

The new PM-1 was essentially a variation of the PN-12, a metal-hull, radial-engine craft with ex-cellent endurance. However, Martin engineers decided to increase the armament to four machine guns. And despite high rudder forces, they also elected to keep the original tail unit with its aero-dynamically balanced rudder. By August 1930 the first few PM-1s were operating with Patrol Squadron VP-8S. In 1931 Martin edged out the competition for a second contract to construct an additional 25 PM-2s. They were similar to the earlier version but differed in possessing a new twin-rudder system. Moreover, they were powered by new Wright Cyclone R-1820 radial engines and possessed new fuel tanks that stretched across the hull. During flight, crew members were now required to crawl along the top of the fuselage while moving between forward and aft compartments! After rendering useful service, the Martin boats were all replaced by more modern Consolidated P2Ys and PBYs in 1938.

**Type:** Torpedo-Bomber

**Dimensions:** wingspan, 56 feet, 6 inches; length, 37 feet, 8 inches; height, 14 feet, 8 inches
**Weights:** empty, 5,007 pounds; gross, 8,422 pounds
**Power plant:** 1 × 585–horsepower Wright T-3 radial engine
**Performance:** maximum speed, 103 miles per hour; ceiling, 8,000 feet; maximum range, 1,018 miles
**Armament:** 1 × 1,618–pound torpedo
**Service dates:** 1924–1928

The SC was designed by the Navy, assembled by Curtiss, and mass-produced by Martin. Like most planes in its class, it was ponderous and slow—but effective.

During the early 1920s, as the Navy gathered more experience in operating aircraft, it began placing a higher priority on torpedo-bombers. By 1922 it was looking to replace the Douglas DT, and the Naval Aircraft Factory (NAF) came up with a new design. Like most planes in its class, the NAF model was large and possessed straight, unstaggered wings, although the lower wing was somewhat longer than the upper one. Power was provided by a liquid-cooled Wright T-3 engine, and the lengthy fuselage held a three-member crew (a pilot and gunner in open cockpits, a bombardier/radio operator buried beneath). And like most aircraft of this period, it could alternately be fitted with wheels or floats. Armament consisted of a single torpedo slung underneath the fuselage. When bids for actual construction went out, they were won by Curtiss, which went on to build six machines under the designation CS-1. They were followed by two examples of an improved version, the CS-2, which featured greater fuel capacity. Throughout 1923 the Navy extensively tested these multirole craft as scouts, bombers, and torpedo planes—and liked the results. However, when Martin managed to underbid Curtiss, it received authority to construct 35 aircraft.

The production models were subsequently renamed SC-1s and were virtually identical to the Curtiss machine. They entered into service in 1924, and the following year Martin fitted a new engine to the craft to produce the SC-2; a total of 40 was acquired. The SCs served with Torpedo Squadrons VT-1 and VT-2 and Scout Squadron VS-1 by 1925, but two years later all SCs were replaced by the newer, more capable Martin T3M.

**Type:** Torpedo-Bomber

**Dimensions:** wingspan, 53 feet; length, 35 feet, 7 inches; height, 14 feet, 9 inches
**Weights:** empty, 3,931 pounds; gross, 8,071 pounds
**Power plant:** 1 × 525–horsepower Pratt & Whitney R-1690 radial engine
**Performance:** maximum speed, 114 miles per hour; ceiling, 10,150 feet; maximum range, 363 miles
**Armament:** 1 × .30–caliber machine gun; 1 × 1,800–pound torpedo
**Service dates:** 1926–1937

The T3M and its successors were some of the largest single-engine aircraft to operate from carriers. Slow and underpowered, they served capably before being replaced by modern monoplane designs.

By 1924 Martin's experience in building the Curtiss-designed CS-1 prompted it to offer an improved version to the Navy. A contract was signed, and in 1925 the new XT3M emerged. It was superficially similar to the earlier design but sat pilot and bombardier side by side in a cockpit well forward of the wings. The gunner was placed well aft, separated from crewmates by a large radiator. Like its predecessor, the craft possessed a lower wing that was longer than the upper one and could be operated with either wheels or floats. The Navy agreed to purchase 24 new machines, which became operational in 1926 as the T3M-1. Before this run was finished, Martin proposed additional refinements, including a more powerful engine, three cockpits

arranged in tandem, and wings of equal length. Consequently, a total of 100 T3M-2s was also built.

However, the Navy became convinced that radial engines not only were as powerful as liquid-cooled ones but also cheaper and easier to maintain. Accordingly, it directed Martin to construct a new aircraft utilizing this more desirable power plant. The T4M rolled out in 1927, and it boasted, along with a Hornet radial engine, shorter wings and a redesigned rudder. Because of the engine switch, the new craft was a full ton lighter and enjoyed better performance. The Navy acquired 102 machines from Martin before it sold its Cleveland, Ohio, plant to Great Lakes Aircraft Corporation. That company manufactured an additional 18 TG-1s and 32 TG-2s, which differed only in motor variations. This hulking torpedo-bomber flew from carriers for several years before being replaced by the Douglas TDB *Devastator* in 1937.

**Type:** Trainer

---

**Dimensions:** wingspan, 38 feet, 8 inches; length, 24 feet, 4 inches; height, 9 feet, 4 inches
**Weights:** empty, 1,320 pounds; gross, 1,720 pounds
**Power plant:** 1 × 90–horsepower Curtiss OX-2 liquid-cooled engine
**Performance:** maximum speed, 96 miles per hour; ceiling, 9,500 feet; maximum range, 443 miles
**Armament:** none
**Service dates:** 1914–1917

By adopting the Martin TT in 1914 the Army saved its pilot-training program. It was the first modern American trainer and possessed excellent performance for its day.

Since the invention of the airplane in 1903, the Army's pilot-training program had contended with obsolete and dangerous pusher-type aircraft, little changed from the Wright brothers' original Flyers. When several trainees were killed by accidents in 1914, the Army seriously considered ending its pilot-training program. However, Grover C. Loeing, the military's first aeronautical engineer, grounded the obsolete pusher craft and contracted with Glenn L. Martin to design a modern tractor trainer (that is, a plane with the propeller in front). The ensuing Martin TT was an extremely clean design for its time. It featured unstaggered, two-bay wings, a fully enclosed fuselage, and a metal-cowled engine. Student and instructor were seated in roomy, tandem cockpits. Unusual features included extended front wheels to prevent noseovers and control surfaces suspended between the two wings. The first few examples acquired by the Army in 1914 possessed excellent performance, and a total of 17 TTs was acquired. They were operated exclusively out of North Island Airfield in San Diego, California.

The TTs represented a big improvement in trainer technology, and during the first year of operations no deaths or injuries occurred. It was also a high-performance aircraft that broke several records. In 1915 Sergeant William Ocker reached 5,200 feet in only 10 minutes, quite a distinction. That same year, Lieutenant Byron Q. Jones, with two passengers, stayed aloft for 8 hours, 53 minutes, a feat that won him the prestigious Mackay Trophy. In 1915 pilot Oscar Brindley won the Curtiss Marine Trophy in a TT for flying a record 443 miles nonstop. It was not until 1917 that Curtiss fielded its legendary JN-4 *Jenny* trainer, which was similar in design and performance. The well-worn Martin TTs were gradually retired following America's entry into World War I.

# ☆ McDonnell F2H *Banshee*

**Type:** Fighter

**Dimensions:** wingspan, 44 feet, 10 inches; length, 47 feet, 6 inches; height, 14 feet, 6 inches
**Weights:** empty, 12,790 pounds; gross, 19,000 pounds
**Power plant:** 2 × 3,600–pound thrust Westinghouse J34 turbojet engines
**Performance:** maximum speed, 610 miles per hour; ceiling, 44,800 feet; maximum range, 2,000 miles
**Armament:** 4 × 20mm cannons; 4,000 pounds of bombs or rockets
**Service dates:** 1947–1959

The *Banshee* was the first jet designed by McDonnell to see combat. They acquitted themselves well in Korea and enjoyed a long postwar career as reconnaissance craft.

With the apparent success of the newly acquired FH-1 *Phantom*, the Navy wanted to move quickly on to its second generation of jet fighters. In 1945 it authorized McDonnell to design a scaled-up version of the existing craft. The company answered in 1947 with the XF2H, which bore a distinct family resemblance to the FH-1. However, the new plane was larger and heavier, with more powerful engines and markedly better performance. More importantly, it retained the slow approach speed necessary for carrier landings. The Navy purchased an initial batch of 56 F2H-1s, and in 1948 they entered service as the *Banshee*. Shortly thereafter, the F2H-2 version appeared, which featured a lengthened fuselage and fixed wingtip tanks for greater range. A night-fighter version, the F2H-2N, and a photo plane,

the F2H-2P, were also developed. Pilots were delighted by the strength and maneuverability of the craft and affectionately dubbed it the "Banjo." A total of 800 was built.

The Korean War broke out in 1950, and naval aviation was committed to battle during the first month of combat. Flying alongside the more numerous Grumman F9F *Panthers*, the F2H performed well as a fighter-bomber. They were also fast enough to serve as escort-fighters and guarded B-29 bombers on several missions. After the war, McDonnell introduced the F2H-3 and F2H-4 variants, featuring improved radar, engines, and fuel capacity. By mid-decade the *Banshee* was being phased out by more modern types, but the speedy reconnaissance version remained in service until 1965.

In 1955 the Navy transferred 60 F2H-3s over to the Royal Canadian Navy, which employed them as late as 1965. They were the last fighter jets of the Naval Air Service.

# ✪ McDonnell F3H *Demon*

**Type:** Fighter

---

**Dimensions:** wingspan, 35 feet, 4 inches; length, 59 feet; height, 14 feet, 7 inches
**Weights:** empty, 21,287 pounds; gross, 33,424 pounds
**Power plant:** 1 × 14,250–pound thrust Allison J71 turbojet engine
**Performance:** maximum speed, 727 miles per hour; ceiling, 42,640 feet; maximum range, 1,370 miles
**Armament:** 4 × 20mm cannons; 4 × *Sparrow* missiles
**Service dates:** 1954–1965

---

The much-maligned *Demon* was the first swept-wing Navy fighter to be armed with missiles. Though initially beset by engine problems, it ended its career with a fine reputation.

In 1948 the Navy sent out a proposal to build a carrier-based fighter with performance equal to any land-based Air Force jet. The need was illustrated throughout the Korean War, when swept-wing MiG-15s enjoyed distinct superiority over more conventional Navy craft. McDonnell accepted the challenge by designing its first single-engine jet fighter, the XF3H, in 1953. It was a modern-looking aircraft, with a streamlined fuselage and broad, highly swept wings. However, it was powered by the notoriously unreliable Westinghouse J40 engine. Test-trials revealed the prototype to be somewhat underpowered, but the Navy ordered 61 F3H-1s, which entered service in 1954 as the *Demon*. Almost immediately, the aircraft was plagued by a series of 11 crashes, and so

it was grounded. The remaining 21 jets, representing a $30 million investment, were thereafter restricted to training duties. McDonnell was financially imperiled by this development and promised to upgrade the *Demon* by incorporating the more reliable J71 engine. When the new F3H-2 was found more desirable, production resumed; 519 machines were produced.

Despite its engine problems, the F3H was rugged, maneuverable, and well-liked by pilots. Its fine low-speed characteristics made it ideal for carrier operations. Starting in 1958 it was the first Navy fighter to be equipped with radar-guided *Sparrow I* air-to-air missiles, conferring a quantum jump in aerial firepower. However, as early as 1958 they were surpassed in overall performance by the supersonic Vought F-8 *Crusader* and McDonnell's own twin-engine F-4 *Phantom II*. The *Demon* nonetheless saw widespread service throughout the fleet until the last models were retired in 1965.

# ✪ McDonnell F-101 *Voodoo*

**Type:** Fighter; Reconnaissance

**Dimensions:** wingspan, 39 feet, 8 inches; length, 67 feet, 4 inches; height, 18 feet
**Weights:** empty, 28,000 pounds; gross, 46,700 pounds
**Power plant:** 2 × 14,880–pound thrust Pratt & Whitney J57 turbojet engines
**Performance:** maximum speed, 1,220 miles per hour; ceiling, 52,000 feet; maximum range, 1,700 miles
**Armament:** 4 × 20mm cannons; 3 × AIM *Falcon* missiles or 2 × *Genie* nuclear-tipped missiles
**Service dates:** 1957–1983

At the time of its introduction, the *Voodoo* was the heaviest fighter ever accepted by the Air Force. It did especially useful service in Cuba and Vietnam as a high-speed reconnaissance craft.

In 1948 McDonnell rolled out its prototype XF-88, which was designed as a long-range escort-fighter for the Convair B-36 *Peacemaker*. Weak engines and lack of range led to its cancellation, but in 1951 the Air Force requested McDonnell to redesign a similar aircraft. The XF-101 first flew in 1954 with twice the range and three times the engine power of its predecessor. It was a low-wing monoplane with swept wings and tail surfaces and twin engines jutting out from the bottom of the fuselage. Performance was excellent, and when the Strategic Air Command canceled the concept of a long-range escort-fighter, the airplane was adopted by the Tactical Air Command as the F-101 *Voodoo*. It was the first McDonnell design accepted by the Air Force and the largest fighter employed to that date.

The F-101A was extremely fast for its day and set several speed and distance records. A later version, the F-101B, was a two-seat bomber-interceptor employed by the Air Defense Command, unique in being the first armed with nuclear-tipped *Genie* air-to-air missiles. Several reconnaissance versions were also built, and it was an RF-101 that first discovered the presence of Soviet missiles in Cuba in 1961. Throughout the Vietnam War, the RF-101 rendered valuable service by virtue of its high speed and long range. The Air Force began phasing out the fighter versions in 1970, although RF-101s flew with the Air National Guard through 1985. The Royal Canadian Air Force was also equipped with its own version, the CF-101, which also enjoyed a long service life.

# ✪ McDonnell FH-1 *Phantom*

**Type:** Fighter

**Dimensions:** wingspan, 40 feet, 9 inches; length, 38 feet, 9 inches; height, 14 feet, 2 inches
**Weights:** empty, 6,683 pounds; gross, 12,035 pounds
**Power plant:** 2 × 1,600–pound thrust Westinghouse J30 turbojet engines
**Performance:** maximum speed, 479 miles per hour; ceiling, 41,100 feet; maximum range, 980 miles
**Armament:** 4 × .50–caliber machine guns
**Service dates:** 1947–1953

The *Phantom* was the Navy's first jet fighter and was the first jet to land on a carrier. Though pleasant to fly, it was underpowered and quickly superseded by more advanced designs.

In 1943 the Navy decided to pursue the new field of jet aviation by developing a counterpart to the Bell P-59 *Airacomet*. It turned to a relatively young company, McDonnell of St. Louis, because of its reputation for innovation. A relatively conservative design emerged that featured a thick, low-set, straight wing; slanted tailplanes to avoid the jet efflux; and widetrack tricycle landing gear. The prototype, initially designated XFD-1, was assembled by 1944 but could not fly owing to a shortage of jet engines. In fact, the first flight took place in January 1945 on one engine because others could not be found! The first two-engine flight occurred in March, and the Navy placed an order for 100 machines. After the war, production was cut back to 60, and it entered the service in 1947 as the FH-1 *Phantom*.

Once operational it became apparent that the *Phantom*, though easy to fly and service, was too underpowered to be a successful fighter. Nonetheless, it established a number of important precedents. On July 26, 1946, it became the first jet aircraft to land on a carrier, the USS *Franklin D. Roosevelt*. The following year, it equipped Fighting Squadron VF-17, which became the first operational jet squadron in Navy history. In 1949 additional machines were handed over to two Marine Corps squadrons, thereby becoming the first jet-equipped squadron in that service. The handsome, docile *Phantom* was rapidly overtaken by the Grumman F9F *Panther* and the McDonnell F2H *Banshee* that year, and by 1950 it left frontline service. The remaining machines flew with Navy Reserve units until 1953, the first in a long line of distinguished McDonnell warplanes.

# McDonnell-Douglas AV-8 *Harrier*

**Type:** Fighter-Bomber

**Dimensions:** wingspan, 30 feet, 4 inches; length, 46 feet, 4 inches; height, 11 feet, 8 inches
**Weights:** empty, 13,086 pounds; gross, 31,000 pounds
**Power plant:** 1 × 21,700–pound thrust Rolls-Royce F402-406 turbofan engine
**Performance:** maximum speed, 668 miles per hour; ceiling, 50,000 feet; maximum range, 748 miles
**Armament:** 1 × 25mm GAU cannon; 17,000 pounds of bombs or rockets
**Service dates:** 1971–

The *Harrier* is currently the only jet in the American arsenal capable of vertical takeoff and landing (VTOL). The Marine Corps employs it as a close-support weapon and demonstrated its effectiveness during the 1991 Gulf War.

The British perfected a military craft capable of VTOL during the early 1960s through the employment of vectored-thrust nozzles under the fuselage. The Marine Corps desired such an aircraft, as it could operate free of landing zones and carriers in direct support of amphibious landings. In 1968 the Americans evaluated the *Harrier* for their own purposes and found it to be a useful, if limited, tool for ground support. The Marine Corps started taking deliveries in 1971, although the first 102 machines, the AV-8A, proved somewhat skittish to fly and possessed only modest range and payload capacities. However, by the time this first batch retired in 1986,

the Marines had a working knowledge of VTOL attack craft and ways to enhance their performance.

In 1978 McDonnell-Douglas entered a joint venture with British Aerospace to design and produce an improved *Harrier* for both countries, the AV-8B. It featured an enlarged wing made of light yet strong carbonfibre epoxy composites at a considerable savings in weight. The increased wing area allowed more fuel and armament to be carried, and the new craft was a marked improvement over the first model while still utilizing the identical engine. The first AV-8Bs were accepted in 1985, and by 1991 four squadrons were in service. During Operation Desert Storm they flew 3,567 sorties and dropped more than 3,000 tons of ordnance with lethal results to Iraqi tanks. Only four were lost in combat. Continuous electronics and engine upgrades will keep the AV-8Bs flying well into the 21st century.

# ⭐ McDonnell-Douglas C-17 *Globemaster III*

**Type:** Transport

**Dimensions:** wingspan, 165 feet; length, 175 feet, 2 inches; height, 55 feet, 1 inch
**Weights:** empty, 269,363 pounds; gross, 580,000 pounds
**Power plant:** 4 × 40,400–pound thrust Pratt & Whitney F117 turbofan engines
**Performance:** maximum speed, 518 miles per hour; ceiling, 45,000 feet; maximum range, 5,412 miles
**Armament:** none
**Service dates:** 1993–

The *Globemaster III* is currently the world's most advanced military transport. It is capable of carrying virtually any piece of Army equipment to anywhere in the world and once flew a 30-foot whale to Iceland.

During the late 1970s the Air Force realized it would need a new transport to update its global airlift capacities. It announced a "Cargo Experimental" (CX) competition for an aircraft that combined the payload capacity of the C-5 *Galaxy* with the forward airstrip ability of the C-130 *Hercules*. After several bids, McDonnell-Douglas was announced the winner in 1980, and work commenced in earnest. The new aircraft suffered from a prolonged and controversial gestation and was almost canceled on account of cost overruns. However, when the prototype finally flew in 1991, a new age in military airlift was born. The XC-17 was sleek and modern in appearance, possessing a rotund fuselage; a high, swept-back wing; and high-mounted tail surfaces. Furthermore, its four podded engines are de-

signed to blow exhaust directly into the large wing flaps, thereby generating additional lift. The aircraft's payload is 170,000 pounds, which can include 102 paratroopers, several helicopters, a score of trucks and jeeps, or a single M-1 *Abrams* heavy tank. Such payloads can be delivered at short, unprepared airstrips anywhere in the world thanks to inflight refueling. Despite its ponderous girth, the craft has automated flight systems and handles like a fighter. It entered service in 1993 with the title *Globemaster III*.

On September 9, 1998, the C-17 was called upon to fly probably the most unusual humanitarian mission of any aircraft in history. A *Globemaster III* became tasked with ferrying Keiko, a 10,000-pound killer whale, from his tank in Oregon to the Westman Islands, Iceland. The nonstop flight proved uneventful, and Keiko was comfortably delivered to his new home for eventual release, although the C-17 blew several tires upon landing. A total of 120 *Globemaster IIIs* is to be constructed by 2005.

# McDonnell-Douglas F-4 *Phantom II*

**Type:** Fighter-Bomber; Reconnaissance

**Dimensions:** wingspan, 38 feet, 5 inches; length, 58 feet, 3 inches; height, 16 feet, 3 inches
**Weights:** empty, 30,776 pounds; gross, 56,000 pounds
**Power plant:** $2 \times 17{,}900$–pound thrust General Electric J79 turbojet engines
**Performance:** maximum speed, 1,450 miles per hour; ceiling, 71,000 feet; maximum range, 1,841 miles
**Armament:** $1 \times 20$mm cannon; 16,000 pounds of bombs, rockets, or missiles
**Service dates:** 1960–

Nicknamed "Rhino" and "Double Ugly," the angular *Phantom* is perhaps the most classic jet design of all time. This incredibly rugged and versatile aircraft has served with distinction for some 40 years in a wide variety of capacities.

In 1952 McDonnell was tasked with producing a supersonic fighter-bomber for Navy carrier operation to replace the McDonnell F3H *Demon*. The prototype emerged in 1958 as the AH-1, incorporating one of the most distinctive appearances ever given a warplane. The new craft was a twin-engine, swept-back monoplane with upswept wingtips and downturned tailplanes. The crew consisted of a pilot in front and a weapon systems operator in back. Its sinister appearance belied world-class ability, however, and in 1960 it entered naval service as the *Phantom II*. Two years later it made history by becoming the first Navy jet to be adopted by the U.S. Air Force.

The F-4 was the workhorse of the Vietnam War and served as fighter, bomber, and reconnaissance platform. In April 1966 a *Phantom* won the world's first supersonic dogfight by shooting down a North Vietnamese MiG-21. Significantly, the only Navy and Air Force aces of this war, Randy Cunningham and Steve Ritchie, flew the hulking aircraft to victory. In 1968 a new version was introduced, the F4G *Wild Weasel*, which was specifically designed to knock out enemy radar and antiaircraft defenses.

By the time production of the F-4 ended, more than 5,000 had been built—2,600 for the Air Force and 1,200 for the Navy and Marine Corps. The rest were employed by Germany, Japan, Greece, Iran, Israel, Egypt, Spain, Turkey, and South Korea. During the 1991 Gulf War, F4G *Wild Weasels* flew 2,683 sorties against Iraqi defenses without loss. Though retired from frontline American service in 1996, updated *Phantoms* continue flying with Marine Corps Reserve and Air National Guard units.

# ★ McDonnell-Douglas F-15 *Eagle*

**Type:** Fighter

**Dimensions:** wingspan, 42 feet, 9 inches; length, 63 feet, 9 inches; height, 18 feet, 5 inches
**Weights:** empty, 30,300 pounds; gross, 68,000 pounds
**Power plant:** 2 × 23,450–pound thrust Pratt & Whitney F100 turbofan engines
**Performance:** maximum speed, 1,665 miles per hour; ceiling, 65,000 feet; maximum range, 3,450 miles
**Armament:** 1 × 20mm Gatling gun; 4 × AIM-7 *Sparrow* missiles; 4 × AIM-9 *Sidewinder* missiles; 15,000 pounds of bombs
**Service dates:** 1974–

The *Eagle* was the first American air-superiority fighter since the F-86 *Sabre* and has already served for a quarter-century. It combines high performance, gut-wrenching agility, and state-of-the-art electronics into a single deadly package.

During the late 1960s the Air Force began contemplating a replacement for its superb but aging F-4 *Phantom II*. Whereas most warplanes of the 1960s were actually multirole fighter-bombers, the new aircraft was intended specifically as an air-superiority fighter. McDonnell-Douglas won the design competition, and in July 1972 it rolled out the prototype XF-15. Unlike the F-4, this was a single-seat fighter with twin engines and tails and all-moving horizontal tail surfaces. Moreover, because the craft possessed more engine thrust than weight, it was the first American fighter able to accelerate during vertical climb. Its broad, sharp, swept wing ensured low wing loading (the ratio of weight to wing area),

so that it enjoyed high maneuverability. In 1974 the F-15A entered into service as the *Eagle*; since then nearly 1,000 have been deployed.

The F-15 enjoys heads-up displays, which are state-of-the-art instruments viewed through the canopy so a pilot can monitor the craft and never take an eye off the target. Furthermore, advanced electronics and radar enable the *Eagle* to detect enemy aircraft at great distances and engage them before visual contact is established. During the 1980s a two-seat ground-attack version, the F-15E *Strike Eagle*, was developed; it remains a highly effective bomber. The F-15 enjoyed a brilliant career in Israeli hands and in one skirmish claimed 60 Syrian MiGs without loss. During the 1991 Gulf War, *Eagles* shot down 35 Iraqi jets in exchange for two F-15Es lost to ground fire. This superb fighter, one of the best ever built, will be flying well into the next century.

# McDonnell-Douglas F/A-18 *Hornet*

**Type:** Fighter-Bomber

**Dimensions:** wingspan, 37 feet, 6 inches; length, 56 feet; height, 15 feet, 3 inches
**Weights:** empty, 23,050 pounds; gross, 49,224 pounds
**Power plant:** $2 \times 17,600$–pound thrust General Electric F404 turbofan engines
**Performance:** maximum speed, 1,190 miles per hour; ceiling, 50,000 feet; maximum range, 2,303 miles
**Armament:** $1 \times 20$mm Gatling gun; 17,000 pounds of bombs or rockets
**Service dates:** 1983–

The formidable *Hornet* is one of the most effective attack aircraft currently in use. With minor changes in programming it is equally adept as a fighter.

In 1974, once the Air Force's quest for a new lightweight fighter was fulfilled by the General Dynamics F-16, the Navy took a hard look at the losing aircraft, Northrop's F-17, as a possible replacement for several of its own aging warbirds. Impressed by its performance, the Navy authorized McDonnell-Douglas to refine it further into the nation's first strike aircraft, that is, a pure fighter that also functions like a bomber. The new XF-18 first flew in 1978 and was immediately ordered into production. Like its predecessor, it was a twin-engine design with two rudders and a broad, unswept wing. It handled crisply as a fighter and also showed great promise as a "bomb truck." Furthermore, the plane was easily flown by computerized fly-by-wire systems, and the liquid-crystal cockpit displays greatly reduced pilot workload. In 1983 the F-18 entered service as the *Hornet*. The Navy acquired 1,168 aircraft for carrier and Marine Corps squadrons; the Navy's *Blue Angels* aerial demonstration team has operated *Hornets* since 1987.

The multimission F-18 was designed to replace the F-4 *Phantom* and F-14 *Tomcats* as fighters, the A-7 *Corsair II* and A-4 *Skyhawk* as attack planes, and the A-6 *Intruder* as a night bomber. From the standpoint of maintenance, it contains several thousand fewer parts than the airplanes it replaces, and its sophisticated electronics are easily changed thanks to plug-in modules. The F-18 demonstrated its value during the 1991 Gulf War when more than 5,000 sorties were completed with the loss of only two planes. With constant upgrades, the *Hornet* will remain the mainstay of Navy attack aviation for the next several decades.

**Type:** Fighter-Bomber

**Dimensions:** wingspan, 44 feet; length, 60 feet; height, 16 feet
**Weights:** empty, 30,564 pounds; gross, 66,000 pounds
**Power plant:** 2 × 22,000–pound thrust General Electric F414 turbofan engines
**Performance:** maximum speed, 1,100 miles per hour; ceiling, 50,000 feet; maximum range, 2,700 miles
**Armament:** 1 × 20mm Gatling gun; 17,750 pounds of rockets or bombs
**Service dates:** 2001–

The *Super Hornet* is the Navy's latest attack aircraft. It is five times more effective than earlier models and is expected to serve for at least three decades into the next century.

Faced with declining military budgets, the Navy chose to upgrade the F/A-18 *Hornet* C/D fighter-bomber rather than incur the expense of a totally new aircraft. In 1992 McDonnell-Douglas was contracted to redesign the existing craft in several areas of performance. The prototype F-18E first flew in 1996 and displayed a marked similarity to the earlier craft, although it was 25 percent larger. The most notable difference is the enlarged wing area, which was created both to carry more weapons and provide slower landing speed for carrier operations. The new craft now has 11 hardpoints on which a bewildering array of bombs and rockets are slung. The wing is also considerably strengthened, which means that three times the ordnance payload can be safely landed back on

deck for reuse. Another visible difference is the octagonal air inlets that have been carefully engineered to reduce radar signature. In fact, the entire new aircraft emits less than one-tenth the signal of earlier F-18s. Fuel capacity has also been increased by 33 percent, with commensurate increases in the *Super Hornet*'s combat radius and loiter time.

Despite this makeover, the F-18E still shares 90 percent of existing avionics with older models. However, the new cockpit is totally updated to include the latest touch-sensitive displays to ease pilot workload. As situated, the F-18E and the two-seat F version possess greater range, endurance, payload, and survivability than the F-18C/Ds. The Navy hopes to acquire up to 1,000 of them, and the first operational carrier unit is expected to deploy in 2001. The *Super Hornet* will serve the fleet for the next 30 years and replace such superlative designs as the F-14 *Tomcat* and the A-6 *Intruder*.

# ⭐ McDonnell-Douglas KC-10 *Extender*

**Type:** Tanker; Transport

**Dimensions:** wingspan, 165 feet, 4 inches; length, 181 feet, 7 inches; height, 58 feet, 1 inch
**Weights:** empty, 240,026 pounds; gross, 590,000 pounds
**Power plant:** 3 × 52,500–pound thrust General Electric F103 turbofan engines
**Performance:** maximum speed, 600 miles per hour; ceiling, 30,000 feet; maximum range, 4,370 miles
**Armament:** none
**Service dates:** 1981–

The massive *Extender* is currently the world's most advanced tanker aircraft. It also enjoys a cargo capacity second only to the C-5 *Galaxy* and C-17 *Globemaster III*.

During the mid-1970s the Air Force decided it needed a new plane to replace its aging fleet of KC-125 *Stratotankers*. For economic reasons, an advanced tanker/cargo aircraft competition was held to utilize an existing wide-body commercial jet. In 1977 the McDonnell-Douglas DC-10 airliner was announced as the winner, and three years later the first KC-10 *Extender* was completed for evaluation. The craft employed the same wing as the commercial model but underwent extensive internal modifications for its intended role. The bottom half of the fuselage was fitted with seven rubber fuel cells holding 18,125 gallons of jet fuel. The fuel can in turn be disgorged via a tanker boom capable of pumping out 1,500 gallons per minute. Thus situ-ated, the KC-10 can fly a distance of 2,200 miles, re-fuel several aircraft, and return to base. The upper half of the fuselage is also easily convertible for cargo purposes and can carry a 170,000-pound pay-load, including 75 passengers. Its girth notwith-standing, the KC-10 is equipped with a digital fly-by-wire system and is as responsive to controls as a fighter. The first *Extender* was delivered in 1981; a total of 60 has been acquired.

It is estimated that a fleet of only 17 KC-10s can transport and service an entire fighter squadron overseas, a workload previously requiring 40 KC-135s. In service, the type has established a phe-nomenal 99 percent operational reliability rate. Dur-ing the 1991 Gulf War, KC-10s flew 380 missions, de-livered 1,000 passengers and 12,400 tons of cargo, and refueled innumerable warplanes en route to the Persian Gulf. *Extenders* are expected to serve for the next several decades.

# McDonnell-Douglas T-45 *Goshawk*

**Type:** Trainer

**Dimensions:** wingspan, 30 feet, 9 inches; length, 39 feet, 3 inches; height, 13 feet, 6 inches
**Weights:** empty, 9,335 pounds; gross, 12,700 pounds
**Power plant:** 1 × 5,450–pound thrust Rolls-Royce Adour Mk.851 turbofan engine
**Performance:** maximum speed, 561 miles per hour; ceiling, 50,000 feet; maximum range, 1,400 miles
**Armament:** none
**Service dates:** 1988–

The *Goshawk* is the most advanced trainer in Navy history and part of a comprehensive computerized training regimen. It is designed to produce superior pilots with less time and lower costs than traditional training methods.

In 1977 the Navy began looking for an advanced basic trainer to replace its T-2 *Buckeyes* and TA-4 *Skyhawks*. It sought a relatively high-performance aircraft that was also durable and inexpensive. The aircraft chosen for the task was the British Aerospace *Hawk*, a multipurpose trainer/light ground-attack design that first flew in 1974. This compact, nimble craft has a low, swept wing, excellent performance for its size, and two crew members under a spacious bubble canopy. In 1978 McDonnell-Douglas contracted with the British to coproduce an American navalized version called the *Goshawk*. The new craft required a minimum of aerodynamic modifications but was fitted with strengthened landing gear and an arrester hook for carrier training. The first T-45As were delivered in 1988 and were followed by the more advanced T-45C in 1998. These latter planes differ by being fitted with the latest digital Navy cockpit, known as Cockpit 21, which closely mimics controls found on the F-18 *Hornet* and AV-8 *Harrier*. A total of 187 *Goshawks* will be procured by 2004.

The T-45 is part of a complete training-systems package that also includes advanced flight simulators and computer-assisted programs for instruction. Before actually flying the aircraft, students acquire realistic training through state-of-the-art projection systems that closely simulate flight. The entire training program is also administered and recorded on a computerized basis to reduce operating expenses. This integrated approach is intended to meet Navy demands for quickly trained, highly competent pilots on a very cost-effective basis.

# ⭐ Naval Aircraft Factory N3N

**Type:** Trainer

**Dimensions:** wingspan, 34 feet; length, 25 feet, 6 inches; height, 10 feet, 10 inches
**Weights:** empty, 2,090 pounds; gross, 2,792 pounds
**Power plant:** 1 × 235–horsepower Wright R-760 radial engine
**Performance:** maximum speed, 126 miles per hour; ceiling, 15,200 feet; maximum range, 470 miles
**Armament:** none
**Service dates:** 1936–1945

The vaunted "Yellow Peril" was one of the Navy's most popular trainers. After World War II hundreds ended up in civilian hands, and the U.S. Naval Academy maintained a small fleet until 1961.

The Naval Aircraft Factory (NAF), established in 1918 to provide the Navy its own manufacturing and test facilities, had by the 1930s become an important design center. In 1934 the Navy sought to replace its aging Consolidated NY trainers and instructed the NAF to come up with an indigenous aircraft of its own. Because more than 1,000 obsolete Wright J-5 radials were being held in stock, the new craft would utilize that power plant. In 1935 the XN3N prototype was unveiled and successfully flown. It was a conventional biplane in appearance with staggered wings of equal length. However, the new craft possessed all-metal construction, a metal fuselage, a single integral wing, and a fuel tank placed ahead of the front cockpit. Another interesting feature was that the entire right side of the aircraft could be opened in panels for maintenance. That year, the Navy authorized construction of 175 N3N-1s to be used as primary trainers. This was followed by an additional 816 N3N-3s powered by the modern Wright R-760 radial engine. Earlier models were subsequently refitted with this engine.

As a trainer, the N3N possessed delightful flying qualities. However, owing to its poor taxiing qualities and bright-yellow paint scheme, it was popularly referred to as the "Yellow Peril." In the years leading up to World War II, thousands of Navy pilots cut their teeth in the front cockpit of an N3N. After 1945 hundreds of surplus N3Ns found their way into civilian hands as private aircraft and crop dusters, with many still in use today. The U.S. Naval Academy in Annapolis, Maryland, also maintained a small fleet of N3Ns, equipped as floatplanes, for the benefit of its cadets. They were actively employed in training until 1961, the last Navy biplanes in service.

**Type:** Patrol-Bomber

**Dimensions:** wingspan, 72 feet, 10 inches; length, 49 feet, 2 inches; height, 16 feet, 9 inches
**Weights:** empty, 7,669 pounds; gross, 14,122 pounds
**Power plant:** 2 × 525–horsepower Wright R-1750 radial engines
**Performance:** maximum speed, 114 miles per hour; ceiling, 10,900 feet; maximum range, 1,310 miles
**Armament:** 1 × .30–caliber machine gun; 4 × 230–pound bombs
**Service dates:** 1922–1929

The PN series was part of a small family of experimental flying boats intended to advance the state of naval aviation. Despite outward similarities, all evolved into different classes of Navy patrol-bombers.

When World War I ended it fell upon the Naval Aircraft Factory (NAF) in Philadelphia to modernize the technology associated with flying boats. It started in 1922 by mating an old Curtiss F-5L flying boat hull with entirely new wings to produce the first PN-7. Dissatisfaction with the power plants led to two PN-8s featuring an all-new, metal hull. One of these then became the first of two PN-9s, which sported revised tail surfaces, nacelles, and nose radiators. Next, four PN-10s with water-cooled V-12 engines were produced, although the last two were subsequently redone as PN-12s sporting Wright Cyclone radial engines. In 1928 these craft set a world seaplane duration

record, covering 1,243 miles in 18 hours, and served as the basis for the Douglas PD-1, the Keystone PK-1, and the Martin PM-1 and PM-2. However, the PN-11 finally abandoned the proven F-5L hull shape for a slimmer design, minus the traditional flared sponsons. This, in turn, became a prototype for the more modern Hall PH-1.

Undoubtedly, the most famous NAF flying boat was the PN-9. In 1928 it set an endurance record, remaining aloft over Philadelphia for 28 hours, 35 minutes, and was chosen to fly a historic nonstop flight from San Francisco to Hawaii. In September 1925, Commander John Rodgers lifted off as planned, but his PN-9 covered only 1,841 miles of the 2,400-mile trip before running out of fuel. He spent the next nine days floating at sea, but rather than waiting to be rescued, his crew stripped canvas from the wings, fashioned a crude sail, and sailed the remaining 559 miles to Hawaii!

# Noorduyn UC-64 *Norseman*

**Type:** Transport

**Dimensions:** wingspan, 51 feet, 6 inches; length, 34 feet, 3 inches; height, 10 feet, 1 inch
**Weights:** empty, 5,020 pounds; gross, 7,540 pounds
**Power plant:** 1 × 600–horsepower Pratt & Whitney R-1340 radial engine
**Performance:** maximum speed, 162 miles per hour; ceiling, 17,000 feet; maximum range, 442 miles
**Armament:** none
**Service dates:** 1942–1952

The *Norseman* was a widely used transport of World War II and one of the few Canadian-designed aircraft employed by the United States. It was a simple and capable plane that served for a decade.

The *Norseman* was built in 1935 by Noorduyn Aviation, Ltd., of Montreal, Quebec, as an aircraft for service in the rugged Canadian bush country. In design it was something of a throwback to an earlier age, being constructed partly of metal, partly of wood, and largely fabric-covered. Its high wing was supported by external bracing, making it look even more antiquated, but the *Norseman* proved simple to repair and operate under difficult conditions. It first came to the attention of the United States in 1942 when noted Norwegian explorer Bernt Balchen volunteered to establish a ferry route to England across northeastern Canada, Greenland, and Iceland. He selected seven *Norsemen* for the difficult journey, and

the aircraft performed flawlessly using wheels and skis. The Army Air Force was so impressed that it ordered 749 examples into service as the UC-64. The same airplane was also widely deployed by the Royal Canadian Air Force in much the same capacity.

During the war six *Norsemen* were allotted to the Army Corps of Engineers, which operated float-equipped versions as general utility transports. The Navy also acquired three with the designation JA-1. Unfortunately, the craft gained a degree of notoriety when the *Norseman* carrying famed bandleader Glenn Miller disappeared on a flight from England to France on December 15, 1944.

The *Norseman* remained on active duty as an air ambulance and a navigation trainer through the Korean War. Although it was soon replaced by another noted Canadian design, the De Havilland L-20 *Beaver*, the *Norseman* remained in production up to 1959.

# North American A3J/A-5 *Vigilante*

**Type:** Bomber; Reconnaissance

**Dimensions:** wingspan, 53 feet; length, 75 feet, 10 inches; height, 19 feet, 5 inches
**Weights:** empty, 38,000 pounds; gross, 80,000 pounds
**Power plant:** 2 × 17,860–pound thrust General Electric J79 turbojet engines
**Performance:** maximum speed, 1,385 miles per hour; ceiling, 67,000 feet; maximum range, 3,200 miles
**Armament:** 1 nuclear weapon
**Service dates:** 1961–1980

The *Vigilante* was one of the largest and heaviest airplanes to operate from a carrier deck. Though originally designed as a bomber, it performed extremely useful service as a high-speed reconnaissance craft.

In 1955 the Navy issued specifications for a new supersonic attack bomber to replace the Douglas A3D *Skywarrior*. The new plane would have to possess all-weather capability and be equipped with nuclear weapons. In 1956 North American proposed its Model NA-247, and a contract was awarded to build several prototypes. They were rolled out in 1958 as twin-engine, high-wing designs incorporating several novel features. Foremost among them were computer-controlled air inlets and exhaust nozzles, as well as a linear bomb bay sandwiched between the engines. The weapons carried, be they nuclear or conventional, would be ejected rearward out of a long tunnel. The XR3J was also unique in having a comprehensive radar-inertial navigation system installed for hitting targets in the worst pos-

sible weather. Furthermore, the new plane was extremely fast and set several world records during testing. The Navy was suitably impressed, and in 1961 the plane entered service as the A3J *Vigilante*. The following year the new designation A-5 was granted. A total of 59 was acquired.

At length the Navy dispensed with the *Vigilante's* nuclear strike capability and elected to adopt a reconnaissance version, the RA-5C, of which 150 were built. Unlike previous models, this machine featured a distinct hump behind the canopy that housed additional fuel and electronics. The new design also carried side-looking radar under the fuselage, as well as a multiple-lens camera and comprehensive electronic countermeasures for operations in hostile airspace. The *Vigilante* did extremely capable work throughout the war in Vietnam and emerged as the Navy's best tactical reconnaissance craft. After the war it equipped several reserve squadrons until being phased out in 1980. Surprisingly, no carrier aircraft of similar performance has replaced it.

**Type:** Light Bomber

**Dimensions:** wingspan, 42 feet; length, 29 feet; height, 12 feet, 2 inches
**Weights:** empty, 4,520 pounds; gross, 6,700 pounds
**Power plant:** 1 × 785–horsepower Wright Cyclone R-1820 radial engine
**Performance:** maximum speed, 250 miles per hour; ceiling, 28,000 feet; maximum range, 800 miles
**Armament:** 5 × .30–caliber machine guns; 400 pounds of bombs
**Service dates:** December 1941

The A-27 was a bomber version of the famous AT-6 military trainer. The Army Air Corps acquired several by default, and they disappeared from the inventory after a few weeks of service.

In 1937 North American sought to expand sales of its basic AT-6 design by providing a military version for export. The resulting prototype, the NA-44, was a low-wing monoplane like the trainer, with an all-metal fuselage, integral wing tanks, and retractable landing gear. The pilot and gunner were seated in tandem underneath a glass greenhouse canopy. It was armed with two machine guns in the cowl, two in the wings, and a single weapon in the rear cockpit. After successful trial flights in 1938, the NA-44 was put up for sale; in November 1939 ten were purchased by Siam (Thailand) as NA-69s. The following year Brazil placed an order for 30 machines under the designation NA-72, and Chile also acquired 12 as NA-74s.

The NA-44, though modern in appearance, was underarmed, underpowered, and clearly never intended for service with U.S. forces. However, as the shipment of machines to Siam was under way, politics intervened. When that country was suddenly occupied by Japanese troops in 1941, the decision was made to seize the aircraft rather than have them fall into the hands of a potential adversary. Once the transport vessel had anchored in the Philippines, the NA-44s were commandeered and transferred to the Army Air Corps. The aircraft were then uncrated, assembled, and pressed into service as A-27 light bombers.

The ten A-27s were present during the December 8, 1941, Japanese attack on the Philippines and had the distinction of being the first American light bombers to see action in World War II. They are presumed to have been destroyed in action shortly thereafter.

# ✪ North American A-36 *Apache*

**Type:** Dive-Bomber

**Dimensions:** wingspan, 37 feet; length, 32 feet, 3 inches; height, 12 feet, 2 inches
**Weights:** empty, 6,300 pounds; gross, 10,000 pounds
**Power plant:** 1 × 1,325–horsepower Allison V-1710 liquid-cooled engine
**Performance:** maximum speed, 365 miles per hour; ceiling, 25,100 feet; maximum range, 550 miles
**Armament:** 6 × .50–caliber machine guns; 1,000 pounds of bombs
**Service dates:** 1942–1945

The *Apache* was a lesser-known dive-bomber version of the more famous P-51 *Mustang*. It served capably in Italy and Burma throughout World War II but was hindered in performance by a low-altitude engine.

In 1940 the British Purchasing Commission requested that North American design a new fighter aircraft within a 120-day deadline. The result was the NA-73, the first aircraft to utilize a low-drag laminar airfoil wing to increase range and performance. The British liked the result and ordered 620 copies, the *Mustang I*. The Army Air Force also expressed interest and bought an additional 310 machines under the designation P-51A. However, because the U.S. military lacked an efficient ground-attack aircraft, North American was asked to modify several *Mustangs* into dive-bombers. It accordingly fitted the P-51A with air brakes, four machine guns in the wings, and two more on each side of the engine cowling. Dubbed the A-36 *Apache*, 500 were completed and delivered to the Army Air Force by March 1943. Like the early *Mustangs*, it was highly maneuverable and delightful to fly, but its low-power Allison engine suffered at high altitudes.

The *Apaches* first saw combat during the closing phases of the North African campaign in 1943 and performed well. As part of the 27th and 86th Bombardment Groups, they also rendered valuable service supporting ground operations during the campaigns in Sicily and Italy. In two and a half years of combat, A-36s delivered 16 million pounds of bombs during 23,400 sorties and shot down 84 Axis aircraft. Only 177 *Apaches* were lost during combat, establishing one of the lowest loss rates of any American aircraft. Two squadrons of A-36s also flew from India and fought in Burma. By 1945 they were phased out by more modern P-51s and P-47s and dropped from the inventory entirely.

# North American AJ *Savage*

**Type:** Bomber; Tanker

**Dimensions:** wingspan, 75 feet, 2 inches; length, 63 feet, 10 inches; height, 20 feet, 5 inches
**Weights:** empty, 29,203 pounds; gross, 59,750 pounds
**Power plant:** 2 × 2,300–horsepower Pratt & Whitney R-2800 Double Wasp radial engines;
   1 × 4,600–pound thrust Allison J33 turbojet engine
**Performance:** maximum speed, 472 miles per hour; ceiling, 45,000 feet; maximum range, 1,670 miles
**Armament:** 10,500 pounds of bombs or nuclear weapons
**Service dates:** 1949–1965

The multiengine *Savage* was one of the first Navy planes to operate both piston and jet engines. Though overshadowed by more advanced designs, it spent its final days as a useful aerial tanker.

Immediately after World War II the Navy sought an advanced attack craft that could operate from the larger carriers then under construction. The new bomber would have to possess long range, high speed, and nuclear capacity. North American was then authorized to develop its Model NA-147 prototype, which first flew in 1946. This was a twin-engine, high-wing design, unique in having a booster jet engine installed in the rear of the fuselage. Through this expedient, it was hoped that the XAJ-1 would enjoy a high-speed run over the target, after which the jet could be shut down to conserve fuel. The Navy approved the final product in 1949, and the AJ entered service as the *Savage*. It was intended to replace the Lockheed P2V *Neptune*, which could not operate from carriers, as the fleet's main bomber. A long-range reconnaissance version, the AJ-2P, was also developed in 1953 with up to 30 camera stations. Despite prolonged teething problems, the *Savage* turned out to be a capable, dependable aircraft with a long service life. The Navy acquired 182 of various models.

As jet technology matured, it was apparent that the AJ had rapidly grown obsolete in its role as a nuclear bomber. Because the excellent Douglas A3D *Skywarrior* was under development, the Navy rejected a faster turbine version of the *Savage*, the XA2J. Consequently, the remaining stocks of AJs were converted into aerial tankers by equipping them with a hose-and-reel system installed in the bomb bay. They remained in operation until 1965, when they were finally replaced by *Skywarriors* outfitted for the same role.

**Type:** Trainer

**Dimensions:** wingspan, 42 feet; length, 29 feet; height, 11 feet, 9 inches
**Weights:** empty, 3,900 pounds; gross, 5,155 pounds
**Power plant:** 1 × 600–horsepower Pratt & Whitney R-1340 radial engine
**Performance:** maximum speed, 210 miles per hour; ceiling, 24,200 feet; maximum range, 629 miles
**Armament:** none
**Service dates:** 1936–1958

The AT-6 was the most important Allied training machine of World War II. Thousands were built and flown, and it remained in service for several decades.

This famous aircraft began life in response to a 1937 Army Air Corps design competition for an advanced trainer (AT). The military was beginning to discontinue biplane trainers (and their pleasant flying characteristics) in favor of more modern, difficult-to-fly craft that mimicked the new warplanes being deployed. North American responded with its NA-26, which was basically a BT-9 with retractable landing gear. In 1938 the Army purchased an initial batch of 180 aircraft, known as BC-1s, although by 1940 they had been redesignated as AT-6 *Texans*. The Navy also acquired many examples, calling them SNJs. Furthermore, the Royal Air Force, then engaged in World War II, ordered several hundred copies for British and Commonwealth

pilots as the *Harvard;* for Australians it was known as the *Wirraway.*

By the time the United States entered World War II the AT-6 and all its derivatives had become the most significant trainer in the world. In just four years, 50,000 Army and 40,000 Navy pilots mastered the art of flying in this airplane—not to mention countless others in 34 other countries. Ultimately, 10,057 AT-6s and 4,800 SNJs were constructed and deployed. After the war, several thousand AT-6s were remanufactured as T-6s and sold abroad to no less than 54 nations. During the Korean War in 1950, the T-6s were employed on "mosquito," or spotter, missions to mark targets with smoke rockets for aerial bombardment. It remained in service in the United States until 1958, finally being replaced by the T-28 *Trojan* and the T-34 *Mentor.* The AT-6 is regarded as history's most influential training aircraft; several hundred still fly today in private hands.

# North American B-25 *Mitchell*

**Type:** Medium Bomber

**Dimensions:** wingspan, 67 feet, 7 inches; length, 54 feet, 1 inch; height, 15 feet, 9 inches
**Weights:** empty, 21,000 pounds; gross, 35,000 pounds
**Power plant:** 2 × 1,700–horsepower Wright Cyclone R-2600 radial engines
**Performance:** maximum speed, 284 miles per hour; ceiling, 27,000 feet, maximum range, 1,500 miles
**Armament:** up to 12 × .50–caliber machine guns and 1 × 75mm cannon; 4,000 pounds of bombs
**Service dates:** 1940–1959

The B-25 was built in larger quantities than any other twin-engine U.S. aircraft during World War II and gained immortality after completing a daring first air raid against Japan. It was fast and rugged and served in every theater of the war.

In 1938 North American responded to an Army Air Corps requirement for a new bomber with the Model NA-62, a twin-engine, twin-rudder design capable of high-speed mid-altitude bomb runs. The Army was suitably impressed and ordered 187 of the new craft directly off the drawing board. The B-25 first flew in January 1939 and was christened the *Mitchell* in honor of U.S. airpower prophet General William "Billy" Mitchell. By all accounts it was fast, versatile, and relatively easy to maintain. During World War II the B-25 was widely exported abroad and saw service with Australian, British, Chinese, and Russian forces.

In December 1941 a *Mitchell* operating from the West Coast sank the first Japanese submarine of the war. Five months later, in April 1942, 16 B-25s under Colonel James H. Doolittle staged a brilliant raid from the deck of the American carrier USS *Hornet* against Tokyo and four other Japanese cities. Damage was slight and all the bombers subsequently crashed in China, but the attack was an enormous psychological boost for the United States. B-25s went on to replace the more sophisticated Martin B-26 *Marauders* in the Southwest Pacific for ease of maintenance. There they underwent the most drastic rearmament of any aircraft in the American inventory. Starting with the B-25G, a 75mm cannon was fitted to fire through a solid nose. This was augmented by up to 12 .50-caliber machine guns in nose packs for deadly low-altitude strafing. A total of 11,000 B-25s was built during the war, and many functioned as transports until 1959.

**Type:** Light Bomber

**Dimensions:** wingspan, 89 feet, 6 inches; length, 75 feet, 4 inches; height, 25 feet, 2 inches
**Weights:** empty, 49,000 pounds; gross, 110,000 pounds
**Power plant:** 4 × 5,200–pound thrust General Electric J47 turbojet engines
**Performance:** maximum speed, 560 miles per hour; ceiling, 40,000 feet; maximum range, 1,200 miles
**Armament:** 2 × .50–caliber machine guns; 22,000 pounds of nuclear or conventional bombs
**Service dates:** 1948–1958

The *Tornado* was the first four-engine American jet to fly and the first produced for the Air Force. It established many aeronautical records and served capably for a decade.

In 1944 the Army Air Force laid out specifications for a high-performance, multiengine jet bomber, although this was announced before German swept-wing technology became available. Consequently, when North American unveiled its XB-45 in 1947, it was a relatively conventional aircraft with straight, shoulder-mounted wings and four engines in two underslung pods. Although Boeing's XB-47 ultimately won the contest, its deployment would be delayed for five years owing to problems during development. Hence, by default, the B-45A *Tornado* became America's first jet bomber. It was fast and pleasant to fly, although several were lost due to engine and flight-control malfunctions. In 1951 the B-45 became the first jet to test-drop an atomic weapon in Nevada. Consequently, *Tornados* were

sent to Sculthorpe, England, with the Tactical Air Command's 47th Bombardment Group as NATO's first nuclear attack unit. They functioned there for six years before being replaced by the Douglas B-66 *Destroyer* in 1958.

In 1948 ten B-45Cs were built, featuring strengthened airframes and wingtip tanks. They were followed by 33 RB-45Cs, which had 12 high-speed cameras and could be refueled in midair. This version flew actively throughout the Korean War with the Strategic Air Command and made the first American penetrations of Soviet and communist Chinese airspace. In July 1952 an RB-45C won the Mackay Trophy for flying 3,640 miles nonstop from Alaska to Japan. Other *Tornados* with British crews also overflew Russia on a number of secret missions. Although little remembered today, the B-45 was an important transitional aircraft that rendered valuable service during the early Cold War period.

# ✪ North American BT-9/BT-14 *Yale*

**Type:** Trainer

**Dimensions:** wingspan, 42 feet; length, 27 feet, 7 inches; height, 13 feet, 7 inches
**Weights:** empty, 3,314 pounds; gross, 4,471 pounds
**Power plant:** 1 × 400–horsepower Wright R-975 radial engine
**Performance:** maximum speed, 170 miles per hour; ceiling, 19,750 feet; maximum range, 765 miles
**Armament:** none
**Service dates:** 1936–1940

The BT-9 marked North American's debut into the military trainer market. It was fast and modern, a precursor to the more famous AT-6.

In 1935 North American entered its NA-16 prototype into a competition for a new Army Air Corps basic trainer (BT). It was evaluated that year at Wright Field, Ohio, and was found to possess performance approximating the tactical aircraft of the day. In 1936 the Army decided to purchase 42 of the new craft, which received the designation BT-9. These were low-wing monoplanes with fixed landing gear and an enclosed glass canopy for the student and instructor. To spare use of strategic materials, the plane was built with low-metal-alloy tubing, wooden parts, and fabric covering. The Army was pleased by the result and followed up its initial order by taking 40 more BT-9As. They differed from the earlier version by possessing a for-

ward-firing .30-caliber machine gun, a gun camera, and a flexible .30-caliber mount in the rear cockpit for gunnery training. North American then constructed 117 of a slightly modified form, the BT-9B, followed by 67 BT-9Cs. Production concluded with the Navy obtaining 40 BT-9s, which went into service as NJ-1s.

A significant variation from the BT-9 was the BT-14, which featured tail surfaces developed for the new BC-1 trainer (AT-6). This craft also differed from the BT-9 in that it was completely metal-covered and featured a more powerful engine. In 1940 the French ordered 200 BT-19s for the Armée de l'Air, but France was overrun by German forces before deliveries could take place. The aircraft were then shunted over to Great Britain and Canada as trainers, where they were known as the *Yale*. A total of 251 was constructed.

# North American F-82 *Twin Mustang*

**Type:** Fighter; Night Fighter

---

**Dimensions:** wingspan, 51 feet, 3 inches; length, 39 feet, 1 inch; height, 13 feet, 10 inches
**Weights:** empty, 15,997 pounds; gross, 25,591 pounds
**Power plant:** 2 × 1,900–horsepower Allison V-1710 liquid-cooled engines
**Performance:** maximum speed, 461 miles per hour; ceiling, 38,900 feet; maximum range, 2,240 miles
**Armament:** 6 × .50–caliber machine guns; 4,000 pounds of bombs or rockets
**Service dates:** 1946–1953

---

The *Twin Mustang* was the last propeller-driven fighter acquired by the U.S. Air Force. It also scored the first air-to-air kill of the Korean War.

The ocean expanses characterizing the Pacific theater during World War II convinced the Army Air Force that it needed a truly long-range escort-fighter. Two engines and a second crew member were considered highly desirable to ensure safety and reduce pilot fatigue during lengthy missions. In April 1945 North American test-flew its XP-82, which at first glance appeared to be two P-51 fuselages spliced onto the same wing. In fact, the innovative design was an entirely new aircraft. The pilot sat in the left cockpit with the flight instruments, and the copilot/navigator occupied the right cockpit. For flying purposes dual controls were installed, and six machine guns were concentrated in the center wing section. The Army placed an order for 500 aircraft, but when the war ended the bulk of the contract was canceled.

In 1946 the Army decided to formalize production of the new fighter and purchased 273 of various models. Most notable among them was the P-82G, a night-fighter variant with a radar pod mounted midwing between the fuselages. In 1948 the new Air Force redesignated these aircraft the F-82, and within a year they had replaced the Northrop P-61 *Black Widows* as night fighters. When the Korean War broke out, F-82s stationed in Japan were committed to battle, and on June 27, 1950, they scored the first American aerial victory by downing a Yak-9. *Twin Mustangs* flew continuously during the next two years as fighters and bombers, completing 1,868 sorties. They were withdrawn from combat in 1952 and retired from active service the following year.

## ⭐ North American F-86 *Sabre*

**Type:** Fighter

---

**Dimensions:** wingspan, 37 feet, 1 inch; length, 37 feet, 6 inches; height, 14 feet, 8 inches
**Weights:** empty, 13,836 pounds; gross, 24,296 pounds
**Power plant:** 1 × 7,500–pound thrust General Electric J47 turbojet engine
**Performance:** maximum speed, 692 miles per hour; ceiling, 50,000 feet; maximum range, 850 miles
**Armament:** 6 × .50–caliber machine guns or 4 × 20mm cannons; 2,000 pounds of bombs
**Service dates:** 1949–1960

---

The mighty *Sabre* was America's first swept-wing jet and the world's first air-superiority fighter. Throughout the Korean War it dominated the sky and shot down formidable Russian MiGs at a 10:1 ratio.

Toward the end of World War II the Army Air Force initiated development of a second-generation jet fighter. Unlike previous aircraft, which were tested and flown without knowledge of German swept-wing technology, North American designed the first such U.S. jet in 1947. The prototype XP-86 was a beautiful aircraft with an air scoop in the nose, a large bubble canopy well ahead of the wings, and equally swept tail surfaces. Performance and maneuverability were outstanding for the time, so in 1948 it entered production as the F-86A *Sabre*. During testing the *Sabre* established many world speed and altitude records; during one shallow dive it became the first American jet to break the sound barrier.

When the Korean War erupted in 1950, early American jets had little difficulty handling the propeller-driven warplanes they encountered. However, when the superlative Russian MiG-15 intervened that November, they were hard-pressed by that swept-wing dervish. The following month, F-86s were rushed into combat, and on December 17, 1950, a MiG-15 was shot down in the world's first clash between competing swept-wing designs. During the next two and a half years, *Sabres* racked up MiG kills at an astounding 10:1 ratio, shooting down 792 while losing only 76. It thus became the first air-superiority fighter in history.

Postwar refinements culminated in the F-86H, which was strengthened for ground-attack missions and also capable of dropping nuclear weapons. The nimble fighter was widely exported abroad and ultimately served with 20 other air forces. They remained in American service through 1960, at which point 5,375 *Sabres* had been constructed. One of the classic warplanes of all times.

# ☆ North American F-86D *Sabre*

**Type:** Fighter

**Dimensions:** wingspan, 37 feet, 1 inch; length, 40 feet, 4 inches; height, 15 feet
**Weights:** empty, 12,470 pounds; gross, 19,000 pounds
**Power plant:** 1 × 7,650–pound thrust General Electric J47 turbojet engine
**Performance:** maximum speed, 690 miles per hour; ceiling, 50,000 feet; maximum range, 1,200 miles
**Armament:** 24 × 2.74–inch *Mighty Mouse* folding-fin rockets
**Service dates:** 1951–1961

The *Sabre Dog* was the most numerous and most important version of this famous fighter. It was also the first Air Force jet armed entirely with missiles and the first single-seat all-weather interceptor in history.

Faced with the prospect of Soviet bombers attacking over the North Pole, in 1949 the Air Force decided to enhance continental defenses by upgrading the F-86 *Sabre* into an all-weather interceptor. This was no simple task, for the aircraft had to carry the elaborate and heavy APS-6 radar/fire-control system. At length North American modified the F-86 airframe by fitting the radar into a prominent nose bulge. The air inlet was placed below the dome and the fuselage was widened slightly to accommodate a more powerful engine. Because the traditional armament had been displaced by new electronics, a chin tray that housed a battery of 24 *Mighty Mouse*

unguided rockets was fitted. These would be lowered and fired automatically by the radar. The new craft was so different from other *Sabres* that it received the temporary designation YF-95A, but at length it became known as the F-86D. Pilots simply and unofficially referred to it as the *Sabre Dog*.

The XF-86D first flew in 1949 with excellent results, and production was authorized. It thus became the first Air Force jet armed entirely with rockets and the first all-weather interceptor flown by a pilot without a radar operator. Despite the increased weight over other *Sabres*, the *Dog* was fast, and in 1951 it overtook itself in two speed records. Ultimately, 2,504 F-86Ds were constructed, more than any other version. In 1956 the Air Force upgraded 981 *Sabre Dogs* into F-86Ls by splicing onto them the longer F-86H wing. They remained in service with the Air Defense Command until the early 1960s.

# North American F-100 *Super Sabre*

**Type:** Fighter

**Dimensions:** wingspan, 38 feet, 9 inches; length, 49 feet, 6 inches; height, 15 feet
**Weights:** empty, 21,000 pounds; gross, 34,832 pounds
**Power plant:** 1 × 17,000–pound thrust Pratt & Whitney J57 turbojet engine
**Performance:** maximum speed, 864 miles per hour; ceiling, 50,000 feet; maximum range, 1,970 miles
**Armament:** 4 × 20mm cannons; 6,000 pounds of bombs or rockets
**Service dates:** 1954–1979

The *Super Sabre* was the first Air Force fighter to cruise at supersonic speeds. Though designed as an interceptor, it gained renown as a fighter-bomber during the Vietnam War.

In 1948 North American began planning an advanced version of its successful F-86 *Sabre* jet. It proposed a larger aircraft, with wings sharply swept at 45 degrees and a more powerful engine. It was anticipated such a craft could operate at sustained speeds above the sound barrier. The Air Force authorized a prototype, which emerged in 1953 as a sleek machine with low-set wings, a distinct oval air intake, and a slab tailplane. On its first flight the YF-100 broke the world speed record, easily reaching 750 miles per hour. This made it the world's fastest fighter with the possible exception of the MiG-19, then under development. In 1954 the new craft entered into production as the F-100A *Super Sabre;* it gained a reputation as a

"hot" plane to fly, especially upon landing. Many were lost due to pilots' unfamiliarity with supersonic flight, but most liked it and nicknamed it the "Hun," short for "Hundred."

The most numerically important version was the F-100D, which featured strengthened wings for work as a tactical fighter-bomber. It also came equipped with the first low-altitude bombing system, and it was extensively used during the Vietnam War. "Huns" became renowned for their ability to accurately deliver ordnance at high speed, and their services were in great demand. After the war, most were turned over to Air National Guard units, where they lingered in service until 1979. F-100s also equipped the Air Force's famed *Thunderbirds* aerobatic team for 13 years. The Air Force eventually acquired 2,394 *Super Sabres,* many of which were transferred to the Greek and Turkish air forces. Several are still employed as aerial target drones.

**Type:** Fighter

**Dimensions:** wingspan, 38 feet, 2 inches; length, 34 feet, 5 inches; height, 14 feet, 10 inch
**Weights:** empty, 8,182 pounds; gross, 12,135 pounds
**Power plant:** 1 × 4,000–pound thrust General Electric J35 turbojet engine
**Performance:** maximum speed, 542 miles per hour; ceiling, 47,400 feet; maximum range, 1,393 miles
**Armament:** 6 × .50–caliber machine guns
**Service dates:** 1948–1953

The squat, unappealing *Fury* was the first Navy jet deployed at sea and the last armed solely with machine guns. After a brief service life it was passed over for more modern designs.

In January 1945 North American offered to build a new jet fighter for the Navy to compete with designs under construction by McDonnell and Vought. The proposed XFJ-1 was a conventional-looking aircraft with straight, laminar-flow wings and a tubby fuselage. Curiously, the Army Air Force also expressed interest and requested a version called the XP-86. Authorization to proceed was acquired, and in September 1946 the first example flew. The new craft was somewhat rotund yet streamlined, with a circular air intake, and the pilot seated above the ducting. It was also equipped with a nosewheel that could be semiretracted, enabling the fighter to "kneel" for better carrier storage. The

Navy had originally placed an order for 100 of the craft, but it was readily overtaken by more advanced designs; procurement was scaled back to only 30. In 1948 they entered into service as the FJ-1 *Fury*.

Despite its looks the FJ-1 flew rapidly, and for a brief time it was the Navy's fastest aircraft. It was also the last carrier-based fighter armed with six machine guns; thereafter four 20mm cannons became the standard array. The *Furies* served only with one squadron, VF-5A, onboard the carrier USS *Boxer*, the first jet squadron functioning operationally at sea. Several landing accidents prompted removal of the "kneeling" front gear in place of a stronger, conventional one. Fourteen months later the *Fury* was removed from frontline service and used to train Navy Reserve pilots. The last FJ-1s were finally dropped from the inventory in 1953 and scrapped.

# North American FJ-2/4 *Fury*

**Type:** Fighter

**Dimensions:** wingspan, 39 feet, 1 inch; length, 36 feet, 4 inches; height, 13 feet, 11 inches
**Weights:** empty, 13,210 pounds; gross, 23,700 pounds
**Power plant:** 1 × 7,700–pound thrust Wright J64 turbojet engine
**Performance:** maximum speed, 680 miles per hour; ceiling, 46,800 feet; maximum range, 2,020 miles
**Armament:** 4 × 20mm cannons; 3,000 pounds of bombs or rockets or 4 × *Sidewinder* missiles
**Service dates:** 1954–1964

The FJ-2/4 was one of a handful of land-based fighters adopted for carrier use. It evolved into several distinct versions that ultimately had little in common with its F-86 ancestor.

The superiority of Russian swept-wing fighters during the Korean War forced the Navy to adapt similar high-performance aircraft for carrier use. The logical choice was North American's classic F-86 *Sabre*, which had easily dominated the MiG-15 in armed combat. In 1951 the Navy authorized construction of several navalized F-86s that flew later that year as XFJ-2s. They were essentially identical to the Air Force version save for strengthened landing gear, folding wings, and an arrester hook for carrier landings. It also featured four 20mm cannons as standard armament. This extra equipment added 1,000 pounds of weight and adversely affected the aircraft's performance, but the Navy rushed ahead by purchasing 200 FJ-2s and deploying them in 1952.

A new model, the FJ-3, soon followed. It had the movable leading-edge slats removed in favor of fixed, extended leading edges, for better low-speed handling, and a bigger engine. It was also the first *Fury* equipped to handle the new AIM-9 *Sidewinder* heat-seeking missile. But in 1954 the definitive model arrived. In an attempt to increase range, the new plane was fitted with a fattened fuselage to accommodate more fuel, and it had a broadened, strengthened wing with six hardpoints for ordnance. The wing also served as an integral fuel tank that boosted range. Furthermore, the cockpit was raised and featured a distinct dorsal spine running down to the tail. The FJ-4 was heavily armed and could carry six *Bullpup* guided missiles or a single tactical nuclear weapon. These *Furies* remained in frontline service through the early 1960s and were declared obsolete by 1965. A total of 1,162 of all versions had been acquired.

**Type:** Reconnaissance

**Dimensions:** wingspan, 46 feet, 4 inches; length, 33 feet, 7 inches; height, 12 feet, 2 inches
**Weights:** empty, 5,980 pounds; gross, 7,636 pounds
**Power plant:** 1 × 975–horsepower Wright R-1820 radial engine
**Performance:** maximum speed, 221 miles per hour; ceiling, 23,200 feet; maximum range, 400 miles
**Armament:** none
**Service dates:** 1937–1942

The O-47 was the world's first modern observation craft. Though obsolete by World War II, it set the technological standards for what would follow.

From the end of World War I through the 1930s, there had been few advances in reconnaissance craft, either in appearance or performance. This changed in 1934 when the General Aviation Corporation answered an Army competition to build a new photo plane. Headed by James H. "Dutch" Kindleberger, a design emerged that was unlike any previous reconnaissance aircraft. It was a large and somewhat rotund, all-metal, midwing monoplane with fully retractable landing gear. Unlike the two-seat biplanes of the era, the XO-47 sat three crew members under a spacious greenhouse canopy. While the pilot and gunner remained topside, the photographer was given a station deep in the lower fuselage. From this post he was given an excellent and unobstructed view of proceedings below. Another important ad-

vantage was speed: Despite its girth, the XO-47 could cruise along at more than 220 miles per hour, faster than most fighters. In 1936 the Army contracted with North American Aviation, the successor to General Aviation, to build 164 machines; the following year they entered service as the O-47A. It was North American's first military design.

After a few months the Army purchased an additional 74 examples of an improved version, the O-47B. It featured a stronger engine, along with greater fuel capacity and endurance. However, advances in fighter technology soon made the O-47 a sitting duck in air combat, and by 1941 the majority had been turned over to Army National Guard units. Several had been caught at Pearl Harbor and the Philippines during the Japanese attacks, their service careers quickly ending. Most surviving O-47s were subsequently employed as trainers and target tows until replaced by more modern types.

# North American P-51 *Mustang*

**Type:** Fighter

---

**Dimensions:** wingspan, 37 feet; length, 32 feet, 2 inches; height, 13 feet, 8 inches
**Weights:** empty, 7,125 pounds; gross, 11,600 pounds
**Power plant:** 1 × 1,590–horsepower Packard V-1650 liquid-cooled engine
**Performance:** maximum speed, 437 miles per hour; ceiling, 41,900 feet; maximum range, 2,080 miles
**Armament:** 6 × .50–caliber machine guns; 1,000 pounds of bombs or rockets
**Service dates:** 1941–1953

---

The *Mustang* was probably the finest all-around fighter of World War II. Curiously, it came about through the marriage of a superb American airframe to a high-performance British engine.

In 1940 the British Air Purchase Commission approached North American for a new fighter to replace its Curtiss P-40s. The resulting Model NA-86 appeared in less than 120 days and was the first fighter to incorporate wings with a low-drag laminar airfoil. The prototype flew in 1940 and was immediately adopted by the Royal Air Force, which christened it the *Mustang*. The U.S. Army also expressed interest and purchased several as P-51A fighters and A-36 *Apache* dive-bombers.

In Europe the *Mustang* was a fine mid-altitude fighter, but its American-built Allison engine lacked power. The British countered this deficiency by fitting the *Mustang* with a high-performance Rolls-Royce Merlin 61 engine in 1942. The resulting fighter outflew the famous *Spitfire* and all its German adversaries. Because the P-51 also possessed tremendous range, it could now be employed as a fighter-escort during the strategic bombing campaign over Germany. The most numerous version, the P-51D, was distinctive in having a glass bubble canopy for better vision. Its appearance spelled doom for the German Luftwaffe, and by 1945 *Mustangs* had shot down 4,950 German planes in the air and 4,131 on the ground at a loss of only 2,520. The P-51s also served with distinction in the Pacific and escorted B-29 raids over Japan from Iwo Jima. The final model, the P-51H, was the fastest, reaching speeds of 487 miles per hour.

The *Mustang* was the only World War II fighter to remain in the Air Force inventory, and it provided valuable service as a fighter-bomber during the Korean War. It was phased out of American service in 1953. A total of 15,586 *Mustangs* was built, seeing service with 55 air forces around the world.

**Type:** Fighter

**Dimensions:** wingspan, 37 feet, 3 inches; length, 27 feet; height, 9 feet
**Weights:** empty, 4,660 pounds; gross, 5,990 pounds
**Power plant:** 1 × 870–horsepower Wright Cyclone R-1820 radial engine
**Performance:** maximum speed, 270 miles per hour; ceiling, 27,500 feet; maximum range, 635 miles
**Armament:** 2 × .30–caliber machine guns; 2 × 20mm cannons; 750 pounds of bombs
**Service dates:** 1941–1942

A handful of P-64s were constructed, only to be seized to prevent them from falling into enemy hands. Slow and underarmed, they were employed as advanced trainers for a short period.

In 1938 North American began exploring the possibility of manufacturing a simple "lightweight" fighter based upon its BC-1 trainer for the export market. Beginning with a stock BC-1, engineers added a more powerful motor, shortened the fuselage by 2 feet, reduced the wingspan by 5 feet, 4 inches, and built up the fuselage behind the flight deck. Armament consisted of two .30-caliber machine guns on the engine cowling. The resulting NA-50 was inexpensive and marginally effective as a modern fighter. The Peruvian government was sufficiently impressed to order seven copies, which were delivered during 1938–1939. They fought during the brief border war with Ecuador in 1941; two were lost during combat.

In 1939 the government of Siam (Thailand) took notice of the NA-50 and expressed an interest in buying it. However, the new version, the NA-68, was modified with a more angular tail, revised landing gear, and the addition of two pod-mounted 20mm cannons. The added weight and drag hurt performance, but nonetheless Siam ordered six copies. They were constructed and shipped during the fall of 1941, then anchored at Hawaii when the Japanese attacked Pearl Harbor and occupied Siam. Fearful that the fighters would fall into enemy hands, the U.S. government confiscated them. Sent home, they were pressed into service as the P-64 advanced trainer. By 1943 they had been replaced by better aircraft and served the last of their days as liaison craft with the Trainer Command at Luke Field, Arizona. Only one survives in private hands today.

# ☆ North American T-28 *Trojan*

**Type:** Trainer

**Dimensions:** wingspan, 40 feet, 1 inch; length, 33 feet; height, 12 feet, 8 inches
**Weights:** empty, 6,424 pounds; gross, 8,500 pounds
**Power plant:** 1 × 1,425–horsepower Wright R-1820 radial engine
**Performance:** maximum speed, 343 miles per hour; ceiling, 35,500 feet; maximum range, 1,060 miles
**Armament:** 2 × .50–caliber machine guns
**Service dates:** 1950–1984

The *Trojan* was the first U.S. military trainer with tricycle landing gear and was extensively employed by both the Air Force and Navy. Many were subsequently reequipped as fighter-bombers and fought in Southeast Asia and North Africa.

In 1947 the Air Force set out specifications for a new trainer to replace its aging fleet of AT-6 *Texans*. The following year, North American responded with its Model NA-159, which first flew in 1949. Like its predecessor, the XT-28 was a low-wing design that housed its occupants in a long bubble canopy, but it was unique in having tricycle landing gear. It was powered by an 800-horsepower engine turning a two-blade propeller. The Air Force approved the new craft, and in 1950 it was accepted as the T-28A *Trojan*. However, it was considered overpowered for novices, and the Air Force decided to transition cadets in the gentler Beech T-34 *Mentor* first. A total of 1,194 T-28As was purchased.

By 1952 the Navy decided to standardize its training equipment with the Air Force, so it ordered a new version, the T-28B. It featured a much stronger engine, a three-blade propeller, and a redesigned two-piece canopy. Another model, the T-28C, had an arrester hook to practice carrier landings. The Navy ultimately acquired 788 of both versions, and they served until 1984.

The Air Force retired its last T-28s during the late 1950s when the jet-powered Cessna T-37 *Tweety Bird* became available. North American then converted 321 of these into T-28D *Nomads*, which were heavily armed counterinsurgency fighter-bombers. They saw active duty for many years in Southeast Asia and formed the backbone of the South Vietnamese Air Force. The French also acquired T-28s, which they called the *Fennec*, and employed them against Algerian rebels during 1960–1962. The *Trojan* still flies as a trainer and an attack craft in Argentina, Bolivia, Laos, and Thailand.

**Type:** Strategic Bomber

**Dimensions:** extended wingspan, 136 feet, 8 inches; length, 147 feet; height, 34 feet
**Weights:** empty, 192,000 pounds; gross, 477,000 pounds
**Power plant:** 4 × 30,000–pound thrust General Electric F101 turbofan engines
**Performance:** maximum speed, 823 miles per hour; ceiling, 60,000 feet; maximum range, 7,455 miles
**Armament:** 59,000 pounds of nuclear or conventional bombs and cruise missiles
**Service dates:** 1986–

The stealthy and capable B-1 represents a milestone in strategic-bomber design. Though smaller than the B-52 it replaces, it carries more weapons while emitting only one-tenth the radar signature.

In 1965 the Air Force announced the advance manned strategic aircraft requirement for a high-altitude supersonic bomber capable of penetrating the Soviet Union's formidable air defenses. A contract was awarded to North American to build such a plane, and in 1974 the first prototype emerged. It was a unique design with movable wings that could sweep back along the blended airframe. The four engines were podded in pairs under the wing, and through careful engineering the B-1 gave off approximately one-tenth the radar signature of the old B-52. Despite the plane's promising performance, President Jimmy Carter canceled the aircraft in 1977 to concentrate on production of air-launched cruise missiles. However, he permitted four prototypes to continue flying for research purposes.

In 1981 President Ronald Reagan reactivated the B-1 program, which had undergone many modifications in four years. Its mission profile had changed from high-altitude bombing to low-altitude, high-speed penetration, which required a new suite of aerodynamics and electronics equipment. The new version, designated the B-1B *Lancer*, enjoyed redesigned wing slots, fixed engine inlets, and radar-absorbing materials to reduce the aircraft's signature. Currently, the B-1B has a radar cross-section of only three square feet, not much larger than a swan. It also incorporates enhanced electronic countermeasures to ensure survival while operating in hostile airspace. For weaponry, the *Lancer* can drop an assortment of conventional or nuclear weapons and carries several cruise missiles in a rotary bomb bay. The Air Force was allowed to purchase 100 of the big planes, which will form the backbone of American airborne deterrence for decades to come.

# North American/Rockwell OV-10 *Bronco*

**Type:** Fighter-Bomber; Reconnaissance

**Dimensions:** wingspan, 40 feet; length, 44 feet; height, 15 feet, 2 inches
**Weights:** empty, 6,893 pounds; gross, 14,444 pounds
**Power plant:** $2 \times 1,040$–horsepower Garrett T76 turboprop engines
**Performance:** maximum speed, 288 miles per hour; ceiling, 30,000 feet; maximum range, 228 miles
**Armament:** $1 \times 20$mm cannon; 1,200 bounds of bombs or rockets
**Service dates:** 1968–

The low-tech, hard-hitting *Bronco* was the first aircraft designed specifically for counterinsurgency (COIN) operations. One of the most versatile warplanes of the Vietnam War, it was fast, easy to handle, and could absorb great damage.

Having opted out of the Grumman OV-1 *Mohawk* program in 1959, the Marine Corps started looking for a light observation plane to replace its existing inventory of Cessna L-19s *Bird Dogs*. It specified a craft that was fast, easily maintained, and able to carry considerable armament for counterinsurgency warfare. By 1964 a contract was awarded to North American for its unusual Model NA-300. The prototype emerged in 1967 as a high-wing aircraft with two engines and twin booms. A podded fuselage carried two crew members who sat in tandem under a high-visibility canopy. To the rear sat a storage compartment capable of holding five para-troopers or 3,200 pounds of cargo. The new aircraft exhibited excellent short takeoff and landing characteristics and could become airborne in only 750 feet. In 1968 it went into production as the OV-10 *Bronco*, with the Marines acquiring 114 and the Air Force an additional 157.

The OV-10 proved its value in Vietnam in a variety of missions. The Air Force used it widely for forward air control to call in air strikes, and the Marines employed it as a ground-attack aircraft. This version was heavily armed with 7.62mm gunpods and a host of rockets. After the war the Air Force slowly retired the *Bronco*, but the Marines refined theirs into the OV-10D by 1980. This version features nighttime surveillance equipment and a 20mm cannon. Several fought during the 1991 Gulf War; others are still operated by Thailand, South Korea, and Germany.

**Type:** Trainer

**Dimensions:** wingspan, 38 feet, 2 inches; length, 38 feet, 8 inches; height, 14 feet, 9 inches
**Weights:** empty, 8,115 pounds; gross, 13,180 pounds
**Power plant:** 2 × 2,950–pound thrust General Electric J85 turbojet engines
**Performance:** maximum speed, 535 miles per hour; ceiling, 45,200 feet; maximum speed, 1,069 miles
**Armament:** none
**Service dates:** 1959–

The *Buckeye* is the Navy's oldest and most successful jet trainer. It owes its long service life to fighterlike performance and for imparting a wide variety of skills on fledgling naval aviators.

In 1956 the Navy began searching for a modern all-purpose trainer capable of taking a student from the first jet flight through carrier landings. That same year, North American proffered its Model NA-241 as a possible prototype, and a contract was awarded. The finished product rolled out in 1958 as a small, single-engine, midwing jet with student and instructor housed in tandem under a long glass canopy. To reduce design expenses, the craft employed a wing similar to the FJ-1 *Fury* and utilized control panels from the T-28 *Trojan* trainer. A novel feature was in elevating the instructor's seat over the student's seat so that both had equally good vision through the windshield. Like all trainers, the new plane was responsive to controls and delightful to fly, so the Navy authorized construction of 217 T-2J-1s. They entered into service as the *Buckeye*, so nicknamed for Ohio, where the craft were assembled.

In 1962 the *Buckeye* received the new designation T-2A. That same year, North American began experimenting with a more advanced version, the T-2B, which had two Pratt & Whitney J60 turbojet engines in place of the single Westinghouse J34. In 1966 the Navy accepted delivery of 97 of these new machines. Two years later North American rolled out the T-2C, which featured two General Electric J85 engines; an additional 231 machines were purchased. The T-2As were phased out during the early 1970s, but the Bs and Cs have only recently begun to be replaced by the McDonnell-Douglas T-45 *Goshawk*. A total of 545 *Buckeyes* had been constructed, making it one of the most successful jet trainers in Navy history.

# Northrop A-17 *Nomad*

**Type:** Light Bomber

**Dimensions:** wingspan, 47 feet, 8 inches; length, 32 feet, 5 inches; height, 9 feet, 9 inches
**Weights:** empty, 5,370 pounds; gross, 8,949 pounds
**Power plant:** 1 × 1,200–horsepower Wright Cyclone GR-1820 radial engine
**Performance:** maximum speed, 265 miles per hour; ceiling, 32,000 feet; maximum range, 910 miles
**Armament:** 5 × .30–caliber machine guns; 1,800 pounds of bombs
**Service dates:** 1935–1938

When it appeared, the A-17 was the world's most advanced attack aircraft. However, it was rapidly outpaced by better technology and rendered obsolete in only a few years.

Jack Northrop founded the Northrop Aircraft Company in 1932 and gained fame by designing the sleek, all-metal Gamma and Delta commercial aircraft. In concert with talented designer Ed Heinemann, he set out to design a modern attack plane as a private venture. The resulting XA-13 was a streamlined, low-wing monoplane that housed two crew members under an extended canopy. It also possessed fixed front wheels enclosed by attractive fairings. The Army, then in need of a new light bomber, took interest in the craft, but tests revealed that it was overpowered. Northrop then fitted it with a 750-horsepower Wright Cyclone radial to produce a better-flying aircraft, and in 1935 the Army purchased 110 machines as the A-17. The following year,

Northrop conceived of a more powerful version with retractable landing gear, and they went into production as the A-17A. A total of 131 was constructed.

During the late 1930s the A-17 formed the backbone of Army Air Corps attack aviation on account of its speed, armament, and bomb load. However, the appearance of the twin-engine Douglas A-20 *Havoc* in 1939 made it obsolete, and that year the Army cleared the A-17 for export. Northrop concocted a more powerful version, the 8A, which was bought in quantity by China, Peru, and Argentina. When the United States entered World War II several 8As were seized and renamed A-33s. Numbers were sent to Britain and France, who did not want them, and many ended up serving with the South African Air Force. The British dubbed them *Nomads* on the basis of these wanderings. A handful were retained by the Army Air Force for training purposes, and all were gone by 1942.

**Type:** Strategic Bomber

**Dimensions:** wingspan, 172 feet; length, 69 feet; height, 17 feet
**Weights:** empty, 158,000 pounds; gross, 376,000 pounds
**Power plant:** 4 × 19,000–pound thrust General Electric F118 turbofan engines
**Performance:** maximum speed, 600 miles per hour; ceiling, 50,000 feet; maximum range, 7,600 miles
**Armament:** 8 × B61 nuclear weapons, 8 cruise missiles, or 40,000 pounds of conventional bombs
**Service dates:** 1993–

The futuristic *Spirit* is the world's first stealth bomber and virtually invisible to radar. With a price tag of $1.5 billion apiece, it is also the most expensive aircraft ever built.

With the advent of stealth technology in the late 1970s the Air Force turned to Northrop to build a high-performance bomber that could penetrate Soviet defenses without being detected. Previously, the company had designed a number of so-called flying wings during the late 1940s and enjoyed an established reputation for technical innovation. When the prototype XB-2 rolled out in 1988 it was a flying wing—but unlike any ever built before. The new craft possessed a sharply swept wing, its trailing edges forming a double-*W* configuration. The fuselage, by contrast, is smoothly blended into the wings and houses a crew of two and a weapons bay. Four engines are employed in pairs, mounted above the wings and terminated well short of the trailing edge to reduce infrared signatures. Vertical stabilizers are completely absent, as advanced fly-by-wire computer systems automatically provide stable flight.

For all its innovations, the B-2's most impressive aspect is its stealth technology. It has been carefully machined, down to the most minute parts, to minimize the radar signature. The entire craft is also coated with radar-absorbing materials, so that it gives off the same radar cross-section as a bumblebee. Unlike the low-altitude B-1, the *Spirit* is specifically designed for high-altitude penetration of enemy defenses and can accurately deliver a range of conventional or nuclear weapons. Given its tremendous range, B-2s can hit targets anywhere in the world with only one inflight refueling. A total of 20 has been constructed; these ultrasophisticated, ultraexpensive weapons will be operational well into the 21st century.

# ✪ Northrop BT

**Type:** Dive-Bomber

---

**Dimensions:** wingspan, 41 feet, 6 inches; length, 31 feet, 8 inches; height, 9 feet, 11 inches
**Weights:** empty, 4,606 pounds; gross, 7,197 pounds
**Power plant:** 1 × 825–horsepower Pratt & Whitney R-1535 radial engine
**Performance:** maximum speed, 222 miles per hour; ceiling, 25,300 feet; maximum range, 1,150 miles
**Armament:** 1 × .50–caliber machine gun; 1 × .30–caliber machine gun; 1 × 1,000–pound bomb
**Service dates:** 1938–1943

The BT was the Navy's first monoplane dive-bomber. It was never well liked operationally but served as forerunner to a very famous aircraft.

In 1934 the Navy set out specifications for a new carrier-based dive-bomber. Northrop, which had just begun development of its soon-to-be-famous A-17, began working on such a craft under the direction of Ed Heinemann. At length the Northrop entry, the XBT-1, beat out competing entries from such well-known firms as Brewster, Curtiss, Great Lakes, Grumman, and Vought. The winning design was a radial-engine, low-wing monoplane covered entirely by stressed metal. It seated two crew members under a lengthy greenhouse canopy and sported retractable landing gear. They withdrew into two large pods beneath the wings that in an emergency could also be landed upon. It also made imaginative use of split flaps, along the wing's trailing edge, that could be utilized conven-

tionally to slow the plane's approach while landing or as dive-flaps to control descent. Because the flaps initially caused heavy buffeting when extended, they were perforated to improve airflow and worked well.

In 1937 Northrop delivered 54 machines to the Navy that became operational as the BT-1. They equipped two squadrons: VB-5 onboard the carrier USS *Yorktown*, and VB-6 with the carrier USS *Enterprise*. Compared to the docile biplanes they replaced, the BT-1s were a handful and initially disliked by pilots and crew. With greater experience, however, the dive-bomber gained wider acceptance. In 1938 Northrop refined a successor, the BT-2. By that time, however, the company had been taken over by Douglas, and the new craft was christened the SDB *Dauntless*. BT-1s remained in frontline service until 1941 and served two more years as trainers before being scrapped.

**Type:** Transport

**Dimensions:** wingspan, 86 feet, 6 inches; length, 67 feet, 1 inch; height, 23 feet, 1 inch
**Weights:** empty, 26,700 pounds; gross, 41,900 pounds
**Power plant:** 3 × 1,200–horsepower Wright R-1820 radial engines
**Performance:** maximum speed, 207 miles per hour; ceiling, 12,200 feet; maximum range, 1,856 miles
**Armament:** none
**Service dates:** 1950–1955

Though conceived as an advanced tactical transport, the *Raider* looked more like a throwback to an earlier age. Grossly underpowered, it served mainly as a trainer for mechanics.

After World War II, Army Air Force dissatisfaction with troop transport gliders caused it to look for a powered replacement. In 1947 Northrop advanced the idea of militarizing its novel N-23 *Pioneer* commercial transport. By that time the newly formed U.S. Air Force agreed, and in 1949 a prototype was flown. The new craft, designated the YC-125, was a trimotor design that harkened back to the 1920s. It possessed a high wing and a horizontal stabilizer placed midway through the high vertical tail. Landing gear were fixed and arranged so that the rear of the fuselage, which formed a loading ramp, would run parallel with the ground. The crew numbered four: pilot, copilot, navigator, and radio operator. As a troop transport, the YC-125 had been designed to be towed to its objective, like a large glider, or to fly under its own power. It possessed good short takeoff and landing characteristics and could operate from relatively unprepared landing strips. Payload consisted of either 32 fully armed troops or 11,000 pounds of cargo.

In 1950 the YC-125 entered production as the *Raider* in two versions. The C-125A was a light assault transport, of which 13 were built. However, the Air Force also acquired ten C-125Bs, which were specially modified Arctic rescue aircraft with special preheating equipment for the engines. However, while in service the *Raider* was found to be underpowered, and its intended tasks were better fulfilled by newly arriving helicopters. Within months all 23 aircraft became mechanical trainers at Sheppard Air Force Base, Texas, and were declared surplus in 1955.

**Type:** Fighter

**Dimensions:** wingspan, 26 feet, 8 inches; length, 47 feet, 4 inches; height, 13 feet, 4 inches
**Weights:** empty, 9,723 pounds; gross, 24,722 pounds
**Power plant:** 2 × 5,000–pound thrust General Electric J85 turbojet engines
**Performance:** maximum speed, 1,082 miles per hour; ceiling, 51,800 feet; maximum range, 656 miles
**Armament:** 2 × 20mm cannons; 2 × *Sidewinder* missiles; 7,000 pounds of bombs or rockets
**Service dates:** 1962–

Despite more than three decades of service, the F-5 family of fighters still flies in 20 air forces around the world. It combines high performance and low cost into an extremely capable package.

By the late 1950s it became apparent that the expensive, complicated warplanes constructed by the United States and its Western allies were beyond the financial and technical means of poorer, less developed countries. Northrop tackled the problem head-on by designing a lightweight fighter based upon its successful T-38 trainer. The new design was a compact, twin-engine craft with delta-shaped wings and tail surfaces. The prototype flew in 1959 and exhibited delightful maneuverability, along with easy maintenance and the ability to operate off improvised airfields. It also possessed breathtaking climbing ability, reaching 40,000 feet in just four minutes. In 1962 it entered production as the F-5A *Freedom Fighter.* Under the auspices of the Military

Assistance Program, F-5s were acquired by South Korea, Greece, Iran, Norway, and a host of other nations. However, the U.S. Air Force acquired only a single squadron for evaluation purposes. Several were deployed in South Vietnam, where they proved useful as fighter-bombers.

In 1970 a successor to the *Freedom Fighter* was sought, and Northrop countered with a more powerful version, the *Tiger II.* Outwardly similar to the F-5A, the new craft had stronger engines, better avionics, and greatly enhanced performance. It was also relatively cheap and was exported to a wide variety of countries. However, as before, the Air Force acquired only a handful of the new F-5Es. They were utilized in "aggressor squadrons" to simulate Soviet MiG-21s in realistic training exercises. More than 4,000 *Freedom Fighters* and *Tiger IIs* were built between 1962 and 1986. They remain in frontline service around the globe.

# ⭐ Northrop F-89 *Scorpion*

**Type:** Fighter

---

**Dimensions:** wingspan, 60 feet, 5 inches; length, 53 feet, 10 inches; height, 17 feet, 6 inches
**Weights:** empty, 24,194 pounds; gross, 46,780 pounds
**Power plant:** 2 × 5,440–pound thrust Allison J33 turbojet engines
**Performance:** maximum speed, 636 miles per hour; ceiling, 49,200 feet; maximum range, 1,367 miles
**Armament:** 4 × 20mm cannons, 52 × 2.75–inch *Mighty Mouse* rockets, or 6 × *Falcon* radar-guided missiles
**Service dates:** 1950–1959

---

The *Scorpion* was the first all-weather jet fighter specifically designed for that role. It was also the last Air Force fighter possessing a wingspan exceeding the fuselage length.

In 1945 the Army Air Force put out specifications for a new interceptor that could guard the northernmost approaches to the United States in any kind of weather. Northrop, which had previous experience designing the successful P-61 *Black Widow*, submitted a proposal that won the competition in 1946. The prototype emerged in 1948 as a twin-engine, midwing jet with two crew members seated in tandem under a long canopy. Although swept-wing technology was by then being incorporated into other aircraft, Northrop elected to retain a straight wing to maximize low-speed handling in bad weather. It also employed a novelty known as "decelerons," that is, ailerons that split open to act as air brakes. The XF-89 first flew in 1948 and possessed excellent performance for a first-generation jet. It was ordered into production the following year as the F-89A *Scorpion*, a reference reflecting the plane's high, thin tail.

The first three versions of the F-89 featured fixed wingtip tanks and an armament of four 20mm cannons. However, in 1952 the F-89D was introduced, with wing tanks and cannons being deleted in favor of wingtip pods carrying 52 unguided *Mighty Mouse* rockets. In 1956 the latest F-86H model sported nine radar-guided *Falcon* missiles, three in the fuselage and six in both pods. In July 1957 an F-89H also test-fired and detonated a *Genie* nuclear-tipped air-to-air missile, the first such occurrence in history. *Scorpions* were almost exclusively used to patrol the skies of Alaska from Soviet attack, but beginning in 1957 they were phased out by the Convair F-102 *Delta Dart*. However, a handful of these reliable fighters flew with the Wisconsin Air National Guard as late as 1969. A total of 1,050 had been built.

# ⭐ Northrop P-61 *Black Widow*

**Type:** Night Fighter

---

**Dimensions:** wingspan, 66 feet; length, 48 feet, 11 inches; height, 14 feet, 2 inches
**Weights:** empty, 20,965 pounds; gross, 32,400 pounds
**Power plant:** 2 × 2,250–horsepower Pratt & Whitney Double Wasp R-2800 radial engines
**Performance:** maximum speed, 369 miles per hour; ceiling, 33,100 feet; maximum range, 1,000 miles
**Armament:** 4 × .50–caliber machine guns; 4 × 20mm cannons; 6,400 pounds of bombs
**Service dates:** 1944–1952

---

Big, powerful, yet easy to fly, the *Black Widow* was the world's first aircraft specifically designed for night fighting. It was a complex forerunner of today's all-weather interceptors.

By 1940 the British experience with night fighting prompted the Army Air Corps to consider acquiring a specialized aircraft for that task. Northrop responded with a design true to the company's reputation for innovation. The XP-61 was a robust, twin-boom aircraft with a heavy armament and a central fuselage pod that housed a pilot, a radar operator, and a gunner. Its long nose housed the latest airborne interception radar; armament consisted of four cannons under the belly and four machine guns in an electrically controlled dorsal turret. Despite its size—rivaling that of a medium bomber—it flew well and was especially adept at tight turning. As such it could locate enemy aircraft in total darkness and deftly maneuver for an attack. The Army liked

the design, and in 1941 it placed an initial order for 150 P-61As. Owing to the planes' gloss-black camouflage, they were promptly christened *Black Widow* after the poisonous spider.

The P-61s were ready for deployment in mid-1944, arriving as a welcome change to the inadequate Douglas P-70s. Because the first models suffered from buffeting, the top turrets were usually removed. *Black Widow* squadrons in both Europe and the Pacific scored early on and established the plane as the best and most versatile night fighter of World War II. Equipped with four 1,600-pound bombs, they also served as capable night intruders. By 1945 a total of 706 P-61s had been delivered. An additional 36 reconnaissance versions, the F-15A *Reporter*, were built in 1946. The redoubtable *Black Widow* served as a night fighter and trainer until 1952, when it was replaced by jet aircraft.

**Type:** Trainer

**Dimensions:** wingspan, 25 feet, 3 inches; length, 46 feet, 4 inches; height, 12 feet, 10 inches
**Weights:** empty, 7,410 pounds; gross, 11,761 pounds
**Power plant:** 2 × 2,680–pound thrust General Electric J85 turbojet engines
**Performance:** maximum speed, 805 miles per hour; ceiling, 45,000 feet; maximum range, 975 miles
**Armament:** none
**Service dates:** 1961–

The *Talon* was the Air Force's first supersonic jet trainer. Safe, dependable, and pleasant to fly, it continues in this capacity after nearly 40 years.

By the mid-1950s the Air Force wanted to replace its subsonic Lockheed T-33s with a jet trainer that mimicked the high-performance fighters being deployed. It so happened that Northrop had been developing a lightweight fighter concept that would be equally applicable to training purposes. The prototype was constructed in 1959 as a compact, low-wing jet with students and instructors seated in tandem under a long canopy. Some questioned the wisdom of exposing inexperienced fliers to a potentially dangerous supersonic trainer, but in every respect the XT-38 was docile to fly and control, even at high speeds. Production commenced in 1960, and the following year it entered service as the T-38 *Talon*. By the time production ended in 1970, 1,187 had been built.

Despite its reputation for high performance, the T-38 became renowned for reliability, ease of maintenance, and a safety record second to none. They are used exclusively by undergraduate pilots during the final stages of pilot training, which includes aerobatics, night flying, formation flying, and navigation. The Air Force acquired 1,139 T-38s; 46 went to West Germany. It is conservatively estimated that more than 60,000 pilots have since earned their wings by training in *Talons*. The five T-38s obtained by the Navy went into its famous Top Gun fighter-pilot program for use as aggressor aircraft. The craft was also selected by the Air Force's *Thunderbirds* aerobatic team, which flew them between 1974 and 1982. Furthermore, the National Aeronautical and Space Administration selected the T-38 for astronaut proficiency training and purchased 24 machines. With constant engine, fuselage, and electronics upgrades, most *Talons* are expected to fly until after 2010.

**Type:** Fighter

**Dimensions:** wingspan, 33 feet; length, 21 feet, 5 inches; height, 8 feet, 4 inches
**Weights:** empty, 1,908 pounds; gross, 2,820 pounds
**Power plant:** 1 × 300–horsepower Hispano-Suiza H liquid-cooled engine
**Performance:** maximum speed, 139 miles per hour; ceiling, 12,450 feet; maximum range, 340 miles
**Armament:** 2 × .30–caliber machine guns
**Service dates:** 1920–1922

The Orenco D was the first American-designed fighter to enter production. It exhibited excellent performance but failed to gain wide acceptance.

Throughout World War I the massive American political and military bureaucracies prevented the United States from developing and fielding domestically designed warplanes. Consequently, U.S. air units that fought in Europe had to be equipped with French and English machines. During this period the Ordnance Engineering Corporation (Orenco) of Baldwin, Long Island, New York, began designing and marketing warplanes on its own. The first craft, the Orenco A, was a two-seat biplane trainer whereby pilot and instructor sat side by side. When the plane failed to attract orders, Orenco switched its attention to the Type B, a single-bay biplane fighter similar to the French Spad. The Army Air Service ordered four Type Bs for evaluation and five more of the Type Cs, which were similar but outfitted for training and reconnaissance.

By the end of 1918 Orenco had perfected its Type D fighter, and four prototypes were built. It was a conventional, double-bay biplane, the only American model with an all-plywood fuselage. Powered by a 300-horsepower liquid-cooled motor, it possessed climbing and turning ability equal to the latest Sopwith Snipe, Nieuport 28, and Spad 13 fighters. In 1919 the Army reacted to these glowing reports by considering the Orenco D for production. However, because of the practice of encouraging companies to bid on other manufacturers' products, the contract was awarded to Curtiss. The 50 production models produced were somewhat heavier than the original prototypes, and their performance was consequently downgraded. For reasons that are not completely known, the promising Model D was superseded by the Thomas-Morse MB-3, a less imaginative design. Curtiss later manufactured a single-bay version called the PW3, but they never went beyond ground testing. Nonetheless, to Orenco's Model D goes the distinction of being the first American-designed fighter to reach production status.

**Type:** Fighter

**Dimensions:** wingspan, 41 feet, 7 inches; length, 25 feet, 3 inches; height, 10 feet, 7 inches
**Weights:** empty, 2,561 pounds; gross, 3,746
**Power plant:** 1 × 425–horsepower Liberty liquid-cooled engine
**Performance:** maximum speed, 133 miles per hour; ceiling, 21,500 feet; maximum range, 320 miles
**Armament:** 4 × .30–caliber machine guns
**Service dates:** 1918–1924

Although no U.S.-designed land aircraft saw combat during World War I, the LUSAC 11 did arrive in France before the Armistice. It never achieved operational status but did establish several world altitude records during the postwar period.

When the United States entered World War I in April 1917, it possessed no modern combat aircraft. Consequently, American air units that fought in France did so flying aircraft of French or British manufacture. To offset this embarrassing disadvantage, the U.S. Army Engineering Division sought to capitalize upon European expertise by having a French officer participate in a joint design effort. The man chosen was Captain Georges Lepere, who was attached to the French Aeronautical Mission in Washington, D.C. The craft Lepere helped design became known by its initials as the LUSAC 11, for "Lepere United States Army Combat." Consequently, the final design possessed a great degree of Gallic influence. The LUSAC 11 was a handsome, two-seat fighter with staggered, two-bay wings. The use of box struts made it possible to dispense with the usual bracing wires. Constructed of wood and fabric, it was powered by the famous Liberty engine and exhibited excellent performance. Consequently, the Army contracted with the Packard Motor Car Company of Detroit, Michigan, to manufacture 3,525 machines, but only 28 had been completed by the time the war ended. The bulk of the order was then canceled, but two LUSAC 11s did arrive in France for training purposes, the only U.S.-built land planes to do so.

After the war, most of the LUSAC 11s lingered at the Army Engineering Laboratory at Cook Field, Ohio, as test vehicles. In 1920 one became the first Army aircraft equipped with a turbosupercharger. Thus modified, between 1920 and 1924, this craft established three altitude records by clawing its way up to 33,000, 34,000, and 41,000 feet respectively. The army also built three examples of the LUSAC 21, which was powered by a 16-cylinder Bugatti engine, but they failed to enter production.

# Piasecki H-21 *Workhorse/Shawnee*

**Type:** Transport Helicopter

---

**Dimensions:** rotor span, 44 feet, 6 inches; length, 52 feet, 4 inches; height, 15 feet, 1 inch
**Weights:** empty, 8,700 pounds; gross, 13,500 pounds
**Power plant:** 1 × 1,425–horsepower Wright Cyclone R-1820 radial engine
**Performance:** maximum speed, 130 miles per hour; ceiling, 9,280 feet; maximum range, 300 miles
**Armament:** 2 × .50–caliber machine guns; 4 × .30–caliber machine guns; 24 × 2.75–inch rockets
**Service dates:** 1953–1965

---

The H-21 was the first tandem-rotor helicopter acquired by the U.S. Air Force. A similar version also served with the Army and fought during the initial stages of the Vietnam War.

In 1948 the Navy asked Piasecki to develop an improved, all-metal version of its HRP-1 "Flying Banana." The new craft, dubbed HRP-2, was completely redesigned and now seated two crew members side by side rather than in tandem. The Navy acquired only five machines, but the Air Force soon expressed interest in the design. In 1953 the helicopter entered service as the H-21A *Workhorse*, of which 38 were outfitted for Arctic rescue service. This was soon followed by the H-21B, a tactical transport version, which featured armor, an autopilot, and the capacity to carry 14 troops or 12 stretchers. The Air Force ultimately purchased 138 of these.

In 1952 the Army also began looking for an advanced twin-rotor helicopter to serve as a medium utility transport. The Army encouraged production of a third version, the H-21C *Shawnee*, which retained the armor and troop conveyance of the Air Force model but also carried a 4,000-pound belly sling hook for cargo. The Army ordered 338 H-21Cs; another 150 made their way into French, German, and Japanese service.

Despite its ungainly appearance, the *Shawnee* was a rugged aircraft with pleasant flying characteristics, and it broke several world records. In 1956 an H-21 named "Amblin' Annie" became the first helicopter to fly across the United States nonstop while being refueled in the air. In 1961 H-21s became the first American helicopter to fight in Vietnam as transports and makeshift gunships. By 1965 they were replaced in both roles by the more modern Bell UH-1 *Iroquois* and retired from service.

**Type:** Transport Helicopter

**Dimensions:** rotor span, 41 feet; length, 48 feet, 2 inches; height, 12 feet, 6 inches
**Weights:** empty, 5,150 pounds; gross, 8,000 pounds
**Power plant:** 1 × 600–horsepower Pratt & Whitney Wasp R-1340 radial engine
**Performance:** maximum speed, 105 miles per hour; ceiling, 8,500 feet; maximum range, 265 miles
**Armament:** none
**Service dates:** 1947–1953

Though much derided as the "Flying Banana," the HRP was a revolutionary aircraft. It was the world's first practical tandem-rotor helicopter and, at the time of its appearance, the world's largest.

In 1944 helicopter pioneer Frank N. Piasecki accepted the Navy's invitation to construct a new utility and rescue aircraft. The prototype emerged three years later as the XHRP-1 and was unlike any helicopter built up to that time. The most obvious difference was the use of two tandem-mounted three-bladed rotors at either end of the fuselage. This approach offered more flexibility with regard to the aircraft's center of gravity and cargo placement. The large rotors were powered by a single radial engine mounted in the rear of the craft, which seated a crew of two in tandem and carried eight passengers or six stretchers. The fuselage itself was distinctly bent upward toward the aft section, sported twin tails, and was partially covered by fabric. It acquired

the nickname "Flying Banana" for obvious reasons. Despite its bizarre appearance, however, the HRP represented a quantum jump in lifting, range, and hovering capacities and could also be fitted with flotation gear for water landings. In 1946 the Navy ordered 20 machines, which entered into service as the HRP-1 *Rescuer*.

The bulk of HRPs was turned over to the Marine Corps, which used them to develop aerial assault tactics from the light carrier USS *Saipan*. A handful also ended up with the Coast Guard, where they served several years as search-and-rescue aircraft. All HRPs were finally withdrawn from service in 1953. However, in 1948 the Navy ordered five examples of a new version, the HPR-2, which featured cleaner lines and was entirely metal-covered. Though not adopted outright, this craft served as the basis of the famous H-21 *Shawnee* helicopter.

# Piasecki HUP *Retriever*/H-25 *Army Mule*

**Type:** Transport Helicopter

**Dimensions:** rotor span, 35 feet; length, 31 feet, 10 inches; height, 12 feet, 6 inches
**Weights:** empty, 4,214 pounds; gross, 6,000 pounds
**Power plant:** 1 × 525–horsepower Continental R-975 radial engine
**Performance:** maximum speed, 119 miles per hour; ceiling, 10,200 feet; maximum range, 275 miles
**Armament:** none
**Service dates:** 1950–1964

The HUP was the first helicopter fitted with an autopilot and the first able to fly and hover on instruments alone. A modest performer, it rendered useful service throughout the Korean War.

In 1945 the Navy put forward specifications for a small helicopter to be flown from carriers and large warships for the purpose of rescuing downed pilots in the water. Piasecki, which had already achieved considerable success with its HRP "Flying Banana," began working on the XHJP-1. In 1948 it emerged as a tandem-rotor design with three fixed wheels. Moreover, the rotors, being staggered in height, overlapped, resulting in a relatively short, all-metal fuselage. The cockpit housed a crew of two seated side by side, and a total of five passengers or three stretchers could be carried. The Navy approved the design, and in 1950 it accepted delivery of 32 machines as the HUP-1 *Retriever*. In action, pilots would be rescued by means of a winch that

lifted them to the cabin door. Shortly thereafter the HUP-2 was developed, an antisubmarine warfare version that featured a dipping sonar for detecting enemy vessels. It was also the first helicopter to be fitted with an autopilot to assist hovering in any weather. Technical snags prevented deployment of this model until 1953; a total of 165 was built.

Meanwhile, in 1953 the Army began looking at the HUP as an interim transport while waiting for the bigger H-21C *Shawnee*. This version, designated the H-25 *Army Mule*, was basically the same machine outfitted with power-assisted controls, a strengthened cargo floor, and enlarged doors. The Army acquired 70 machines, but by 1955 they were deemed unsuited for fieldwork, and most were handed over to the Navy as HUP-3s. Throughout the Korean War, the HUPs did exemplary service by rescuing downed Allied pilots. They were retained in fleet service until 1964.

# ★ Piper O-59/L-4 *Grasshopper*

**Type:** Liaison

**Dimensions:** wingspan, 34 feet, 3 inches; length, 22 feet, 4 inches; height, 6 feet, 8 inches
**Weights:** empty, 695 pounds; gross, 1,220 pounds
**Power plant:** 1 × 65–horsepower Continental air-cooled engine
**Performance:** maximum speed, 87 miles per hour; ceiling, 9,500 feet; maximum range, 250 miles
**Armament:** none
**Service dates:** 1942–1945

The L-4 was the most numerous and successful of the Army *Grasshoppers*. It flew its first mission of World War II from the deck of a carrier.

In 1941 the Army began investigating the possibility of employing light, civilian-style cabin planes as military liaison and utility craft. That year Piper lent the Army four of its popular J-3 *Cubs* for evaluation under the designation YO-59. They were simply constructed machines consisting of a welded steel-tube frame and wooden spars covered by fabric. The YO-59s demonstrated their worth as observation and artillery spotting aircraft during the famous Louisiana maneuvers of 1941, and so the Army ordered an additional 40 machines as O-59s. Along with similar craft from Aeronca, Interstate, Stinson, and Taylorcraft, the Pipers were passed into service as *Grasshoppers*, so named for their ability to fly and land virtually anywhere.

World War II witnessed a dramatic expansion of liaison craft use, and the Piper O-59 became the most numerous model. Renamed L-4 in mid-1942, it flew its first combat mission that fall when three L-4s were launched from the carrier *Ranger* during the invasion of North Africa. Thereafter, the slow and dependable Pipers became a common site on the battlefields of Europe and Asia. Despite their simple construction, L-4s were rugged and easy to fly and maintain. In addition to artillery spotting they functioned in a variety of roles, including pilot training, courier service, and frontline scouting. No less than 5,413 L-4s were built, including 250 Navy NE-1s. An important variation was the TG-8, a glider trainer whereby the engine section of a standard L-2 was replaced by a canopy. The L-4 was gradually phased out of active service after the war, but some lingered on well into the 1950s. Several hundred remain in civilian hands today.

# ✪ Republic F-84 *Thunderjet*

**Type:** Fighter-Bomber

**Dimensions:** wingspan, 36 feet, 5 inches; length, 38 feet, 1 inch; height, 12 feet, 7 inches
**Weights:** empty, 11,095 pounds; gross, 23,525 pounds
**Power plant:** 1 × 5,600–pound thrust Wright J35 turbojet engine
**Performance:** maximum speed, 622 miles per hour; ceiling, 40,500 feet; maximum range, 2,000 miles
**Armament:** 6 × .50–caliber machine guns; 6,000 pounds of conventional or nuclear bombs
**Service dates:** 1947–1956

The *Thunderjet* was the first fighter-bomber to carry nuclear weapons. It was conceived as a jet-powered successor to the famous P-47 *Thunderbolt* and acquired equal fame in the same role.

In 1944 Republic began development of a jet aircraft to succeed its legendary *Thunderbolt*. In 1946 the slim and elegantly simple prototype emerged with straight wings, tricycle landing gear, and a large bubble canopy. In September 1946 it broke the world speed record of 611 miles per hour and entered into production the following year as the P-84 *Thunderjet*. In 1948 it was redesignated F-84 once the "Pursuit" category was dropped in favor of "Fighter."

In service, the F-84 proved fast, rugged, and dependable. These features were put to outstanding use during the Korean War, where *Thunderjets* were used for a variety of missions. They frequently escorted B-29 raids over North Korea and tangled with

superior, swept-wing MiG-15s. However, F-84s distinguished themselves as close-support aircraft, bombing, rocketing, and strafing enemy targets on a daily basis. In May 1953 massed formations of up to 90 *Thunderjets* destroyed two important dams and deprived North Korea of all its electrical power. By war's end they had flown more than 86,000 missions and dropped more than 50,000 tons of bombs.

The final version, the F-84G, was the first single-seat fighter-bomber in history able to carry tactical nuclear weapons. The craft was also unique in having pioneered the art of aerial refueling, and in 1950 a *Thunderjet* became the first jet fighter to cross the Atlantic Ocean nonstop. In 1953 the famous Air Force *Thunderbirds* aerobatic team was formed, and it was initially equipped with F-84s. By the time production ended in 1953, a total of 4,457 F-84s had been built. They left frontline service beginning in 1956.

**Type:** Fighter-Bomber

**Dimensions:** wingspan, 33 feet, 7 inches; length, 43 feet, 4 inches; height, 14 feet, 4 inches
**Weights:** empty, 13,645 pounds; gross, 28,000 pounds
**Power plant:** 1 × 7,220–pound thrust Wright J65 turbojet engine
**Performance:** maximum speed, 620 miles per hour; ceiling, 46,000 feet; maximum range, 2,200 miles
**Armament:** 6 × .50–caliber machine guns; 6,000 pounds of bombs or rockets
**Service dates:** 1954–1961

Although still carrying the designation F-84, the *Thunderstreak* had little in common with its straight-wing predecessor. It was nonetheless an agile craft and was once considered for use as a parasite fighter.

By 1949 it was apparent that straight-wing jets were on the verge of obsolescence thanks to developments in swept-wing technology, and Republic began work on a swept-wing successor to the F-84 *Thunderjet.* It began as a company project owing to a lack in defense funding, but as the Air Force developed interest more money became available. The first prototype XF-84F flew in 1950, equipped with a low-thrust J35 engine. Its performance remained decidedly subsonic, so the Air Force suggested that a larger J65 engine be utilized instead. This change necessitated heightening the fuselage seven inches, giving it a more oval shape. A streamlined canopy and smaller air intake were also provided. The new prototype flew in 1951 with impressive results, and

production was authorized. In 1954 the first of 2,711 F-84Fs went into service as the *Thunderstreak.*

Like the *Thunderjet,* the F-84F was rugged, dependable, and an excellent ground-attack aircraft. Because NATO airpower was then in need of bolstering, the *Thunderjet* became the first American jet widely exported under the Military Assistant Program. West Germany acquired 480 F-84Fs, Italy 200, Belgium 197, France 150, Norway 175, and the Netherlands 75. As these aircraft were phased out by Lockheed's F-104G during the mid-1960s, many F-84Fs were passed along to Greece and Turkey. The *Thunderstreak* was also taken into consideration for use as parasite fighters strapped to the wingtips of giant Convair B-36 bombers. Development of inflight refueling made this expedient unnecessary, and so the idea was dropped. The remaining American F-84Fs lingered until 1961, when they were finally supplanted by F-100 *Super Sabres.*

# ⭐ Republic F-105 *Thunderchief*

**Type:** Fighter-Bomber

**Dimensions:** wingspan, 34 feet, 11 inches; length, 69 feet, 7 inches; height, 20 feet, 2 inches
**Weights:** empty, 28,393 pounds; gross, 54,027 pounds
**Power plant:** 1 × 24,500–pound thrust Pratt & Whitney J75 turbojet engine
**Performance:** maximum speed, 1,480 miles per hour; ceiling, 32,000 feet; maximum range, 2,390 miles
**Armament:** 1 × 20mm Gatling gun; 14,000 pounds of bombs or rockets
**Service dates:** 1958–1980

The mighty *Thunderchief* was the largest single-seat, single-engine fighter-bomber in history and the first to exceed Mach 2. Known variously as the "Thud" and the "Lead Sled," it bore the brunt of the air war over North Vietnam, flew the most missions, and took the heaviest losses.

In 1951 Republic undertook a private venture to develop a supersonic successor to its F-84F *Thunderstreak*. The new design was intended to deliver nuclear or conventional ordnance at high speeds and low altitudes in any weather. The Air Force became interested, and a contract for several prototypes was signed. They rolled out in 1955 as the biggest fighter-bombers ever built. The XF-105 was a swept-wing jet with unusual forward-pointing air intakes and low-mounted, swept tailplanes. Possessing a large internal bomb bay, it also had air brakes that doubled as secondary afterburners. Fully loaded, the craft could carry a staggering 14,000 pounds—seven tons—of ordnance aloft,

more payload than the World War II–era Boeing B-17 bomber. During its first flight, the XF-105 broke the sound barrier and was ordered into production as the F-105 *Thunderchief* in 1958. A total of 833 was acquired.

Throughout the Vietnam War, highly automated *Thunderchiefs* gained a legendary reputation as a ground-attack aircraft. Flying fast and low, it accurately bombed scores of heavily defended targets, and its rugged construction kept losses to less than 1 percent per mission. In 1972 the two-seat F-105F version was introduced for "Wild Weasel" antimissile missions and was highly successful. Ultimately, *Thunderchiefs* flew 101,000 strike missions and dropped 202,596 tons of bombs. A total of 382 was shot down, but sometimes the hulking fighters struck back, and they are credited with 25 MiG kills. The few remaining battle-scarred *Thunderchiefs* were transferred to reserve units in 1980 and were finally retired four years later.

# ✪ Republic P-43 *Lancer*

**Type:** Fighter

**Dimensions:** wingspan, 36 feet; length, 28 feet, 6 inches; height, 14 feet
**Weights:** empty, 5,654 pounds; gross, 7,935 pounds
**Power plant:** 1 × 1,200–horsepower Pratt & Whitney R-1830 radial engine
**Performance:** maximum speed, 349 miles per hour; ceiling, 38,000 feet; maximum range, 800 miles
**Armament:** 2 × .50–caliber machine guns; 2 × .30–caliber machine guns
**Service dates:** 1940–1942

The *Lancer* was a failed attempt to improve upon the earlier P-35. However, the lessons learned were incorporated into a truly great fighter—the P-47 *Thunderbolt*.

In 1938 Seversky engineers embarked upon a private venture in an attempt to update the performance of the existing P-35 fighter. They fitted a stock fuselage with a supercharged Pratt & Whitney Twin Wasp radial engine for better all-around performance, especially at high altitude. The AP-4 prototype registered marked improvements in speed and altitude, so in May 1939 the Army ordered 13 examples for evaluation as YP-43s. This happened just before the Seversky venture changed its name to the Republic Aircraft Corporation. After delivery and testing in 1941, 54 P-43s and 80 P-43As (which had a slightly different engine) were ordered as the *Lancer*.

The P-43 bore the trademark elliptical wing of its P-35 forebears, but it possessed greater streamlining and inwardly retracting landing gear. A new variant, the P-43A-1, was also developed with a better engine; this resulted in an order for an additional 125 of the new machines. The *Lancer* was an improvement over many existing designs, but judging from reports coming from Europe its performance remained inferior to contemporary English and German aircraft. Therefore, P-43s only served as a photoreconnaissance aircraft with the Army Air Corps. However, of the total 272 planes produced, no less than 108 of them had been offered as lend-lease fighters to the Nationalist Chinese Air Force. They fought several years against better Japanese aircraft and proved mediocre at best. Fortunately for Republic, it used the experience with the *Lancer* to develop a new and better airplane, the P-47, which carried the basic design to its ultimate and most successful conclusion.

# ⭐ Republic P-47 *Thunderbolt*

**Type:** Fighter

**Dimensions:** wingspan, 40 feet, 9 inches; length, 34 feet, 10 inches; height, 14 feet, 2 inches
**Weights:** empty, 10,700; gross, 19,400 pounds
**Power plant:** 1 × 2,000–horsepower Pratt & Whitney R-2800 Double Wasp radial engine
**Performance:** maximum speed, 428 miles per hour; ceiling, 38,000 feet; maximum range, 1,900 miles
**Armament:** 8 × .50–caliber machine guns; 2,500 pounds of bombs or rockets
**Service dates:** 1942–1955

The P-47 was the largest single-engine craft built during World War II, and the Army Air Force acquired it in greater numbers than any other fighter. The *Thunderbolt*'s ability to absorb incredible damage and stay aloft was legendary, and pilots affectionately referred to it as the "Jug."

This famous craft was a further development of the mediocre P-43 *Lancer*. It was built around a 2,000-horsepower Pratt & Whitney radial engine and carried a supercharger in the aft section of the fuselage. The prototype XP-47 flew for the first time in May 1941 and showed great promise, but a succession of technical problems delayed production until spring 1942.

When the *Thunderbolt* finally reached England in January 1943, its lumbering size was greeted with skepticism by many pilots. In combat, however, the P-47 possessed fine high-altitude performance and, by dint of great weight, could outdive any German fighter. But the *Jug*'s finest attribute was sheer strength. A *Thunderbolt* could sustain tremendous damage to wings, engine, and fuselage yet carry itself and pilot safely back home. The most numerous model, the P-47D, introduced a bubble canopy to improve pilot vision and a broad-blade propeller for better performance.

Lack of range prevented P-47s from enjoying success as a fighter-escort over Germany, and when P-51 *Mustangs* began undertaking escort duty the *Thunderbolts* were unleashed as ground-attack fighters. They excelled in that role, given their high speed and heavy armament, and shot up tanks, airfields, and locomotives with deadly effect. To overcome the range deficiencies, a new model, the P-47N, featured an enlarged wing housing additional fuel, and it successfully escorted B-29 raids over Japan from Iwo Jima. A total of 15,579 *Thunderbolts* was constructed, and they remained in service with Air National Guard units until 1955. Several South and Central American air forces maintained P-47s up through the 1960s.

**Type:** Reconnaissance

**Dimensions:** wingspan, 33 feet, 7 inches; length, 47 feet, 7 inches; height, 15 feet
**Weights:** empty, 14,025 pounds; gross, 27,000 pounds
**Power plant:** 1 × 7,800–pound thrust Wright J65 turbojet engine
**Performance:** maximum speed, 620 miles per hour; ceiling, 46,000 feet; maximum range, 2,200 miles
**Armament:** 4 × .50–caliber machine guns
**Service dates:** 1954–1972

The *Thunderflash* was the first modern jet fighter converted into a photoreconnaissance aircraft. It was the final variant of a long and distinguished family.

In 1952 Republic began work on a reconnaissance version of the F-84F *Thunderstreak*, then still under development. Republic accomplished this by transferring the oval air intake to the wing roots and extending the nose. The new craft could then be fitted with a battery of aerial and dicing cameras for close-ups of individual targets. Or it could be configured with an elaborate Trimetrogon camera for taking horizon-to-horizon photographs. The XRF-84F was also the first reconnaissance fighter equipped with camera-control systems and viewfinders that enabled the pilot to act as a trained camera operator. The prototype was successfully flown in February 1952 and ordered into production as the RF-84F *Thunderflash*. It was the first modern swept-wing fighter jet outfitted for photographic purposes and greatly enhanced the flexibility of tactical reconnaissance. A total of 715 was constructed, of which 386 were exported to various NATO countries.

A significant variant was the GRF-84K, which was developed in 1953. This craft had a hook installed in the nose and horizontal tailplanes set at extreme downward angles. This was to ensure that the fuselage could be carried in the bomb bay of a specially designed GRB-36 reconnaissance bomber. The *Thunderflash* would be lowered by means of a mechanical trapeze, fly off on a low-altitude, high-speed mission, then reunite with the mother ship. At length the fighter-conveyor concept was deemed too dangerous and impractical for wartime, but the 25 RF-84Ks subsequently equipped a standard reconnaissance squadron. After 1958 the RF-84s were removed from frontline service, but they functioned with Air National Guard units as late as 1972.

# ✪ Ryan FR-1 *Fireball*

**Type:** Fighter

---

**Dimensions:** wingspan, 40 feet; length, 32 feet, 4 inches; height, 13 feet, 7 inches
**Weights:** empty, 7,915 pounds; gross, 10,595 pounds
**Power plant:** 1 × 1,425–horsepower Wright Cyclone R-1820 radial engine; 1 × 1,600–pound thrust General Electric J31 turbojet engine
**Performance:** maximum speed, 426 miles per hour; ceiling, 43,100 feet; maximum range, 1,030 miles
**Armament:** 4 × .50–caliber machine guns; 1,000 pounds of bombs
**Service dates:** 1945–1947

---

The hybrid *Fireball* was the Navy's first attempt at harnessing jet power for carrier aviation. An unremarkable aircraft, it had a brief and inconspicuous service life yet imparted many useful lessons.

In 1942 the Navy sought to adapt newly emerging jet technology for its own uses. Because contemporary jet aircraft required long takeoffs and high landing speeds, they were initially deemed unsuitable for carrier operations. The remedy pointed to a hybrid aircraft, which would take off and land using its propeller but use the jet engine for climbing and combat. Nine companies responded when specifications were issued in 1943, but the contract was awarded to Ryan, which had never designed a combat aircraft. The prototype XFR-1 was very conventional-looking, a low-wing monoplane with tricycle landing gear and a bubble canopy. A small jet engine was also at the rear of the fuselage, with the air intakes at the wing roots. The XFR-1 was successfully flown in 1944, and the Navy ordered 1,300 aircraft as the *Fireball*. The first squadron, VF-66, was equipped in early 1945, but the war ended before training had finished. Consequently, the contract was canceled with only 66 FR-1s built. Most were retained as test aircraft.

During the fall of 1945, 16 FR-1s were handed over to VF-41 for carrier qualifications onboard the USS *Wake Island*. On November 1, 1945, a *Fireball* made history by conducting the first jet-powered landing on a carrier deck when its piston engine failed! By that time the pure-jet McDonnell FH-1 *Phantom* was being evaluated, and it offered clear performance advantages over hybrid designs. Although much had been learned from the FR-1s, they were unceremoniously mustered out in 1947.

**Type:** Trainer

**Dimensions:** wingspan, 30 feet, 1 inch; length, 22 feet, 5 inches; height, 6 feet, 10 inches
**Weights:** empty, 1,313 pounds; gross, 1,860 pounds
**Power plant:** 1 × 160–horsepower Kinner R-540 radial engine
**Performance:** maximum speed, 131 miles per hour; ceiling, 15,500 feet; maximum range, 352 miles
**Armament:** none
**Service dates:** 1940–1944

The *Recruit* was the Army's first monoplane trainer. It was acquired in several versions and served extensively throughout World War II.

By 1939 the Army was faced with expanding its pool of trained pilots in anticipation of fighting in World War II. That same year, it approached the Ryan Aircraft Corporation of San Diego, California, for one of its noted STA civilian trainers. This low-wing, streamlined aircraft with open cockpits and sleek, spatted landing gear was ostensibly one of the most beautiful aircraft ever flown. It featured a mixed construction of metal fuselage, wooden wing spars, fabric covering, and external wire bracing. The Army saw potential in the aircraft and ordered 15 copies as the YPT-16, the Army's first monoplane trainer. The following year, it ordered 40 more PT-20s, which were slightly revised versions with larger cockpits and some stiffening of the fuselage.

As World War II approached, the Army Air Force was in dire need of great numbers of trainers. The PT-16/20 flew well, but constant use was wearing out their Menasco inline engines; the spatted landing gear was another source of trouble. It was decided to refit the existing fuselage with a larger, more reliable Kinner radial engine. The new Ryan design was called the PT-21, of which 100 were purchased. However, when war broke out the Army ordered 1,023 examples of yet another version, the PT-22 *Recruit*. It featured a more powerful Kinner radial engine and had the wheel spats replaced by simple landing struts for ease of maintenance. The Navy also acquired 100 machines under the designation NR-1. Both types were employed at civilian-operated flight-training schools around the country before their eventual retirement in mid-1944. Several Ryan trainers have been carefully restored and are still operational.

# ★ Seversky AT-12 *Guardsman*

**Type:** Trainer

---

**Dimensions:** wingspan, 41 feet; length, 27 feet, 8 inches; height, 9 feet, 9.5 inches
**Weights:** empty, 4,750 pounds; gross, 6,433 pounds
**Power plant:** 1 × 1,050–horsepower Pratt & Whitney Cyclone R-1820 radial engine
**Performance:** maximum speed, 285 miles per hour; ceiling, 28,000 feet; maximum range, 1,000 miles
**Armament:** 3 × .30–caliber machines guns; 1,350 pounds of bombs
**Service dates:** 1940–1945

---

The Army Air Force acquired the AT-12 by default. Although designed as a two-seat fighter-bomber, it served during World War II as a trainer and squadron hack.

Between 1938 and 1939 Seversky developed a two-seat "escort fighter" version of its successful P-35. It was based upon the previous airframe but featured a more powerful engine, longer wings, and a rear gunner. The new design, the Model 2PA *Guardsman*, could also carry nearly 7 tons of bombs and function as a dive-bomber. When the Army Air Force displayed no interest in the type, Seversky offered it on the export market. Japan purchased 20 of the big machines, which subsequently served with a fighter regiment in China. However, the biggest customer turned out to be Sweden, then desperately in need of new warplanes. Seversky contracted to build 50 planes for that country, but only two had been delivered when World War II broke out and a ban on exports was enacted. Sweden loudly protested this seizure, but U.S. Secretary of State Cordell Hull feared that the country would be conquered by Germany, and so the ban was enforced. Consequently, all 50 of the 2PAs, fully assembled and paid for, remained at the Seversky factory until further notice.

At length the Army decided to adopt the *Guardsman* as AT-12 advanced trainers. To this end, the bomb rack and armament were removed, and they functioned in this capacity until replaced by the better-suited North American AT-6. Thereafter, the need arose for a high-speed courier to ferry senior Air Force officials from field to field to attend conferences. Thus, many AT-12s became the personal aircraft of various base commanders. By 1945 the bulk of these craft had all been wrecked in the line of duty or junked outright. A single AT-12 has survived in flying condition and is based at the Planes of Fame Museum in Chino, California.

**Type:** Trainer

**Dimensions:** wingspan, 36 feet; length, 24 feet, 4 inches; height, 8 feet, 10 inches
**Weights:** empty, 3,017 pounds; gross, 4,050 pounds
**Power plant:** 1 × 400–horsepower Pratt & Whitney R-985 radial engine
**Performance:** maximum speed, 175 miles per hour; ceiling, 15,000 feet; maximum range, 742 miles
**Armament:** none
**Service dates:** 1937–1939

The BT-8 was the Army Air Corps's first all-metal monoplane trainer. Though underpowered and prone to stalling, it set the stage for later trainers.

Throughout the 1930s Alexander P. De Seversky, a former Russian fighter ace, became renowned for producing aircraft of increasingly bold design. In 1933 his most recent machine, the SEV-3, set a world speed record for amphibian aircraft. Two years later, when the Army announced specifications for a new, all-metal, low-wing trainer, Seversky decided to modify the SEV-3 for the task. The new craft was a sleek monoplane with fully enclosed canopies for student and instructor. It was also fitted with conspicuous streamlined wheel fairings. During extensive testing the Seversky design outperformed all rival entries, and in 1936 the Army ordered 30 machines to serve as the BT-8. This was the first "basic" trainer that was not simply a modified biplane or a souped-up holdover from the primary trainer category. It represented a great step forward in aerial instruction technology.

The bulk of the BT-8s was deployed at Randolph Field, Texas, which had long served as the West Point of the Army Air Corps. Students and instructors alike came to appreciate the fine flying qualities of the Seversky craft, as well as the enclosed canopies shielding them from exposure to the elements. However, owing to Army regulations that no trainer should exceed 400 horsepower, the relatively heavy BT-8 was distinctly underpowered. It climbed slowly and, if stalled at low altitude, would invariably crash with fatal results. It also possessed a disturbing tendency to ground-loop (flip over) while being landed by inexperienced hands. Nonetheless, the BT-8 gave the Army Air Corps its first real experience with modern training machines and techniques. By 1939 the Seversky had been superseded by another fine trainer, the North American BT-9. The worn-out BT-8s were summarily grounded and cut up for scrap; none survived.

# Seversky P-35

**Type:** Fighter

---

**Dimensions:** wingspan, 36 feet; length, 26 feet, 10 inches; height, 9 feet, 9 inches
**Weights:** empty, 4,575 pounds; gross, 6,723 pounds
**Power plant:** 1 × 1,050–horsepower Pratt & Whitney R-1830 radial engine
**Performance:** maximum speed, 290 miles per hour; ceiling, 31,400 feet; maximum range, 950 miles
**Armament:** 2 × .50–caliber machine guns; 2 × .30–caliber machine guns; 350 pounds of bombs
**Service dates:** 1937–1941

---

The P-35 was the Army Air Corps's first metal monoplane fighter to feature a retractable undercarriage. Obsolete by World War II, it was a direct predecessor of the famous P-47 *Thunderbolt*.

In 1935 the Army announced a competition for a new generation of all-metal fighters to replace the Boeing P-26. It so happened that Seversky had privately developed an experimental two-seat fighter, the SEV-2XP. It crashed in 1935 and was redesigned by Russian born-engineer Alexander Kartveli as the single-seat AP-1. The new craft possessed an elliptical wing with large, streamlined trouser fairings into which the landing gear retracted. It was also fitted with a fully enclosed canopy and presented a highly streamlined appearance. In 1935 the AP-1 was flown against the competing Curtiss Hawk 75. Neither design achieved 300 miles per hour as promised by their manufacturers, but the Army declared the AT-1 the winner. It purchased 77 machines as the P-35, which became the Army Air Corps's first truly modern fighter.

The P-35 proved delightful to fly, but it suffered from a lack of armament, armor, and speed. To rectify this, Seversky developed a more powerful version for the export market, the EP-106. It featured more guns, a stronger engine, and slightly more speed. Sweden particularly liked the design and ordered 120 aircraft. However, only 60 had been delivered when the outbreak of World War II caused the American government to confiscate the remainder. Those were pressed into service as the P-35A; the Army shipped 48 of them to the Philippines in anticipation of war with Japan. But Japan's surprise attack against the Philippines on December 8, 1941, destroyed most P-35As on the ground, and after two days of fighting only eight survived intact. This concluded the service of Seversky's little fighter, although under Kartveli's direction the design evolved into the famous P-47 *Thunderbolt*.

# Sikorsky CH-3/HH-3 *Jolly Green Giant*

**Type:** Transport Helicopter

---

**Dimensions:** rotor span, 62 feet; length, 73 feet; height, 18 feet, 1 inch
**Weights:** empty, 12,423 pounds; gross, 22,050 pounds
**Power plant:** 2 × 1,500–horsepower General Electric T58 turboshaft engines
**Performance:** maximum speed, 164 miles per hour; ceiling, 13,600 feet; maximum range, 760 miles
**Armament:** 3 × 7.62mm miniguns
**Service dates:** 1963–1995

In 1962 the Air Force acquired three Navy SH-3 *Sea Kings* as support aircraft for its offshore "Texas Towers" radar sites. The experiment was deemed successful, and three more were acquired with the designation CH-3B. However, these aircraft, being almost identical to the Navy versions, were better suited for overwater operations than for land use. Therefore, the Air Force approached Sikorsky to design a new helicopter to meet long-range rescue requirements. In 1963 a new machine, the CH-3C, flew for the first time. Although it retained the same engines, rotors, and power train of its predecessor, the fuselage had been totally redesigned. It dispensed with sponsons and the boat-shaped hull in favor of a loading ramp, a higher tail, and retractable tricycle landing gear. The CH-3 could also carry up to 25 combat troops or 12 stretchers. The Air Force was pleased by the changes and ordered 41 CH-3Cs. In

1966 the CH-3E was introduced with stronger engines. The Air Force accepted 42 of those and rebuilt all its CH-3Cs to the new standard.

Mounting American involvement in the Vietnam War prompted the Air Force to reconfigure 50 CH-3s for work with its elite Aerospace Rescue and Recovery Service. The new version, the HH-3, was fitted with titanium armor, an inflight refueling drogue, self-sealing tanks, and fast-firing miniguns for self-defense. They were deployed to Vietnam as *Jolly Green Giants* and gained renown for an ability to rescue downed American pilots in any weather or terrain. Furthermore, in 1967 a pair of HH-3s became the first helicopters to cross the Atlantic nonstop, being refueled nine times in the air. During the 1991 Gulf War, HH-3s flew 251 combat missions with a reserve squadron. By 1995 the *Jolly Green Giant* was finally retired, replaced by the H-53 *Sea Stallion*.

# Sikorsky CH-53/HH-53 *Sea Stallion*

**Type:** Transport Helicopter

**Dimensions:** rotor span, 72 feet, 3 inches; length, 88 feet, 3 inches; height, 24 feet, 11 inches
**Weights:** empty, 23,485 pounds; gross, 42,000 pounds
**Power plant:** 2 × 3,925–horsepower General Electric T64 turboshaft engines
**Performance:** maximum speed, 196 miles per hour; ceiling, 21,000 feet; maximum range, 257 miles
**Armament:** 3 × 7.62mm miniguns
**Service dates:** 1966–

The powerful *Sea Stallion* is one of the West's largest helicopters, the first helicopter to possess lifting capacity rivaling airplanes of comparable size. It has rendered distinguished service in every American conflict since Vietnam.

During the late 1950s the Marine Corps began seeking a large assault helicopter but decided against adopting the Army's CH-47 *Chinook*. Sikorsky answered by designing its largest-ever helicopter, the massive S-65. The new craft was actually a hybrid, for it employed a scaled-up fuselage from the earlier S-61 and the power train of the CH-54. Like the earlier helicopter, the S-65 employs a watertight hull for water operations, and two sponsons hold the retractable landing struts. The S-65 is powered by two turbine engines fitted on the roof above the cargo hold, driving an enormous six-blade propeller and a four-blade tail rotor. This arrangement also freed the fuselage from obstructions, and consequently it can carry up to 38 armed troops or 24 stretchers or a variety of trucks, jeeps, and missiles weighing up to 8,000 pounds. Alternately, a 13,000-pound payload can be externally slung beneath the aircraft. The Navy and Marine Corps were delighted with the results, and in 1967 they accepted deliveries as the CH-53 *Sea Stallion*. Ultimately, 265 of these giant machines were purchased.

As the war in Vietnam escalated, the Air Force also sought a larger craft than its current HH-3 *Jolly Green Giant* for its Aerospace Rescue and Recovery Service. In 1966 it began modifying several *Sea Stallions* with stronger engines, armor, and three miniguns. The new HH-53 *Super Jollys* subsequently distinguished themselves by recovering several hundred pilots downed behind communist lines. A total of 72 was acquired. The newest Marine Corps version, the CH-53D, can carry up to 68 fully armed troops and is capable of minesweeping operations. Germany and Israel also operate this impressive craft in large numbers.

# Sikorsky CH-53E *Super Stallion*/MH-53 *Sea Dragon*

**Type:** Transport Helicopter

**Dimensions:** rotor span, 79 feet; length, 73 feet, 4 inches; height, 27 feet, 9 inches
**Weights:** empty, 33,226 pounds; gross, 73,500 pounds
**Power plant:** 3 × 4,380–horsepower General Electric General Electric T64 turboshaft engines
**Performance:** maximum speed, 196 miles per hour; ceiling, 18,500 feet; maximum range, 518 miles
**Armament:** none
**Service dates:** 1981–

The three-engine *Super Stallion* is currently the West's most powerful lifting helicopter. It can easily transport 93 percent of the heavy equipment utilized by a Marine Corps division.

By the 1970s advances in engine and computer technology made it possible to improve and enhance existing helicopter designs. In 1973, when the Marine Corps announced specifications for a machine capable of lifting 16 tons, Sikorsky answered with the S-80, an enlarged version of its already successful *Sea Stallion*. In essence, the new helicopter is simply a lengthened CH-53 airframe fitted with three motors. As before, the motors are located on the cabin roof but now drive an extended, seven-blade rotor. The tail section has also been redesigned and sports a 20-foot, four-blade tail rotor and a canted horizontal stabilizer. Thus, by increasing the *Super Stallion*'s power by a full third, the lifting capacity— up to 36,000 pounds—was doubled over earlier versions. This ability will be useful for retrieving battle-

damaged aircraft from carrier decks or delivering heavy equipment to mobile construction battalions. Also, being equipped for inflight refueling, its range is virtually unlimited. The CH-53E entered production in 1981; 100 are currently in service with Navy and Marine Corps units.

A significant subtype is the MH-53 *Sea Dragon*, of which 15 have been deployed. This version features enlarged sponsons on the hull sides for increased fuel capacity and can cruise for up to six hours. The *Sea Dragon*'s mission is minesweeping, and it has been outfitted with a host of computers and detection arrays for this essential task. It is employed by both the American and Japanese navies.

*Super Stallions* debuted in combat during the 1991 Gulf War, flying 2,045 combat sorties without incident. Reputedly, MH-53Es placed secret reconnaissance teams behind enemy lines before hostilities commenced. Both versions will be actively employed as heavy-lift platforms for decades to come.

# ⭐ Sikorsky H-18/HO5S

**Type:** Transport Helicopter; Reconnaissance Helicopter

**Dimensions:** rotor span, 33 feet; length, 27 feet, 5 inches; height, 8 feet, 8 inches
**Weights:** empty, 1,650 pounds; gross, 2,700 pounds
**Power plant:** 1 × 245–horsepower Franklin air-cooled engine
**Performance:** maximum speed, 110 miles per hour; ceiling, 15,800 feet; maximum range, 290 miles
**Armament:** none
**Service dates:** 1952–1958

The diminutive H-18 was the first American helicopter to employ metal rotor blades and at one time held several international speed and altitude records. It served principally with the Marine Corps in Korea as an observation and evacuation craft.

Design work on the Sikorsky civilian S-52-1 began in 1945 once lessons from the R-4 and R-6 helicopters had been fully absorbed. The new craft possessed an all-metal, egg-shaped fuselage seating two passengers and landed on fixed quadricycle landing gear. Powered by a 178-horsepower Franklin engine, it featured an improved rotor head, whereby flapping and drag hinges were closely coordinated, ensuring better control. It was also the first American helicopter to be equipped with all-metal blades for the main and tail rotors. The S-52-1 first flew in 1947 and set several world records for speed (129 miles per hour) and altitude (21,220 feet).

In 1949 the S-52-1 became the first Sikorsky helicopter evaluated by the Army; encouraged by the performance, it purchased four examples as the H-18. However, by 1950 the craft's power and payload were judged unsatisfactory, and it declined to purchase more. However, the Navy displayed considerable interest in a new version, the S-51-2, which featured an enlarged cabin seating four and a stronger 245-horsepower engine. To enhance stability, ventral fins were also fitted at the rear of the tail boom. In 1952 the Navy acquired 89 examples and employed them as the HO5S. They served actively in the Korean War as spotter and rescue craft, and one squadron, VMO-6, staged the first nighttime helicopter evacuations from Pusan. By 1953 their HO5Ss helped remove a total of 7,137 wounded men to safety. Several were also employed by the Coast Guard in search-and-rescue operations. By 1958 all HO5s had been withdrawn and replaced by more advanced machines.

**Type:** Transport Helicopter

**Dimensions:** rotor span, 49 feet; length, 41 feet, 8 inches; height, 13 feet, 4 inches
**Weights:** empty, 5,250 pounds; gross, 6,800 pounds
**Power plant:** 1 × 700–horsepower Wright R-1300 radial engine
**Performance:** maximum speed, 105 miles per hour; ceiling, 15,000 feet; maximum range, 350 miles
**Armament:** none
**Service dates:** 1950–1964

The *Chickasaw* was the first helicopter with a nose-mounted engine and was the first effective troop carrier. Actively employed by all three services, it was also widely exported abroad.

In 1949 Sikorsky undertook development of a large helicopter capable of lifting ten passengers. That same year, the S-55 prototype emerged, representing a breakthrough in helicopter technology. It was an all-metal pod-and-boom design, unique in having a nose-mounted engine. This made for easy servicing through clamshell doors and also kept the cargo hull uncluttered. Furthermore, the crew of two was seated above the passenger cabin and enjoyed excellent forward and side vision. The long boom, which canted downward in later models, possessed a two-blade antitorque rotor and small stabilizing fins.

Sikorsky's new craft was immediately adopted by the Navy and Marine Corps as the HO4S and HRS, respectively. The Navy employed it for transport and rescue duties, but the HRS was used to help develop airmobile doctrine during the Korean War. Marines practiced and refined the vertical assault and envelopment tactics that transformed helicopters into valuable instruments of modern warfare. In 1950 the Air Force also bought a quantity of machines, known as H-19 *Chickasaws*, for search-and-rescue operations. They became famous for retrieving Allied pilots deep behind enemy lines during the Korean War and once hauled back a damaged MiG-15 fighter. By 1952 the Army likewise ordered a quantity of *Chickasaws*, which saw active service during the last few months of the war. A total of 1,067 was built.

In July 1952 a pair of Air Force H-19s made the first crossing of the Atlantic by helicopter in five stages. The *Chickasaw* proved itself to be so rugged and versatile that it was manufactured under license in Japan, France, and Great Britain and was flown by 34 nations. Several examples were active during initial stages of the Vietnam War before being retired in 1964.

# Sikorsky H-34 *Choctaw*/HSS *Sea Horse*

**Type:** Transport Helicopter

---

**Dimensions:** rotor span, 56 feet; length, 46 feet, 9 inches; height, 14 feet, 3 inches
**Weights:** empty, 7,650 pounds; gross, 13,000 pounds
**Power plant:** 1 × 1,525–horsepower Wright R-1820 Cyclone radial engine
**Performance:** maximum speed, 120 miles per hour; ceiling, 9,500 feet; maximum range, 247 miles
**Armament:** 2 homing torpedoes
**Service dates:** 1955–1970

---

The *Choctaw* was the first large helicopter deemed safe enough to transport the president of the United States. Like its predecessor, it was employed by all branches of the armed forces and was also marketed overseas.

By 1952 Navy dissatisfaction with the HSL-1 and the H-19 *Chickasaw* as antisubmarine warfare (ASW) helicopters led it to approach Sikorsky for a new aircraft. In 1954 the prototype S-58 first flew. It appeared to share many characteristics with the older *Chickasaw* but was a larger, more powerful machine. The S-58 had a nose-mounted engine driving a four-blade rotor, but the fuselage configuration was characterized by a downward-sloping boom and tricycle landing gear. This arrangement, coupled with a stronger engine, enabled the XHSS-1 to carry up to 16 passengers or 5,000 pounds of cargo. In 1955 they entered production as the Navy HSS-1 *Sea Bat* and Marine Corps HUS-1 *Sea Horse*. A total of 927 was acquired.

As good as the HSS-1 was, it still lacked sufficient lifting power to carry both detection gear and weapons. Therefore, *Sea Bats* were usually employed in pairs, with one using a dipping sonar to detect targets, the another unleashing torpedoes. When this arrangement was also deemed unsatisfactory, Sikorsky combined both functions into the H-3 *Sea King*.

In 1954 the Army acquired 437 H-34 *Choctaws* and employed them as troop transports during the opening phases of the Vietnam War. However, because of its size and strength, the H-34 became the first helicopter to be assigned duties as a presidential transport. In 1957 Army aircraft selected for the Executive Flight Detachment were refitted with soundproofing, better communications, and a plush interior. The surviving H-34s were released from reserve duty in 1970. All told, 2,187 of the rugged, durable *Choctaws* were constructed at home or under license in France and England.

# Sikorsky H-37/HR2S *Mojave*

**Type:** Transport Helicopter

---

**Dimensions:** rotor span, 72 feet; length, 64 feet, 3 inches; height, 22 feet
**Weights:** empty, 20,831 pounds; gross, 31,000 pounds
**Power plant:** 2 × 2,100–horsepower Pratt & Whitney R-2800 air-cooled engines
**Performance:** maximum speed, 130 miles per hour; ceiling, 8,700 feet; maximum range, 145 miles
**Armament:** none
**Service dates:** 1955–1967

At the time of its debut, the mighty *Mojave* represented major advances in helicopter technology. Despite bulky appearances, it was the largest and fastest chopper of its kind in the world.

The Korean War added great impetus to helicopter development, and in 1950 the Marine Corps posted specifications for a large assault transport capable of carrying 26 fully armed troops. By 1953 Sikorsky responded with the S-56, an impressive and very capable machine. It was a twin-engine design driving a single, five-blade rotor. However, to keep the cargo hold unobstructed, the engines were mounted in two pods on either side of the fuselage. It was also the first large helicopter to be equipped with fully retractable landing gear. The spacious hull could easily carry 26 troops, three jeeps, or up to 10,000 pounds of cargo, loaded and disembarked through large clamshell doors in the nose. Because the cockpit was placed high above the cargo bay, the crew of two also enjoyed good

all-around vision. In 1955 the Marine Corps accepted the first of 55 machines as the HR2S. At the time of its debut it was the largest and fastest helicopter in the world.

In 1956 the Army evaluated a single HR2S and was greatly impressed. The following year it placed orders for 94 machines, which became known as the H-37A *Mojave*. By 1962 all had been brought up to H-37B standards with the introduction of autostabilization, self-sealing tanks, and improved cargo doors. In 1963 four *Mojaves* were briefly in Vietnam, and within four months they recovered downed aircraft worth $7.5 million. By 1967 both Army and Marine Corps versions had been replaced by the modern turbine-powered H-54 *Tarhe*.

The Navy also conducted an interesting experiment with two HR2Ss by outfitting them as airborne early warning pickets. They were fitted with a huge, bulging radar dome under the nose, but excessive vibration resulted in their cancellation.

# Sikorsky H-52 *Sea Guardian*

**Type:** Rescue Helicopter

**Dimensions:** rotor span, 53 feet; length, 44 feet, 6 inches; height, 14 feet, 2 inches
**Weights:** empty, 4,903 pounds; gross, 8,100 pounds
**Power plant:** 1 × 1,250–horsepower General Electric T58 turboshaft engine
**Performance:** maximum speed, 109 miles per hour; ceiling, 11,200 feet; maximum range, 474 miles
**Armament:** none
**Service dates:** 1963–1988

The Coast Guard *Sea Guardian* is the most successful rescue machine in aviation history. In 25 years of distinguished service it saved more than 15,000 lives.

During the late 1950s Sikorsky began developing a smaller, less expensive version of its S-61 helicopter for the commercial market. The maiden flight occurred in 1958, and the S-62 became the first turbine-powered helicopter cleared for commercial use. Like its predecessor, the new craft possessed a watertight, boat-hull fuselage and twin stabilizing sponsons astride the cockpit. It was powered by a single engine and utilized the proven rotor and transmission system of the earlier and successful S-55. Furthermore, the S-62 had retractable landing gear and could easily operate from land or water. In 1962 an example underwent service trials by the Navy, which purchased four machines for the Coast Guard as the H-52A. They differed from civilian machines by having a military-rated engine, a fold-down rescue platform on the fuselage, and a 600-pound winch by the left cabin door. A total of 99 H-52s was subsequently acquired by the Coast Guard as the *Sea Guardian* to slowly replace its fleet of aging H-34s. It also purchased the H-52B version, which featured an improved engine, shorter blades, and a rotor system from the S-58.

Beginning in 1963 the venerable *Sea Guardian* was a common sight in skies along America's coasts and lakes. For 25 years it was heavily engaged in maritime search-and-rescue operations and is conservatively credited with saving more than 15,000 lives. When Hurricane Betsy slammed New Orleans in 1965, H-52s evacuated 1,200 people, snatching many from rooftops. In view of this success, Sikorsky prepared an export version, the S-62C, which was also manufactured under license in Japan. The last H-52s were retired in 1988 and replaced by the twin-engine, French-built Aerospatiale H-65 *Dolphin*.

**Type:** Transport Helicopter

**Dimensions:** rotor span, 72 feet; length, 70 feet, 3 inches; height, 18 feet, 7 inches
**Weights:** empty, 19,800 pounds; gross, 47,000 pounds
**Power plant:** 2 × 4,800–horsepower Pratt & Whitney T73 turboshaft engines
**Performance:** maximum speed, 126 miles per hour; ceiling, 9,000 feet; maximum range, 230 miles
**Armament:** none
**Service dates:** 1964–

Despite its ungainly, mantislike appearance, the 30-year-old *Skycrane* remains one of the world's great lifting helicopters. It rendered impressive service throughout the Vietnam War and is still deployed with reserve units.

During the late 1950s Sikorsky began exploring the concept of a heavy-lift helicopter and constructed the S-60, an early flying crane. It crashed in 1961, but soon an enlarged machine emerged, the S-64. It was an extremely unusual, even homely design but proved to be a record-breaker. The S-64 consisted of a small cockpit mounted just below an extremely thin fuselage. Two turbine engines were placed midway on the fuselage top, driving a five-blade, fully articulated rotor. Moreover, the craft was fitted with two pairs of spindly landing gear that raised the body 18 feet, allowing bulky cargoes to be placed beneath it. The landing gear was also flexible, enabling the entire craft to "kneel" and discharge its load. The Army was impressed with the S-64's lifting capacities, and in 1963 it ordered six examples as the H-54 *Skycrane*.

In 1966 four H-54s were deployed in Vietnam for field-evaluation purposes. Happily, they exceeded expectations and proved extremely valuable for lifting heavy loads to seemingly impossible places. This included placing heavy artillery batteries on mountaintops, transporting construction bulldozers to difficult ridges, and recovering damaged equipment. In this manner more than 300 aircraft and helicopters, worth some $210 million, were salvaged. The *Skycrane* was also the only helicopter capable of carrying the 10,000-pound *Daisy Cutter*, a bomb that could carve out helicopter landing zones in the heart of forbidding jungle terrain. The Army ultimately purchased 54 CH-54As, followed by an additional 37 CH-54Bs, which featured stronger engines and drive trains. They subsequently set many payload and altitude records that endured until only recently. Since then, the *Skycrane* has been replaced by the even more capable CH-47 *Chinook*, although several examples continue flying with reserves and the National Guard.

# ✪ Sikorsky JRS

**Type:** Transport

---

**Dimensions:** wingspan, 86 feet; length, 51 feet, 2 inches; height, 17 feet, 8 inches
**Weights:** empty, 12,750 pounds; gross, 19,096 pounds
**Power plant:** 2 × 750–horsepower Pratt & Whitney Hornet R-1690 radial engines
**Performance:** maximum speed, 190 miles per hour; ceiling, 20,700 feet; maximum range, 775 miles
**Armament:** none
**Service dates:** 1937–1944

---

The JRS was adapted from a highly capable commercial aircraft. With minor modifications, it continued the tradition of excellence that characterized Sikorsky products.

Beginning in the 1920s, amphibious aircraft became conspicuous fixtures of naval aviation and would remain so until the 1960s. These aircraft were useful to the Navy because they could service distant oceanic posts that lacked regular landing facilities. The first modern all-metal flying boats reached the commercial sector by 1930 and were a quantum improvement over earlier designs. The Sikorsky S-43 was such a craft and became a financial success for that company. It was a big, twin-engine design with a spacious two-step boat hull, a pylon-mounted wing, and two wingtip floats. It was also fully amphibious, with landing gear that retracted into wells on either side of the fuselage. While still in its prototype stage, the S-43 broke several international seaplane records and was acquired by airlines around the world.

Naturally, an aircraft of such outstanding performance attracted military attention, and in 1936 the Navy acquired seven examples under the designation JRS. They differed from civilian models only in having militarized versions of the Hornet radial engine, and they found immediate favor as utility transports. In 1938 ten more were acquired. At least eight found their way into a single squadron, VJ-1, based at San Diego, California, which maintained regular operations to the Hawaiian Islands. Two were also allocated to the Marine Corps, and JRS flying boats were conspicuously employed throughout the Pacific theater during World War II. In 1937 the Army acquired five S-42s, which it operated as the Y1OA-8. All S-42 craft were finally relieved of duty in 1944, and one is preserved at the National Air and Space Museum, Smithsonian Institute.

**Type:** Rescue Helicopter

**Dimensions:** rotor span, 36 feet; length, 48 feet, 11 inches; height, 12 feet, 5 inches
**Weights:** empty, 2,020 pounds; gross, 2,535 pounds
**Power plant:** 1 × 165–horsepower Warner Super-Scarab R-500 radial engine
**Performance:** maximum speed, 77 miles per hour; ceiling, 8,000 feet; maximum range, 220 miles
**Armament:** none
**Service dates:** 1944–1947

The modest R-4 was the world's first military helicopter and the first to be mass-produced in the United States. Despite limitations, it demonstrated the feasibility of vertical-lift technology and pointed the way to the future.

In May 1940 inventor Igor Sikorsky finally perfected his first functional helicopter, the VS-300. After the craft was successfully test-flown, the Army Air Corps announced specifications for an operational military design. In May 1942 the VS-316A emerged, which laid the groundwork for most future helicopter designs. It consisted of a lengthy fabric-covered fuselage that mounted a main rotor directly behind the cockpit section. A 165-horsepower motor drove the three-blade main rotor as well as a smaller antitorque rotor on the tail boom. The craft was landed on three fixed gear, but it could also be outfitted with pontoons for water operation. To demonstrate its efficiency and safety, the prototype was flown 761 miles from Stratford,

Connecticut, to Wright Field, Ohio, in only 16 hours of flying time.

After further evaluation, the Army purchased three preproduction models as the YR-4A. It was followed by an additional 27 YR-4Bs to conduct additional Arctic and tropical trials. Ultimately, the Army purchased 100 R-4s, of which 22 went to the Navy as HNS-1s; 45 ended up in British hands as the *Hoverfly I*. The R-4 witnessed only limited service abroad, but in 1944 it performed the first aerial helicopter rescue by lifting four British soldiers out of a Burmese jungle. That same year, a Navy HNS-1 made the first helicopter landing at sea by alighting upon the deck of the tanker USS *Bunker Hill*. After the war, the little R-4s distinguished themselves in a number of civilian rescue missions, thereby validating the potential use of helicopters. As better machines were introduced, the R-4s were relegated to training duties and finally withdrawn in 1947. The total production run was 131.

# ✪ Sikorsky R-5/HO3S

**Type:** Observation Helicopter; Rescue Helicopter

**Dimensions:** rotor span, 48 feet; length, 57 feet, 1 inch; height, 13 feet
**Weights:** empty, 3,780 pounds; gross, 4,825 pounds
**Power plant:** 1 × 450–horsepower Pratt & Whitney R-985 radial engine
**Performance:** maximum speed, 106 miles per hour; ceiling, 14,400 feet; maximum range, 360 miles
**Armament:** none
**Service dates:** 1945–1957

The HO3S was the first Navy helicopter to replace scouting aircraft at sea. It performed exemplary service during the Korean War and enjoyed a long service life.

In 1943 the Army requested Sikorsky to develop a follow-on observation machine to supplant the limited R-4. The prototype XR-5 was unveiled in 1944 as a completely new design. Although incorporating the basic rotor and engine drive, the new craft possessed a streamlined hull and a glass nose that seated two crew members in tandem. The new craft was covered with molded plywood panels instead of fabric and was equipped with a reverse-tricycle landing-gear system. Two medical stretchers could also be fixed to either side of the fuselage. Testing proceeded smoothly, and in 1945 the Army ordered 27 experimental YR-5s, followed by 34 production machines. Two were turned over to the Navy as HO2S-1s.

In 1946 Sikorsky expanded the basic design into the S-51, an all-metal, four-seat commercial heli-copter. In addition to some mechanical refinements, the most noticeable difference from early versions was the regular tricycle landing gear. The Air Force quickly obtained 66 of the new machines under various designations. The Navy was also particularly interested in the craft as a replacement for the Curtiss SC-1 *Seahawks*, then flying off cruisers and battleships. In addition to scouting, they were expected to perform search-and-rescue operations at sea and on land. The Navy acquired 46 HO3S-1s, four of which performed well enough during Admiral Richard E. Byrd's Antarctic expedition (1946–1947) to merit additional orders. The HO3S-1 was active throughout the Korean War, performing search-and-rescue operations and retrieving many Allied pilots from behind enemy lines. It was also the first helicopter constructed in Britain and the first one the British employed in combat during the Malaysian insurrection (1950–1956). The last of the HO3Ss were removed from service in 1957 after 379 had been built.

**Type:** Rescue Helicopter

**Dimensions:** rotor span, 38 feet; length, 38 feet, 3 inches; height, 10 feet, 4 inches
**Weights:** empty, 2,590 pounds; gross, 2,900 pounds
**Power plant:** 1 × 240–horsepower Franklin 0-405 radial engine
**Performance:** maximum speed, 96 miles per hour; ceiling, 10,000 feet; maximum range, 305 miles
**Armament:** none
**Service dates:** 1945–1948

The R-6 was basically a refinement of the earlier R-4 and displayed some improvement. It equipped the Navy's first helicopter squadron but was quickly overtaken by more capable designs.

The R-6 was developed in an attempt to enhance the marginal performance of the R-4. Although utilizing the same rotor and transmission of the earlier craft, the XR-6 possessed a totally redesigned, streamlined, all-metal fuselage as well as an open Plexiglas cockpit for greater visibility. In addition to fixed quadricycle landing gear, the craft could be outfitted with pontoons for water landings. Provisions were also made to attach medical stretchers to either side of the fuselage.

During an early test-flight the XR-6 set new distance, endurance, and altitude records for helicopters, traveling 387 miles from Washington, D.C., to Wright Field, Ohio, climbing to 5,000 feet over the Allegheny Mountains. In 1944 the Army and Navy accepted several YR-6s for evaluation purposes, and in April 1945 the Coast Guard operated the first helicopter stationed at sea from the cutter *Cobb*. Subsequent models were fitted with more powerful motors and went into production as the Army R-6 and the Navy HOS-1. Several of the latter equipped the Navy's first helicopter squadron in 1946. Great Britain also acquired 40 R-6s through a lend-lease agreement; they were equally divided between Royal Navy and Royal Air Force squadrons as the *Hoverfly II*.

In service, the R-6 proved a pleasant-handling machine but was beset by engine problems. It also inherited the speed and payload limitations of the R-4, which restricted its usefulness as a rescue craft. In view of these difficulties, the R-6 and HOS-1 were quickly supplanted by the more capable R-5, which had been developed at the same time. A total of 228 were constructed.

# Sikorsky SH-3 *Sea King*

**Type:** Antisubmarine Helicopter; Rescue Helicopter

**Dimensions:** rotor span, 62 feet; length, 72 feet, 8 inches; height, 16 feet, 10 inches
**Weights:** empty, 9,763 pounds; gross, 18,626 pounds
**Power plant:** 2 × 1,400–horsepower General Electric T58 turboshaft engines
**Performance:** maximum speed, 166 miles per hour; ceiling, 14,700 feet; maximum range, 625 miles
**Armament:** either 870 pounds of torpedoes and depth charges or 2 × 7.62mm miniguns
**Service dates:** 1961–

The *Sea King* was the first helicopter to combine both hunter and killer functions for antisubmarine warfare. Several examples continue serving as VIP transports for the president of the United States.

In 1957 the Navy requested Sikorsky to build a combined-function hunter/killer helicopter to replace its aging fleet of SH-34 *Choctaws*. A prototype flew in 1959 as the S-61 and proved to be a record-breaking aircraft. True to its naval origins, the new design consisted of a waterproof boat-shaped hull. Stabilizing sponsons were fitted on either side of the forward cabin and housed the retractable landing gear. The S-61 also possessed a large, five-blade propeller and two turboshaft engines mounted directly on the fuselage roof. This arrangement kept the fuselage unobstructed so that a variety of sonar detectors and homing torpedoes could be carried. In 1961 the S-61 became operational as the SH-3S *Sea King*. Being able to fly in any kind of weather, it was a formidable addition to the Navy's antisubmarine warfare capabilities. A total of 255 was purchased.

In 1966 the Navy acquired 73 SH-3Ds featuring upgraded engines. It also converted nine of the earlier SH-3As into RH-3As, which were outfitted for minesweeping operations. However, the most famous mission for the *Sea King* was as a presidential transport. By 1975 no less than 11 specially equipped VH-3Ds were on hand in Washington, D.C., to whisk the president and Cabinet out of danger should the capital be threatened. A final version of the *Sea King* appeared during the Vietnam War, the HH-3 (no relation to the Air Force version), which was outfitted as an armed search-and-rescue helicopter. This versatile aircraft was also manufactured under license in Japan, Italy, and Great Britain for several years.

**Type:** Antisubmarine Helicopter

**Dimensions:** rotor span, 53 feet, 8 inches; length, 64 feet, 10 inches; height, 17 feet
**Weights:** empty, 13,648 pounds; gross, 21,884 pounds
**Power plant:** 2 × 1,713–horsepower General Electric T700 turboshaft engines
**Performance:** maximum speed, 207 miles per hour; ceiling, 13,800 feet; maximum range, 781 miles
**Armament:** 2 × Mk.46 homing torpedoes
**Service dates:** 1984–

The costly, complex *Sea Hawk* carries an impressive array of mission avionics and sensors. Deployed from small warships, it is probably the most effective antisubmarine helicopter ever flown.

The success of Kaman's H-2 *Seasprite* as part of the light airborne multipurpose system (LAMPS I) was limited by the fact that it was too small to accept the next generation of advanced antisubmarine warfare (ASW) technology. Therefore, in 1977 the Navy closely examined the Sikorsky H-60 *Black Hawk*, then under development for the Army, as a replacement. Extensive testing prompted it to adopt a navalized version as the LAMPS III aircraft. The new machine was fitted with more powerful engines, an automatic rotor folding system and folding tail section for onboard storage, and flotation features. However, the most distinguishing features are the complicated electronics. It is fitted with sophisticated navigational and search radars, a magnetic anomaly detector (MAD) boom, and up to 125 dis-

posable sonobuoys. For armament, two lightweight Mk.46 homing torpedoes are also carried. The LAMPS III program was judged to be an outstanding success, and in 1984 the Navy accepted the first of 204 machines as the SH-60 *Sea Hawk*.

Unlike previous ASW helicopters, the *Sea Hawk* is part of a totally integrated sensor system. It is designed to operate from destroyers and frigates while remaining electronically tethered to their sonar arrays. On its own, the SH-60 will then fly up to 200 miles after launching and further pinpoint the location of enemy submarines and shipping. In this manner up to 30,000 square miles of ocean can be quickly and effectively scanned for targets. A subsequent version, the SH-60F *Ocean Hawk*, is specially designed for carriers to protect the inner zone of a carrier battle group from attack. The Navy has acquired 175 of these elaborate machines; both versions will remain operational well into the next century.

# ⭐ Sikorsky UH-60 *Black Hawk*

**Type:** Transport Helicopter

**Dimensions:** rotor span, 53 feet, 8 inches; length, 50 feet; height, 12 feet, 4 inches
**Weights:** empty, 10,624 pounds; gross, 20,250 pounds
**Power plant:** 2 × 1,560–horsepower General Electric T700 turboshaft engines
**Performance:** maximum speed, 184 miles per hour; ceiling, 19,000 feet; maximum range, 375 miles
**Armament:** 2 × 7.62mm machine guns; 16 × *Hellfire* laser-guided missiles; 250 aerial antitank mines
**Service dates:** 1979–

The *Black Hawk* is currently the Army's main assault helicopter. Fast and dependable, it can also be used for a variety of reconnaissance, rescue, and command-and-control missions.

By the late 1960s the Army was searching for a new machine to replace the UH-1 *Iroquois* and announced a competition for its utility tactical transport aircraft system. Among the many requirements were seating for 11 soldiers, high survival under fire, and the ability to squeeze into a C-130 *Hercules* transport. Several companies responded, and in 1976 the Sikorsky entry was declared the winner.

The new aircraft was unlike anything Sikorsky had previously designed. It was streamlined, possessed fixed landing struts, and employed an airplanelike horizontal stabilizer on the tail boom. Two turbine engines were mounted on top of the fuselage pod, driving a four-blade rotor. The blades themselves were made from bullet-resistant composite materials and designed to survive hits from 23mm

cannon shells. For crew and passenger survival, the fuselage is also crash-resistant, able to withstand relatively fast ground impacts. The Army was pleased with the new machine, and in 1979 it accepted deliveries of the first UH-60 *Black Hawks*. Eventually, 1,715 will be constructed. They rendered valuable service during the 1983 invasion of Grenada, the 1989 invasion of Panama, and the 1991 Gulf War.

An important variant is the EH-60A, which is dedicated to electronic warfare. It carries sophisticated electronic countermeasure equipment that can monitor, jam, and pinpoint the location of enemy transmissions. Production totaled 132 units.

The Air Force also deploys its own version, the HH-60 *Night Hawk*. They are all-weather rescue craft for retrieving pilots behind enemy lines. They are heavily automated and equipped with terrain-following radar for high-speed, low-altitude night flying. The Air Force intends to purchase up to 90 of these sophisticated machines.

**Type:** Liaison

**Dimensions:** wingspan, 20 feet; length, 17 feet, 9 inches; height, 6 feet, 9 inches
**Weights:** empty, 623 pounds; gross, 862 pounds
**Power plant:** 1 × 60–horsepower Lawrence J-4 radial engine
**Performance:** maximum speed, 96 miles per hour; maximum range, 500 miles
**Armament:** none
**Service dates:** 1920–1923

The diminutive *Messenger* was the smallest aircraft ever operated by the Army Air Service. Although regarded as a useful and reliable craft, it accidentally claimed the life of its manufacturer.

In 1919 the Army decided it needed a small liaison aircraft to function as the airborne equivalent of a motorcycle dispatch rider. The desired plane had to be inexpensive, simple to maintain, and able to land on rough strips of land. That year, noted engineer Alfred Verville, who worked for the Engineering Division at McCook Field, Ohio, designed a small wooden biplane with staggered, single-bay, fabric-covered wings. It was fully aerobatic despite its small size and could take off at only 45 miles per hour. The new craft was supposed to deliver messages between field commanders, hence it acquired the official name M-1 *Messenger*. When the final design had been approved, construction bids were announced, and the lowest bidder was the Sperry Aircraft Corpora-

tion of Farmingdale, New York. In 1920 a contract was signed to construct five machines.

The owner of Sperry Aircraft Corporation, Elmer Sperry, was another ingenious inventor. In addition to constructing *Messengers*, he was authorized to convert several into radio-controlled, pilotless assault drones—a forerunner to today's air-to-ground missile. In fact, to gain publicity for his new craft, Sperry flew one personally to Washington, D.C., intending to land upon the U.S. Capitol lawn. However, Sperry certainly gained national attention when a sudden gust of wind blew his M-1, which lacked brakes, right up the stairs of Congress! The incident had the desired effect, and the Army soon ordered Sperry to build another 37 *Messengers*. In the fall of 1924 an M-1 made the first successful launch and hookup with an Army dirigible. Unfortunately, Sperry lost his life while flying over the English Channel on December 13, 1923—his M-1 ditched, and he drowned. The *Messengers* were retired from active duty soon thereafter.

# ✪ Standard E-1

**Type:** Trainer

**Dimensions:** wingspan, 24 feet; length, 18 feet, 11 inches; height, 7 feet, 10 inches
**Weights:** empty, 838 pounds; gross, 1,144 pounds
**Power plant:** 1 × 100–horsepower Gnome rotary engine
**Performance:** maximum speed, 85 miles per hour; ceiling, 14,800 feet; maximum range, 160 miles
**Armament:** 1 × .30–caliber machine gun
**Service dates:** 1918–1919

Having failed as a fighter design, the diminutive E-1 was pressed into service as an advanced trainer. It enjoyed little success in that role and soon disappeared from the Army's inventory.

During World War I the Standard Aircraft Corporation of Elizabeth, New Jersey, manufactured European-designed aircraft for the Army Air Service. However, in 1917 it rolled out the prototype for a light fighter of its own. Called the *M-Defense*, it was a standard biplane with staggered, two-bay wings, wooden construction, and fabric covering. For armament it carried a single .30-caliber machine gun and was powered by a French Gnome rotary engine. After testing, the Army decided the craft possessed adequate stability and maneuverability, but it was too slow and underpowered to serve as a fighter. Therefore, in 1918 it contracted with Standard to construct 460 examples as an advanced fighter-trainer called the E-1.

By August 1918 the Air Service had acquired 93 E-1s, but the U.S.-manufactured Gnome rotary engines needed constant maintenance. Accordingly, it decided to switch engines, and the next 75 aircraft were fitted with an 80-horsepower Le Rhone engine. In service the E-1 was unpopular with pilots on account of its marginal characteristics and poor visibility. It was joked that a pilot trained on the E-1 was not merely a good pilot—from then on he could fly anything! When the war ended in November 1918, the remaining contract orders were canceled, and within a few years the E-1 was struck from the Army's inventory. During this period, however, Elmer Sperry converted three E-1s into some of the earliest radio-controlled aerial torpedoes by lengthening the fuselage to accommodate the new equipment. A similar experiment was carried out using several Sperry *Messengers*.

**Type:** Trainer

**Dimensions:** wingspan, 43 feet, 10 inches; length, 26 feet, 7 inches; height, 10 feet, 10 inches
**Weights:** empty, 1,557 pounds; gross, 2,070 pounds
**Power plant:** 1 × 100–horsepower Hall-Scott A-7 liquid-cooled engine
**Performance:** maximum speed, 70 miles per hour; ceiling, 5,800 feet; maximum range, 235 miles
**Armament:** none
**Service dates:** 1916–1918

During World War I the J-1 was a lesser-known contemporary of the famous Curtiss JN. It was fitted with a better engine during the postwar period and eclipsed its former rival as a barnstorming aircraft.

In 1916 the Standard Aircraft Company improved upon the Sloan H series of biplane trainers to produce the Model J-1. This was done in response to the Army's need for acquiring new military trainers in the event of war. The J-1 was a standard biplane design with unstaggered, swept-back wings and wood-and-fabric construction. It closely resembled its close competitor, the Curtiss JN-4 *Jenny*, save for the addition of a small front wheel to prevent noseovers in soft sand. In the opinion of some pilots it was a better, more forgiving aircraft than the JN series but had the misfortune of being powered by the Hall-Scott A-7 engine. That power plant was notoriously unreliable and prone to catching fire while in the air, so as more and more JN-4s be-

came available the military eventually grounded all its J-1s. By 1918 Standard had manufactured 1,932 J-1s, but most remained crated during the war and were subsequently sold off as surplus.

Once in the hands of private collectors, the J-1's reputation underwent a dramatic transformation. Private owners discarded the balky Hall-Scott engines and fitted them instead with better and more powerful Hispano-Suizas and Curtiss OXs. The result was the best barnstorming aircraft of the 1920s that eclipsed, at least in terms of popularity if not numbers, the more famous *Jenny* in that role. One reason was that while the JN-4 could carry a pilot and a single passenger, the Standard labored aloft with four. Fully loaded, J-1s easily flew from the small hayfields that frequently served as airports. For many years they thrilled audiences with the usual routine of acrobatics, wing-walking, and other aerial stunts. Several are preserved in flying condition to this day.

**Type:** Trainer

**Dimensions:** wingspan, 32 feet, 2 inches; length, 24 feet, 10 inches; length, 9 feet, 8 inches
**Weights:** 2,635 pounds
**Power plant:** 1 × 220–horsepower Continental R-670 radial engine
**Performance:** maximum speed, 135 miles per hour; ceiling, 13,200 feet; maximum range, 450 miles
**Armament:** none
**Service dates:** 1935–1945

The beloved *Kaydet* was the most widely produced biplane in aviation history. Almost every Army and Navy pilot of World War II, plus thousands of others from foreign countries, first experienced flight in these rugged, dependable trainers.

In 1934 the Stearman Company, a subsidiary of Boeing, designed a new biplane trainer as a private venture. The Model 70 was a clean, if conventional, biplane, with fixed landing gear, dual controls in tandem cockpits, and exceptionally gentle flying characteristics. It featured a mixed construction of steel tubing, wooden wings, and fabric covering. In 1935 the Navy took interest and ordered 70 machines powered by a 225-horsepower Wright engine, which passed into service as the NS-1. The following year the Army Air Corps followed suit by obtaining 26 versions powered by 215-horsepower Lycoming engines, designating them PT-13s. In time, Stearman trainers became celebrated for their robust construction and forgiving spin and stall characteristics.

In the years up to and including World War II, the Stearman became the most important training aircraft in the American inventory. Almost 100,000 pilots passed through its cockpits en route to winning their wings. The Army fielded an improved version fitted with a 220-horsepower Continental radial engine that became officially known as the PT-17, whereas the Navy deployed the identical craft as the N2S. The Canadians also purchased 300 of a variant known as the PT-27, which was simply a standard Stearman outfitted with a canopy to protect pilots from cold weather. The Stearman remained in production until mid-1945, by which time some 10,346 of all kinds had been produced. After the war they were declared surplus and placed on the civilian market. In private hands *Kaydets* continue flying as aerobatic stunt planes and crop dusters.

## ⭐ Stinson O-49/L-1 *Vigilant*

**Type:** Liaison

**Dimensions:** wingspan, 50 feet, 11 inches; length, 34 feet, 3 inches; height, 10 feet, 2 inches
**Weights:** empty, 2,670 pounds; gross, 3,400 pounds
**Power plant:** 1 × 295–horsepower Lycoming R-680 radial engine
**Performance:** maximum speed, 122 miles per hour; ceiling, 12,800 feet; maximum range, 280 miles
**Armament:** none
**Service dates:** 1940–1945

The *Vigilant* was an intermediary type between the heavy observation craft of the 1930s and the lighter *Grasshoppers* of World War II. It possessed excellent takeoff and landing qualities and was widely employed by the United States and Great Britain.

By 1940 the U.S. Army was reevaluating its policy toward aircraft that could cooperate closely with units in the field. It sought lighter, less expensive designs with better rough-field performance. That year, Stinson entered its two-seat Model 74 light plane into competition against prototypes from Bellanca and Ryan. This was an all-metal, high-wing, enclosed-cabin aircraft designed for low-speed, high-lift performance. To accomplish this, the Model 74's wings had automatic slats on the leading edge, and the trailing edge was fitted with pilot-operated, slotted flaps. Consequently, the Model 74 possessed superb short takeoff and landing performance, and the Army purchased 142 machines with the designa-

tion O-49. Soon, the Army also obtained 182 O-49As, which differed in having a slightly longer fuselage and minor equipment changes.

In 1942 the Army dropped the "Observation" designation entirely and substituted the "Liaison" class. The O-49 thereafter became known as the L-1, of which 324 were ultimately built. A number were exported to Great Britain under Lend-Lease, where they were christened the *Vigilant*. L-1s saw service around the world and in a number of capacities, including artillery spotting, courier duty, emergency rescue, and even dropping off agents behind enemy lines. Some aircraft were fitted with a variety of skis and floats for winter and water operations. However, the Army was more interested in the lighter, cheaper, less complicated Aeronca, Piper, and Taylorcraft *Grasshoppers*, so the *Vigilant* was never acquired in great numbers. They performed admirably throughout the war years before being declared surplus in 1945 and discarded.

# ✪ Stinson O-62/L-5 *Sentinel*

**Type:** Liaison

**Dimensions:** wingspan, 34 feet; length, 24 feet, 1 inch; height, 7 feet, 11 inches
**Weights:** empty, 1,550 pounds; gross, 2,020 pounds
**Power plant:** 1 × 185–horsepower Lycoming air-cooled engine
**Performance:** maximum speed, 130 miles per hour; ceiling, 15,800 feet; maximum range, 420 miles
**Armament:** none
**Service dates:** 1942–1955

The *Sentinel* was the second most widely used *Grasshopper* employed by the United States. It served with distinction as an artillery spotter and flying ambulance in two wars.

In 1941 the Army began contemplating the use of light civilian aircraft for liaison and light transport duties, so it acquired six Stinson Model 105 *Voyagers* for evaluation. It was a high-wing, three-seat, cabined plane of metal-tube construction, wooden control surfaces, and fabric covering. They went into service briefly as YO-54s, at which point the Army ordered a further 275 machines under the designation O-62. These craft were modified from the civilian version by carrying only two passengers, seated in tandem, and increasing the fuselage size. In 1942 the aircraft was redesignated the L-5, and 302 were delivered to the Marine Corps as OY-1s. Several hundred were also exported to Great Britain, where they acquired the unofficial name *Sentinel*.

During World War II L-5s were purchased in quantity and served along every front, in every capacity. This included artillery spotting, medical evacuation, light transport, courier duty, and laying communications wire. Like all *Grasshoppers*, the *Sentinel* could land and take off from just about anywhere. By 1945 no less than 3,284 L-5s were built, making it the second most popular liaison craft after the Piper L-4. The majority of *Sentinels* were declared surplus when hostilities ceased, and they were sold to the public. However, several remained in use with reserve forces until the advent of the Korean War in 1950. It was a Stinson L-5 that evacuated South Korean President Syngman Rhee from Seoul during the first days of the war. For many months into that conflict, the L-5 formed the backbone of Army aviation units until it was eventually replaced by the more modern Cessna L-19 *Bird Dog*. A handful of *Sentinels* served with the Air Force until 1955.

**Type:** Liaison

**Dimensions:** wingspan, 35 feet, 5 inches; length, 22 feet, 9 inches; height, 8 feet
**Weights:** empty, 875 pounds; gross, 1,300 pounds
**Power plant:** 1 × 65–horsepower Continental air-cooled engine
**Performance:** maximum speed, 88 miles per hour; ceiling, 10,000 feet; maximum range, 230 miles
**Armament:** none
**Service dates:** 1941–1945

The L-2 was the third most popular *Grasshopper* craft employed for liaison purposes. A sizable number were also utilized to train glider pilots.

In 1941 Taylorcraft was one of four companies contracted by the U.S. Army to provide light airplanes for evaluation as light utility craft. The aircraft submitted was the popular Model D, a high-wing, enclosed-cabin airplane with fixed landing gear and tandem arrangements for two passengers. Three passed into service as YO-57s during the famous Louisiana maneuvers of that year and were chosen for production. Accordingly, the Army ordered 140 additional craft as O-57s, which were nearly identical to the civilian version. However, on the 336 O-57As that followed, the trailing edge was cut out of the wing roots to improve all-around vision.

During World War II the Army dropped the "Observation" category of aircraft and adopted "Liaison" in its place. Hence, the O-57 became officially known as the L-2, and it served in military campaigns around the world with distinction. Like all other *Grasshoppers*, the L-2 became renowned for its ability to take off and land on short, unprepared airstrips. This greatly enhanced its ability to serve as an artillery spotter, a reconnaissance craft, an aerial ambulance, and a courier transport. As the war progressed a specialized version, the L-2B, was fitted with special equipment for closer service with the field artillery. The final production variant, the L-2M, featured a closely cowled motor and wing spoilers to improve low-speed performance. During the war a total of 1,911 Taylorcraft was produced.

Because of the need for glider pilots, Taylorcraft also constructed a glider version of the L-2 called the TG-6. This consisted of a stock L-2 that had its engine replaced by a cabin for an additional crew member. A total of 253 was built for the Army; three ended up in Navy hands for evaluation purposes.

**Type:** Trainer

**Dimensions:** wingspan, 29 feet, 10 inches; length, 30 feet, 7 inches; height, 10 feet, 10 inches
**Weights:** empty, 3,139 pounds; gross, 4,400 pounds
**Power plant:** 1 × 920–pound thrust Continental J-69 turbojet engine
**Performance:** maximum speed, 345 miles per hour; ceiling, 32,000 feet; maximum range, 276 miles
**Armament:** none
**Service dates:** 1957–1960

The tiny *Pinto* was the first primary jet trainer accepted into service by the U.S. armed forces. It served only briefly but demonstrated the value of early exposure to advanced aeronautics.

After World War II the Temco Aircraft Corporation of Dallas, Texas, enjoyed great commercial success in marketing its attractive *Swift* passenger airplane. At that point it decided to enter the military training field with a similar design, the T-35. When it was defeated by the famous Beech T-34 *Mentor*, Temco submitted a modified form to the Navy called the *Plebe*. Although it was a splendidly acrobatic aircraft, no orders were forthcoming. Undeterred, in fall 1954 Temco proposed modifying the *Plebe* into its first primary jet trainer. The Navy proved so receptive to the idea that it encouraged Beech to do the same with its T-34.

Temco was determined to finally beat its established competitor and in March 1956 unveiled the new TT-1 design. This was a tiny, single-engine jet with straight high-mounted wings and a long glass canopy. However, it featured many standard features of operational jet fighters, like ejection seats, liquid oxygen equipment, and speed brakes. Moreover, the TT-1 possessed instrument panels and controls similar to those found on the jet fighters that students would soon fly. The TT-1 was somewhat slow and underpowered for a jet, but it was fully aerobatic, responsive, and a joy to fly. For this reason it easily beat Beech's entry, the Model 73 *Jet Mentor*. In July 1957 a ceremony was held whereby actress Jayne Mansfield publicly christened the TT-1 with its official designation, the *Pinto*. Only 14 were built. The TT-1s served only a few years due to limited range, and by 1960 they were replaced by the North American/Rockwell T-2 *Buckeye*. However, several *Pintos* have since found their way to the commercial market and still fly in private hands.

**Type:** Fighter

**Dimensions:** wingspan, 26 feet; length, 20 feet; height, 7 feet, 8 inches
**Weights:** empty, 1,716 pounds; gross, 2,539 pounds
**Power plant:** 1 × 300–horsepower Wright H-3 liquid-cooled engine
**Performance:** maximum speed, 140 miles per hour; ceiling, 21,200 feet; maximum range, 270 miles
**Armament:** 2 × .30–caliber machine guns
**Service dates:** 1920–1927

The MB-3 was the Army's first standardized, mass-produced fighter. It offered few advantages over prevailing European designs, yet it was strongly built and maneuverable.

A failure to manufacture warplanes in America during World War I prompted the Army's decision to end its dependence upon European designs during the postwar period. As early as 1918 it encouraged the Thomas-Morse Aircraft Corporation of Ithaca, New York, to construct a plane with superior performance to the Spad XIII then in use. The following year it fielded the MB-3, destined to be the first American fighter produced in large numbers. This was an all-wood, fabric-covered biplane with single-bay, unstaggered wings. It possessed unusually clean lines owing to the placement of the radiator in the upper wing section. The design was also kept as deliberately small as possible to ensure a good power-to-weight ratio. Consequently, the MB-3 exhibited lively performance but suffered from a cramped canopy, poor pilot vision, and constant maintenance problems. Nonetheless, the Army pressed it into production by purchasing 50 machines, which began equipping pursuit squadrons by 1920.

The MB-3 was no world-beater, but it did give the fledgling Air Service experience in designing and serving its own aircraft. General William "Billy" Mitchell outfitted one as his personal aircraft. Satisfaction with the MB-3 culminated in a 1922 order for 200 additional machines, which would prove the largest procurement of fighter craft until the Curtiss P-36 in 1937. However, owing to competitive bidding, the production order went to an upstart company—Boeing of Seattle. It introduced a new version, the MB-3A, which featured a revised cooling system, four-blade propellers, and other refinements. Furthermore, the last 50 units were fitted with a taller, revised tail section. MB-3s rendered useful frontline service until 1926, when they began to be supplanted by more advanced Boeing PW-9s and Curtiss PW-8s. Several examples lingered on as trainers as late as 1928.

# ★ Thomas-Morse O-19

**Type:** Reconnaissance

**Dimensions:** wingspan, 39 feet, 9 inches; length, 28 feet, 4 inches; height, 10 feet, 6 inches
**Weights:** empty, 2,722 pounds; gross, 3,800 pounds
**Power plant:** 1 × 450–horsepower Pratt & Whitney R-1340 radial engine
**Performance:** maximum speed, 137 miles per hour; ceiling, 20,500 feet; maximum range, 462 miles
**Armament:** 2 × .30–caliber machine guns
**Service dates:** 1928–1935

The O-19 was the first Thomas-Morse military design to feature a metal fuselage. An excellent aircraft, it functioned as the secretary of war's personal transport.

Throughout most of the 1920s the Thomas-Morse Aircraft Corporation experimented with metallurgy in an attempt to create better, more durable airplanes. The perseverance paid off in 1926, when the Army Air Corps authorized Thomas-Morse to construct two all-metal versions of the redoubtable Douglas O-2 observation plane. The Army displayed no interest in the aircraft, designated the O-6, so Thomas-Morse engineers reconfigured a new design with smaller dimensions, revised wing bracing, and an all-metal fuselage. The fuselage was covered with wraparound corrugated metal sheets but the wing, though framed in metal, remained fabric-covered. The new XO-19 was fast and strong, and in 1929 an order for 70 O-19Bs was received. The following year the Army purchased 71 additional O-19Cs, which featured a ring cowling and a tail wheel. The final order was submitted in 1931, when 30 O-19Es, with a stronger engine and an increased upper wingspan, were delivered.

Like the Douglas design they were based upon, O-19s were rugged, dependable aircraft; they equipped four scouting squadrons in the United States and four more deployed in Hawaii, the Philippines, and the Panama Canal Zone. Such was the reputation of this craft that a single example, the O-19D, was rigged with plush seating, dual controls, and the O-19E engine to function as a staff transport for the U.S. secretary of war. Total production amounted to 180 machines. Furthermore, the YO-20, the XO-21, and the YO-23 were all experimental O-19s fitted with differing engines and cooling systems. By 1935 reconnaissance biplanes had been rendered obsolete by the newest all-metal monoplanes, and the O-19s were retired.

**Type:** Trainer

**Dimensions:** wingspan, 26 feet, 6 inches; length, 19 feet, 9 inches; height, 8 feet, 1 inch
**Weights:** empty, 963 pounds; gross, 1,330 pounds
**Power plant:** 1 × 80–horsepower Le Rhone rotary engine
**Performance:** maximum speed, 97 miles per hour; ceiling, 15,000 feet; maximum range, 300 miles
**Armament:** 1 × .30–caliber machine gun
**Service dates:** 1917–1919

The *Tommy* was a popular trainer during World War I. Light and maneuverable, it enjoyed great success as a civilian barnstormer throughout the postwar era.

The Thomas-Morse Aircraft Corporation of Ithaca, New York, came about in 1917 through the merger of the Thomas Brothers and Morse Chain companies. That year it developed a sprightly fighter design called the S-4. It was a typical biplane of the period with single-bay, staggered wings, wooden construction, and fabric covering. Thomas-Morse evaluated the S-4 that year as a possible production fighter craft and found it highly maneuverable—but too underpowered for consideration. However, because the United States had declared war on Germany that April, the Army adopted the S-4 as an advanced fighter-trainer to supplant the nearly obsolete Curtiss JN *Jenny*. Production models differed from the prototype only in possessing a shortened fuselage. To pilots, the aircraft simply became known as the *Tommy*.

In 1918 the Air Service received the first of 100 S-4Bs, which were immediately used for training large numbers of fighter pilots. However, the original 100-horsepower Gnome rotary engine leaked oil and was a source of constant maintenance problems. Consequently, the next 1,050 S-4Cs on order were fitted with a less powerful, but more reliable, Le Rhone rotary engine. The Navy also received a handful of *Tommies* fitted with floats and redesignated S-5s. When the war ended in November 1918, further production was canceled, so that the final tally of S-4s reached 597 units.

During the postwar period hundreds of S-4s were declared surplus and put up for sale. Former military pilots purchased them in droves, and over the next decade the beloved *Tommy* was a common sight at air shows around the nation. During the 1930s many found their way into various Hollywood war films, and several examples remain in flying condition to this day.

# ⭐ Timm N2T *Tutor*

**Type:** Trainer

**Dimensions:** wingspan, 36 feet; length, 24 feet, 10 inches; height, 10 feet, 8 inches
**Weights:** empty, 1,940 pounds; gross, 2,725 pounds
**Power plant:** 1 × 220–horsepower Continental R-670 radial engine
**Performance:** maximum speed, 144 miles per hour; ceiling, 16,000 feet; maximum range, 400 miles
**Armament:** none
**Service dates:** 1943–1944

The *Tutor* was the first airplane made almost entirely of plastic-bonded plywood. It served briefly as a formation-flying trainer with the Navy during World War II before lapsing into obscurity.

As the United States geared up for war in 1940, the Army and Navy experienced a need for training aircraft to instruct a great number of pilots in short order. Especially sought was a craft that did not employ strategic resources, like metal, in its construction. This freed light alloys to be used for military combat aircraft. That same year, the Timm Aircraft Corporation of Van Nuys, California, patented a plastic-bonded plywood called Aeromold that was strong and light. It then designed a two-seat airplane built almost entirely of Aeromold, the S-160-K, which the government awarded an Approved Type Certificate in April 1941.

The Navy, eager to conserve its alloy stocks, expressed interest in Timm products and ordered two aircraft, called the XN2T *Tutor*, for evaluation. The *Tutor* was a wooden low-wing monoplane with fixed landing gear, an exposed engine, and extremely clean lines. Being made almost entirely of Aeromold, the *Tutor* was a unique aircraft in that it lacked rivet heads or surface fixtures of any kind. The fuselage was made entirely without metal and consisted of plastic-bonded formers and stringers covered not by fabric, like those in most trainers, but rather by a molded-wood skin. The result was a pleasant-looking aircraft, its smooth lines interrupted only by the Continental radial engine. This engine drove a two-blade, variable-pitch propeller. The *Tutor* was extremely easy to fly, steady as a rock in flight, and utilized by the Navy to teach formation flying. A total of 260 N2Ts was built by 1943, and they remained in service until the end of the following year. Only two examples survive today.

**Type:** Bomber

**Dimensions:** wingspan, 38 feet, 9 inches; length, 46 feet, 1 inch; height, 16 feet
**Weights:** empty, 18,942 pounds; gross, 42,000 pounds
**Power plant:** 1 × 15,000–pound thrust Allison TF41 turbofan engine
**Performance:** maximum speed, 698 miles per hour; ceiling, 51,000 feet; maximum range, 2,871 miles
**Armament:** 1 × 20mm Gatling gun; 15,000 pounds of bombs or rockets
**Service dates:** 1967–1993

Known affectionately as SLUF (Short Little Ugly Fellow), the *Corsair II* was the first deliberately subsonic aircraft accepted by the Navy and Air Force. It served with distinction as a bomber throughout the Vietnam War.

During the early 1960s the Navy issued specifications for a new attack aircraft to replace the aging Douglas A-4 *Skyhawk*. This was a mounting priority since the war in Vietnam demonstrated the need for a low-speed attack aircraft possessing considerable loiter time. In 1964 a proposal was advanced by Vought for a bomber based partially upon its proven F-8 *Crusader* design. A contract was signed, and in 1965 the prototype was tested. Like its forebears, the new craft had an air inlet under the radar dome and a bubble canopy set well forward of the wing. However, it was shorter than the *Crusader* and had a fixed, less-swept-back wing and no afterburner. In view of the nature of guerrilla warfare, accurate

bombing and loiter time above a battlefield were more important than speed. The Navy liked the results, and in 1967 it entered into production as the A-7 *Corsair II*. More than 1,500 of all models were constructed.

Curiously, the Air Force was also in the market for a low-cost, accurate ground-support aircraft to replace its F-100 *Super Sabres*, and in 1968 the A-7 became one of few Navy designs accepted into that service. In combat the A-7 lived up to its reputation as a rugged, dependable bomb truck that accurately delivered ordnance from low altitude. In August 1973 a pair of A-7s flew the final mission of the war by striking targets in Cambodia. Since that time the *Corsair II* received numerous engine and avionics upgrades and was active in Grenada, Lebanon, and the 1991 Gulf War. It was finally released from Air National Guard service in 1993, although both Greece and Portugal continue to operate A-7s.

# ★ Vought F4U *Corsair*

**Type:** Fighter

**Dimensions:** wingspan, 40 feet, 11 inches; length, 33 feet, 8 inches; height, 14 feet, 9 inches
**Weights:** empty, 9,900 pounds; gross, 14,079 pounds
**Power plant:** 1 × 2,850–horsepower Pratt & Whitney Double Wasp radial engine
**Performance:** maximum speed, 462 miles per hour; ceiling, 44,000 feet; maximum range, 1,000 miles
**Armament:** 6 × .50–caliber machine guns or 4 × 20mm cannons; 2,000 pounds of bombs
**Service dates:** 1942–1952

The F4U, better known as the "Bent-wing Bird," was the longest-produced World War II fighter. It served brilliantly in two conflicts and was the first propeller-driven aircraft to shoot down a jet.

In 1938 the Chance Vought Corporation started designing a new naval fighter that mounted a powerful R-2800 radial engine around the smallest possible fuselage. Because the engine was intended to drive a huge propeller, the engineers used an inverted gull wing that shortened the length of landing gear necessary to clear the ground. The resulting prototype XF4U took to the air in May 1940 and reached 404 miles per hour, faster than any American fighter. The following year the Navy authorized production, and the plane entered service as the F4U *Corsair*.

Though fast and powerful, the *Corsair* experienced visual and landing problems and was not qualified to operate from carriers. It therefore flew from island airstrips and compiled a brilliant record as a combat aircraft. By 1945 F4Us had established an 11:1 kill ratio, shooting down 2,140 Japanese aircraft while losing only 138 *Corsairs*. One famous Marine squadron, the "Black Sheep," produced no less than ten aces. By war's end, better canopies and landing struts enabled *Corsairs* to operate from carrier decks. The Japanese christened the formidable fighter "Whistling Death" on account of its distinct sound.

After the war the F4U remained the only World War II Navy fighter still under production. It served with distinction throughout the Korean War as a ground-attack bomber, and later models could carry 4,000 pounds of bombs and four 20mm cannons. In 1952 an F4U became the first propeller-driven aircraft to shoot down a modern MiG-15 jet. The last of 12,571 F4Us rolled off the assembly lines in 1952, but it served in foreign air forces up through the 1970s. Only the McDonnell-Douglas F-4 *Phantom* enjoyed a longer service life.

**Type:** Fighter

**Dimensions:** wingspan, 30 feet, 2 inches; length, 32 feet, 10 inches; height, 11 feet, 9 inches
**Weights:** empty, 5,876 pounds; gross, 9,306 pounds
**Power plant:** 1 × 3,000–pound thrust Westinghouse J34 turbojet engine
**Performance:** maximum speed, 530 miles per hour; ceiling, 40,900 feet; maximum range, 1,285 miles
**Armament:** 4 × 20mm cannons
**Service dates:** 1949–1950

The ugly and short-lived *Pirate* was Vought's first venture into jet aviation. Underpowered and unstable, it ended up as a teaching aid for mechanics.

In 1944 the Navy began looking for a viable jet fighter that could operate off carriers. Vought responded by proposing an airframe around the Westinghouse J33 jet engine. The Navy agreed to a prototype, and in 1946 the first XF6U was flown. It was a somewhat tubby design with straight wings, air inlets under the wing roots, a bubble canopy, and a high-set tail. An important innovation was use of Metalite skin, a core of balsa sandwiched between two layers of aluminum. Another weight-saving composite, Fabrilite, which consisted of balsa and fiberglass, was also employed in the vertical tail and air ducts. These materials strengthened the overall structure and enabled the airframe to be lightened considerably. However, initial flights demonstrated that the craft was underpowered and inherently unstable. Tail surfaces were revised no less than five times and a more powerful engine was installed, yet improvements were minimal. Ultimately, auxiliary fins had to be added to the tail surfaces. In May 1948 the XF6U also became the first Navy jet to employ an afterburner for enhanced speed, although it consumed great quantities of fuel. Performance remained marginal, yet the design looked promising, so the Navy authorized construction of 30 aircraft as the F6U *Pirate*.

The F6Us were deployed in 1949 but demonstrated less performance than the F2H *Banshees* and F9F *Panthers* already flying. They consequently only served with an experimental squadron, VX-3, and spent their entire operational career helping to develop arresting gear and barriers for carrier-deck operations. Active duty ceased in 1950; they served the rest of their days as technical trainers.

# Vought F7U *Cutlass*

**Type:** Fighter

**Dimensions:** wingspan, 38 feet, 8 inches; length, 44 feet, 3 inches; height, 14 feet, 7 inches
**Weights:** empty, 18,210 pounds; gross, 31,642 pounds
**Power plant:** 2 × 4,600–pound thrust Westinghouse J46 turbojet engine
**Performance:** maximum speed, 680 miles per hour; ceiling, 40,000 feet; maximum range, 660 miles
**Armament:** 4 × 20mm cannons or 4 *Sparrow I* missiles
**Service dates:** 1950–1959

The futuristic *Cutlass* was the first tailless American jet-powered warplane and the first designed with twin afterburners. Fast and maneuverable, it was also unforgiving, unreliable, and the source of many accidents.

At the end of World War II the acquisition of advanced German aeronautics research prompted Vought to propose a radically different fighter for the Navy, one combining high speed and maneuverability with small size for carrier storage. The Navy expressed interest, and three prototypes were authorized. They first flew in 1948 and were completely different from any American fighter built to date. The XF7U was a tailless, twin-jet design with twin rudders and two built-in afterburners, another aeronautical first. It also possessed an extremely long nose gear, which lifted the nose high for carrier takeoffs. In flight the new craft was extremely fast, maneuverable, and structurally strong—but also in-

herently unstable. All three prototypes crashed, but the Navy was sufficiently intrigued to order it into production as the F7U-1 *Cutlass* before all the bugs were worked out.

In service the F7U was a sparkling performer, but it was also prone to engine failure and inexplicable crashes. Rather than ground the craft, the Navy introduced the new F7U-3 in 1953 with extensively redesigned fuselage and canopy sections. This version chalked up a better safety record than earlier machines, yet it was never completely trusted by pilots. At length the final model, the F7U-3M, was the first Navy fighter to be armed solely with radar-guided *Sparrow I* air-to-air missiles. The *Cutlass* was retained in frontline service until being replaced and surpassed in 1959 by the splendid Vought F8U *Crusader* in 1959. A total of 400 of all versions had been built, which claimed the lives of four test pilots and 21 Navy pilots.

**Type:** Fighter

**Dimensions:** wingspan, 35 feet, 2 inches; length, 54 feet, 6 inches; height, 15 feet, 9 inches
**Weights:** empty, 19,700 pounds; gross, 34,000 pounds
**Power plant:** 1 × 18,000–pound thrust Pratt & Whitney J57 turbojet engine
**Performance:** maximum speed, 1,105 miles per hour; ceiling, 42,900 feet; maximum range, 455 miles
**Armament:** 4 × 20mm cannons; 4 × *Sidewinder* missiles; 4,000 pounds of bombs
**Service dates:** 1957–1977

The shark-nosed *Crusader* was yet another non-traditional concept from Vought, one that proved overwhelmingly successful. It scored the highest kill ratio of any craft during the Vietnam War, earning the nickname "MiG Master."

In 1952 the Navy issued specifications for its first supersonic fighter, and Vought's proposal was chosen from among eight other contenders. The choice was curious, as Vought's two previous Navy designs—the F6U *Pirate* and the F7U *Cutlass*—were unsatisfactory aircraft. Nonetheless, the prototype XF8U flown in 1955 demonstrated such spectacular results that it entered production only six months later. The new craft was an extremely streamlined design with an unusual high wing that could be canted upward 7 degrees to assist carrier takeoffs and landings. Because this device always kept the fuselage parallel to the ground, very small landing gear could be fitted. The pilot was placed well forward of the wing, just behind the nose intake, and

was afforded excellent frontward vision. In 1956 it became the first American fighter to exceed 1,000 miles per hour. The Navy was understandably quite enthusiastic about the new craft, and in 1957 it accepted the first deliveries as the F8U *Crusader*. The total of all models constructed was 1,259.

As a fighter, the F8U possessed tremendous powers of speed and maneuverability. Throughout the Vietnam War, it was the airplane of choice for many fighter pilots, and it is attributed with destroying 21 Russian-built MiGs. A reconnaissance version, the RF-8, was also widely employed, although, being obliged to fly in straight lines while photographing, it took considerable losses. Because of the *Crusader*'s excellent carrier-deck characteristics, in 1964 the French Navy also ordered 42 to serve on its small carriers *Foch* and *Clemenceau*. The last F8Us were phased out of American service during the late 1970s, but the French will keep upgraded versions flying until the year 2000.

# ⭐ Vought O2U *Corsair*

**Type:** Reconnaissance

**Dimensions:** wingspan, 34 feet, 6 inches; length, 24 feet, 5 inches; height, 10 feet, 1 inch
**Weights:** empty, 2,342 pounds; gross, 3,635 pounds
**Power plant:** 1 × 450–horsepower Pratt & Whitney R-1340 radial engine
**Performance:** maximum speed, 150 miles per hour; ceiling, 18,700 feet; maximum range, 608 miles
**Armament:** 3 × .30–caliber machine guns
**Service dates:** 1926–1932

The *Corsair* was the first airplane designed to utilize the famous Pratt & Whitney Wasp radial engine. For many years it served on virtually every capital ship in the U.S. fleet.

The perfection of Pratt & Whitney's radial engine during the mid-1920s was a technological breakthrough for military aviation. The new power plant offered greater performance at much less weight than the prevailing liquid-cooled engines. In 1926 Vought offered to build a new scout floatplane built around this new engine for the Navy. The prototype O2U was a standard biplane configuration, one of the first from Vought possessing steel-tube construction for the fuselage. The wings were of wooden construction, and in latter models the lower wings were given a slight dihedral. A crew of two sat in tandem open cockpits, and the plane could be fitted with either landing gear or floats. While still in testing, the prototype broke four international records for floatplanes. The

Navy was clearly delighted with the new craft and that year ordered 130 examples as the O2U *Corsair*. This was the first Vought machine to bear that famous name.

With wheels or floats, the O2U proved itself an outstanding aircraft, and it became standard equipment on virtually every American cruiser and battleship. *Corsairs* also earned a measure of fame in 1927 fighting in Nicaragua with the Marines. One aviator, Lieutenant Christian F. Schilt, won the Congressional Medal of Honor for landing under fire to rescue fellow Marines. The type's excellent service led to additional models that sported minor refinements. The Navy ultimately acquired a total of 289 O2Us. Vought also enjoyed considerable success exporting the *Corsair* abroad to Argentina, China, Mexico, and Peru. Commencing in 1930, the O2U was slowly phased out by the more advanced O3U, but a handful remained at Pensacola as trainers until the late 1930s.

**Type:** Reconnaissance

**Dimensions:** wingspan, 36 feet; length, 27 feet, 5 inches; height, 11 feet, 4 inches
**Weights:** empty, 3,312 pounds; gross, 4,765 pounds
**Power plant:** 1 × 600–horsepower Pratt & Whitney R-1690 radial engine
**Performance:** maximum speed, 167 miles per hour; ceiling, 18,600 feet; maximum range, 680 miles
**Armament:** 3 × .30–caliber machine guns
**Service dates:** 1930–1941

The O3U was another rugged, dependable Navy scout. They served for a decade up through the advent of World War II.

In 1930 Vought capitalized upon its success with the O2U by introducing an improved model, the O3U-1. This version featured revised wings with greater dihedral and sweep, as well as a Grumman-developed amphibious float. The Navy acquired 87 of these machines, all of which served on capital ships in the U.S. fleet.

Subsequent purchases of *Corsairs* resulted in greater streamlining and variations. The next model, the O3U-2, was fitted with a new Hornet engine and a cowling to reduce drag. It also sported a modified tailfin and simple, straight-axle landing gear. Vought constructed 29 of this version; upon being handed over to the Marine Corps they received the designation SU-1, for "Scout, Utility." Onboard the USS *Saratoga* and *Lexington*, these planes equipped VS-14 and VS-15, the only carrier-based Marine Corps squadrons during this period.

Another model, the O3U-3, returned to using the Wasp engine and obtained a rounder rudder. The Navy acquired 76 of these machines before authorizing construction of 65 O3U-4s with long-chord cowls and other equipment changes. As before, these were supplied to the Marines as SU-2s and SU-3s. The 40 examples of the SU-4 revived the short-chord cowling and were also fitted with larger tail surfaces. The final variant, the O3U-6, resumed the long cowl and introduced a partial canopy between the cockpits. As before, Vought enjoyed considerable success exporting the *Corsair* abroad, and numbers were either purchased or manufactured under license by Argentina, China, Mexico, and Thailand.

Like its predecessors, the O3U/SU series was versatile and enjoyed careers of unusual longevity. Even though they were biplanes, 141 *Corsairs* were still in service by the time Japan attacked Pearl Harbor in December 1941. Many ended their days serving as radio-controlled drones with tricycle-style landing gear.

# ☆ Vought OS2U *Kingfisher*

**Type:** Scout

---

**Dimensions:** wingspan, 35 feet, 11 inches; length, 33 feet, 10 inches; height, 15 feet, 1 inch
**Weights:** empty, 4,123 pounds; gross, 6,000 pounds
**Power plant:** 1 × 450–horsepower Pratt & Whitney R-985 Wasp Junior radial engine
**Performance:** maximum speed, 164 miles per hour; ceiling, 13,000 feet; maximum range, 805 miles
**Armament:** 2 × .30–caliber machine guns; 325 pounds of bombs
**Service dates:** 1940–1945

---

The *Kingfisher* was the Navy's first monoplane scout aircraft to be catapulted at sea. It was widely used throughout World War II and served as the eyes of the fleet.

In 1937 Vought began work on a replacement for its aging O3U *Corsair* biplane scouts. The following year, a monoplane prototype emerged, using innovative construction techniques like spot-welding. The XOS2U was fitted with a large central float and stabilizing floats on the wingtips, but they could be detached and substituted with fixed landing gear for ground operations. The Navy initially ordered 54 examples under the designation *Kingfisher*, and deliveries began reaching the U.S. fleet in August 1940. They were followed by 158 OS2U-2s in 1941, which featured a slightly different engine.

During World War II the OS2U, nicknamed "Old, Slow, and Ugly," served capably from battle-ship and cruiser catapults as well as land bases. They were active as scouts for the fleet but became better known for harrowing air-sea rescue operations. It was a *Kingfisher* that saved World War I ace Eddie Rickenbacker when his B-17 crashed into the Pacific in October 1942. The OS2U was also active in antisubmarine work and participated in the destruction of at least two U-boats in the Atlantic. At least 100 were also delivered to the Royal Air Force, which employed them throughout the Caribbean for similar purposes. The Dutch forces in the East Indies were slated to receive 24, but when those islands fell to the Japanese, the Australians acquired them by default. Production ended in 1942 with Vought having delivered 1,006 OS2Us; the Naval Aircraft Factory completed another 300. All were phased out of active service as of 1945 in favor of more modern types.

**Type:** Scout-Bomber

**Dimensions:** wingspan, 42 feet; length, 34 feet; height, 10 feet, 3 inches
**Weights:** empty, 5,634 pounds; gross, 9,421 pounds
**Power plant:** 1 × 825–horsepower Pratt & Whitney Twin Wasp Junior R-1535 radial engine
**Performance:** maximum speed, 243 miles per hour; ceiling, 23,600 feet; maximum range, 1,120 miles
**Armament:** 2 × .50–caliber machine guns; 1,000 pounds of bombs
**Service dates:** 1938–1942

The *Vindicator* was the Navy's first monoplane scout-bomber. Fast and modern for its day, it was obsolete by World War II and quickly removed from service.

By 1934 the Chance Vought Corporation was designing a replacement for its SBU scout-bomber. It emerged as the XSB2U, a radical departure from the biplanes then in use. The new craft was a low-wing monoplane with retractable landing gear and folding wings for ease of storage onboard carriers. However, like the biplanes it was intended to replace, the XSB2U was partially constructed of metal and partly covered in fabric. The prototype first flew in 1936, by which time the Navy contracted to acquire 54 machines. This was followed by orders for 58 SB2U-2s in 1938 and 57 SB2U-3s in 1940. The latest model was the first to be officially called the *Vindicator*, and it equipped four squadrons aboard the carriers *Lexington*, *Saratoga*, *Wasp*, and *Ranger.* An export model, V-156, was also purchased by France in anticipation of World War II.

The *Vindicator*'s combat career was short but violent. *Vindicators* equipped two squadrons of the French Aeronautique Maritime and fought well until France was overrun by Germany in May 1940. Great Britain also ordered 50 V-156s, christened *Chesapeakes*, which were found too bulky for small British carriers and assigned to training duty. However, after the Japanese attack on Pearl Harbor in December 1941, the aging SB2Us were necessarily pressed into frontline service. In spring 1942 they fought alongside Douglas SBDs and TBDs in various raids along the Caroline and Marshall Islands. However, their greatest test came in June 1942 during the decisive Battle of Midway, where they took heavy losses at the hands of Japanese *Zero* fighters. All SB2Us were quickly phased out of active duty in favor of more modern machines.

# ★ Vought SBU *Scout*

**Type:** Dive-Bomber

---

**Dimensions:** wingspan, 33 feet, 3 inches; length, 27 feet, 10 inches; height, 11 feet, 11 inches
**Weights:** empty, 3,645 pounds; gross, 5,520 pounds
**Power plant:** 1 × 700–horsepower Pratt & Whitney R-1535 radial engine
**Performance:** maximum speed, 205 miles per hour; ceiling, 23,700 feet, maximum range, 548 miles
**Armament:** 2 × .30–caliber machine guns; 1 × 500–pound bomb
**Service dates:** 1935–1940

The SBU was the last fixed-wheel biplane to operate from Navy carriers and the first to introduce air-cooled cowlings. Excellent dive-bombers, they served until World War II erupted.

In 1932 the Navy revived the category of two-seat fighter for possible production, and Vought responded with the XF3U-1. However, War Department politics forced the Navy to abandon that outdated category and substitute it with "VSB" for "Scout, Bomber." Because the XF3U-1 displayed excellent aerial qualities, Vought decided to modify it for the new role. The new XSBU-1 was a standard biplane with a metal fuselage and fabric-covered wings. However, it had a fully enclosed canopy for the crew and a unique, air-cooled cowling. This device featured adjustable "gills" on the cowl's trailing edge that could be opened and shut to better control air flowing over the engine cylinders. This soon became a standard feature on most radial-engine cowlings. The XSBU-1

also sported fixed landing gear and provisions to drop a 500-pound bomb. The Navy was pleased with the airplane's performance—it was the first dive-bomber to exceed 200 miles per hour in level flight—and in 1935 purchased 84 examples as the SBU-1. This was one of few Vought designs not to receive either a company- or Navy-inspired nickname.

In service the SBU equipped Scouting Squadrons VS-1B, VS-2B, and VS-3B and performed admirably from a number of carriers. In 1936 the Navy purchased an additional 40 examples as SBU-2s, delivered directly to reserve squadrons. Vought also exported 14 SBU-1s to Argentina, which promptly dubbed them "Corsarios." This handsome scout was gradually replaced by the Vought SB2U *Vindicator* beginning in 1938; they were retired from frontline line service in 1940. Many SBUs remained as training craft during World War II and were finally retired in 1944.

**Type:** Torpedo-Bomber

**Dimensions:** wingspan, 56 feet, 11 inches; length, 39 feet, 2 inches; height, 15 feet, 6 inches
**Weights:** empty, unknown; gross, 18,488 pounds
**Power plant:** 1 × 2,000–horsepower Pratt & Whitney Double Wasp R-2800 radial engine
**Performance:** maximum speed, 306 miles per hour; ceiling, 27,200 feet; maximum range, 1,500 miles
**Armament:** 4 × .50–caliber machine guns; 1 × .30–caliber machine gun; 1 × 2,000–pound torpedo
**Service dates:** 1944–1945

The *Sea Wolf* was far and away the best torpedo-bomber developed by the United States during World War II. However, production problems delayed its deployment until 1944, and it never saw combat.

In 1939 Vought entered a Navy competition to design a more modern torpedo-bomber. Its entry was awarded a contract in 1940, and the following year a prototype was completed and flown. The new design was a low-wing monoplane of all-metal construction and featured retractable wheels and a long greenhouse canopy terminating in a power gun turret. The crew consisted of pilot, radio operator, and gunner. The bomb bay was also totally enclosed and could be fitted with either torpedoes or bombs. Unlike the Grumman TBM *Avenger*, the closest competitor, the wings were fixed and did not fold for carrier storage. However, tests showed that the Vought TBU possessed much higher performance and was a much faster aircraft than the lumbering *Avenger*.

The Navy was sufficiently impressed to place an order for 1,100 TBUs, which it dubbed the *Sea Wolf*, in 1943. However, because Vought production facilities were overflowing with work on the much-needed F4U *Corsair* fighter, it was decided to contract construction out to Consolidated. By this time the war in the Pacific had taken dramatic turns in favor of the Allies, and the urgency for new and more torpedo-bombers slackened. Therefore, the Navy canceled the contract with Consolidated after only 180 TBYs (the new designation) were delivered. The capable *Sea Wolf* was initially delivered to the Navy during fall 1944, but all were retained stateside as training aircraft and never served operationally. All were scrapped shortly after the war ended.

# Vought UO/FU

**Type:** Reconnaissance; Fighter

---

**Dimensions:** wingspan, 34 feet, 3 inches; length, 24 feet, 5 inches; height, 8 feet, 9 inches
**Weights:** empty, 1,494 pounds; gross, 2,305 pounds
**Power plant:** 1 × 200–horsepower Wright J-3 radial engine
**Performance:** maximum speed, 124 miles per hour; ceiling, 18,800 feet; maximum range, 398 miles
**Armament:** none
**Service dates:** 1922–1932

The UO had a long, distinguished career as a two-seat scout and a brief, peculiar period as a single-seat fighter. It was also the last American warplane to employ World War I–era building concepts.

By 1921 the Navy was looking to replace its World War I–vintage VE-7s with a more modern successor. Specifically, it wanted an airplane that utilized the lighter and less complicated radial engine technology that was better suited for sea duty. Rather than design a new plane, Vought offered an updated version of the trusted VE-7. In 1922 it rolled out the first VO-1, which was a standard two-seat biplane based on the earlier craft. The wood-and-wire fuselage was much rounder and now possessed streamlined cheek tanks behind the engine. The vertical tail was also taller, and the new craft could fly from land and sea by using interchangeable wheels and floats. The Navy liked the changes and purchased 150 machines as the UO-1. Within a few years they had displaced all other types of aircraft as the eyes of the fleet.

In 1925, before aircraft carriers were fully operational, the Navy became sold on the concept of battleship fighters, which could be catapulted off capital ships in order to defend the ships. Accordingly, the Navy asked Vought to modify the UO-1 into a single-seat floatplane-fighter. This was accomplished by fairing over the front cockpit, strengthening the wings for high-stress maneuvers, and fitting two .30-caliber machine guns on the nose. The Navy purchased 20 of these fighters, designated FU-1s, which deployed at sea with the Pacific Fleet in 1926. They proved to be responsive, acrobatic aircraft, but pilots complained about poor visibility from the former rear cockpit. At length the Navy acknowledged the FU-1's inadequacies and reconverted the aircraft back into FU-2 two-seat trainers. Meanwhile, the UO-1s continued serving the fleet well for a decade before being replaced by high-performance O2U *Corsairs*.

**Type:** Fighter; Reconnaissance

**Dimensions:** wingspan, 34 feet, 1 inch; length, 24 feet, 5 inches; height, 8 feet, 7 inches
**Weights:** empty, 1,505 pounds; gross, 2,100 pounds
**Power plant:** 1 × 180–horsepower Wright E-2 liquid-cooled engine
**Performance:** maximum speed, 117 miles per hour; ceiling, 15,000 feet; maximum range, 291 miles
**Armament:** 2 × .30–caliber machine guns
**Service dates:** 1918–1928

Originally built as a trainer, the VE-7 became the Navy's first fighter and proved that Americans could construct world-class warplanes. It was also the first naval aircraft to be launched from an aircraft carrier.

When the United States entered World War I, its aviation industry was woefully unprepared for production of anything but European-designed aircraft. Nonetheless, the military establishment encouraged American manufacturers to develop their own craft in order to break this dependency. In 1917 Chance E. Vought submitted plans for the VE-7 advanced trainer. It was a standard biplane with two-bay, slightly staggered wings, a Hispano-Suiza engine, and an oval radiator that made it resemble the French Spad XIII. When the prototype flew in 1918 it displayed sterling qualities, and the Army ordered 1,000 copies. However, only 14 had been delivered by the time the war ended that November, and the remainder was summarily canceled.

Fortunately for the young Chance Vought Corporation, the Navy had tested the VE-7 and adopted it as its first fighter. To accomplish this, the front cockpit of the VE-7 was faired over and two .30-caliber machine guns were mounted. Vought manufactured 129 copies in several versions, and by 1920 it equipped VF-1 and VF-2, the Navy's first fighter squadrons. In May 1922 a VE-7 became the first aircraft to be catapulted off an American battleship. On October 17 of that year, Lieutenant Virgil C. Griffen flew a VE-7 off the carrier USS *Langley* for the first time in history. This craft possessed such good performance that several examples were also built as two-seat, float-equipped observation planes. Still others were equipped with inflatable bags tucked under the wings that were deployed in the event of a crash landing at sea. The VE-7s rendered excellent service for a decade and were finally replaced by 1928. More importantly, they established Vought's long-standing relationship with the Navy, which lasted for more than 60 years.

# Vultee A-31/A-35 *Vengeance*

**Type:** Dive-Bomber

**Dimensions:** wingspan, 48 feet; length, 39 feet, 9 inches; height, 14 feet, 6 inches
**Weights:** empty, 9,900 pounds; gross, 15,600 pounds
**Power plant:** 1 × 1,600–horsepower Wright Cyclone R-2600 radial engine
**Performance:** maximum speed, 279 miles per hour; ceiling, 22,000 feet; maximum range, 600 miles
**Armament:** 5 × .50–caliber machine guns; 2,000 pounds of bombs
**Service dates:** 1942–1944

This modern and accurate dive-bomber was regarded by many as a waste of resources, and it never saw service with American forces. However, the British put it to good use in Burma.

In 1940 the British Purchasing Commission approached Vultee to design a new dive-bombing aircraft for the Royal Air Force. Vultee responded with the V-72, an outgrowth of its earlier and widely exported V-11. This was a midwing, all-metal airplane with an internal bomb bay and a crew of two. Its most distinctive feature was the angular, cranked main wing that featured dive brakes and a swept-back leading edge. The prototype first flew in July 1941 and proved to be strongly built and fully aerobatic. The British placed an initial order for 500, which entered service as the A-31 *Vengeance*. However, dive-bombing had passed from the European scene, as the tactic was regarded as too vulnerable to fighter opposition. Therefore, those A-31s that were not retained in England as target tugs were deployed to Burma as dive-bombers.

As of 1942 the Army Air Force also expressed an interest in the *Vengeance*, and that year it acquired 583 Americanized versions, designated A-35s. These differed from the British model mainly by having either four or six machine guns mounted in the wings. However, the Army found the A-35 too slow and vulnerable and restricted it to target towing. The British, meanwhile, ultimately received a total of 1,319 A-31s, which continued flying in Burma up through 1944. Though slow, the *Vengeance* was a highly accurate diving platform and did useful work hitting jungle targets. By 1944 it had been surpassed by more modern designs and was relegated to second-line duties. Brazil also acquired 29 A-35s; it flew antisubmarine patrols until the end of the war.

**Type:** Trainer

**Dimensions:** wingspan, 42 feet; length, 28 feet, 10 inches; height, 11 feet, 6 inches
**Weights:** empty, 3,375 pounds; gross, 4,496 pounds
**Power plant:** 1 × 450–horsepower Pratt & Whitney R-985 Wasp Junior radial engine
**Performance:** maximum speed, 180 miles per hour; ceiling, 21,650 feet; maximum range, 725 miles
**Armament:** none
**Service dates:** 1940–1945

During World War II the BT-13 was acquired in greater numbers than any other basic trainer. It became known to crew members as the "Vultee Vibrator" on account of its rattling canopy.

In 1938 Vultee responded to an Army competition for new training aircraft by fielding the Model 54. This was a modern, all-metal, low-wing monoplane with fabric control surfaces, retractable landing gear, and a spacious, if loosely fitting, canopy. Vultee intended it for the "Basic Training" (BT) category, midway between "Primary Training" (PT) and "Advanced Training" (AT) stages. The Army liked the result and ordered 300 of the craft in 1939, which at that time was the largest order ever placed for basic trainers. Designated the BT-13 *Valiant*, production models differed from the prototype in having fixed landing gear and a lower-powered engine. The Navy also expressed interest, and in 1940 it acquired several aircraft under the designation SNV.

In service, the *Valiant* proved stable but tricky to fly for inexperienced pilots. Its sometimes vicious stall characteristics caused many fatalities and gave the craft the reputation as a "cadet killer." Nonetheless, during World War II it was the most numerous basic trainer acquired by U.S. armed forces, and almost 100,000 pilots passed through its cockpits. When engine shortages required Vultee to switch to a Wright R-975 engine, that version was officially labeled the BT-15. By 1945 more than 10,375 *Valiants* had been purchased for the Army, with a further 2,000 ending up in Navy hands. After the war the BT-13 and all its variants were declared obsolete and either scrapped or sold. This was because the three-tiered training system was abandoned in favor of the single designation "T" for "Trainer." Many BT-13s ended up in private hands, where they continue flying as heavily modified crop dusters.

# ★ Vultee P-66 *Vanguard*

**Type:** Fighter

---

**Dimensions:** wingspan, 36 feet; length, 28 feet, 5 inches; height, 9 feet, 5 inches
**Weights:** empty, 5,235 pounds; gross, 7,384 pounds
**Power plant:** 1 × 1,200–horsepower Pratt & Whitney Twin Wasp R-1830 radial engine
**Performance:** maximum speed, 340 miles per hour; ceiling, 28,200 feet; maximum range, 950 miles
**Armament:** 2 × .50–caliber machine guns; 4 × .30–caliber machine guns
**Service dates:** 1941–1942

The *Vanguard* was an export fighter version of the famous BT-13 trainer. Though fast and maneuverable, it was rejected by the United States and Great Britain but saw service in China.

In 1938 Vultee began developing a fighter from the basic design of its BT-13 trainer. Called the Model 48, it was a low-wing, all-metal design with fully retractable landing gear and tail wheel. The prototype first flew in 1939 with a tight-fitting engine cowl and a large bullet spinner for streamlining, but cooling problems necessitated adoption of a conventional open cowl. Subsequent testing resulted in larger tail and control surfaces, and by the time Model 48 was ready for export it was a delightfully aerobatic little fighter.

Sweden was the first country to express interest in the Vultee design and in February 1940 placed an order for 140 Model 48s. However, the U.S. government, fearful that Sweden was about to be overrun by Germany, slapped on an export embargo. The aircraft then received the designation P-66 *Vanguard* and were offered to Great Britain through the Lend-Lease program. However, the Royal Air Force deemed them unsuitable for combat operations, as did the Canadians. Consensus was then reached to export 129 *Vanguards* to the Nationalist government in China, which was being severely pummeled by Japanese airpower. Before this could transpire, Pearl Harbor was bombed and the U.S. government seized the P-66 for its own use. Several ended up serving the 14th Pursuit Group for several weeks, its pilots thoroughly enjoying its flying characteristics. By February 1942, however, all had been crated and sent to Karachi, India. There they were assembled and flown to Kunming, China, rendering undistinguished service for several years.

# ★ Vultee V-11

**Type:** Light Bomber

---

**Dimensions:** wingspan, 50 feet; length, 37 feet; height, 10 feet
**Weights:** empty, 6,415 pounds; gross, 9,863 pounds
**Power plant:** 1 × 850–horsepower Wright Cyclone GR-1820 radial engine
**Performance:** maximum speed, 238 miles per hour; ceiling, 28,000 feet; maximum range, 2,380 miles
**Armament:** 6 × .30–caliber machine guns; 2,000 pounds of bombs
**Service dates:** 1937–1945

---

The V-11 was a widely exported light bomber during the 1930s. Although rejected by the Army Air Corps, it saw extensive frontline service in China.

In 1934 Vultee decided to develop a single-engine light bomber from its existing V-1 transport design. The new craft was an all-metal, low-wing monoplane with retractable landing gear and an internal bomb bay. The crew of two sat in tandem under an extended greenhouse canopy. The prototype V-11 first flew in September 1935, and the Nationalist Chinese government expressed interest in acquiring the design. Accordingly, 30 of the craft were assembled and delivered between July 1937 and April 1938. They entered service at Hangkow with the 14th Squadron, a short-lived international formation of American and French pilots with Chinese gunners. They saw action against Japanese forces through 1938 before being disbanded.

Though somewhat slow and underpowered,

the V-11 was a reliable and rugged airplane. Vultee continued refining the basic design, and in 1937 it offered the V-11GB on the world market. It differed from earlier models by having a third crew member who functioned as a tailgunner. The Soviet Union acquired four V-11GBs along with the right to manufacture more under license. Furthermore, Turkey ordered 40 VT-11s, Brazil requested 26, and China purchased an additional 26. In June 1938 the Army Air Corps also ordered seven examples, which received the designation YA-19. They were evaluated as possible light bombers and were fitted with a more powerful 1,200-horsepower Pratt & Whitney Twin Wasp R-1830 engine. Despite these modifications, V-11s were found to be less promising than new aircraft about to enter service, and no orders were forthcoming. However, the machines exported or built in China and Russia remained in service throughout World War II as bombers and transports.

# ⭐ Waco CG-4 *Haig/Hadrian*

**Type:** Glider

**Dimensions:** wingspan, 83 feet, 8 inches; length, 48 feet, 3 inches; height, 12 feet, 7 inches
**Weights:** empty, 3,790 pounds; gross, 7,500 pounds
**Power plant:** none
**Performance:** maximum towing speed, 138 miles per hour; stalling speed, 38 miles per hour
**Armament:** none
**Service dates:** 1942–1948

The CG-4 was the only mass-produced American glider of World War II. It served extensively in Europe and Burma with both United States and British forces.

The 1941 German airborne assault against Crete convinced the U.S. Army that gliders were a practical method of transporting troops. Accordingly, it opened competition for an assault glider capable of carrying 15 fully armed troops, including pilot and copilot. Of four models entered, the Waco XCG-4 was deemed the most promising. It was a high-wing design and constructed of wood, a steel-tube frame, and fabric covering. The landing gear were jettisoned after takeoff, and landings would be conducted on a single skid beneath the fuselage. Two or three of the gliders, known in U.S. service as the *Haig*, could be towed behind C-46 or C-47 troop transports. Several also served with the British, who dubbed them *Hadrian*. Once grounded, the cockpit area, which was hinged, could swing up to disgorge troops, a quarter-ton jeep, or a 75mm howitzer.

The CG-4 saw its baptism of fire during the near-disastrous airborne assault on Sicily in 1943. Launched during stormy weather, nearly one-third of the gliders crashed at sea, whereas the rest scattered far from their objectives. Better luck was obtained in Burma in March 1944, when CG-4s successfully conveyed General Orde Wingate's "Chindits" 150 miles behind Japanese lines. Three months later hundreds of *Haigs* were released over Normandy during D day and again that fall during Operation Market Garden in Holland. They were also present during the invasion of southern France and the crossing of the Rhine in 1945. After the war, many were declared surplus and sold to civilians, who cut them up for their valuable wood. A total of 12,400 CG-4s was built by no less than 16 companies. A handful remained in service until 1948.

# AIRCRAFT BIBLIOGRAPHY

**Aeromarine**

Model 39B

Matt, Paul R. "Aeromarine Tractor Trainer," *Historic Aviation Album* 9 (1971): 184–197.

**Aeronca**

Hollenbaugh, Bob. *Aeronca: A Photo History.* Destin, FL: Aviation Heritage Books, 1993.

L-3 *Grasshopper*

Holcomb, Mal. "Send the Grasshopper," *Wings* 13 (February, 1983): 40–49.

**Beech**

Pelletier, Alain J. *Beech Aircraft and Their Predecessors.* Annapolis, MD: Naval Institute Press, 1995.

AT-10 *Wichita*

Kennedy, W. H. "Memoirs of a Wartime Student Pilot," *Air Classics* 16 (June, 1980): 40–45, 81–82.

C-45 *Expediter*

Ball, Larry A. *The Immortal Twin Beech.* Indianapolis: Ball Publications, 1995.

Huston, Fred. "Bombardier," *Air Power* 15 (March, 1985): 46–48, 53.

Sloat, Chuck. "Salute to the Bug Smasher," *Warbirds International* 7 (January/February, 1988): 48–56.

T-34 *Mentor*

Drendel, Lou. *T-34 Mentor in Action.* Carrollton, TX: Squadron/Signal Publications, 1990.

**Bell**

Matthews, Birch. *Cobra! The Bell Aircraft Corporation, 1934–1946.* Atglen, PA: Schiffer Publishing, 1996.

Pelletier, Alain J. *Bell Aircraft since 1935.* Annapolis, MD: Naval Institute Press, 1992

AH-1 *Cobra*

Mutza, Wayne. *AH-1 Cobra in Action.* Carrollton, TX: Squadron/Signal Publications, 1998.

Peacock, Lindsay T. *AH-1 Cobra.* London: Osprey, 1987.

Peoples, Kenneth. *Bell AH-1 Variants.* Arlington, TX: Aerofax, 1988.

Verier, Mike. *Bell AH-1 Cobra.* London: Osprey, 1990.

H-13

Mutza, Wayne. *H-13 Sioux.* Carrollton, TX: Squadron/Signal Publications, 1995.

H-58 *Kiowa*

Dorr, Robert F. "Kiowa Warrior," *World Air Power* 15 (Winter, 1993): 26–35.

HSL

Andrews, Hal. "Naval Aircraft: HSL," *Naval Aviation News* (September, 1980): 24–25.

P-39 *Airacobra*

McDowell, Ernie. *P-39 Airacobra in Action.* Carrollton, TX: Squadron/Signal Publications, 1980.

Mitchell, Rick. *Airacobra Advantage: The Flying Cannon.* Missoula, MT: Pictorial Histories Publishing Company, 1992.

P-59 *Airacomet*

Carpenter, David. *Flame Powered: The Bell XP-59A Airacomet.* Jet Pioneers of America, 1992.

Furler, E. H. "America's First Jet Fighter," *Air Classics* 21 (February, 1985): 28–39.

P-63 *Kingcobra*

Furler, E. H. "Kingcobra," *Air Classics* 19 (November/December, 1983): 14–21, 38–45.

O'Leary, Michael. "Super Cobra," *Air Classics* 14 (April, 1978): 50–59.

UH-1 *Iroquois*

Chant, Christopher. *Bell UH-1.* Newbury Park, CA: Haynes, 1985.

Drendel, Lou. *Huey.* Carrollton, TX: Squadron/Signal Publications, 1983.

Mutza, Wayne. *UH-1 Huey in Action.* Carrollton, TX: Squadron/Signal Publications, 1986.

Scutts, Jerry. *UH-1 Iroquois/AH-1 Cobra.* London: Ian Allen, 1984.

V-22 *Osprey*

Brown, David A. *The Bell Helicopter/Textron Story: Changing the Way the World Flies.* Arlington, TX: Aerofax, 1995.

Larsen, George C. "Extreme Machine," *Air & Space Smithsonian* 13 (October/November, 1998): 26–35.

**Berliner-Joyce**

"The Fighters of Berliner-Joyce," *Air Classics Quarterly Review* 1 (Fall, 1974): 66–71.

Westburg, Peter W. "Berliner-Joyce: The Story of an Aircraft Company," *Air Classics* 14 (July, 1978): 18–23, 68–73.

OJ-2

Andrews, Hal. "Naval Aircraft: OJ-2," *Naval Aviation News* (August, 1978): 24–25.

P-16

Westburg, Peter W. "Berliner-Joyce: The Story of an Aircraft Company," *Air Classics* 14 (August, 1978): 16–21, 60–63.

**Boeing**

Bowers, Peter M. *Boeing Aircraft Since 1916.* Annapolis, MD: Naval Institute Press, 1989.

B-17 *Flying Fortress*

Ethell, Jeffrey L. *B-17 Flying Fortress.* Osceola, WI: Motorbooks International, 1995.

Freeman, Roger A. *The B-17 Flying Fortress Story: Design, Production, History.* London: Arms and Armour Press, 1998.

Hess, William N. *Great American Bombers of World War II: B-17 Flying Fortress.* Osceola, WI: Motorbooks International, 1998.

**B-29** *Superfortress*

Campbell, John B. *Boeing B-29 Superfortress.* Atglen, PA: Schiffer Publishing, 1997.

Davis, Larry. *B-29 Superfortress in Action.* Carrollton, TX: Squadron/Signal Publications, 1992.

Marshall, Chester. *B-29 Superfortress.* Osceola, WI: Motorbooks International, 1993.

Vander Meulen, Jacob. *Building the B-29.* Washington, DC: Smithsonian Institution Press, 1996.

**B-47** *Stratojet*

Drendel, Lou. *B-47 Stratojet in Action.* Carrollton, TX: Squadron/Signal Publications, 1976.

Peacock, Lindsey T. *Boeing B-47 Stratojet.* Osceola, WI: Motorbooks International, 1987.

Wilson, Stewart. *Vulcan, Boeing B-47 & B-52.* Fyshwick, Eng.: Aerospace Publications, 1997.

**B-50** *Superfortress*

Bourgeois, Harold. "Lucky Lady's Flight," *Aviation Quarterly* 6 (Summer, 1980): 180–191.

Boyne, Walter J. "The Anonymous Peacemaker," *Air Classics* 4 (August, 1968): 8–17, 70–74.

Stinson, Patrick. "Around the World Nonstop," *Air Power History* 36 (March, 1989): 24–30.

**B-52** *Stratofortress*

Boyne, Walter J. *Boeing B-52: A Documentary History.* Atglen, PA: Schiffer Publishing, 1994.

Dorr, Robert F., and Lindsay Peacock. *B-52 Stratofortress: Boeing's Cold War Warrior.* London: Osprey, 1995.

Francillon, Rene. *B-52: Aging Buffs, Youthful Crews.* Osceola, WI: Motorbooks International, 1989.

**E-3** *Sentry*

*An Illustrated Data Guide to Modern Reconnaissance Aircraft.* London: Tiger Books International, 1997.

Trimble, Robert L. "Big Brother Is Watching," *Air Combat* 10 (September, 1982): 6–15.

**F2B**

Bowers, Peter M. "The Fleet's In," *Air Power* 9 (May, 1979): 30–41, 53.

**F3B**

Andrews, Hal. "Naval Aircraft: F3B," *Naval Aviation News* (October, 1978): 22–23.

**F4B**

Barrow, Jess C. "Teething Problems with F4B-1s: A New Fighter Joins the Fleet," *AAHS Journal* 16 (Summer, 1971): 98–104.

Bowers, Peter M. "The First Boeing P-12," *Aero Album* 4 (Winter, 1968): 9–12.

———. "Recollections of the Boeing F4B-4," *AAHS Journal* 38 (Spring, 1993): 138–145.

**FB-5**

Bowers, Peter M. "Sea-Going Boeing," *Air Power* 7 (September, 1977): 44–55.

**KC-97** *Stratotanker*

Bowers, Peter M. "Stratofreighter," *Air Power* 29 (July, 1999): 18–49.

McCarthy, Dan B. "The C-97," *Air Classics* 8 (August, 1972): 14–21, 28–50, 58–59.

**KC-135** *Stratotanker*

Dorr, Robert F. *Boeing KC-135 Stratotanker.* London: Ian Miller, 1987.

Hopkins, Robert S. *Boeing KC-135 Stratotanker: More Than Just a Tanker.* North Branch, MN: Specialty Press, 1997.

Logan, Don. *The Boeing C-135 Series: Stratotanker, Starlifter, and Other Variants.* Atglen, PA: Schiffer Publishing, 1998.

**NB**

Van Deurs, George. "Fly Before Buy: The Boeing NB-1 Occasionally Went into Flat Spins, Whirling Like a Maple Leaf," *Aerospace Historian* 21 (Fall, 1974): 139–143.

**P-12**

Bradley, Mark. "The Boeing P-12," *Aerospace Historian* 32 (December, 1985): 239–245.

Davis, Larry. *P-12/F4B in Action.* Carrollton, TX: Squadron/Signal Publications, 1993.

Wallick, S. L. *Flying the P-12.* Seattle, WA: Classic Publications, 1982.

**P-26** *Peashooter*

Davis, Larry. *P-26.* Carrollton, TX: Squadron/Signal Publications, 1994.

Maloney, Edward T. *Boeing P-26 Peashooter.* Fallbrook, CA: Aero Publishers, 1973.

**PW-9**

Bowers, Peter M. "Boeing's First Fighter," *Wings* 7 (August, 1977): 42–55.

Cavanagh, Robert L. "Boeing PW-9s in the Navy," *AAHS Journal* 7 (Summer and Winter, 1962): 110–114, 285–287.

**Boeing-Vertol**

**CH-46** *Sea Knight*

Andrews, Hal. "Naval Aircraft: Sea Knight," *Naval Aviation News* (February, 1978): 20–21.

**CH-47** *Chinook*

Anderton, David. *Boeing Helicopters: CH-47 Chinook.* Arlington, TX: Aerofax, 1988.

Mutza, Wayne. *CH-47 Chinook in Action.* Carrollton, TX: Squadron/Signal Publications, 1989.

**Brewster**

Maas, Jim. "Fall From Grace: The Brewster Aeronautical Corporation, 1932–1942," *AAHS Journal* 30 (Summer, 1985): 118–135.

**F2A** *Buffalo*

Ford, Daniel. "The Sorry Saga of the Brewster Buffalo," *Air & Space Smithsonian* (April, 1996): 26–37.

Maas, Jim. *F2A Buffalo in Action.* Carrollton, TX: Squadron/Signal Publications, 1987.

**SB2A** *Buccaneer*

Geminhardt, Fritz, David Lucabaugh, and Bob Martin. "The Brewster 'Blaster,'" *AAHS Journal* 37 (Spring, 1987): 58–73.

SBN

Dean, Jack. "Dive Bomber: The Brewster Blunders," *Wings* 15 (April, 1985): 10–17.

Smith, Peter C. "Brewster SBA Series," *Fly Past* 37 (August, 1984): 60–63.

## Cessna

Shiel, Walt. *Cessna Warbirds: A Detailed and Personal History of Cessna's Involvement in the Armed Forces.* Iola, WI: James Publishing, 1995.

A-37 *Dragonfly*

Love, Terry. *A-37/T-37 Dragonfly in Action.* Carrollton, TX: Squadron/Signal Publications, 1991.

AT-17/UC-78 *Bobcat*

Matt, Paul R. "Cessna T-50 Bobcat," *Historic Aviation Album* 17 (1984): 81–88.

L-19/O-1E *Birddog*

Adcock, Al. *O-1 Birddog in Action.* Carrollton, TX: Squadron/Signal Publications, 1988.

Thompson, Warren. *L-19 Bird Dog: The Lovable One-Niner.* Paducah, KY: Turner Publishing, 1996.

O-2 *Skymaster*

Sims, Don. "Forward Air Controller," *Air Classics Quarterly* 6 (Spring, 1979): 63–72.

T-37 *Tweety Bird*

Trimble, Robert L. "Cessna's Tough Two-seater," *Air Combat* 10 (July, 1982): 38–47.

T-41 *Mescalero*

Clark, Charles. *The Cessna 172.* Blue Ridge Summit, PA: Aero, 1987.

## Consolidated

Wagner, William. *Reuben Fleet and the Story of Consolidated Aircraft.* Fallbrook, CA: Aero Publishers, 1976.

B-24 *Liberator*

Bowman, Martin W. *The Consolidated B-24 Liberator, 1939–1945.* New York: Sterling Press, 1989.

Campbell, John M. *Consolidated B-24 Liberator.* Atglen, PA: Schiffer Publishing, 1993.

Johnsen, Frederick A. *Consolidated B-24 Liberator.* North Branch, MN: Specialty Press, 1996.

Lloyd, Alwyn T. *Liberator: America's Global Bomber.* Missoula, MT: Pictorial Histories Publishing Company, 1993.

B-32 *Dominator*

Harding, Steve. *Dominator: The Story of the Consolidated B-32 Bomber.* Missoula, MT: Pictorial Histories Publishing Company, 1984.

———. "Flying Terminated Inventory," *Wings* 23 (April, 1993): 38–49.

Johnsen, Frederick A. "Last and Unluckiest of the Hemispheric Bombers," *Wings* 4 (February, 1974): 8–17.

Y'Blood, William T. "The Second String," *AAHS Journal* 13 (Summer, 1968): 80–92.

P2Y *Ranger*

Matt, Paul R. "Consolidated P2Y Flying Boat," *Historic Aviation Album* 9 (1971): 198–214.

P-30/PB-2

Dean, Jack. "Legion of the Lost," *Wings* 4 (October, 1974): 36–45.

Teliczan, Raymond J. "PB-2A: An Insider's Story," *Aero Album* 12 (Winter, 1970): 8–13.

PB2Y *Coronado*

Bowers, Peter M. "The Ghost of Coronado: The Ultimate Patrol Bomber," *Wings* 2 (February, 1972): 36–49.

PB4Y *Privateer*

Arnold, Rhodes. *The B-24/PB4Y in Combat: The World's Greatest Bomber.* Reserve, NM: Pima Paisano Publications, 1994.

Johnsen, Frederick A. *Bombers in Blue: PB4Y-2 Privateers and PB4Y-1 Liberators.* Glendale, CA: Aviation Book Company, 1979.

Sullivan, Dick. "The Scourge of the Sealanes: The PB4Y Privateer," *Air Classics* 8 (October, 1972): 10–19, 64.

PBY *Catalina*

Creed, Roscoe. *PBY: The Catalina Flying Boat.* Annapolis, MD: Naval Institute Press, 1985.

Hendrie, Andrew. *Flying Cats: The Catalina Aircraft in World War II.* Annapolis, MD: Naval Institute Press, 1988.

Sullivan, Jim. *PBY Catalina in Action.* Carrollton, TX: Squadron/Signal Publications, 1983.

## Convair

Yenne, Bill. *Into the Sunset: The Convair Story.* Lyme, CT: Greenwich Publishing Group, 1995.

B-36 *Peacemaker*

Ford, Daniel. "B-36: Bomber at the Crossroads," *Air & Space Smithsonian* 11 (January, 1996): 42–51.

Jacobsen, Meyers K. *Convair B-36: A Comprehensive History of America's "Big Stick."* Atglen, PA: Schiffer Publishing, 1998.

Johnsen, Frederick A. *Thundering Peacemaker: The B-36 Story in Words and Pictures.* Tacoma, WA: Bomber Books, 1978.

B-58 *Hustler*

Machat, Mike. "Supersonic Spearhead," *Wings* 23 (April, 1993): 16–39, 50–52.

Miller, Jay. *Convair B-58 Hustler: The World's First Supersonic Bomber.* Leicester, Eng.: Midland Publishing, 1997.

C-131 *Samaritan*

Bell, Mark S. "So Long Old Greasy," *Air Combat* 18 (February, 1990): 46–51.

Ginter, Steve, and Nick Williams. *Convair T-29 Flying Classroom, R4Y/C-131 Samaritan, and CC-109 Cosmopolitan.* Simi Valley, CA: Steve Ginter, 1987.

Williams, Nicholas M. "The Convair YC-131C Turboliners," *AAHS Journal* 25 (Winter, 1980): 255–258.

F-102 *Delta Dart*

Mendenhall, Charles A. *Delta Wings: Convair's High Speed Planes of the Fifties and Sixties.* Osceola, WI: Motorbooks International, 1983.

Ragay, J. D. *F-102 Delta Dagger in Europe.* Carrollton, TX: Squadron/Signal Publications, 1991.

Thompson, Warren. "Unsheathing the Dagger," *Wings* 21 (February, 1991): 22–43.

**F-106 *Delta Dagger***

Carson, Don, and Lou Drendel. *F-106 Delta Dart in Action.* Carrollton, TX: Squadron/Signal Publications, 1974.

Deal, Duane W. "F-106: Biggest Deal of the Century Series," *Wings* 14 (June, 1984): 20–29; 48–55.

Holder, William G. *Convair F-106 Delta Dart.* Fallbrook, CA: Aero Publishers, 1977.

**R3Y *Tradewind***

Ginter, Steve. *Convair P5Y and R3Y Tradewind.* Simi Valley, CA: Steve Ginter, 1999,

O'Leary, Michael. "Flying Landing Craft," *Air Classics* 22 (November, 1986): 62–65.

Poling, George F. "On the Trail of the Tradewind," *Air Power* 8 (May, 1978): 11–24, 62.

**Curtiss**

Bowers, Peter M. *Curtiss Aircraft, 1907–1947.* Annapolis, MD: Naval Institute Press, 1979.

Eltscher, Louis R., and Edward M. Young. *Curtiss-Wright: Greatness and Decline.* New York: Twayne of Macmillan, 1998.

**A-3/O-1 *Falcon***

Boyne, Walter J. "Bent Wing Falcon," *Air Power* 2 (January, 1972): 8–16.

Westburg, Peter. "The Unforgettable Curtiss Falcon," *Air Classics* 9 (November, 1975): 66–81.

**A-8 *Shrike***

Jeffries, Walter M. "The Curtiss Shrikes," *AAHS Journal* 10 (Summer, 1965): 129–139.

Westburg, Peter. "Curtiss A-8 Shrike," *Air Classics* 11 (December, 1975): 14–25.

**A-12 *Shrike***

Dean, Jack. "The Secret of the Shrike," *Air Power* 9 (September, 1979): 8–17, 54.

**AT-9 *Jeep***

Boyne, Walter J. "Curtiss AT-9," *Wings* 4 (February, 1974): 18–26, 29.

Matt, Paul R. "Curtiss AT-9," *Historic Aviation Album* 2 (1965): 82–85.

**B-2 *Condor***

Boyne, Walter J. "Curtiss B-2 Condor," *Air Power* 2 (March, 1972): 4–21, 62–66.

McCorrison, Sears. "Curtiss B-2 Condor Bomber," *Historic Aviation Album* 18 (1987): 4–19.

**C-46 *Commando***

Christy, Joe. "Commando Extraordinaire," *Air Power* 3 (May, 1973): 22–33.

Davis, John M. *The Curtiss C-46 Commando.* 2 Vols. Hornchurch, Eng.: Air Britain, 1978.

Trimble, Robert L. "Big-assed Bird," *Air Classics* 17 (July, 1981): 14–26, 75.

Westell, Freeman. "Fast Freight," *Air Power* 28 (May, 1998): 40–55.

**F5L**

"U.S.A. Navy F-5-L Flying Boat," *Over the Front* 5 (Summer, 1990): 145–153.

**F6C/P-1 *Hawk***

Bowers, Robert M. *Curtiss Navy Hawks in Action.* Carrollton, TX: Squadron/Signal Publications, 1995.

Boyne, Walter. "P for Pursuit, or, the Pigeon in Hawk's Clothing," *Air Power* 6 (March, 1976): 8–23.

Davis, Larry. *Curtiss Army Hawks in Action.* Carrollton, TX: Squadron/Signal Publications, 1992.

"Early Army Hawks," *Skyways* 5 (January, 1988): 2–21.

Shamburger, Page, and Joe Christy. *The Curtiss Hawks.* Kalamazoo, MI: Wolverine Press, 1974.

**F7C *Seahawk***

Andrews, Hal. "Naval Aircraft: F7C-1," *Naval Aviation News* (August, 1979): 20–21.

**F8C/O2C *Helldiver***

Bowers, Peter M. "Helldiver," *Wings* 12 (April, 1982): 10–25.

**F8C/OC *Falcon***

Andrews, Hal. "Naval Aircraft: OC Falcon," *Naval Aviation News* (July, 1981): 24–25.

**F9C *Sparrowhawk***

Andrews, Hal. "The Sparrowhawk: The Airship Fighter," *Naval Aviation News* (April/May, 1980): 22–27; 20–25.

Nye, Willis L. "Genealogy of the Curtiss Sparrowhawk 'Dirigible Fighters,'" *AAHS Journal* 3 (April/June, 1958): 70–109.

**F11C *Goshawk***

Larkins, William C. "The Curtiss Goshawk," *AAHS Journal* 9 (Spring, 1964): 58–63.

Mizrahi, J. V. "Carrier Fighter," *Air Power* 2 (September, 1972): 18–29.

**H-16**

Bowers, Peter M. "Sea Wings," *Air Power* 5 (September, 1975): 38–52.

**HS**

Molson, K. M. *The Curtiss HS Flying Boats.* Annapolis, MD: Naval Institute Press, 1995.

**JN-4 *Jenny***

Lincke, Jack R. *Jenny Was No Lady: The Story of the JN-4D.* New York: W. W. Norton, 1970.

**MF**

"Curtis MF," *World War I Aero* 49 (December, 1974): 5–12.

**N-9**

Van Deurs, George. "The N-9," *Air Classics* 8 (November, 1972): 44–49.

**NC**

Smith, Richard K. *First Across! The U.S. Navy's Transatlantic Flight of 1919.* Annapolis, MD: Naval Institute Press, 1973.

Trimble, Robert L. "Nancy Boats Versus the Atlantic," *Air Progress Aviation Review* 4 (January, 1980): 12–23, 96.

Wilbur, Ted. *The First Flight Across the Atlantic, May 1919.* Washington, DC: Smithsonian Institution Press, 1969.

**O-52 *Owl***

Glasebrook, Rick. "Flying the North American O-47 and the Curtiss-Wright O-52," *Aerospace Historian* 25 (January, 1970): 5–11.

P-6E *Hawk*
Boyne, Walter J. "'P' for Pursuit," *Wings* 6 (April, 1976): 38–53.
Dean, Jack. "Curtiss P-6E Hawk," *Air Power* 24 (March, 1994): 22–33.
Westburg, Peter. "Curtiss P-6E," *Air Classics* 14 (March and May, 1978): 18–25, 70; 18–24, 68.

P-36 *Hawk*
Bowers, Peter M. "Hawk 75: Evolution of the Curtiss P-36 Series," *Air Classics* 6 (August, 1970): 6–23.
Hyer, Charles J. "Curtiss P-36 in Squadron Service," *AAHS Journal* 33 (Winter, 1988): 242–257.

P-40 *Warhawk*
Christy, Joe, and Jeffrey L. Ethell. *P-40 Hawks at War.* New York: Scribner, 1980.
Johnsen, Frederick A. *P-40 Warhawk.* Osceola, WI: Motorbooks International, 1998.
McDowell, R. Ernest. *Curtiss P-40 in Action.* Carrollton, TX: Squadron/Signal Publications, 1976.

PW-8
Boyne, Walter J. "The Great P-Shooter Shoot Out!" *Air Classics* 7 (March, 1971): 40–49.

SBC *Helldiver*
Bowers, Peter M. "The Forgotten Dive Bomber," *Wings* 1 (December, 1971): 18–29, 58–59.
Doll, Thomas E. *SBC Helldiver in Action.* Carrollton, TX: Squadron/Signal Publications, 1995.

SB2C *Helldiver*
McCullough, Anson."The Beauty of the Beast," *Air Power* 27 (May, 1997): 8–37.
Smith, Peter C. *Curtiss SB2C Helldiver.* Shrewsbury, Eng.: Airlife, 1998.
Stern, Robert C. *SB2C Helldiver in Action.* Carrollton, TX: Squadron/Signal Publications, 1982.

SC-2 *Seahawk*
"Curtiss SC-1 and -2 Sea Hawk," *Historic Aviation Album* 1 (1965): 32–35.
Ginter, Steve. *Curtiss SC Seahawk.* Simi Valley, CA: Steve Ginter, 1999.
Scutts, Jerry. *Fantail Fighters.* St. Paul, MN: Phalanx Publishing Company, 1995.

SNC *Falcon*
"Curtiss SNC Falcon," *Aero Album* 7 (Fall, 1969): 38–41.
Trimble, Robert L. "Last of the Falcons," *Air Classics Quarterly Review* 5 (Winter, 1978): 12–18.

SO3C *Seamew*
Andrews, Hal. "Naval Aircraft: Seagull," *Naval Aviation News* (June, 1977): 20–21.
Gunston, Bill. "Last of the Seagulls," *Aeroplane Monthly* 4 (December, 1976): 620–625.

SOC *Seagull*
Bowers, Pete M. "Sea Scouts: The Eyes of the Fleet, From Curtiss SOC to Seagull and Sea Hawk," *Wings* 15 (February, 1985): 32–52.
Brazelton, David. "The Curtiss SOC Seagull," *AAHS Journal* 3 (July/September, 1958): 167–174.
Semmes, Raphael. "A Seaplane Built for Two," *Aerospace Historian* 26 (Summer, 1979): 102–107.

T-32 *Condor*
"Curtiss-Wright T-32 Condor," *Historic Aviation Album* 1 (1965): 24–27.
Eltscher, Lou. "A Tale of Two Condors," *Skyways* 14 (April, 1990): 2–18.
Matthews, William R. "Curtiss Condor II," *AAHS Journal* 12 (Spring, 1967): 3–27.
McCorrison, Sears. "Curtiss B-20 Condor Transport," *Historic Aviation Album* 18 (1987): 20–35.

TS-1
Andrews, Hal. "TS-1," *Naval Aviation News* 78 (January/February; March/April, 1996): 38–39; 34–35.
Bowers, Peter M. "The Fleet's First Fighter," *Wings* 14 (April, 1984): 42–50.

**Curtiss/Wright**

CW-21 *Demon*
Bowers, Peter M. "Demons by the Dozen," *Wings* 11 (October, 1981): 36–51.

**De Havilland**

Hannah, Donald. *De Havilland.* Stamford, Eng.: Key, 1982.

DH-4
Bowers, Peter M. "That Damnable DH-4," *Wings* 10 (December, 1980): 36–45.
Boyne, Walter J. *De Havilland DH-4: From Flaming Coffin to Living Legend.* Washington, DC: Smithsonian Institution Press, 1984.
Gemeinhardt, Walter. "DH-4s in Marine Corps Service," *AAHS Journal* 7 (Winter, 1962): 243–253.
Rust, Ken C. "The DH-4B and DH-4M WW I De Havilland DH-4," *Aero Album* 14 (Summer, 1971): 11–18.

**De Havilland—Canada**

CV-2/C-7 *Caribou*
Mutza, Wayne. *C-7 Caribou in Action.* Carrollton, TX: Squadron/Signal Publications, 1993.

L-20/U-6 *Beaver*
Rossiter, Sean. *The Immortal Beaver: The World's Greatest Bush Plane.* Vancouver, BC: Douglas and McIntyre, 1996.
Siuru, William. "Leave It to Beaver!" *Air Power* 11 (September, 1981): 46–51.

**Douglas**

Stelpflug, Steve. *McDonnell Douglas/Douglas Aircraft Company, 1st 75 Years.* Long Beach, CA: South Coast Publishing, 1995.

A3D *Skywarrior*
Cunningham, Bruce. *Douglas A3D Skywarrior.* Simi Valley, CA: Steve Ginter, 1999.
Francillon, Rene, and Edward H. Heinemann. *Douglas A-3 Skywarrior.* Arlington, TX: Aerofax, 1978.
Pace, Steve. "Birds of a Feather," *Air Power* 18 (July, 1988): 10–37.

Sullivan, Jim. *A-3 Skywarrior in Action.* Carrollton, TX: Squadron/Signal Publications, 1995.

A-4 *Skyhawk*

Drendel, Lou. *A-4 Skyhawk in Action.* Carrollton, TX: Squadron/Signal Publications, 1973.

Kilduff, Peter. *Douglas A-4 Skyhawk.* Osceola, WI: Motorbooks International, 1983.

Peacock, Lindsay T. *A-4 Skyhawk.* London: Osprey, 1987.

A-20 *Havoc*

Bowers, Peter M. "Dog of War," *Air Power* 26 (January, 1996): 10–47.

Hess, William N. *A-20 Havoc at War.* New York: Scribner, 1980.

Mesko, Jim. *A-20 Havoc in Action.* Carrollton, TX: Squadron/Signal Publications, 1994.

Williams, Robert E. "Douglas DB-7/A-20 Boston/Havoc," *AAHS Journal* 35 (Spring, 1990): 2–15.

A/B-26 *Invader*

Bowman, Martin W. "To Hell and Back," *Air Classics* 30 (March, 1994): 34–61.

Gallemi, Francis. *Warbird Profile: A-26/B-26 Invader.* Vandreuil, Quebec: Aries Publications, 1994.

Mesko, Jim. *A-26 Invader in Action.* Carrollton, TX: Squadron/Signal Publications, 1993.

AD/A-1 *Skyraider*

Hughes, Kris. *Douglas A-1 Skyraider.* North Branch, MN: Specialty Press, 1997.

Johnsen, Frederick A. *Douglas A-1 Skyraider: A Photo Chronicle.* Atglen, PA: Schiffer Publishing, 1994.

Sullivan, Jim. *Skyraider in Action.* Carrollton, TX: Squadron/Signal Publications, 1983.

B-18 *Bolo*

Enyedy, Tony. "Douglas' Reluctant Warriors," *Air Classics* 3 (March, 1967): 26–33, 63.

Johnsen, Frederick A. "The Great Bolo Boondoggle," *Wings* 3 (August, 1973): 8–19.

Trimble, Robert L. "Bolo: America's Forgotten Warrior," *Air Classics* 16 (May, 1980): 22–33, 62–67.

B-23 *Dragon*

Bowers, Peter M. "The Reluctant Dragon," *Air Power* 10 (November, 1980): 24–41.

O'Leary, Michael. "A Dragon's Last Flight," *Air Classics* 22 (April, 1986): 34–41.

B-66 *Destroyer*

Francillon, Rene J. *Douglas B-66 Destroyer.* Arlington, TX: Aerofax, 1988.

Schrader, Richard K. "The USAF Destroyer," *Air Classics* 24 (April, 1988): 20–22, 78.

BTD

Kowalski, Robert. *Douglas XSB2D-1 and BTD Destroyer.* Simi Valley, CA: Steve Ginter, 1999.

C-21/RD *Dolphin*

Bowers, Peter M. "The Douglas RD Dolphin," *Air Power* 12 (November, 1982): 10–25, 49–50.

C-39

Daniels, C. M. "Douglas DC," *Wings* 3 (June, 1973): 18–31.

Trimble, Robert L. "The Silver-Winged Thoroughbred," *Air Classics* 21 (May, 1985): 28–29, 60–61, 82.

C-47 *Skytrain*

Davis, Larry. *C-47 Skytrain in Action.* Carrollton, TX: Squadron/Signal Publications, 1995.

Glines, Carroll V. *The Amazing Gooney Bird: The Saga of the Legendary DC-3/C-47.* Atglen, PA: Schiffer Publishing, 1996.

O'Leary, Michael D. *DC-3 and C-47 Gooney Birds.* Osceola, WI: Motorbooks International, 1992.

C-54/R5D *Skymaster*

Daniels, C. M. "Skymaster," *Air Power* 4 (January, 1974): 46–60.

Grant, Robert B. "The Four," *Air Classics* 22 (March, 1986): 28–37.

Williams, R. E. "Skymaster: The Douglas DC-4/C-54/R5D," *AAHS Journal* 37 (Winter, 1992): 288–299.

C-74 *Globemaster I*

Williams, Nicholas. "Globemaster: The Douglas C-74," *AAHS Journal* 25 (Summer, 1980): 82–106.

C-118/R6D *Liftmaster*

Whittle, John A. *The Douglas DC-6 and DC-7 Series.* London: Air Britain, 1966.

C-124 *Globemaster II*

Dean, Jack. "Old Shaky," *Wings* 22 (February, 1992): 44–52.

DT

Bowers, Peter M. "Around the World in 175 Days," *Wings* 4 (December, 1974): 8–15, 48–53.

MacKay, Ernest A. *World to Conquer: The Epic Story of the First Around the World Flight.* New York: Arco, 1981.

F3D *Skyknight*

Amody, Francis J. "Skynights, Nightmares, and MiGs," *AAHS Journal* 34 (Winter, 1989): 308–313.

Ginter, Steve. *Douglas F3D Skyknight.* Simi Valley, CA: Steve Ginter, 1982.

O'Rourke, G. G., and E. T. Wooldridge. *Night Fighter over Korea.* Annapolis, MD: Naval Institute Press, 1998.

F4D *Skyray*

Francillon, Rene. *Douglas F4D.* Arlington, TX: Aerofax, 1985.

Hackett, Peter. "Killer Rays," *Wings* 27 (December, 1997): 20–46.

Williams, Nick. *Douglas F4D Skyray.* Simi Valley, CA: Steve Ginter, 1986.

O-2

Boyne, Walter J. "Fly Off!" *Air Power* 9 (September, 1979): 32–44.

O-25

Westburg, Peter. "The Falcon's Stepsister," *Air Power* 2 (November, 1972): 58–63.

———. "The Douglas Observation Monoplanes: The O-25," *Air Classics* 13 (May, 1977): 82–101, 114–116.

O-31

Westburg, Peter. "The Douglas Observation Monoplanes: The YO-31A/O-31B," *Air Classics* 21 (November, 1976): 18–25, 68–77.

O-38

Bowers, Peter M., and Ken C. Rust. "Douglas Biplane Observation Type Aircraft," *Historic*

*Aviation Album* 11 (1972): 22–43; 12 (1973): 72–98.

Westburg, Peter. "O-38, the Douglas Dobbin," *Air Power* 3 (March, 1973): 50–57.

———. "The Douglas Observation Biplanes: The O-38," *Air Classics* 13 (June, 1977): 94–111.

O-43

"Douglas O-43A," *Skyways* 1 (January, 1987): 22–29.

Westburg, Peter. "The Douglas Observation Monoplanes: The O-43A," *Air Classics* 13 (January, 1977): 16–26, 68–74.

Westburg, Peter, and Peter M. Bowers. "The Parasols of Santa Monica," *Wings* 3 (October, 1973): 50–65; 4 (April, 1974): 56–67.

O-46

Westburg, Peter. "Douglas Observation Monoplanes," *Air Classics* 13 (March, 1977): 20–31, 83–90.

P-70

Pape, Garry R., and Ronald C. Harrison. *Queen of the Midnight Skies: The Story of America's Air Force Night Fighters.* West Chester, PA: Schiffer Publishing, 1992.

Thompson, Warren. "Night Hunter," *Wings* 16 (June, 1986): 44–55.

———. "P-70 in the Pacific," *Wings of Fame* 9 (1997): 106–115.

PD-1

Andrews, Hal. "Naval Aircraft: Douglas PD-1," *Naval Aviation News* (July, 1975): 20–21.

SBD *Dauntless*

Stern, Robert C. *SBD Dauntless in Action.* Carrollton, TX: Squadron/Signal Publications, 1984.

Tillmann, Barrett. *The Dauntless Dive Bomber of World War II.* Annapolis, MD: Naval Institute Press, 1976.

Wildenberg, Thomas. *Destined for Glory: Dive Bombing, Midway, and the Evolution of Carrier Air Power.* Annapolis, MD: Naval Institute Press, 1998.

TBD *Devastator*

Adcock, Al. *TBD Devastator in Action.* Carrollton, TX: Squadron/Signal Publications, 1989.

Ashley, John. "Torpedo One," *Air Power* 21 (November, 1991): 44–53.

McCullough, Anson. "Torpedo Bomber Devastator," *Air Classics* 5 (January/February, 1968): 28–43.

**Fairchild**

Mitchell, Kent A. *Fairchild Aircraft, 1926–1987.* Santa Ana, CA: Markiewicz/Thompson, 1997.

A-10 *Thunderbolt II*

Logan, Don. *Republic's A-10 Thunderbolt: A Pictorial History.* Atglen, PA: Schiffer Publications, 1997.

Smallwood, William L. *Warthog: Flying the A-10 in the Gulf War.* Washington, DC: Brassey's, 1993.

Stevens, Rick. *Fairchild A-10: Fighting Warthog.* London: Aerospace, 1995.

AT-21 *Gunner*

Mitchell, Kent A. "The Saga of the Fairchild AT-21," *AAHS Journal* 32 (Fall, 1987): 162–171.

Pendragon, Donald. "Those Other Wooden Wonders," *Air Classic Quarterly Review* 6 (Winter, 1979): 26–26.

Rawls, Ramsey. "Fairchild's Ghost Bomber," *Air Classics* 8 (March, 1972): 28–33.

C-82 *Packet*

McCullough, Anson. "Load 'Em Up!" *Air Power* 26 (November, 1996): 8–32.

Mitchell, Kent A., "The Fairchild C-82 Packet." *American Aviation Historical Society Journal* 44 (Spring, 1999): 2–15.

C-119 *Flying Boxcar*

Lloyd, Alwyn T. *C-119 Flying Boxcar.* Castro Valley, CA: Pacific Aero Press, 1996.

Trimble, Robert L. "Boxcar on New Tracks," *Air Classics* 13 (December, 1977): 58–61.

C-123 *Provider*

Adcock, Al. *C-123 Provider in Action.* Carrollton, TX: Squadron/Signal Publications, 1992.

Dean, Jack. "Payload!" *Wings* 19 (October, 1989): 36–55.

McGowan, Sam. "The Provider: The Fairchild C-123 Provider Series," *Air Classics* 24 (July, 1988): 60–65.

Mitchell, Kent A. "The C-123 Provider," *AAHS Journal* 37 (Fall, 1992): 162–186.

PT-19/23 *Cornell*

Mitchell, Kent A. "Fairchild 'Cornell' Trainer," *AAHS Journal* 37 (Winter, 1992): 264–273.

Puckett, Herb L. *Sherman Fairchild's PT-19: Cradle of Heroes.* Tony, WI: Flambeau Litho Corporation, 1980.

UC-61 *Forwarder*

Ames, Bob. "Fairchild 24," *Air Classics* 2 (September/October, 1965): 10–13.

**Fokker**

Weyl, A. R. *Fokker: The Creative Years.* New York: Funk and Wagnalls, 1965.

C-2

Bowers, Peter M. "The Flight of the Question Mark," *Air Power* 9 (May, 1979): 44–52.

Renfro, Robert B. "Question Marks's Flight," *AAHS Journal* 34 (Summer, 1989): 136–143.

T-2

Casey, Louis S. *The First Nonstop Coast to Coast Flight and the Historic T-2 Airplane.* Washington, DC: Smithsonian Institution Press, 1964.

Scrivner, John H. "The Impossible Has Happened," *Aerospace Historian* 14 (Summer, 1967): 103–109.

Wallace, Sally M. *John Macready: Aviation Pioneer.* Manhattan, KS: Sunflower University Press, 1998.

**Ford**

C-4/RR *Trimotor*

Holden, Henry M. *The Fabulous Ford Trimotors.* Blue Ridge Summit, PA: TAB/Aero, 1992.

Larkins, William T. *The Ford Tri-motor.* West Chester, PA: Schiffer Publishing, 1992.

Weiss, David S. *The Saga of the Tin Goose: The Story of the Ford Trimotor.* New York: Cumberland Enterprises, 1996.

**General Dynamics**

Wegg, John. *General Dynamics and Their Predecessors.* Annapolis, MD: Naval Institute Press, 1992.

EF-111 *Raven*

Thompson, Warren. "Jammers," *Wings* 17 (June, 1987): 46–56.

F-16 *Fighting Falcon*

Drendel, Lou. *F-16 Fighting Falcon in Action.* Carrollton, TX: Squadron/Signal Publications, 1982.

Richardson, Doug. *F-16 Fighting Falcon.* New York: Salamander, 1990.

Shaw, Robbie. *F-16 Fighting Falcon.* Osceola, WI: Motorbooks International, 1996.

Sweetman, Bill, and Robert F. Door, eds. *Lockheed Martin F-16 Flying Falcon.* Westport, CT: AIRtime Publishing, 1999.

F-111 *Aardvark*

Davies, Peter E. *F-111 Aardvark.* Marlborough, Wilshire, Eng.: Crowood Press, 1997.

Halberstadt, Hans. *F-111 Aardvark.* London: Windrow and Greene, 1992.

Logan, Don. *General Dynamics F-111 Aardvark.* Atglen, PA: Schiffer Publishing, 1998.

Thornborough, Anthony M. *F-111: USAF's Ultimate Strike Aircraft.* London: Osprey, 1993.

**Great Lakes**

BG-1

Westburg, Peter. "Old Wings and a Prayer," *Air Power* 9 (November, 1979): 36–52.

**Grumman**

Francillon, Rene. *Grumman Aircraft Since 1929.* Annapolis, MD: Naval Institute Press, 1989.

Hardy, M. J. *Sea, Sky, and Stars: An Illustrated History of Grumman Aircraft.* New York: Sterling Publishing Company, 1987.

A-6 *Intruder*

Dorr, Robert F. *Grumman A-6 Intruder.* Osceola, WI: Motorbooks International, 1987.

Drendel, Lou. *Intruder.* Carrollton, TX: Squadron/Signal Publications, 1991.

Michaels, Joe. *A-6 Intruder in Action.* Carrollton, TX: Squadron/Signal Publications.

AF-2 *Guardian*

Johnson, Scott O. "Hunter, Killer," *Air Power* 10 (March, 1980): 30–34, 50–51.

Kolalski, Robert J. *Grumman AF Guardian: Hunter-Killer ASW Aircraft.* Simi Valley, CA: Steve Ginter, 1991.

Miska, Kurt H. "The Development of the Grumman XTB3F and the AF Guardian," *AAHS Journal* 18 (Winter, 1973): 218–225.

C-1 *Trader*

Mitchell, Kent A. "Grumman C-1A Trader." *American Aviation Historical Society Journal* 40 (Winter, 1995): 276–281.

C-2 *Greyhound*

"Carrier Onboard Delivery," *Air Combat* 8 (September, 1980): 64–69.

E-1 *Tracer*

Andrews, Hal. "Naval Aircraft: Tracer," *Naval Aviation News* (July, 1971): 20–21.

Sims, Donald. "Goodbye, Willie Fudd," *Air Combat* 5 (March, 1977): 48–57, 82.

E-2 *Hawkeye*

Clauser, Charles A. "The Grumman E-2C Hawkeye," *Air Power* 20 (July, 1990): 20–29, 44–52.

*An Illustrated Data Guide to Modern Reconnaissance Aircraft.* London: Tiger Books International, 1997.

EA-6 *Prowler*

Francillon, Rene. *Grumman EA-6A/B.* Arlington, TX: Aerofax, 1984.

Jenkins, Dennis R. *Grumman EA-6A Intruder and EA-6B Prowler.* Arlington, AT: Aerofax, 1989.

Wogstad, James. *EA-6A Intruder and EA-6B Prowler.* San Antonio, TX: Aerophile, 1985.

F2F

Dann, Richard S. *Grumman Biplane Fighters in Action.* Carrollton, TX: Squadron/Signal Publications, 1996.

Tillman, Barrett. "Grumman's Flying Beer Barrels," *Wings* 4 (February, 1974): 32–47.

F3F

"The Grumman F3F Biplane Fighter," *Air Classics* 7 (May, 1971): 20–35.

Seybel, Roger. "Three-time Prototype," *Wings* 19 (February, 1989): 30–41, 54.

F4F *Wildcat*

Linn, Don. *F4F Wildcat in Action.* Carrollton, TX: Squadron/Signal Publications, 1984.

Tillman, Barrett. *Wildcat: The F4F in World War II.* Annapolis, MD: Naval Institute Press, 1990.

F6F *Hellcat*

Sullivan, Jim. *F6F Hellcat in Action.* Carrollton, TX: Squadron/Signal Publications, 1979.

Tillman, Barrett. *Hellcat: The F6F in World War II.* Annapolis, MD: Naval Institute Press, 1988.

F7F *Tigercat*

Carr, Orrin I. "Fire Cat," *Air Classics* 12 (September, 1976): 38–47.

Scarborough, William E. *F7F Tigercat in Action.* Carrollton, TX: Squadron/Signal Publications, 1986.

F8F *Bearcat*

Chant, Christopher F. *Grumman F8F Bearcat.* Osceola, WI: Motorbooks International, 1988.

Jackson, B. R., and Tom E. Doll. *Grumman F8F Bearcat.* Fallbrook, CA: Aero Publishers, 1970.

Schrivner, Charles L. *F8F in Action.* Carrollton, TX: Squadron/Signal Publications, 1990.

F9F *Cougar*

Foxworth, Thomas G. "F9F Cougar," *Aero Album* 5 (January, 1972): 30–37.

F9F *Panther*

Sullivan, Jim. *F9F Panther/Cougar in Action.* Carrollton, TX: Squadron/Signal Publications, 1982.

F11F *Tiger*

Allen, Francis J. "Grumman's Reluctant Tiger," *Wings* 14 (June, 1984): 30–41.

Meyer, Corwin. *Grumman F11F-1 Tiger.* Simi Valley, CA: Steve Ginter, 1999.

Trimble, Robert L. "F11F Tiger," *Air Classics* 16 (November, 1980): 32–37, 70–71.

F-14 *Tomcat*

Baker, David. *Grumman F-14 Tomcat.* Marlborough, Wiltshire, Eng.: Crowood, 1998.

Gillcrist, Paul T. *Tomcat! The Grumman F-14 Story.* Atglen, PA: Schiffer Publications, 1994.

Jenkins, Dennis R. *Grumman F-14 Tomcat: Leading U.S. Navy Fleet Fighter.* Leicester, Eng.: Aerofax, 1997.

Lake, John, ed. *Grumman F-14: Shipborne Superfighter.* Westport, CT: AIRtime Publishing, Inc., 1998.

FF/SF

Baxter, Leroy. "The Pioneer Fighter Everyone Forgot: The Grumman FF-1," *Air Classics* 8 (December, 1971): 15–25.

Dean, Jack. "Grumman's Biplanes," *Wings* 24 (February, 1994): 10–19, 43–52.

Matt, Paul R. "Grumman FF-1," *Aero Album* 12 (Winter, 1970): 32–37.

Mayborn, Mitch. *History of the Pre-War Grumman Fighters.* Dallas: Flying Enterprise Publications, 1976.

JF/J2F *Duck*

Gault, Owen. "The Duck That Roared," *Air Classics* 8 (March, 1972): 16–27.

Hosek, Timothy. *Grumman JF Duck.* Carrollton, TX: Squadron/Signal Publications, 1996.

JF4/OA-18 *Widgeon*

"Grumman G-44 Widgeon," *Historic Aviation Album* 5 (1967): 239–245.

JRF/OA-9 *Goose*

Dean, Jack. "Grumman's Seabirds," *Wings* 24 (August, 1994): 8–31, 48–54.

OV-1 *Mohawk*

Colucci, Frank. "Mohawk," *Air Power* 11 (November, 1981): 24–37.

Love, Terry. *OV-1 Mohawk in Action.* Carrollton, TX: Squadron/Signal Publications, 1989.

S-2 *Tracker*

Redman, Rod. "Twilight of the Stoof: Grumman S2F Tracker," *Air Classics* 8 (June, 1972): 41–47.

Sullivan, Jim. *S2F Tracker in Action.* Carrollton, TX: Squadron/Signal Publications, 1990.

SA-16/UF-1 *Albatross*

Ginter, Steve. *Grumman HU-16 Albatross.* Simi Valley, CA: Steve Ginter, 1984.

Migliardi, Robert D. *HU-16 Albatross in Action.* Carrollton, TX: Squadron/Signal Publications, 1996.

Mutza, Wayne. *Grumman Albatross: A History of the Legendary Seaplane.* Atglen, PA: Schiffer Publishing, 1996.

TBF/TBM *Avenger*

Jackson, Berkeley R. *Grumman TBF/TBM Avenger.* Fallbrook, CA: Aero Publishers, 1984.

Scrivner, Carl. *TBM/TBF Avenger in Action.* Carrollton, TX: Squadron/Signal Publications, 1987.

Tillman, Barrett. *Avenger at War.* New York: Scribner, 1980.

**Hall**

Boyne, Walter J. "The Flying Hallmarks," *Wings* 5 (June, 1975): 8–25.

PH

Trimble, Robert L. "Hall's Aluminum Boat," *Air Classics* 19 (July, 1983): 58–63, 78–79.

**Helio**

U-10

Smith, Gene. "Helio Stallion: Warhorse," *Air Progress* 41 (May, 1979): 73–78.

**Hiller**

Spenser, Jay P. *Vertical Challenge: The Hiller Aircraft Story.* Seattle: University of Washington Press, 1992.

UH-12

Mitchell, Kent A. "The Hiller H-23 Raven," *AAHS Journal* 39 (Winter, 1994): 254–259.

**Hughes**

500MD *Defender*

"The 500M-D Defender," *Air International* 15 (July, 1978): 7–14.

AH-64 Apache

Colucci, Frank. *The McDonnell-Douglas Apache.* Blue Ridge Summit, PA: Aero, 1988.

Geddes, J. Philip. *Apache.* Alexandria, VA: International Defense Images, U.S.A., 1989.

Monson, Lyle. *McDonnell Douglas AH-64 Apache.* Arlington, TX: Aerofax, 1986.

Munro, Bob. *McDonnell Douglas AH-64 Apache.* New York: Gallery Books, 1991.

H-6

Porter, Donald. *The McDonnell Douglas OH-6A.* Blue Ridge Summit, PA: Aero, 1990.

**Kaman**

Kaman, Charles H. *Kaman, Our Early Years.* Indianapolis: Curtis Publishing Company, 1985.

HOK/H-43 *Huskie*

Mutza, Wayne. *Kaman H-43: An Illustrated History.* Atglen, PA: Schiffer Publishing, 1998.

SH-2 *Seasprite*

Rice, Christian B. "Performance of the SH-2F Seasprite Helicopter." Master's Thesis, University of Tennessee, Knoxville, 1973.

**Keystone**

LB

Bowers, Peter M. "Keystone Bombers," *Aero Album* 18 (Summer, 1972): 2–22.

———. "From Dusters to Keystone Bombers," *Air Power* 8 (January, 1978): 50–61.

Donnelly, Jon R. "Last of the Keystones," *Air Force Magazine* 66 (July, 1984): 100–102.

Hansell, Haywood S. "The Keystone Bombers: Unhonored and Unloved," *Air Force Magazine* 60 (September, 1977): 130–136.

**Lockheed**

Badrocke, Mike, and Bill Gunston. *Lockheed Aircraft Cutaways.* London: Osprey Publishing, 1998.

Francillon, Rene. *Lockheed Aircraft since 1913*. Annapolis, MD: Naval Institute Press, 1988.

A-28 *Hudson*

Bowers, Peter M. "The Makeshift Armada," *Wings* 14 (April, 1984): 26–41.

Hendrie, Andrew. *Seek and Strike: The Lockheed Hudson in World War II*. London: Kimber, 1983.

Westell, Freeman. "Lockheed's Made-Over Bomber," *Wings* 26 (December, 1996): 46–54.

AC-130 *Specter*

Colucci, Frank. "Night Specter," *Wings* 10 (April, 1980): 30–36.

Cupido, Joe. "A Box with Wings," *Wings* 23 (August, 1993): 46–53.

C-5 *Galaxy*

Barnett, Ned. "The Largest Galaxy in the Sky," *Air Classics* 9 (June, 1973): 60–65, 76.

Ulsamer, Edgar E. "Such a Nimble Giant," *Air Force and Space Digest* 52 (April, 1969): 79–87.

Wilkinson, Stephan. "Big," *Air and Space Smithsonian* 4 (March, 1989): 28–38.

C-69/R70 *Constellation*

Betts, Ed. "Original Connies," *AAHS Journal* 36 (Summer, 1991): 114–123.

Bowers, Peter M. "Constellation," *Air Power* 20 (November, 1990): 10–23, 42–54.

Stringfellow, Curtis K. *Lockheed Constellation*. Osceola, WI: Motorbooks International, 1992.

C-121/R7V *Super Constellation*

Germain, Scott E. *Lockheed Constellation and Super Constellation*. North Branch, MN: Specialty Press, 1998.

Ginter, Steve. *Lockheed C-121 Constellation*. Simi Valley, CA: Steve Ginter, 1983.

C-130 *Hercules*

Dabney, Joseph E. *Herk: Hero of the Skies*. Lakemont, GA: Copple House Books, 1979.

Drendel, Lou. *C-130 Hercules in Action*. Carrollton, TX: Squadron/Signal Publications, 1984.

Mason, Francis K. *Lockheed Hercules*. New York: Sterling, 1985.

Reed, Chris. *Lockheed C-130 Hercules and Its Variants*. Atglen, PA: Schiffer Publishing, 1999.

C-141 *Starlifter*

Martin, Harold H. *Starlifter: The C-141, Lockheed's High Speed Flying Truck*. Brattleboro, VT: S. Greene Press, 1972.

F-22 *Lightning II*

Sweetman, Bill. *F-22 Raptor*. Osceola, WI: Motorbooks International, 1998.

Wallace, Mike, and Bill Holder. *Lockheed Martin F-22 Raptor: An Illustrated History*. Atglen, PA: Schiffer Publishing, 1998.

F-80 *Shooting Star*

Davis, Larry. *P-80 Shooting Star, T-33/F-94 in Action*. Carrollton, TX: Squadron/Signal Publishing, 1980.

McLaren, David. *Lockheed P-80/F-80 Shooting Star: A Photo Chronicle*. Atglen, PA: Schiffer Publishing, 1996.

F-94 *Starfire*

Francillon, Rene. *Lockheed F-94 Starfire*. Arlington, TX: Aerofax, 1986.

Isham, Marty J., and David R. McLaren. *Lockheed F-94 Starfire: A Photo Chronicle*. Atglen, PA: Schiffer Publishing, 1993.

McClaren, David. *Lockheed T-33: A Photo Chronicle*. Atglen, PA: Schiffer Publishing, 1999.

Thompson, Warren. "Night Patrol," *Wings* 18 (April, 1988): 26–44.

F-104 *Starfighter*

Foster, Peter R. *F-104 Starfighter*. New York: Arms and Armours Press, 1987.

Friddell, Phil. *F-104 Starfighter in Action*. Carrollton, TX: Squadron/Signal Publications, 1993.

Pace, Steve. *Lockheed F-104 Starfighter*. Osceola, WI: Motorbooks International, 1992.

F-117A *Nighthawk*

Dorr, Robert F. *Lockheed F-117 Nighthawk*. London: Aerospace Publishing, 1995.

Holder, William G. *Lockheed F-117 Nighthawk: An Illustrated History of the Stealth Fighter*. Atglen, PA: Schiffer Publishing, 1996.

Miller, Jay. *Lockheed Martin F-117 Nighthawk*. Leicester, Eng.: Midland Publishing, 1995.

P2V *Neptune*

Bowman, Martin W. "King of the Seas," *Air Classics* 31 (April, 1995): 36–63.

Mutza, Wayne. *Lockheed P2V Neptune: An Illustrated History*. Atglen, PA: Schiffer Publishing, 1996.

Pace, Steve. "Neptune," *Air Power* 19 (March, 1989): 10–47.

Sullivan, Jim. *Lockheed P2V Neptune in Action*. Carrollton, TX: Squadron/Signal Publications, 1985.

P-3 *Orion*

Reade, David. *The Age of the Orion: The Lockheed P-3 Story*. Atglen, PA: Schiffer Publishing, 1998.

P-38 *Lightning*

Bodie, Warren. *The Lockheed P-38 Lightning*. Hiawassee, GA: Wide Wing Publications, 1991.

Johnsen, Frederick A. *Lockheed P-38 Lightning*. North Branch, MN: Specialty Press, 1996.

Pace, Steve. *Lockheed P-38 Lightning*. Osceola, WI: Motorbooks International, 1996.

PV-1 *Ventura*

Bowers, Peter M. "The Borrowed Bomber," *Wings* 5 (February, 1975): 40–53.

Scrivner, Charles. *PV-1 Ventura in Action*. Carrollton, TX: Squadron/Signal Publications, 1993.

Stanaway, John C. *Vega/Ventura: The Operational History of Lockheed's Lucky Star*. Atglen, PA: Schiffer Publishing, 1996.

PV-2 *Harpoon*

Scrivner, Charles L. "Harpoon," *Air Power* 3 (November, 1973): 50–59.

Veronico, Nick, and John F. Whyte. "Gun-Nosed Harpoon," *Warbirds International* 8 (March/April, 1989): 30–37.

S-3 *Viking*

Elward, Brad. "Air-Sea Warfare: The Future of the S-3B Viking," *Combat Aircraft* 2 (May–June, 1999): 128–137.

Hurlocker, Hal. "Lockheed's S-3A Viking," *Aerophile* 1 (June, 1979): 308–341.